MICHAEL E. VEAL

Dub

SOUNDSCAPES AND SHATTERED

SONGS IN JAMAICAN REGGAE

WESLEYAN UNIVERSITY PRESS

Middletown, Connecticut

Published by Wesleyan University Press, Middletown, CT 06459

www.wesleyan.edu/wespress

5 4 3 2 1

This book has been published with the assistance of the
Frederick W. Hilles Publication Fund of Yale University.

We also gratefully acknowledge assistance from the Manfred Bukofzer
Publication Endowment Fund of the American Musicological Society.

Library of Congress Cataloging-in-Publication Data

Veal, Michael E., 1963–
Soundscapes and shattered songs in Jamaican reggae / Michael E. Veal.
    p.   cm. — (Music/culture)
Includes bibliographical references (p.   ), discography (p.   ), and
index.
ISBN-13: 978-0-8195-6571-6 (cloth : alk. paper)
ISBN-10: 0-8195-6571-7 (cloth : alk. paper)
ISBN-13: 978-0-8195-6572-3 (pbk. : alk. paper)
ISBN-10: 0-8195-6572-5 (pbk. : alk. paper)
1. Dub (Music)—Jamaica—History and criticism. I. Title.
ML3532.V43 2007
781.646'097292—dc22   2006037669

Dub

While the material invention of instruments was still in the hands of a few, their imaginative invention and reinvention were profitably and dangerously in the hands of the many who might expand their significance beyond an inventor's wildest dreams or even against his wishes.

—James Lastra 2000

It happened like this . . . Because of the development of new recording technology, a whole host of compositional possibilities that were quite new to music came into existence. Most of these had to do with two closely related new areas—the development of the texture of sound itself as a focus for compositional attention, and the ability to create with electronics virtual acoustic spaces (acoustic spaces that don't exist in nature). . . . I wanted to suggest that this activity was actually one of the distinguishing characteristics of new music, and could in fact become the main focus of composi- tional attention. . . . [I]t was clear to me that this was where a lot of the action was going to be . . . people like me just sat at home night after night fiddling around with all this stuff, amazed at what was now possible, immersed in the new sonic worlds we could create. . . . [I]mmersion was really the point: we were making music to swim in, to float in, to get lost inside.

—Brian Eno 1996

Space is a prime symbol of the aspirations of a people, permeating architecture, music, and mathematics.

—Marcos Novak, quoted in Moser 1996

Contents

❦

Illustrations

Acknowledgments

My first thanks to the two friends who made me aware of dub music back in 1983, Tony Sims and Willy D. Wallace. I also acknowledge everyone who was interviewed for this book (their names are listed in the bibliography) with particular mention of Michael "Mikey Dread" Campbell, Clive Chin, Dave Hendley, Edward "Bunny" Lee, Desmond Shakespeare, and Bobby Vicious for their assistance at various stages of this project.

Special thanks to Gage Averill, who advised this work through its dissertation stage (2000) at Wesleyan University, and who provided my entry into academia. I also thank Mark Slobin and Su Zheng. Others at Wesleyan who proved invaluable: Hope McNeil of the music department; Allison M. Insall, Beth Labriola, and Barbara Schukoske of the Office of Graduate Student Services; and Dianne Kelly, Alec McLane and Randy Wilson of Olin Library.

Colleagues and friends at various institutions who provided feedback, an exchange of music, ideas, or other valuable information at various stages of this work: Carolyn Abbate (Princeton University), Kofi Agawu (Princeton University), Tahmima Anam (Harvard University), Harris Berger (Texas A&M University), Franya Berkman (Lewis & Clark College), Lucia Cantero (Yale University), Eric Charry (Wesleyan University), Michael Denning (Yale University), Paul Gilroy (Yale University), Lori Gruen (Wesleyan University), Jackson Lears (Rutgers University), Peter Manuel (CUNY), Alondra Nelson (Yale University), and Marc Perlman (Brown University).

I thank my colleagues in the Department of Music at Yale University, and in the Department of African-American Studies at Yale, especially Ellen Rosand, Patrick McCreless, Sarah Weiss, John Halle, Paul Gilroy, Vron Ware, Hazel Carby, John Szwed, Robert Farris Thompson, Alondra Nelson, Elizabeth Alexander and Kellie Jones. I appreciate the efforts of the administrative staff in the Department of Music: Elaine Lincoln, Linette Norbeau, Melissa Capasso, Mary-Jo Warren, and Sharleen Sanchez;

and the administrative staff in the Department of African-American Studies: Geneva Melvin and Janet Giarrantano.

Several students who read the manuscript at various stages and offered valuable commentary and/or music: Lucia Cantero, Hannah Appel, Emily Ferrigno, Richard Leiter, and Daniel Sussman. Matthew Byrnie of Routledge Press and Suzanna Tamminen and Eric Levy at Wesleyan University Press were generous with time and counsel.

Finally, I thank Gary Tomlinson of the Department of Music at the University of Pennsylvania.

I am grateful to my parents, Henry and Yvonnecris Veal; and all the members of the Veal, Smith, Coleman, and Tyson families. And I give a huge shout-out to those friends who have seen me through the writing process: Fleetwood, Catfish Jr. Kennedy, R², Jules, The Irascible Imp, Jon, Greg, A.J., Grubes, Blass, Maria V., Norbu, Ike, Bud Struggle, Nadia, Groove Maneuvers, Damon and Naomi and Jay Hoggard, Goldi, Lauralito, Yomski, Romily, Ingi, Rachael, Suzu, The Quinto Kid, Julius, Luke, Mat, Steve, Tony L., Maya, Trev, Mojay, Tony and Silvie Allen, Alexandre, M. Z, Sheron, Miriam.

Those in Jamaica who offered assistance include Canute Salmon and family; Junior Bailey; Cheryl Chambers at Jammy's; Daniel Jackson, Stephanie Black; Allan Karr; and Tenny and Launa Graham. I extend particular thanks to Drs. Carolyn Cooper and Cecil Gutzmore of the University of the West Indies in Mona for their warmth, kindness, and hospitality during my visits to Jamaica. I also thank Hannah Appel for all her help during my trips to Kingston.

Others in the United States to whom I offer thanks include the staff at Cutler's Records in New Haven, Connecticut; Monica Wint; Geoff Albores; Dressell's Service Station (Granby, Massachusetts); Mystery Train Records (Amherst, Massachusetts); Newbury Comics (Amherst, Massachusetts); Mars Records (Boston, Massachusetts); and Dave Rosencrans of *Experience Music Project* (Seattle, Washington). I would also like to thank James Dutton of Motion Records.

Partial support for this research was provided by a Five College Fellowship for the academic year 1996–97, during which I was in residence in the Department of Music of Mount Holyoke College. I acknowledge the music department, as well as Carol Angus, Lorna Peterson, and Leslie Taylor of Five Colleges, Inc. Additional funding was provided by Yale University through a Griswold Travel Research Grant in 2000, and a Morse Junior Faculty Fellowship in 2003–2004. I also acknowledge the Department of Music at New York University, where I taught for the academic year 1997–98.

Introduction

❦

I.

[T]his is the kingdom of post-civilization, the disintegrated, post-kingdom kingdom in which everything is falling apart, fragmented into atomic bits that look like evidence—clues stacked, sorted, and organized in some purposeless microanalysis. . . . It rather serenely contemplates the moment of civilization's passing away, or its cyclical sinking into a simultaneously pre- and post-literate swamp of representational decay where the center no longer holds, the image no longer holds, language no longer holds . . . this world of disintegration and ruin which also contains an implicit possibility of recombination, renewal, and rebirth . . . is both tarnished relic and anticipatory sign. [The artist] will regain his lost selfhood . . . through a cataclysmic reversal of Western history . . .
—Thomas McEvilley, *"Royal Slumming"*[1]

If you take as your cultural polarities Africa on the one side, and North America on the other side, you have two extremely heavy cultures balancing each other. And there's this one little, tiny connection between the two, in which you can see both. And that connection, I think, is Jamaica. You have a huge quantum of cultural energy on each side, and one small connection that's glowing red-hot. That's Jamaica, glowing like a red-hot wire.
—Filmmaker Perry Henzell, director of *The Harder They Come*[2]

With *Time* magazine voting Bob Marley and the Wailers' *Exodus* as the "album of the 20th century" and with veteran producer Lee "Scratch" Perry receiving a Grammy award in 2003, Jamaica is beginning to be recognized for its influence on world popular music.[3] Like Cuba, Jamaica is a small island culture of the Greater Antilles that has exerted a tremendous influence on the development of post–World War II popular music globally. But even though Jamaica has been making its musical presence felt in mainland American music at least since Louis Armstrong's 1927 recording "King of the Zulus," the structural innovations of its music—unlike those of Cuba's—have yet to be widely acknowledged.[4]

This book is a historical, analytical, and interpretive study of the sub-genre of Jamaican reggae music known as *dub,* which was pioneered by recording studio engineers such as Osbourne "King Tubby" Ruddock (1941–1989), Lee "Scratch" Perry (born 1935), Errol "Errol T." Thompson (1941–2005), and others. Dub music flourished during the era of "roots" reggae (approximately 1968 through 1985),[5] and its significance as a style lies in the deconstructive manner in which these engineers remixed reggae songs, applying sound processing technology in unusual ways to create a unique pop music language of fragmented song forms and reverberating soundscapes. Today, the sounds and techniques of classic dub music have been stylistically absorbed into the various genres of global electronic popular music (such as hip-hop, techno, house, jungle, ambient, and trip-hop), and conceptually absorbed into the now commonplace practice of song remixing. Few people are aware that dub, a style built around fragments of sound over a hypnotically repeating reggae groove, was a crucial forerunner of these genres and that much of what is unique about contemporary dance music is directly traceable to the studio production techniques pioneered in Kingston beginning in the late 1960s. Dub's "fragmenting of the song surface" has become one of the stylistic cornerstones of popular dance music in the digital age, and its fluid reinterpretation of song form laid an important foundation for the amorphous remix culture that is so central to contemporary pop music. It is not overstating the case to suggest that this music has changed the way the world conceives of the popular song. Thus, one of my primary aims in this book is to demonstrate that in the same way that Bob Marley's themes of exile and spiritual conviction have inspired audiences around the world, the production style of Jamaican music has helped transform the sound and structure of world popular music. Further, I intend to show the extent to which this music (despite its creation in the hermetic setting of the recording studio) is in fact a potent metaphor for the society and times within which it emerged, and for global culture at the new millenium.

The Post–World War II Transformation of the Euro-American Popular Song

If we can speak of a transformation of the popular song at the turn of the twenty-first century, it is important to acknowledge that the Jamaican creators of dub were by no means the only musicians responsible. During the 1970s, for example, the experiments of post–World War II composers such as John Cage, Karlheinz Stockhausen, Steve Reich, and LaMonte Young eventually influenced a generation of experimentally inclined popular groups worldwide, who fused popular rhythms with tape-based and electronically generated elements, as well as with formal designs inspired by minimalism and indeterminacy.[6] The irreverent instrumental approaches of British punk musicians in the 1970s aggressively introduced a variety of pure sound elements into the popular song.[7] Brian Eno is an important pioneer of soundscaping in popular music; his experiments with atmospheric textures in the 1970s gradually made their way from the experimental rock underground (via his work with groups such as Roxy Music and Talking Heads) to the pop mainstream with his production of groups such as U2 during the 1980s. Eno's work eventually inspired a younger generation of electronic composers and the consolidation of "ambient" as a recognized genre category.[8] Jazz musicians such as Miles Davis and John Coltrane distilled the harmonic landscape of jazz through their experiments with modalism in the early 1960s in order to facilitate a new type of chromatic improvisation, and these modal innovations in turn formed the harmonic basis for jazz-rock fusion toward the end of the decade. The fusion of harmonic modalism and electronic textures in turn influenced a wide variety of popular musical forms.[9]

In Europe and the United States during the 1970s, dance music producers in various genres tampered with song form in different ways. Generally, the goal was to stretch the boundaries of songs beyond their radio-formatted length of three minutes in accordance with the extended play requirements of dance clubs and discotheques. Producers of disco and house music extended tracks through remixing and the construction of tape loops.[10] Hip-hop musicians in New York City did this by creating "breakbeats," excerpted rhythm grooves that were elongated by turntable scratching and later, by digital sequencing and sampling. What these efforts demonstrate is that outside of the requirements of selling and broadcasting, the duration of commercially recorded dance music is often fixed within highly artificial limits.[11] More important, all of these stylistic streams contributed to a transformation in the structure of the popular song from something that had arguably been fairly fixed to something that—in an age where the remix has become a central compositional paradigm—has become much more fluid and mutable. Jamaican dub is arguably particularly significant and fundamental in this process. As I will chronicle in the book's coda, it was crucial to the formative years of hip-hop in New York City, while it simultaneously played an important role in England through its influence on punk and other spheres of the British popular music underground.

Roots Reggae in Global and Local Perspective, 1970–1985

For many reasons, the influence of dub music must be discussed in the context of the global popularity of roots reggae during the 1970s and early 1980s, much of which is attributable to the influence of Bob Marley. Since 1973, Marley and his band the Wailers had scorched a blazing trail across the concert stages of America, Europe, and Asia, converting audiences to the idiosyncratic and completely unfamiliar religious vision of Rastafari (see section on broader themes) solely on the strength of their music and Marley's personal charisma.[12] The promotional campaign waged on Marley's behalf targeted European and American rock audiences. Marley was tremendously successful in courting this audience but tragically, he became terminally ill just as he was preparing to court African American audiences through a joint tour with Stevie Wonder. Nevertheless his success, as well as the emigration of thousands of Jamaicans to American and British cities after World War II, significantly expanded the market for Jamaican music in the major urban centers of the United States and Europe, and laid the foundation for the structural influence of Jamaican pop on global dance music.

The stylistic evolution of Jamaican popular music along both local and transnational lines was a complex and intertwined process; in terms of the aesthetics of production, however, reggae developed in two general directions during the 1970s. One direction was represented by musicians like Marley, Peter Tosh, Toots and the Maytals, Jimmy Cliff, and others: these were the figureheads anointed by the multinational record industry to introduce Jamaican popular music to the international audience. For this reason, their music was often recorded at better-equipped studios outside of Jamaica and was marked by high-end production values, more sophisticated chord progressions than were the local norm, and rock/pop stylizations such as electronic synthesizers and lead guitar solos. As with most pop music, there was a strong emphasis on singing, and specific songs tended to be associated with specific performers. Song lyrics tended toward themes of social and political justice filtered through the religious vision of Rastafari. The biblical undertones of this vision translated onto the world stage as a universalist sentiment that struck a strong chord with post–World War II American and European rock audiences.[13]

Musicians like Marley and Tosh maintained strong followings at home in Jamaica; stylistically, however, their music gradually grew fairly distinct from the local dancehall culture.[14] Producer/vocalist Michael "Mikey Dread" Campbell worked as a disc jockey for the Jamaican Broadcasting Corporation (JBC), and aired Jamaica's first all-reggae radio format in 1976.

Campbell described Marley's distance from the mainstream of Jamaican music, while emphasizing his breadth of vision and ultimate importance:

[Dancehall audiences] weren't really listening to Bob. They were listening to more rootsier sounds. They were more listening to Dennis Brown and Gregory [Isaacs] and whatever—Sly and Robbie and those things. . . . The kind of music Bob Marley was singing, the rhythm tracks were not like what was currently taking place in Jamaica at that time. 'Cause Bob Marley's music was like, timeless—you don't follow the trend or the fad which is going on now. You don't make music for now, you make music for all time.[15]

Although it also came to sell significantly abroad, another direction in which reggae developed was represented by musicians producing music largely aimed at the local Jamaican audience, associated during the 1970s and early 1980s with producers like Bunny Lee, Linval Thompson, Joe Gibbs, Junjo Lawes, and the Hookim brothers. How did this music differ from that of performers like Marley and Tosh? DJs—vocalists who rapped over rhythm tracks—were becoming nearly as popular as singers inside of Jamaica; in terms of song lyrics, however, the difference was not always so pronounced. The Rastafari-inspired lyrical themes were shared by both camps, such as those addressing African repatriation, the benefits of ganja (marijuana) smoking, the heroism of Marcus Garvey, quotations of Scripture, or the divinity of Ethiopian emperor Haile Selassie. Certain topics tended to be more prevalent in the local sphere, such as the ever-present "slackness" songs (generally sung by DJs) focusing on sexual topics, the "lover's rock" genre of romantic reggae (which actually had roots in the music of Jamaican immigrants in England), the songs addressing the political violence that was engulfing Jamaica, or songs relating to current events in general. One clearly important difference between local and international reggae was in their respective sites of consumption. As opposed to attending the concerts staged abroad by musicians like Marley and Tosh, most Jamaicans enjoyed music in dancehalls and at outdoor dances at which recorded music was provided by mobile entertainment collectives known as *sound systems.*

Possibly the clearest difference between the two types of reggae was in the sound, and it is the sound of Jamaican reggae that I primarily address in this book. In contrast to the music aimed at the international market, the production values and seemingly "virtual" construction of much of the music aimed at Kingston's sound system audiences probably seemed downright errant to many American, European, and upper-class Jamaican listeners at that time, whose listening tastes were conditioned by the naturalist values of much rock and roll and soul music.[16] This music, in contrast, drew attention to itself as a *recording* in a peculiar way. These Jamaican singers did not always conform to the chord changes of a song, and sometimes even sang in a different key altogether than the musicians. Vocalists didn't even always sing; many times they casually rapped over the rhythm tracks as if they were carrying on a conversation in spite of the music underneath. The vocals also sometimes seemed strangely discontinuous; no sooner would a singer complete a stanza of a song, before a different vocalist (usually a DJ) began shouting over the music in apparent disregard of the original vocalist; the varying fidelity made it clear that these vocalists did not record their parts at the same time. The music also seemed oddly mixed. The bass sounded unusually heavy and the equalization strangely inconsistent, as the sound veered back and forth from cloudy and bass-heavy to sharp and tinny. The individual instruments didn't seem to play continuously, but zipped in and out of the mix in a strangely incoherent manner. At a dance or on the radio, it seemed as if you could hear the same rhythm track for hours on end. Reggae historian/curator Dave Hendley, listening from London in the early 1970s, remembered the reception of this music by British audiences a few years prior to its global explosion: "Reggae was ridiculed in the early seventies by the mainstream media as being repetitive, musically impoverished, kind of like idiot's music. That was the kind of perception of it. Because in those times, you had all of those progressive rock bands. So it was very much derided. But a lot of the people that had derided it changed their tune after the advent of Bob Marley."[17]

Essentially, the artist-based marketing of Jamaican musicians to the Euro-American audience by multinational corporations did not prepare one for the often bewildering complexity of a music that, in its natural context, was multiply elaborated by a multitude of voices moving between the fluid sites of stage, studio, and sound system. Even within Jamaica, popular music has moved in and out of phase with radio networks, with music producers and radio programmers sometimes holding strongly contrasting ideas about what constitutes acceptable or appropriate broadcast quality and/or content. It was these rougher qualities that were sometimes deemed in need of "smoothing out" by multinational record labels, in their attempt to market reggae internationally. As such, they are largely absent from the Jamaican music most familiar to non-Jamaicans. Ironically, however, the same musical choices that made local Jamaican music sound so "pre-professional" to mainstream Western ears were simultaneously visionary and deliberate. The approach Jamaican producers and recording engineers took to the production of music would make a subtle, structural, and long-term impact on world popular music in subsequent years, providing openings for new practice in the areas of form, structure, harmony, orchestration, and studio production. It illustrates that postindependence Jamaica has been an important source of material and sound concepts for the international music industry,[18] with reggae itself being, in the words of Louis Chude-Sokei, "a vehicle for the dissemination of larger ideas about sound, oral/aural knowledge, and technical innovation."[19]

2.

"The Half That Never Been Told"

Despite the differences in production values, the locally oriented reggae held an immediate charm for many non-Jamaican listeners. My own fascination with dub music dates to the early 1980s, immediately following the international success of Bob Marley. My epiphanal moment took place one winter evening in New York in 1983 while hanging out with my friend Tony, who had just picked up the Wailing Souls's 1982 LP *Wailing,* a "showcase" album containing songs followed by their dub versions.[20] Tony had a state-of-the art sound system, and the room was filled with the ethereal Jamaican "country" harmonies of Rudolph "Garth" Dennis, Winston "Pipe" Matthews, George "Buddy" Hayes, and Lloyd "Bread" McDonald as they sang "Who No Waan Come Cyaan Stay." The song's title translates from the Jamaican patwa as "Who Didn't Want to Come Can't Stay," and the elegiac lyric, in which the singer promises to prepare a place for his brethren in a heavenly African Zion, is a typical Rastafari-inspired theme of African repatriation, given an obliquely poetic slant:

> It's been long, so long
> I've been warning you
> Yet you're trying hard not to upset my world
> But when the master's calling
> You will find yourself stumbling
> I'll be waiting
> by the wayside . . .
>
> Who no waan come cyaan stay
> You can stay for I am going
> Who no waan come cyaan stay . . .

The song's mystical message was reinforced by the production style, which seemed to depict some sort of dreamy, electro-pastoral paradise. Although the drum pattern was stark and heavy, the singers' voices floated above a bed of subtly reverberating guitar chords, anchored by a ponderous electric bass pattern, colored with enchanting wah-wah guitar melodies, and thrown into a cavernous soundscape. Yet all this, as it turned out, was only half of what the music had to offer. As the song faded, Tony winked at me conspiratorially and said, "Now check *this* out!" Before the last notes had disappeared, the track abruptly began again, in what seemed to be a reprise of the song we had just heard. The singers again harmonized the first notes of the song's wistful melody; then, just as suddenly, their voices evaporated into a reverberating void in the mix, to be heard only fleetingly throughout the rest of the performance. The rhythm section was treated similarly: sometimes audible, at other times dissolving into passages of pure ambient sound. In this remixed version of the song, reverberation seemed to be the central compositional element, as the music moved back and forth between music and echoes of music. Even these echoes were themselves manipulated until the track seemed at times to lapse into clouds of pure noise. At this point the mixer would reintroduce the rhythm section, and the music became once again earthbound. It was as if the music was billowing out from the speakers in clouds, dissolving and reconstituting itself before our ears.

We had just experienced a "Scientific Dub Mix" as crafted by engineer and King Tubby protégé Scientist (Overton H. Brown), and from that moment on I was hooked on dub music. In alternating snatches, dub seemed to convey the stereotypically optimistic and melodious quality of much Caribbean music, the improvisational disposition of jazz, the contemplative dreaminess of pop psychedelia, the ominous undertones of black insurgence, and the futuristic soundscapes of experimental electronic music and science fiction. This fusion of dance music, improvisation, and abstract soundscaping was right in line with my own musical interests, as I listened avidly to reggae, jazz, and experimental electronic music. Rooted in the aesthetics and communal imperatives of black dance music, while foregrounding the creative use (and misuse) of sound technology, this music could satisfy all three tastes.

Boston, where I attended the Berklee College of Music in the early 1980s, was a city with a strong audience for roots reggae music. Some of this interest was traceable to the residual impact of Marley, who had played the city several times, including a legendary benefit concert at Harvard Stadium in 1979;[21] one of his very last concerts was at the Hynes Auditorium in the fall of 1980. Jazz and popular music were the dominant student interests at Berklee, but there was also a strong subculture of reggae enthusiasts. In fact, a number of my classmates joined local reggae bands such as One People, the I-Tones, and Zion Initation, and others went on to play with renowned reggae artists such as Burning Spear, the re-formed Skatalites, and Sugar Minott. But what I remember most is listening to reggae for hours with my friend Willy D. Wallace, analyzing and dissecting the finer points of dub mixes by Scientist, King Tubby, and others. In fact, Willy was studying audio engineering, and had recorded and mixed a song called "E.T." which was inspired by Lee Perry's Black Ark mixing style.

Back home in New York City, the burgeoning Jamaican community provided a great opportunity to hear and buy this music. Besides seeking out the classic work of dub luminaries such as Augustus Pablo and Lee Perry at reggae outlets like VP Records in Queens, Coxsone's Record Mart in Brooklyn, or Brad's Record Shack in the Bronx, expatriate Jamaican producer Lloyd "Bullwackie" Barnes hit a hot streak in the early 1980s, issuing a stream of dub-influenced recordings from his base in the Bronx. The spacey B-side dub mixes of innumerable singles were also played nightly as background for the radio patter of New York–area reggae DJs like Gil Bailey, Clive Hudson, and Earl "Rootsman" Chin. Hearing these fragmented and collaged-sounding Jamaican songs over the very medium—radio— that arguably implanted the aesthetic of the sound collage into the public's sonic imagination made dub music a powerfully organic reflection of the sonic culture of our times. A true music of our modern spheres—if those spheres are understood to be streaked by an infinitude of invisibly competing broadcast signals,[22] intermittently canceling each other out.

Besides the music itself, I found the ethos surrounding it equally intriguing. Recording engineers have certainly never been the star personalities of popular music; like the subterranean graffiti murals that graced subway cars in New York City as they dipped in and out of public view during the 1970s and 1980s, dub mixes seemed to issue from a subaltern location in the most *literal* sense. They seemed to exist as shadow versions of popular themes: sometimes heard, sometimes not, anonymous-sounding in their skeletal spookiness. Who was creating this strange music, and where was it being created? I eventually learned of Lee "Scratch" Perry, eccentric master dancer/producer/engineer/songwriter, mentor of Bob Marley and the Wailers, and the so-called Dalí of reggae who had progressed from funky, soul-inspired reggae rhythms to swirling, psychedelic soundscapes and (allegedly) on to madness. I learned of dub's guiding mystics, Augustus Pablo and Yabby You. The first was an elusive and introspective Rasta producer and session musician whose heavy dub rhythms were graced with his wistful melodica improvisations and whose devout faith imparted to his dub music a feeling of meditation and devotion. The second, a vocalist possessed by postcolonial visions of biblical apocalypse, found in dub a sonic complement to his excoriating sermonizing. I learned of King Tubby, the studio engineer who, in the back of his home in one of Kingston's roughest ghettos, had turned re-mixing into a new and dramatic form of composition that used sound processing to melt the reggae song form into ambient soundscapes. In the context of the rapid corporatization and standardization of the popular song that was taking place during the 1980s, I heard dub music as a radical and refreshingly different conception of what the popular song could sound like. And although (as I shall discuss in the final chapter) most of the techniques of dub music have been subsequently subsumed into the common practice of popular song composition, this music continues to stand out today as a provocative intervention into the global conception of the popular song.

Kingston

It was my enthusiasm for dub music that eventually inspired me to write this book. Part of this project involved getting to know some of the many Jamaican musicians who had emigrated to New York City and other parts of the United States. Eventually, I made several trips to Jamaica between 2000 and 2003. The heart of my visits was a personal pilgrimage of sorts to the Kingston studios (almost all of them now inoperative) in which dub music was created back in the 1970s: King Tubby's studio in Waterhouse, Lee Perry's Black Ark studio in Washington Gardens, the Hoo-Kim brothers' Channel One studio on Maxfield Avenue, Byron Lee's Dynamic studio off Spanish Town Road near Three Miles, Harry Johnson's Harry J. Studio off Hope Road, and Joe Gibbs's studio on Retirement Crescent, where Errol Thompson had worked as chief engineer. Randy's studio, where Thompson did much of his earliest work, had been located on the downtown square known as The Parade, but no longer existed by the time of my first visit.

"Man, we're going into the *heart* of the ghetto!" exclaimed the driver of my cab as we sped down Olympic Way to Bay Farm Road, toward the Waterhouse district of West Kingston where King Tubby's studio had been located. The name "Waterhouse" is a colloquialism that is not always printed on maps; the name refers to an area of Kingston 11 just south of Sandy Gully, bounded by the neighborhoods of Tower Hill on the east, Nanse Pen on the west, Balmagie on the north, and Spanish Town Road on the south. The area struck me as somewhat of a tropical war zone: its crumbling buildings, debris-strewn lots, and treacherously potholed streets would be better traversed by a military jeep than a conventional automobile. The area is in fact a *literal* war zone, one epicenter of a decades-long struggle between Jamaica's two dominant political parties, the Jamaican Labour Party (JLP) and the People's National Party (PNP).[23] The formerly left-leaning PNP seemed dominant in Waterhouse, judging from all the graffiti proclaiming socialism and warning visitors that they were now entering "Moscow." I was lucky to get a cab at all, as many licensed cabbies refused to drive into the area. My cab driver pointed to two indentations above each of his ears, proud of the fact that he had survived a direct gunshot wound to the temple while being robbed in this very area.

Waterhouse is an extremely tough area by American standards, but as long as the political violence was dormant, it didn't seem the hell on earth that many Kingstonians had warned me of. I located King Tubby's old home studio on Dromilly Avenue with the help of the cabdriver, but it no longer evoked the colorful accounts of reggae historians like Dave Hendley who had visited Tubby's during its heyday in the 1970s.[24] Instead, I found a typical Jamaican bungalow that seemed empty, save for the dogs and goats in the front yard. Tubby had been tragically murdered during a robbery in 1989, and his family closed the studio shortly thereafter. On a later visit, however, I was met outside by a young boy returning home from school, who lived in the house with his family. "You a tourist?" he asked me as I raised my camera to take a photo of the famous carved door that still stands at the studio's entrance. "Not exactly," I told him, "I'm writing a book about King Tubby." "He died" was the boy's simple reply.

In a way, that simple sentence became a recurrent theme during my trips to Kingston. The challenges and occasional surreality of researching a music that had reached its social, commercial, and stylistic apogee more than two decades earlier was compounded by the fact that many of its most important practitioners had since perished in the violent climate of Kingston. I had the impression that I was sometimes researching in a ghost town, despite the profusion of life—including musical life—at every turn. Ironically, this impression was reinforced by the reverberating sound of the dub music I listened to following my daily travels around the city.

As far back as my aforementioned college years, my friends and I had remained largely unaware that Jamaica of the early 1980s was a very different place than the Jamaica of the 1970s that had given birth to roots reggae. Some of us were indirectly aware of the violence that accompanied the 1980 elections as Edward Seaga ousted Michael Manley from office, but our awareness of Jamaica was primarily developed through its music, and what we heard was largely Rastafarian-themed music of the roots era. For the most part, the radio stations in New York continued to play a substantial amount of Rasta-themed music, and the Jamaican performers who toured high-profile U.S. venues in the 1980s were the star singers and DJs of the roots and early dancehall era like Dennis Brown, Burning Spear, Gregory Isaacs, Culture, Bunny Wailer, Yellowman, Eek-A-Mouse, Black Uhuru, and British performers such as Steel Pulse and Linton Kwesi Johnson.

For those of us judging the country by its music, our understanding of Jamaica would change dramatically in 1985, when seemingly out of nowhere, the music suddenly went digital, with a sound so radically different from what had preceded it as to shake the foundations of many assumptions we had about Jamaica itself. And this re-visioning had as much to do with the concrete political realities of Jamaican culture as it did the global marketing of Jamaican music at that time. The truth is, since the late 1970s, Jamaica's music had in fact been changing, gradually becoming harder, more urban-sounding, and more reflective of the harsh social and political realities that were transforming the country. And this transformation could be felt far away in New York City, where Jamaican posses were an increasing presence in the city's drug trade, and the city's Jamaican dancehalls were increasingly plagued by political and gang-related violence.

My point here is that, similarly to my friends and me in the early 1980s, many Jamaican music lovers outside of the Caribbean have no idea of the tough climate that spawned the music that so passionately speaks of peace, love, and brotherhood. A mere roll call of the great Jamaican musicians who have met violent deaths will make this clear—and for both economic extremes of the Jamaican music industry. For example, the number of deceased musicians (most never lived to age twenty-five) in Beth Lesser's recent biography of dancehall icon King Jammy shows that violent death is a daily reality in a Jamaican ghetto such as Waterhouse. At the other end of the economic ladder, a skim of the final chapter of Timothy White's revised biography of Bob Marley shows how regularly Jamaica's violence can affect the lives of the most affluent and successful musicians.[25] This book is partially a tribute to the lives and work of these artists, as well as a reminder to audiences outside of Jamaica of the human toll behind the music they so cherish.

King Tubby's Waterhouse legacy can be considered partially inherited by Lloyd "King Jammy" James, his former righthand man, who now presides over a musical empire on nearby St. Lucia Road encompassing a recording complex, a leading sound system, and several record labels. Located in a depressed area, Jammy's complex is probably among the biggest industries in the local Waterhouse economy. Jammy's studio is a mere few blocks away from Tubby's but once inside, you're in a different world entirely. The brightly lit, air-conditioned lobby is gleaming with white tile, furnished with a fish tank, and staffed by a friendly receptionist seated behind a stylishly curved office desk. A long couch awaits visitors, who can kill time by studying the gold records framed on the walls, or the photomontage of Jammy (referred to at the studio as "The King") with the hundreds of top-selling artists he has produced. In fact, King Tubby had also been producing digital music at his studio during the four years prior to his death, but did not live to consolidate this new phase in full. So in both social and sonic terms, King Jammy's Waterhouse empire can be considered Tubby's most direct descendant, even though the digital "ragga" he produces there is quite distinct from the psychedelic-sounding dub music that was issued by Tubby's studio during the 1970s and early 1980s.[26]

A visit to Lee Perry's legendary Black Ark studio was also high on my agenda. Although Perry has lived outside of Jamaica for some twenty-five years now, the remains of his studio still stand in the back of his old home, located at the end of quiet Cardiff Crescent in the Kingston suburb of Washington Gardens. The neighborhood seems a world away from the West Kingston ghetto where King Tubby lived and worked, and reflects the period of affluence Perry enjoyed while he was the producer for such legends of reggae music as Bob Marley, Augustus Pablo, The Meditations, The Heptones, The Mighty Diamonds, and others. A legendary eccentric of Jamaican music, Perry destroyed his studio in 1979; since then he has created a new career in Europe as what might be considered an artist/producer/performance artist. In this new role, he seems to devote as much attention to his eccentric costumes and profuse wordplay as to his music, which has tended toward collaborative efforts with British-based "neo-dub" producers, such as Adrian Sherwood and Neil "Mad Professor" Fraser. The Black Ark studio itself remains a burnt-out, rubble-filled shell of a building, although the carport leading to it has been refurbished with outdoor fish tanks, drawings, paintings, and an array of multicolored light bulbs. For some time, it has been rumored that Perry is on the verge of reviving the Black Ark as an actual recording facility; only time will tell if he will actually bring this to fruition. For the moment, the embers of his brilliance continue to smolder in the eccentric trappings that garnish the charred remains of his studio.[27]

Basically, the neighborhoods of West Kingston are like many other places in the world: tough urban spaces populated by people trying to live their lives with dignity. Both local politics and global economics have extracted a heavy toll here, and it takes a powerful music to transform the harsher aspects of this reality. That is exactly what King Tubby, Lee Perry, and other producers of dub music accomplished during the 1970s. All the talk of circuits, knobs, and switches can distract one from the fundamental reality that what these musicians were doing was synthesizing a new popular art form, creating a space where people could come together joyously despite the harshness that surrounded them. They created a music as roughly textured as the physical reality of the place, but with the power to transport their listeners to dancefloor nirvana as well as the far reaches of the cultural and political imagination: Africa, outer space, inner space, nature, and political/economic liberation. Nevertheless, this book will focus on those knobs and the people who operated them, in order to develop an understanding of the role of sound technology, sound technicians, and sound aesthetics within the larger cultural and political realities of Jamaica in the 1970s.

3.
Broader Themes

Post-Colonial Jamaica

Roots reggae reflected a unique moment in Jamaican history and, as such, intersects with a number of themes that shape this narrative on a broader level. From the period of urbanization that began in the 1930s, Kingston life had progressively differentiated along class lines. By the 1960s, class distinctions between rich and poor were usually referred to by the words "uptown" (affluent, elite, Europhile, light-complexioned) and "downtown" (poor, from rural origins, dark-skinned, and generally of clear African descent).[28] These divisions were reflected in music. While Jamaica is now known worldwide for its popular music forms such as reggae and ska, this music was associated inside Jamaica with the country's urban underclass, and largely spurned by the middle and upper classes. This attitude began to change during the 1970s. The charismatic Michael Manley (1924–1997) and his People's National Party (PNP) had swept to victory in 1972 with a populist mandate to spread the power and the wealth, to provide a voice for the nation's dispossessed, and to acknowledge the nation's overwhelmingly African heritage as part of the creation of a new postcolonial Jamaican identity. Manley's vision defined Jamaica in the 1970s and, in many ways, roots reggae music formed the soundtrack for the Manley era. Early in his campaign, Manley had commissioned musicians to write pro-PNP songs, and he used both reggae and the rhetoric of Rastafari in his campaign to project his populist vision and empathy with the nation's underclass.[29] Pursuing a democratic-socialist agenda, Manley opened diplomatic channels with Cuba and courted Fidel Castro for a state visit (all under the nose of the United States, which grew increasingly uncomfortable at the prospect of "another Cuba" in the hemisphere).

Manley's democratic-socialist experiment ultimately collapsed because of several factors including fluctuating demand for Jamaica's exports, increasing levels of social instability, and alleged subversion by the U.S. government. But what was taking place in Jamaica reflected changes in the world at large. Cultural and political consciousness was on the rise in many developing countries, inspired by the nearby Cuban revolution, the civil rights/Black Power movements in America, and nationalism in other formerly colonized areas (especially Africa). Regional political activists in the Caribbean like Walter Rodney and Maurice Bishop were dismantling the ideological foundations of colonialism and white supremacy, while artists and intellectuals like C. L. R. James, Aimé Césaire, Frantz Fanon, and other Caribbeans had emerged to articulate the postcolonial condition for the black world and beyond.

Rastafari

Jamaica has often been characterized as an extremely religious society,[30] and one place this religiosity is strongly reflected is in the country's popular music—particularly in the strong influence of the Rastafarian faith on reggae of the 1970s. The religion of Rastafari had long been considered a fringe movement of Jamaican society since its inception in the 1930s and *Rastas,* as adherents were known, were generally looked upon with contempt and disdain by the larger society. Nevertheless, the millenarian and utopian aspects of Rasta theology, heralding the destruction of an evil world, the ultimate victory of the weak over the strong and of good over evil, resonated dynamically within the sociopolitical turbulence of post–World War II Jamaica. From the 1930s, the religion grew substantially in popularity and influence and began to make inroads among the urban poor in Kingston, a process that accelerated after leading reggae musicians such as Bob Marley and Peter Tosh became adherents in the late 1960s.[31] Rooted in the epic stories of the Old Testament, Rastafarian belief also drew on the pan-Africanist ideas of Marcus Garvey, which introduced a crucial political component into the religious equation. By the late 1960s, Rastafari began to appeal to those beyond Jamaica's most dispossessed; embraced by artists, students, and intellectuals, it awakened a sense of "communal attachment to a common culture that transcen[ded] social class."[32] Although the actual number of adherents remained low, Rastafari and its ideas became the most provocative articulation of Jamaica's postcolonial ethos by the end of the 1960s, and its newly potent place within Jamaican culture owed much to the dissemination of its ideals through the medium of reggae musicians and dancehall DJs.[33]

Rastafarian belief rejected modern technology in favor of a philosophy of naturalism typified by a rural ("roots") lifestyle and the "dreadlock" hairstyle—at that time, the antithesis of "cultured" ideas of style. Rastafari also held, among other things, that the Old Testament of the Bible was a coded history of black people, that the Messiah prophesied in the biblical book of Revelation was the reigning emperor of Ethiopia, Haile Selassie (1892–1975); that Rastafarians were modern descendants of the Old Testament

Hebrews; that Western civilization (referred to as "Babylon") was evil and doomed to imminent destruction (some prophecies had this taking place by 1983); that marijuana (usually referred to in Jamaica by its East Indian–derived name, *ganja*) was a religious sacrament;[34] and that people of African descent in the Western Hemisphere should prepare for imminent repatriation to the African motherland.

Although there were abundant love songs, novelty songs, slackness songs, and instrumentals, the Rastafarian influence was dominant in the popular reggae of the era. Songs such as the Wailing Souls's "Kingdom Rise, Kingdom Fall" prophesied the end of Western civilization;[35] Horace Andy's "Leave Rasta" condemned political persecution and social marginalization of Rastas;[36] Johnny Clarke's "Be Holy, My Brothers and Sisters" exhorted the faithful to live upstanding lives;[37] Sang Hugh's "Rasta No Born Yah" advised Jamaicans to seek their true home in the African motherland;[38] Burning Spear honored the memory of Marcus Garvey on their famous album of the same name;[39] while Augustus Pablo's instrumental "Israel in Harmony" used biblical imagery to appeal for an end to the political violence plaguing the island. The gruff-voiced DJ Prince Far I even recorded an entire album of himself "chanting" (as he described his DJ style) Old Testament Scripture over reggae rhythm tracks.[40]

Peter Manuel believes that the moment when a musical style of the urban proletariat gains the embrace of all classes of society, is the moment when a truly *national* style is born.[41] Such was the case with reggae in the 1970s, which consolidated as Jamaica's national music in the same moment that Manley preached a vision of inclusion and broadly based empowerment, and the previously marginal religion of Rastafari became an attractive option for a small but influential minority of Jamaicans of different social classes. Eventually, through the medium of music and charismatic reggae performers such as Marley and Tosh, Rastafari grew to become the most globally diffused of all the indigenous Caribbean religions.[42]

The lyrics of roots reggae songs clearly tie into a broader critique of colonial European, neocolonial American, and upper-class Jamaican domination. The musical structure of roots reggae, built upon a hybrid of neo-African and progressively Africanized Euro-American traits, represent a second component; the hybridized redeployment of European musical traits in an Africanized musical agenda is encoded with the self-determination at the heart of the nationalist and postcolonial projects. In this book, I argue that beyond traditional textual and structural concerns, the additional transformations wrought by studio engineers in the mixing of dub music represent a third and, in the long run, profoundly transformative musical arena. At their most radical, the textural and syntactic qualities of the music counteracted the dominance of Westernized musical thinking; ultimately, they helped transform the culture of popular music within the West itself. My goal is not to make any concrete claims about such extramusical associations, but rather to evoke what Raymond Williams would term a particular "structure of feeling"[43] with multiple roots in Jamaican music and history.

The Ganja Factor

As the central sacrament to Rastafarians, the importance of ganja (marijuana) has been well documented and this importance extends into the sphere of Rasta-influenced Jamaican music. Rasta-influenced musicians were often outspoken advocates of ganja smoking, with songs full of exhortations to "smoke the herb": Peter Tosh's "Legalize It," Bob Marley's "Kaya" and "Easy Skanking," Culture's "International Herb," Horace Andy's "Better Collie," Lee Perry's "Free Up the Weed" and "Roast Fish, Cornbread and Collie Weed," and Leroy Horsemouth Wallace's "Herb Vendor" are a mere few of hundreds of such songs. Yet while it would probably be difficult to find a Jamaican musician of the roots era who was avowedly anti-ganja, some Jamaican musicians nevertheless felt that the prominence of this theme led to a distorted view of reggae in the world at large, as musicians played to the expectations of their international audiences. Paul Henton voiced a sentiment common among some Jamaican musicians, who felt that their colleagues sung about ganja at least in part "just because they know that the white people love it. If tomorrow morning the people or the fans say 'Okay, we don't want to hear anymore of this ganja stuff,' they'll stop singing about it and stop promoting it!"[44]

Inside Jamaica, where ganja songs have flourished within several genres of Jamaican popular music (such as roots reggae and ragga), the situation has been more complex. Ganja was declared illegal in Jamaica in 1913 and for the decades since, its illegality has been a primary tool used by the ruling class in the social control of working-class Jamaicans.[45] Correspondingly, it became a combustible element in the constellation of factors (including music, Rastafari, class conflict) that factor into Jamaica's social tensions. As such, it is not surprising that ganja played a central role in the blended class, cultural, and political content that exploded in Jamaica in the 1970s and that arguably found its most powerful and passionate articulation in roots reggae. This centrality can be felt in the comments of legendary drummer Leroy "Horsemouth" Wallace: "The people respect you in Jamaica when you can put forty and fifty bag a ganja on a plane! We don't call that drugs. That is ganja business. . . . We do those things like we are revolutionary. We put forty bag on a plane and feel good. . . . We send those so people in America could smoke the good ganja, not just for money alone."[46]

The symbiotic relationship between ganja and roots reggae helped clear a psychological space for the flourishing of Jamaica's brand of cultural nationalism, but in all likelihood, its significance to Jamaican culture transcended both this and its function as a religious sacrament for Rastas. As Rasta-influenced reggae musicians extolled the virtues of ganja to the international audience, Jamaica, roots reggae, and ganja essentially became interchangeable advertisements for each other, with the latter rivaling legal exports such as bauxite, sugar cane, and bananas. Despite the religious rhetoric, then, a deeper reason for the sacralization of ganja in Jamaica might be the huge economic benefit it brings to the island. Bonham Richardson concluded:

Romanticized by reggae and a sacrament in the island's Rastafarian religious sect, the use of ganja is widespread though illegal in Jamaica. . . . A Jamaican narcotics squad patrols warehouses, sabotages clandestine airstrips, and intimidates growers, and the Jamaican government has sponsored helicopter flights over parts of the island to burn ganja fields. Yet these campaigns from a Jamaican government pressured by US politicians are not appreciated by the majority of Jamaicans; a recent poll indicated that 62 percent of all Jamaicans opposed the curtailment of marijuana exportation to the United States, in part because so many benefit from it.[47]

As a result of this situation, some have suggested that the connection between reggae and ganja may represent the most complex "drug-music nexus" in the sphere of global popular music.[48] But what has been less documented is the role of ganja in the sonic transformation of Jamaican music in the 1970s. As I shall discuss in chapter 2, ganja was an important catalyst in the sound of dub music. For example, some musicians claim a correlation between the sound of the music produced in different recording studios, and various producers' willingness or reluctance to let musicians smoke ganja in their studios. Similar to the case of psychedelic rock music of the 1960s, mind-altering substances were a catalyst in the expansion of Jamaica's sonic imagination in the 1970s, inspiring musicians and engineers to expand their conception of the capabilities of their equipment.

Basically, then, this book is about a particular type of art realized in the recording studios of Kingston: its sound, its broader resonance for Jamaican and diasporic African culture, and its influence on the language of popular music worldwide. The book can be considered a history of a subgenre of reggae music with a substantial oral history component, a sonic analysis of what I hear as unique about Jamaican studio craft, and a work of cultural interpretation. The book examines the impact of dub music on several levels. This introduction delineates some of the book's prominent themes, and will most interest readers who desire an overview of dub music and its general relevance to both post–World War II popular music and several broader themes. Chapter 1 foreshadows the emergence of dub by providing a brief historical overview of Jamaican music and an exploration of the theme of electronic music as viewed through the prism of Jamaican music. Chapter 2 examines the economic, stylistic, and technological forces that were catalysts in the emergence of dub as a genre, the formal strategies of the dub mix, and includes the voices of several of the musicians central to its rise. My musicological approach in this chapter ultimately rests on a notion of the dub mixer as a "songscape" composer concerned with regulating the musical parameters of (electronically manipulated) texture and soundspace as much as the traditional parameters of melody, rhythm, and harmony. Given the extent to which advances in sound technology have opened up new sonic parameters in music, my analysis in chapters 2 though 6 is an attempt (however preliminary and narrative-based) to fashion a language to address the qualities of this music on its own terms. And my own work necessarily ties into similar efforts in the spheres of experimental music, free jazz, various world musics, and other forms of electronic popular music. Chapter 2 will most likely interest readers who wish to understand what distinguishes dub from the rest of roots reggae music, as well as those interested in its processes of realization.

Chapter 2 in turn lays the foundations for the third through sixth chapters, each of which examines the history, equipment, and mixing styles of several of the era's leading studios and engineers: Sylvan Morris (at Studio One and Harry J studio), King Tubby, Philip Smart, King Jammy and Scientist (at King Tubby's studio), Lee "Scratch" Perry (at his Black Ark studio), and Errol Thompson (at Randy's and Joe Gibbs's studios). While this section of the book can be read straight through from beginning to end, it might be more comfortably read a chapter at a time—ideally, while listening to the various dub mixes that are discussed. Unfortunately, clearance issues proved prohibitive in the release of a CD to accompany this book, but CD sources for all music discussed in this text are provided in the notes and the appendix of recommended listenings. These chapters will be most relevant to readers interested in the history and styles of specific studios and engineers, as well as in a close read of stylistic aspects of dub mixing (especially true for the "On the Mix" sections, which examine specific dub mixes in close details and will be of most interest to engineers, music scholars, musicians, and composers).

Chapter 7 briefly chronicles the final years of the roots reggae era, and examines the legacy of dub music in Jamaica and its influence on the digital era of Jamaican music, which began in the mid-1980s. Chapter 8 largely concludes the Jamaica-centered core of the book, and is an interpretive attempt to ground dub music in the particular cultural and historical experience of postcolonial Jamaica, and within certain dominant tropes of African diasporic history. As Veit Erlmann has asserted, "Musical analysis . . . is not about structure per se, or even about semantic content. Rather, it seeks to uncover the processes by means of which certain people—socially-situated and culturally-determined actors—invest certain sounds with meanings."[49] So although portions of this book are concerned with musical analysis of a type, chapter 8 attempts to chart the way in which the strategies of the dub mix may function as sonic markers of certain processes of black culture. Chapter 8 will be of most interest to those readers who approach the topic of dub music with an interest in black cultural studies, diaspora studies, or postcolonial studies.

The book closes with a coda, and it examines dub's stylistic legacy to global popular music. Having moved beyond the boundaries of Jamaican culture, this coda makes a claim for dub as an influential musical subculture of global popular music at the turn of the twenty-first century. Because this book, for the most part, focuses on dub in its original Jamaican context, I do not attempt to examine the non-Jamaican varieties of dub in the same amount of detail as I devoted to the Jamaican context; I merely provide enough material to give the reader an overview of how dub has influenced musical developments outside of Jamaica. In this light, I also use the coda to emphasize dub's significance in the historical soundscape of popular music via a brief comparison with hip-hop, a musical genre that (as I shall discuss) shares a somewhat parallel history with dub, but that has achieved much higher visibility in both academic studies and popular music journalism.[50] The varying amounts of attention paid to the two styles is ironic as both hip-hop and dub worked more or less in tandem (although at different rates) to transform the grammar of global popular music, and both are implicated in a reshaping of sonic values in popular dance music that can be traced at least as far back as the late 1960s. I compare the two styles in a way that takes advantage of the scholarly space opened by hip-hop scholarship's study of issues such as technology and identity, while simultaneously distinguishing dub as a crucial, regionally specific genre that engages a different constellation of musical and extramusical issues, and that deserves serious discussion on its own terms.

In the end, there are two themes in this book. One is the theme of dub music, its evolution, stylistic characteristics, primary innovators, and influence on world popular music. The other is the story of dub music considered as an embodiment of its times, both in Jamaica and to a lesser extent, globally.

Along with the practice of rapping or toasting over prerecorded music, dub's unique approach to production has been among Jamaica's most important contributions to world popular music. The former trait has been addressed by several writers including David Toop (1984), Brian Jahn and Tom Weber (1998), Carolyn Cooper (1995 and 2004), Norman C. Stolzoff (2000), and others, but no substantial study has yet been completed on the sonic, procedural, or conceptual aspects. While there have been a number of chapter-length articles devoted to dub music,[51] there have been no book-length studies to date. The lack of writing about dub probably reflects three factors. First, the difficulty in analyzing music created by electronic technologies; after all, no standardized musicological language exists to discuss these types of music.

Second, for the most part, authors on the subject of Jamaican music have tended to write biographies of individual musicians (T. White 1983, Davis 1985, Katz 2000, Lesser 2002), historical overviews of the genre (Davis and Simon 1982 and 1982, Potash 1997, Foster 1999, Bradley 2000, Katz 2003) or social-scientific studies that are less concerned with musical detail than in the broader social and political forces within which the music was constituted (Waters 1985, Stolzoff 2000, King 2003). It is also true that virtually all Jamaican music of the "roots" era has tended to be viewed through the prism of Rastafari. This strong extramusical influence has made it difficult for the music to be appreciated for its purely musicological, technical, and/or conceptual qualities.

Third, generally speaking, Caribbean music has not been thought of for its conceptual qualities; the dominant stereotypes of the region's music center around ideas of sensuality, physicality, hedonism, and existential optimism.[52] Accordingly, many people have asked me, when they hear of my approach to this music, "Does the music really support the theorizing?" In terms of the music itself, dub won't hold much fascination for those for whom the bass-driven roots reggae sound and its foggy, low-fi aesthetic is monotonous and bottom-heavy. But although it might sometimes sound staid in comparison to its digital descendants of today, dub in its day was messy, unruly, and subversive; its pioneers devised a new system of improvisation and helped transform the recorded popular song from a fixed *product* into a more fluid *process*.

In fact, although dub is certainly a genre of Jamaican music, it might be most accurate to think of it as such a process: a process of song remixing or, more accurately, song re-composition. The fact that the dub mix is a version of a preexisting song that allows fragments of its prior incarnations to remain audible as an obvious part of the final product, makes it conducive to such conceptualizing; it can be linked with similar technology-based processes in other artistic media such as the serial reuse of images, collage, manipulations of texture, and compositional procedures based on chance. So if the real-time, live musician, dance-oriented performance aspects of the music allow it to furnish the usual range of physical, emotional, psychological, and aesthetic pleasures normally expected of pop music, its post-performance manipulation at the hands of recording engineers gives it a conceptual edge that makes it applicable to various modes of abstract theorizing. Thus, I have written this book in a way that simultaneously remains faithful to dub's Jamaican context, allows its technical and conceptual contributions to world sonic art to be acknowledged, and also explores its similarities with a range of non-Jamaican art forms. If comparisons with Western canvas painting, African oral and visual arts, deconstructive architecture, and experimental Euro-American art music seem a bit afield, the text will make it evident that I am not addressing the music in this way in order to "add thrilling new grist to the moribund old elitist mill" (to quote John Corbett).[53] Rather, I hope to make dub music a part of discussions that are global in scope. As much as the music has to tell us about the obvious tropes of race, nation, culture, it has other stories to tell about art, aesthetics, technology, and the nature of modernity.

As such, the book also contributes to a growing body of literature about electronic popular music and the creative history of the recording studio.[54] In addition to the more established area of technical books, articles, and manuals, the study of the studio as a musical and/or cultural institution has grown over the last two decades. The literature can be traced through several disciplines and concerns: histories of recorded sound (Chanan 1995, Lastra 2000, Sterne 2000); philosophies and aesthetics of recording (Eisenberg 1987, Zak 2001, Cunningham 1998, Buskin 1999, Martin 1983); histories of specific studios and studio systems (Cogan and Clark 2003, Bowman 2003, Southall, Vince, and Rouse 2002); biographies of producers, engineers, technicians, and session musicians (Martin 1979, Howard 2004, Repsch 1989, Cleveland 2001, Moore 1999, Dr. Licks 1989); chronicles of the recording history of specific artists (Lewisohn 1998, McDermott, Cox, and Kramer 1996); architectural surveys of recording studios (Grueneisen 2003); and many books devoted to the creation of particularly influential recordings. Ethnomusicologists have tended to approach the recording studio as a site in which to examine a variety of musical and extramusical concerns such as gender (Sandstrom 2000), and the aesthetics and discourses of the studio (Porcello 1996, Porcello and Greene 2005, Meintjes 2003).

My book draws from several of these areas but can be most centrally placed within ethnomusicology as it addresses both music history (who did what when, with which equipment) and analysis (the effects these actions had on song form and structure). It also examines the way this studio-based art functioned during a particular historical moment in Jamaica; in this sense it is also a work of interpretation in which I show the extent to which the recording studio (despite its seemingly hermetic remove from the "real world") is in fact a microcosm of the society within which it exists.[55] Dub music can be defined by a set of core stylistic traits and technical procedures, but as will be discussed in chapter 2, these traits vary slightly from definition to definition. Such variation suggests that, seen from another perspective, dub is not merely a musical genre but a vividly sonic expression of the social, political, and cultural changes affecting Jamaica in the 1970s. This approach allows me to address the theme of political transformation, so central to most other works on roots reggae, from a different but equally effective angle. And several of the the topics explored in this book ultimately intersect with topics that have been prominent in ethnomusicological, anthropological, literary, and art historical studies of the late twentieth-century Caribbean as a cultural sphere: the issue of African retentions, the impact of slavery and colonization, postcoloniality, Caribbeaness as creolization, and the increasing centrality of vernacular forms to the cultural life of the nation.[56]

Given that the academic discussion of much black popular music today tends to be dominated by non–music scholars, this book might strike some as conservative in the sense that it addresses the music in fairly musicological terms. It does not privilege the sociocultural over the aesthetic and the historical, but rather attempts to keep them in complementary balance. What I offer in this book is a discussion of Jamaican popular music that treats "the music" itself as a serious object of study, doing it as much justice as it does the music's broader resonances. And while some might argue that "the music" is itself a problematic construction, I believe that in order to understand a music's broader resonances, we need an informed understanding of the way social codes are sublimated into the codes of musicalized sound, in order to understand the way they are manipulated to produce social meaning.[57] Ultimately, what I have aspired to here is a culturally grounded inquiry of ethnomusicology and a blend of what Guthrie P. Ramsey has discussed as the "musicological" and "literary" tendencies in black music scholarship and criticism.[58]

I want to make it clear that this book is *not* a general history of reggae or of Jamaican music; for that or other reggae-related topics, the reader should consult any of the many excellent studies that have preceded it, including Barrow and Dalton (1997), Bilby in Manuel (1995), Bradley (2000), Chang and Chen (1998), Clarke (1980), Cooper (2004), Davis and Simon (1982 and 1992), Dawes (1999), Foster (1999), Hebdige (1987), Hurford and Kaski

(1987), Katz (2003), Jahn and Weber (1998), Neely (forthcoming), Potash (1997), or Stolzoff (2000). Although the book is concerned with a fairly specialized topic, I believe it will remain relevant to the study of Jamaican music, because Jamaica's most significant contributions to the world's music are based in large part around its studio innovations.

Topically, this book is framed and/or inspired by several works that have preceded it. Even though my own book is written in a very different way, Walter Everett's work on the Beatles provided an inspiring example of the rigor with which popular music scholarship can be undertaken: on the one hand, in terms of depth of analysis; and on the other, in terms of accountability to factors of repertoire and biography (via the search for unauthorized recordings, alternate takes, session logs, and journalistic accounts), which are handled as thoroughly as a historical musicologist's search for letters, scores, and manuscripts in dusty archives in far-flung lands.[59] Robert Farris Thompson's 2005 historical study of the Argentine tango was a threefold inspiration. First, for the way that personal passion for a topic can combine with the rigor of the scholar to paint an enlivened and poetic history of an artistic genre and/or a culture. Second, for the way that nonmusical perspectives (in this case, the art historical) can be used to expand and enrich the discussion of music, expanding the parameters of musical thinking while remaining accountable to the "sound material."[60] Third, for the way Thompson has teased out the Africanist underpinnings of a dance genre heretofore considered to be one of the defining artistic statements of Western modernity. Louise Meintjes's *Sound of Africa* (2003) presents a vivid ethnographic account of the ways that cultural identity becomes embodied in musical sound via the technology of the recording studio. Art historian (and chemistry professor) Philip Ball's *Bright Earth: Art and the Invention of Color* (2001) makes the case that histories, analyses and interpretations of artistic movements are virtually meaningless without close scrutiny of the different materials available to artists in different eras. Ball's colorful (pun intended) history of the synthesis of artist's pigments clearly parallels the synthesis of new sounds made possible by sound processing technologies. Paul Gilroy has consistently used the most innovative forms of black popular music as fruitful points of departure for broader and particularly provocative discussions of race, culture, and history. His challenge to received notions of modernity, expressed most comprehensively in *The Black Atlantic* (1993a), was a touchstone for my work here. The writings of Michael Chanan (1995), James Lastra (2000), and Jonathan Sterne (2003) provided crucial historical contexts for the emergence, evolution, and cultural significance of sound technologies. Finally, any study of reggae must acknowledge the work done by scholars, archivists, and journalists of Jamaican music (Steve Barrow, Kenneth Bilby, Lloyd Bradley, Stephen Davis, Dave Hendley, David Katz, Adrian Sherwood, Roger Steffens and Chris Wilson, to name just a few), who have conducted numerous interviews with the pioneers of reggae music since the 1970s, authored seminal books, founded reissue labels (Heartbeat, Blood & Fire, Pressure Sounds, Motion, Auralux), curated museum exhibitions, and contributed informative liner notes to retrospective compilations of Jamaican music. My study would be inconceivable without their work.

CHAPTER ONE

Electronic Music in Jamaica
Dub in the Continuum of Jamaican Music

However unique it may be in the soundscape of black popular music, dub—like most popular music of the Caribbean—arose as a product of the historical continuum encompassing European conquest, slavery, colonization, industrialization, urbanization, and globalization in the so-called New World. As such, it can be clearly fit into a historical continuum of Jamaican music traceable centuries into the past. Given that the history of Jamaican music is covered in several previous publications, the following historical sketch is deliberately brief and schematic, used to set the stage for this book's primary concerns.

A plantation society similar to the nearby nation of Haiti, colonial Jamaica was characterized by harsh cultural and political repression of the overwhelmingly black majority by a small, white plantocracy. The British rulers (who ended a brief period of Spanish rule in 1655) viewed African cultural expressions with distaste, and attempted to eradicate them through a mixture of legislation, conversion, and coercion. As a result of this, the documentation of "pure" transplanted African cultural expressions in Jamaican music remains fairly basic. What *is* known includes a variety of retained West African songs and other cultural forms that flourished undocumented in the country's interior well into the twentieth century. Those accounted for include *Burru, Etu, Tambu, and Gombe*—all rural-based, neo-African musical genres that traditionally flourished on both plantations and in the country's interior. Fusing African-derived singing, drumming, and religious possession, these styles betrayed little or no European influence,[1] and they share characteristics in varying degrees with other regional neo-African liturgical musics such as Cuban *santería* and *palo* music, Haitian *vodun*, and Trinidadian *shango*.[2] Other styles such as the widespread *Revival* or *Pocomania/Kumina* styles, blended similar drumming styles with Africanized Christian hymnal singing and were more widely practiced; the latter was also used for trance healing ceremonies, and selected elements of both musical traditions would later be adopted by Rastafarians for their own liturgical *Nyabinghi* music and *Kete* drumming.

During the era of slavery from the mid-1600s to 1838, colonial planters also encouraged their subjects to form "slave orchestras" for the masters' entertainment during various slave and Christian holidays. Blending African- and European-derived musical traits, these orchestras represented Jamaica's first documented indigenous musical forms. This hybrid history is reflected in the blend of African-derived structural traits such as rhythmic dynamism, call-and-response song forms, and drumming traditions, with European traits such as various instrument types, chordal harmonies and various song types (for example, Protestant hymns, sea shanties).

Taken together, these traditional religious and folk styles constituted the body of documented musical practice until the urbanization of the 1930s provided a context for the emergence of Jamaican popular music. Kenneth Bilby characterizes the evolution of Jamaica's popular music as being informed by a continuous exchange between the rural and the urban,[3] and many of these musical practices would ultimately be transplanted to the urban context, influencing the evolution of popular music in various ways.

Mento

Growing directly out of the experience of rural migrants to Kingston during the first decades of the twentieth century, the origins of Jamaican popular music—like the traditional forms they grew out of—were considered unworthy of serious attention and/or documentation by the Europhile national elite. As a result, precise origins, influential individuals, and seminal moments have gone largely unaccounted.[4] By most accounts, however, the country's tradition of popular music is widely considered to have begun with *mento*, a style that had flourished since the early decades of the twentieth century and that was first recorded in the early 1950s by the first generation of Jamaican recording entrepreneurs, including Stanley Motta, Ken Khouri, and Baba Tuari.[5]

The term *mento* encompassed a fairly wide range of stylistic practices that drew on all the aforementioned folk traditions in varying degrees. Like many other regional Caribbean styles, it also sometimes blended elements of European ballroom and folk dance (such as *quadrille, lancer,* and *mazurka*) with African-derived percussion and vocal stylizations.[6] Over time, the African elements came to dominate, owing in Bilby's account to the aesthetic preferences of the black musicians and the African-derived instruments on which they performed. By the time the style began to be recorded in the early 1950s, enough standardization had occurred that mento could now be considered a national folk music broadly related to Trinidadian calypso in style, if not origin. During the 1930s and 1940s, this newly commercialized mento was performed by large dance bands who also played American jazz standards to audiences in Kingston and other cities. Song lyrics were usually concerned with love, sex, and hardship, and instrumentation was typically some configuration of banjo, hand drums, guitar, "rhumba box" (a large, bass-register thumb piano of West African origin), bamboo "sax," penny-whistle, and Trinidadian steel pan.[7] In addition to weddings and parties, mento bands often performed for tourists at various resorts. Even today, foreign tourists arriving at Sangster International Airport in Montego Bay are likely to be serenaded by the sounds of a mento band.

The Influence of Rhythm & Blues

While mento was the main local style, the dominant music that urban Jamaicans were dancing to during the 1950s was rhythm and blues imported from the United States. The music could also be heard via radio transmissions, which could be picked up on clear nights from broadcast points in the southern United States such as Miami and New Orleans. It also made its way to Jamaica via migrant workers returning from farmwork in the United States, and through the presence of African American migrant workers and military servicemen stationed on the island.[8] At this time, rhythm and blues was still strongly rooted in blues and gospel music and was dominated by plaintive ballads and shuffle tempos; the Jamaican preference was for the "jump blues" of musicians like Charles Brown, Louis Jordan, and Big Joe Turner, or for balladeers like Nat King Cole, Billy Eckstine, and Arthur Prysock.[9] Sound system operators like Coxsone Dodd traveled frequently to the southern United States to find the hottest and most obscure records to play for their Jamaican audiences.

The emergence of rock and roll as a national craze in America of the late 1950s had consequences for the subsequent development of black American pop. The first wave of proto–rock and roll purveyed by electric blues and/or rhythm-and-blues artists such as Little Richard, Chuck Berry, and Bo Diddley began to be aimed at a more cosmopolitan audience; by the beginning of the 1960s, many black R&B hits were "covered" by white American singers like Elvis Presley and Pat Boone. The white sound was softer, and held less appeal for the Jamaican audiences used to the rawer, more passionate sounds of black R&B. Meanwhile black American musicians, their styles having been co-opted by cover artists, were in the process of either "crossing over" to white audiences, or regrouping before the explosive emergences of Motown, Stax-Volt, and James Brown later in the decade. It was this period of stylistic change that provided the catalyst for the first serious formulations of an indigenous Jamaican popular music. At a loss for appealing African American music at the turn of the decade, sound system proprietors such as Dodd and Reid began to turn at last to local musicians to produce sounds for the local market. In Dodd's account: "What really gave me the idea that we needed to produce some local recording [was that] at about 1960 the rhythm & blues dried up and in came the rock & roll, but rock & roll wasn't so popular in Jamaica. It never went over. So I figured, more or less, then we'd have to get in the studio and get with that heavy dance beat, you know. So that's how we really thought of doing it."[10]

This turn to the local was a significant cultural landmark; as Davis and Simon point out, Jamaica, like other formerly colonized cultures, was then in the grip of a cultural mindset that privileged all things foreign (especially British and American); producers only turned to local musicians as a last resort. In the broad view, however, Jamaican music has often functioned—at least partially—as the most provocative Caribbean commentary on mainland African American popular music. From this period on, Jamaican and African American music would develop in and out of stylistic phase with each other until—with the post-1980s symbiosis of Jamaican ragga and American hip-hop music—the musical influences became almost completely complementary.

Ska

The musicians that local businessmen-cum-producers (for example, Dodd and Duke Reid) turned to were older players such as Val Bennett, Sonny Bradshaw, Roy Coburn, and Bertie King who had made a name for themselves in the Jamaican dance-band scene. They also turned to younger musicians such as guitarist Ernest Ranglin, pianist Jackie Mittoo, or drummer Jah Jerry, some of whom were graduates of the Alpha School in West Kingston, a school that took boys off of the streets and provided them with a solid musical education.[11] In previous decades, the older bands had offered their (mostly elite) audiences a repertoire of American swing music, mixed with the occasional orchestrated mento, Cuban rhumba, Trinidadian calypso, and Dominican merengue. When it became necessary to formulate their own popular music, however, they modeled it directly after rhythm and blues, but with a distinctly local twist. The earliest attempts were directly indebted to the shuffle/swing tempos and plaintive ballads of American R&B, elaborated with various rural Jamaican and local Caribbean influences.[12] But when guitarists and pianists began emphasizing the upbeat (off-beat eighth notes) in the music, the *ska* style, as it came to be known, was born. Like the rhythm-and-blues music upon which it was initially modeled, ska was marked by a bouncy uptempo beat played in either straight or swung time, with the guitar and piano emphasizing the upbeats. This upbeat emphasis, traceable to the "comping" style of piano and/or guitars in rhythm & blues as well as the role of the banjo in mento,[13] would become the most distinctive element of Jamaican music, continuing throughout the successive stylistic phases to the present.[14] The ensemble that emerged as the dominant ska outfit came to be known as the *Skatalites*, under the direction of the late trombonist Don Drummond (1940–1969); the music they would create for producers like Coxsone Dodd, Duke Reid, and Justin Yap remains a high-water mark for Jamaican pop.[15]

The loose ensemble feeling of many ska songs recalls the early, small combo jazz of musicians like Louis Armstrong in New Orleans. The musicians typically conform to set song forms but sometimes take a fair amount of improvisational liberty in playing their individual parts, resulting in a buoyant mood and heterophonic ensemble texture. Some have suggested that this buoyancy was at least partially a form of musical propaganda sponsored by the Jamaican government to foster optimism in the new nation.[16] Nevertheless, it is generally accepted that it was also an organic reflection of the national mood following the nation's independence from England in August 1962. Like the forms highlife in sub-Saharan Africa and soul in Afro-America, the mood of lighthearted abandon in such ska songs as Derrick Morgan's "Forward March" and Jimmy Cliff's "Miss Jamaica" was powered by a wave of national pride and sociopolitical commitment and optimism.[17]

But there was also another side to ska, typified by the tightly orchestrated instrumental pieces composed by musicians like Drummond, saxophonists Tommy McCook and Roland Alphonso, and trumpeter Johnny Moore; these pieces sported such provocative titles as "Fidel Castro," "Exodus," "King Solomon," "Addis Ababa," "Distant Drums," "Yogi Man," and "South China Sea." They hinted at the growing influence of Rastafari, looming political revolution, a culture increasingly looking eastward, and the reemergence of ancestral Africa as a valued cultural symbol.[18] Shepherded by the tragic genius figure of Drummond, this type of ska was Jamaica's local commentary on the emergence of musicians like Charlie Parker, Dizzy Gillespie, and the idea of modern jazz as an Afro-inflected art music of the twentieth-century metropolis.

Rock Steady

By 1966, ska had been transformed into a style known as *rock steady*. The moniker describes several changes in the music: a slower, steadier tempo; a de-emphasis on horns; the foregrounded role of electric bass lines that were now composed from a mixture of rests and syncopations (as opposed to the continuous "walking" pattern of ska) opening up spaces for other instruments to insert counterrhythms;[19] and the introduction of the stubborn "one drop" drumming pattern, which became a highly distinctive feature of Jamaican music.[20] The earliest song in this style is often considered to be Hopeton Lewis's "Take It Easy," and there are varying accounts of the catalysts for the musical change. In Davis and Simon's account, many Jamaicans attributed the change to the unusually hot summer of 1966, in which slower dancing became a necessity in the extreme heat.[21] Producer Clive Chin spoke in more general terms of the move to slow the tempo down from its rhythm-and-blues and ska origins:

Basically what slow it down is that . . . a man like for a more relaxed stage of movement. The foot movement and the jigglin,' it nice but it tired you out . . . you want to feel good and you and your queen just a move steady—you no want a whole heap of foot movement like you get on the dance floor and just create a mash. You just go there and lock and position yourself and rub-a-dub and sip your beer or your spliff or whatever. The whole mood of it—you just cool, you just mellow.[22]

Other accounts attribute the change to a "darker" social mood reflecting the growing culture of "rude boys" (that is, young, unemployed men in the city), an increase in violence and the intensification of political rivalries; this would account for the change in subject matter as well.[23] In general we can observe that, for whatever reasons, the ska model was refashioned over time and rock steady marked the beginning of a process in which Jamaican popular music became slower, more bottom-heavy, less concerned with abandon and more with controlled and repeated syncopations. The accompanying dancing became more controlled as well, with the halting, syncopated bass lines inspiring what David Katz described as "a stationary pose with a rocking body, jerking shoulders, and snapping fingers."[24] The most prolific rock steady session band was the Jets, led by guitarist Lynn Taitt, whose melodious chording (inspired, in some accounts, by the steel pan music from his native Trinidad) embellished the heavy bass lines created by players like Bryan Atkinson, Jackie Jackson, and others.[25]

Reggae

Many people are wondering about the origins of the word reggae. *What we are talking about is the* regality *of the music.*[26]

Reggae means comin' from the people, y'know? . . . Like from the ghetto. From majority. Reggae mean regular people who are suffering, and who don't have what they want.[27]

. . . at that time we was listening to the rebels, and the rebels was the lazy people. Them want something to rock to because them fucking lazy. They want exercise, so we have to take the rhythm down to help.[28]

A beat like this, it get a rich guy very scared. When they hear the horns, is like the horns a say "Hey, one day I'm going to fuck you up! One day I'm going to catch you!" . . . When you hear the drumroll, it's like cutting, making a fight . . . the whole basical truth about it is that the tempo is right. You can never say it's wrong. It's like revolutionary.[29]

Ever since the R&B and ska years, when sound system operators pushed their bass controls to full capacity in order to thrill and traumatize their audiences and have their sounds heard over the widest possible outdoor distances, the electric bass had grown in prominence in Jamaican music.[30] The first Fender bass had been introduced into Jamaica around 1959 by bassist/entrepreneur Byron Lee and by the rock steady period, Jackie Jackson had emerged to define the instrument's role more precisely.[31] As rock steady began to slow down into what became known as *reggae*, it was this instrument that became the key to the new style. Structurally, reggae was partly common practice harmony and song form, and partly a neo-African music of fairly rigid ensemble stratification in which the fundamental ingredients were an aggressive, syncopated bass line, a minimalist (but highly ornamented) drum set pattern, and a chordal instrument (usually guitar and/or piano) playing starkly on each offbeat eighth note, elaborated by a syncopated "shuffle organ" emphasizing the offbeats in sixteenth-note double time. The "one drop" became standardized into a minimalist pattern in which the bass drum emphasized beats 2 and 4, the snare (playing mainly on the rim) alternately doubled the bass drum or improvised syncopations, while the hi-hat kept straight or swung eighth-note time. There were also several other popular patterns and variations, such as the popular "steppers" rhythm in which the bass drum sounded on each beat while the snare played interlocking syncopations, or the "flying cymbal," which imported the offbeat hi-hat splash of disco music and fused it with the one drop.[32]

Although rock steady is generally considered to have "slowed down" into reggae, it actually accelerated (via the double-time shuffle organ) and decelerated (via the half-time drum and bass) simultaneously. It also tightened considerably, as rock steady had at times retained some of the ensemble looseness of ska. Because of this juxtaposition of downbeat and offbeat, along with the tighter ensemble texture, the net effect of "roots" reggae (as it came to be known) was simultaneously of midair suspension and firm grounding, of density and spaciousness, of weightiness and weightlessness. It could be danced as a sensual and subtly interwoven dance for couples, or as a very free step for people dancing alone. As usual, there are varying claims and accounts of the first commercially recorded reggae song. Toots and the Maytals's "Do the Reggay," Lee Perry's "People Funny Boy," and Larry Marshall's "Nanny Goat" are three songs most frequently credited with inspiring the slower tempo.[33]

Reggae was a distinct stylistic phase of the music; structurally speaking, however, it was (as outlined above) actually a refinement of many elements that had been introduced in the ska and rock steady periods. The true significance of the change comes from these musical refinements in conjunction with a dramatic shift in lyrical themes that itself reflected a fundamental shift in the cultural mood. In terms of the new lyrical focus on Africa as cultural homeland, Erna Broadber observed, "a river of sentiment that had been running underground for decades had suddenly surfaced."[34] Songs also began to explore a wider range of social and political topics giving voice to a more critical examination of the new nation-state: poverty, class conflict, homelessness, political violence, Rastafari, the concept of "blackness," and a variety of other social and cultural issues. The infusion of political, class, and religious sentiment reflected the music's roots in the experiences of both rude boys and Rastas, and gave rise to the dynamically contrasting claims for reggae's etymological roots in words such as "raggedy" (that is, lower class) and "regal" (that is, Rastafari). In the view of some historians, it was this thematic shift that actually defined the shift to reggae.[35] Many musicians offered interpretations similar to that of engineer Philip Smart, who claimed that "the tempo of the music had something to do with the revolution at the time."[36] The slower tempo resulted in a brooding mood conducive to the weightier topics; as Lloyd Bradley notes, it also allowed a more relaxed, hymnlike quality of singing for the increasing number of songs with religious or spiritual themes.[37]

Crucial to this generation were the producers who shepherded the new sound: Clement Dodd, Duke Reid, Joe Gibbs, Lee Perry, Bunny Lee, Clive Chin, Jack Ruby, and others who would record the emerging musicians. It is impossible to talk about the music without mentioning these figures, and the story of dub music in particular is a collaborative story between these producers and the studio engineers they worked with: Bunny Lee and Augustus Pablo with King Tubby, Clive Chin and Joe Gibbs with Errol Thompson, Linval Thompson and Junjo Lawes with Scientist, and other similar partnerships.

Finally, there was the new crop of musicians, especially the electric bassists and drum set players who were in the forefront of the new sound: the former included Aston "Family Man" Barrett, Glen Brown, George "Fully" Fullwood, Boris Gardiner, Errol "Flabba" Holt, Lloyd Parks, Robbie Shakespeare, Leroy Sibbles, and Errol "Bagga" Walker;[38] the latter included Carlton "Carlie" Barrett, Warren "Benbow" Creary, Carlton

"Santa" Davis, Lowell "Sly" Dunbar, Mikey "Boo" Richards, Lincoln "Style" Scott, and Leroy "Horsemouth" Wallace. It was these musicians who revolutionized Jamaican music and put an indelible stamp upon world popular music. As Adrian Sherwood claims, "There were half a dozen bass players who for a period of twenty years were putting out fantastic stuff, and the way that their crew of producers and mixers and the musicians interacted is unique. It cannot be compared to anyone else. You cannot compare any huge bulk of music with what came out of Jamaica. It's quite unique."[39]

Although reggae, as performed by this new generation of musicians, would attain unprecedented international popularity by the late 1970s, the foundations of their innovations had been solidly laid in place by the musicians at the Studio One and Treasure Isle studios between the 1960s and early 1970s. From around the time of independence in 1962, these musicians had been charged by producers like Coxsone Dodd and Duke Reid with the task of using their jazz skills to adapt black American R&B into a new local popular music. By the rock steady period at the end of the 1960s, they had blended high musicianship, jazzy solos, accomplished singing, and meticulous songcraft in the synthesis of what might be thought of as Jamaica's "perfectly formed pop song." Even at the turn of the twenty-first century, producer "Computer Paul" Henton could remark on the irony: "Every generation that comes up eventually gets into Studio One music. Why? It was just good music. Every song almost is a sing-along. Cyaan [can't] beat that, it's like Motown."[40]

Dub

Because of a combination of social, political, and technological factors, the neat conception of the pop song would undergo a strange transformation during the 1970s. Roots reggae's unique interplay of density and spareness had set the stage for the texturally and spatially oriented practices of dub, a style in which the Jamaican pop song was electronically deconstructed and reconfigured by a generation of studio engineers who had variously tuned into the potentials of Africa, outer space, nature, psychedelia, and the late modernist machine. Two iconic photos of legendary producer/engineer Lee Perry demonstrate this dramatic change. In the first, a widely circulated publicity shot taken around 1967, Perry poses coolly against a park bench, with a placid pond in the background. He is dressed in a matching ensemble of black shirt, slacks, and sports jacket with polished black shoes and hair trimmed to a short, neat Afro. Like many publicity shots of the mid-1960s, he strikes a stylish and dynamic pose, with his jacket slung over his shoulder. The image is of a successful and stylish music businessman "on the go"; my guess would be that the photo was taken in England.[41]

In a well-known later photo taken by Peter Simon around 1976, Perry has been transformed. He is shown in front of the console of his Black Ark studio, the site of his greatest sonic achievements. The sporty ensemble has been discarded in favor of shorts and a cut-off sleeveless T-shirt. His head and hair—by this time a large Afro on the verge of dreading—are thrown back as if blown by a fan. His hands (one of which holds a burning spliff) are raised in the air in an ecstatic gesture, and his mouth is open as if forming a scream. Perry's expression here is actually quite similar to iconic photos of Little Richard, who blended comic, sexual, and religious absorption into a new construction of rock-and-roll passion.[42] The difference here is that when Perry drops his hands back down, they will not rest upon a piano keyboard, but rather on the knobs, buttons, and dials of a recording console. And for those in the know, it is from this fact that the passion of this photo is constructed; the recording console was Perry's "instrument" in the same way that the jazz orchestra was Duke Ellington's, a vessel for his most sublime and elemental insights.

Perry's personal transformation parallels the transformation in both the music and in Jamaica. The era of "roots" in Jamaica was paralleled throughout the black world as cultures and their artists embraced ideas of Africa, nature, resistance, and blackness and channeled them into local popular music forms. The raw emotion of the photo (especially given the distortion of the image) implies that Perry had found in the ostensibly neutral technology of the studio a potent medium through which to channel the passion, peril, and promise of the times.

What might be thought of as Jamaica's period of musical modernity was arguably bookended by the tragic, lone-genius figure of Don Drummond on one hand, and the techno-deconstructionist figures of Lee Perry and King Tubby on the other. Ska, rock steady and roots reggae were all, to varying extents, invested in traditional conceptions of race, nation, a linear understanding of history, and a clear distinction between good and evil. The advent of dub subverted these constructs, creating a space in Jamaican music (and later world pop) for the postsong, for linguistic, formal, and symbolic indeterminacy. Nevertheless, dub was very much a reflection of the particular society and historical moment in which it arose. If the resounding bass drum patterns of the Kumina traditional healing ceremony were considered sonic "heart strings" that connected the worlds of the living and the dead,[43] the thunderous patterns of the reggae electric bass would similarly serve to reawaken postcolonial Jamaicans to their "dead" past as a people of African descent, as a British slave colony, and their uncertain future as a neocolonial satellite of the United States. The emergence of what Lloyd Bradley described as the "nationalistic swagger"[44] of "drum & bass" to Jamaica's musical forefront paralleled the full flowering of the postcolonial political consciousness and pro-African cultural nationalism that formed roots reggae's symbolic fibre. Within all of this would be contained the first glimpses of a new musical language that at once hearkened backward in cultural time to ancestral Africa and forward to a pancultural, cybersonic future of virtual environments, human-machine interfaces, and digitized sensuality.

Electronic Music in Jamaica
The Recording Studio in Perspective

As a genre of reggae music particularly associated with the recording studio, dub music must be discussed in the context of the global evolution of sound recording technology in the twentieth century. Without a doubt, the technology of sound recording is one of the most profound musical developments of the twentieth century. Magnetic tape recording dates to the late nineteenth century in the Netherlands, and was first standardized in the 1920s in Germany. Recording studios—the primary site for the manipulation of magnetic tape—have existed since just after the turn of the twentieth century. As far back as phonograph inventor Thomas Edison and such early recording pioneers as Fred Gaisberg, Walter Legge, and John Culshaw, engineers have had to make aesthetic as well as technical judgments in their translation of musical performances onto a recorded format that was from its earliest years understood in some quarters to hold more creative potential than a mere passive documentation of a "traditional" musical performance.[45] This idea of the sound recording as an artistic creation in itself—as opposed to a faithful re-creation—developed in stages. It had roots in the 1920s, when the advent of electrical recording allowed a spatial separation between sound source and recorder, typified by the separation in the studio between the performing room and the control room that created an autonomous space for the recording engineer.[46] The idea gained momentum in the 1930s, when a variety of sound processing devices (such as equalization and reverb) began to be used in the production of Hollywood film soundtracks.[47] It was in tandem with these technical advances that the recording engineer began to play a more prominent creative role in the studio-based creation of popular music.

Prior to the 1950s, however, the role of the engineer had nevertheless been widely misunderstood as a purely technical one, concerned mainly with the ostensibly "accurate" translation of musical performances onto a recorded format. This perception began to change with the introduction of multitrack technology; four-channel recorders became available in the 1950s, and eight- and sixteen-channel machines followed in the subsequent decade.[48] Recording engineers now began to be publicly recognized as what Chanan calls "audio artists" (music critic Oliver Daniel coined the term "tapesichordists"), aggressively moving recording out of the realm of the documentary and into the realm of the creative.[49] They were aided in this endeavor by continuing advances in electronic circuitry and sound processing technology, as well as the ability to overdub—a revolutionary byproduct of multitrack technology (generally attributed to guitarist and electronics innovator Les Paul) that loosened recording from the constraints of real time and space and allowed recordings to be perfected as "works of art."[50] By the mid-1960s, aspects of the studio production process began to consolidate into the signature styles of various producers and engineers of popular music in England and America. In England, producers and engineers such as Joe Meek (working at his North London studio), Eddie Kramer (working primarily with Jimi Hendrix at Olympic in London and later, the Record Plant and Electric Lady in New York), George Martin and Geoff Emerick (working with, among other artists, the Beatles at EMI's Abbey Road studios) expanded the palette of popular music through techniques such as backward tape manipulation, tape splicing, overdubbing, the use of sound effects, and sound processing. In America during the same period, Tom Dowd fashioned a unique aesthetic from the stylized roughness of rhythm-and-blues recordings while working as a staff engineer at New York's Atlantic studios.[51] Legendary producer Phil Spector worked with engineers Stan Ross and Larry Levine in New York's Gold Star studios, providing pop music with a sonic sense of grandeur with his "wall of sound" productions. Spector's work in turn inspired Beach Boy Brian Wilson and a series of engineers (including Larry Levine at Gold Star and Chuck Britz at Western Recorders in Hollywood) in the creation of the Beach Boys' influential 1966 recording *Pet Sounds*. In jazz, Teo Macero (who had himself been trained in twentieth-century composition) helped expand the role of the studio in jazz from the purely documentary to the creative while working with Miles Davis on the latter's jazz-rock fusion music between 1968 and 1975.[52]

This history suggests that, as the invention of the grand piano opened up new possibilities for composers of European art music in the nineteenth century, so the advent of multitrack recording represented a similarly transformative advance for popular composers in the late twentieth century.[53] And considering the centrality of the recording studio in the production of virtually all forms of post–World War II music, this evolution also suggests that the class of technicians we normally refer to as "producers" and "engineers" might themselves, in some cases, be more accurately understood as "composers."[54] The technology they use and the controlled studio setting in which they use it has become an integral part of the compositional process, arguably enabling a more "painterly" form of creativity that brings recorded music closer to the solitary arts of painting, sculpture, literature, and poetry.[55] In fact, it is the use of sound processing devices (with their simulations of space and movement) that enabled the emergence of what might be called a "pictorial" dimension in popular music.[56]

In this book, I have placed Jamaican producer/engineers among this group of postwar sound innovators. Their closest English and American counterparts would be multitasking producer/engineer/inventor/entrepreneurs such as Joe Meek, Sam Philips, Norman Petty, and Les Paul who, despite various technical, institutional, and economic limitations, created the aesthetic foundations of entire pop music cultures. Jamaicans such as Sylvan Morris, King Tubby, Errol Thompson, and Lee Perry created dub music at a time when American record companies were expanding their markets into the Caribbean,[57] and recording technology was being gradually adapted outside of the overdeveloped nations in the service of budding local record industries. It also developed at a time when the introduction of stereo radio transmission into Jamaica led to a rise in the broadcasting of foreign music "deemed to sound good in stereo."[58] This new outlet in turn gradually opened a space for the appreciation of Jamaican music with more sophisticated production values.

The innovations described above were by no means limited to the realm of popular music; as mentioned earlier, most of them had in fact been prefigured in the years following World War II in various centers of experimental art music composition in Europe and the United States. As such, the innovations of dub in Jamaica can also be discussed in the context of global developments in electronic music—provided we devise a culturally fluid definition of the term. Originally, the term *electronic music* was quite restrictive, coined after World War II in the studios of Cologne, Germany, to refer to music composed from electronically generated sound signals (*elektronische Musik*). Later, the term was broadened to include the tape-based musique concrète composition associated with French composers such as Pierre Henri and Pierre Schaeffer, and still later, broadened to include works realized with electronic synthesizers. Clearly, dub cannot be defined as "electronic music" in the specific sense that we define the term in the context of these traditions of post–World War II Euro-American experimental art music. If, on the other hand, we define "electronic music" broadly as encompassing either any musical form relying on the electronic generation, processing, amplification, or storage of sound signals or as any prerecorded work intended solely for transmission via loudspeakers, a huge majority of contemporary music making could then be classified as "electronic."[59]

The significance of dub music can be located somewhere between these two definitions. On the one hand, it can be generically discussed as "electronic" in the same way that we discuss other musical forms making use of any electronic technology. But it can also be discussed in more narrowly "electronic" terms, owing to the degree to which Jamaican producers and engineers foregrounded the experimental use of sound technology within the genre. As a form of tape-based composition, for example, dub might be compared to aspects of musique concrète. Its emphasis on repetitive rhythmic structures (which have often been stripped of their harmonic elements) might be compared with the minimalism of composers like Steve Reich and Philip Glass and in fact (as I shall discuss in the coda), the music was adopted as an aesthetic template in the 1990s by a generation of German electronic music composers who had themselves been influenced by minimalism. Dub's electronic manipulation of spatiality can be compared with certain spatially conceived works of composers like Karlheinz Stockhausen. In purely sonic terms, it bears comparison with certain works of composers such as Stockhausen, John Cage, and Vladimir Ussachevsky, who subjected prerecorded musical materials appropriated from mass media (such as commercial recordings or radio broadcasts) to electronic manipulation.[60] Conversely, the Jamaican practice of deejays toasting over prerecorded music fits into a body of work composed for electronics and live musicians that in its broadest sense encompasses everything from pieces like Mario Davidowsky's *Synchronisms No. 1* (composed for live flautist and tape) to karaoke singing.

Any sonic similarities between these very different musical areas probably reflect the fact that to the ear, electronic and tape compositions (many of which were only notated after the fact) seem to share a sonic and conceptual space with popular forms that developed out of traditions of performance and improvisation.[61] It also reflects the rarely discussed fact that composers of the experimental tradition were often influenced by concepts of form, sound, and process found in various jazz, popular, and non-Western traditions.

In the same way that it would be fascinating to hear how composers such as Pierre Schaefer, Pierre Henri, or John Cage might adapt their "pure" sound experimentation to the stylistic demands of popular/dance music, it would be equally fascinating to hear the way Jamaican studio engineers like Scientist or Sylvan Morris would utilize venues specially designed for the performance of spatially oriented "pure sound" works (such as the building built for Stockhausen at the 1970 World's Fair in Osaka, Japan), or studios specifically equipped for the realization of electronic works (such as the Nordwestdeutscher Rundfunk in Cologne, Radiodiffusion Française in Paris, or the Columbia-Princeton Electronic Music Center in New York City). The truth, of course, is that Jamaican engineers never had access to such elaborate technology and it was in light of this lack of technical and institutional access that a recent profile of second-generation dub engineer Mad Professor mused: "Neil Fraser, a.k.a. UK dub producer 'The Mad Professor,' can't wait for audio technology to catch up with the sounds he can hear inside his head. Frustrated by the limitations of our outdated stereo technology, Fraser thinks in quadraphonic, pentatonic, geometric, analgesic, afrodisiac, psychedelic full-screen surround-sound, pushing his equipment to the limit and beyond as he attempts to cram his cutting-edge creations into a format that uses just two puny speakers."[62]

What makes the work of these engineers particularly provocative is what they were able to achieve by pushing the limits of the equipment at their disposal. In any case, Jamaica's musical innovations provide a fascinating example of the way in which similar forms of technology have been applied in different cultural areas, as well as a localized example of what constitutes musical "experimentation," in a Jamaican popular context.

Despite their frequently overlapping associations in post–World War II Western art music, the terms *electronic* and *experimental* are by no means synonymous. To the extent that these terms have often been used interchangeably, however, my use of the term "electronic music" in this text is also a conscious attempt to raise and problematize the concept of an experimental avant-garde in relation to the music cultures of Africa and the African diaspora. This issue has been substantively explored by musician/scholar George Lewis in relation to jazz and other improvised musics, and in this book, I attempt to extend the discussion into the sphere of popular music.[63] The idea of an avant-garde is fairly established in Afro-America, where jazz musicians of the 1960s such as John Coltrane, Albert Ayler, and Cecil Taylor made music that challenged the status quo from various "outsider" artistic stances. But this particular model of outsiderness is not the only aesthetic sphere in which social and/or aesthetic norms have been challenged and/or transformed. With the rise of digital and electronic technologies, in fact (and as jazz has become increasingly associated with elitist and academic values), the experimental envelope in much black music has been frequently pushed in the arena of communal dance musics. And this expansion has in turn opened a space for sophisticated musical discussion by authors willing to engage the idea of experimentalism from the perspective of popular music (or at least to let the two perspectives influence each other). In the United States, this experimentalism was apparent in the work of writers such as John Rockwell and more recently, John Corbett, as well as the generation of jazz critics who came of age concurrently with the jazz avant-garde, such as Amiri Baraka, Stanley Crouch, and Greg Tate. In the last decade, D.J. Spooky (Paul D. Miller) has broadened this discussion through his engagement with dub, hip-hop, and the Western experimental music tradition. In England, a similar contribution has mainly come from music journalists and cultural studies scholars; some of the most insightful musical criticism in this sphere has come from such authors as Kodwo Eshun and David Toop.

In light of all this, it follows that my application of the "experimental" idea in relation to Jamaica will remain grounded in Jamaica's cultural reality; although there is a local tradition of modern jazz (typified by such musicians as Joe Harriott, Monty Alexander, Ernest Ranglin, and Don Drummond) the culture has no tradition of a musical avant-garde in the Euro-American or African American sense of the term.[64] There is, however, a vibrant tradition of electronic music, best typified by dub music. The creators of this music certainly viewed themselves as experimentalists, as their comments and professional monikers indicate: Scientist, Peter Chemist, Professor, and so on. Their work represented the sonic vanguard of Jamaican music in the 1970s and early 1980s, and it later entered into the production of Euro-American popular music in a de facto avant-garde position, its *perceived* low-fidelity aesthetic providing inspiration and justification for various "outsider" musical stances beyond Jamaica.[65]

How, then, might this music factor more broadly into the history of twentieth-century popular and experimental musics and vernacular modernism in general? In the sphere of visual arts, the role of Africanist aesthetics in the formulation of the Western avant-garde has been discussed fairly extensively, allowing Kobena Mercer and Lowery Sims to apply the idea of a de-centered "cosmopolitan modernity" in relation to modernist (visual) artists of the Afro-Caribbean.[66] But despite the "Jazz Age," the "rock and roll revolution," "free jazz," "world beat," and the globalization of hip-hop culture, the acknowledgment of Africanist influences upon Western notions of the musical avant-garde has been slow in coming. Paul Gilroy's conception of the Black Atlantic zone as a symbiotic "counter-culture" of modernity provides an opening here. Based on the idea of modernity having been forged through the diametric but symbiotic opposition between Western Europe and its colonized "others,"

Gilroy's conception of modernity provides the framework through which we can understand Africanist aesthetics of dub as a local articulation of modernist traditions of musical experimentalism. [67]

The Jamaican Sound System

Ultimately, the most relevant and organic context in which to ground any discussion of an electronic aesthetic within Jamaican music (besides the recording studio) is the local institution known as the *sound system*, which has been asserted by many observers as the site of most that is unique to Jamaican music.[68] With a depressed postwar economy, few Jamaicans could afford to purchase recordings on a regular basis, and the enjoyment of music was mainly a communal, public affair. From the 1950s onward, most Kingstonians enjoyed music via these sound systems: mobile outfits playing recorded music in dancehalls or outdoor clearings, which emerged as a more viable economic alternative to the large dance bands that they rapidly replaced; for the most part, the dance bands gradually became associated with the urban upper class in Kingston and the growing tourist trade on Jamaica's north coast.[69] By the mid-1960s, there were dozens of sound systems in operation, but the scene was dominated by the "Big Three" operators: Clement "Coxsone" Dodd (Sir Coxsone's Downbeat), Arthur "Duke" Reid (Trojan), and Vincent "King" Edwards (Giant).[70] These men commanded fierce loyalty among their followers and rivalries between competing systems often erupted into violence. Technically speaking, the sound systems emerged from extremely humble origins. Coxsone Dodd, for example, began his own "Downbeat" sound system in the 1950s by playing imported records for customers on a tiny phonograph in his parents' liquor shop in Kingston; as he explained to Rob Kenner, "in those days, 30 watts was a big thing."[71] Outfits such as this later grew to include a phonograph and extension speakers, typically set up in a "yard": a public clearing for dances that were generally sponsored by an adjoining bar, restaurant, or other business. Despite their humble origins, these systems would eventually grow—under the guidance of Jamaican technicians such as Hedley Jones, Fred Stanford, Jacky Eastwood, Lloyd "Matador" Daley, and their successors—into sonic powerhouses capable of delivering tens of thousands of watts of power, producing sound that could be heard for miles around.[72]

There are several conceptual aspects of the sound system experience that are directly relevant to the growth of dub, and that will be discussed in the next chapter. In the most basic view, it seems plausible to speculate that because of the relative dearth of performing ensembles in Jamaica, emphasis has tended to be placed on verbal and electronic creativity. But the significance of the sound system, which has received thorough cultural grounding in the aforementioned works of Carolyn Cooper and Norman Stolzoff, transcends mere entertainment; it is arguably one of the most powerfully resonant metaphors for postcolonial Jamaica. It has been described as the "community's heartbeat":[73] the place where "a discourse of specifically black identity was celebrated and articulated" in a particularly powerful way.[74] Like the stereotypical village clearing in sub-Saharan Africa or the block party in urban black America, the sound system is a communal space in which many of the nation's most potent myths, tropes, and emotions are dramatized in the act of communal dance. The songscape innovations of dub music, composed in the recording studio with the 1970s sound system experience in mind, are intimately implicated in these same myths despite the largely nonliteral (that is, instrumental) nature of the music.

As such, any "experimental" tendencies evident in dub remained predicated upon the capital-driven setting of the Jamaican recording studio, which was a radically different setting than the radio and university studios that have provided the technical and institutional framework for electronic composition in Europe and America. These tendencies also remained predicated upon the communal imperatives of the sound system and the dancehall, which were themselves radically different settings than the concert halls, galleries, and other spaces we usually associate with the performance of experimental music in Europe and America. Despite its experimental aspects, dub music remained solidly grounded in the reality of Kingston life in the 1970s. As Sebastian Clarke describes:

The sound man [that is, the sound system proprietor] carries his impoverished community with him. The music that he plays appeals to the sensibility and sensuality of the urban impoverished settler. By and large, the sound man's audience consists of an impoverished urban community like Waterhouse (where King Tubby comes from). In this community is a multiplicity of personalities. The hardworking man may be a follower, as well as the "gun man"—the ex-political rebel [sic] rouser-turned-criminal. It is the latter element [who] are prepared to terrorize anybody for the silliest of reasons, who are almost totally responsible for the notoriety of the sound man.[75]

The social polar opposite of the recording studio in its hermetic isolation, the sound system is significant as the site in which studio experimentation acquires its cultural grounding. In his insightful essay on Orientalism in the Western experimental tradition, John Corbett notes how "the notion of experimentation rhetorically carries into the musical process a connotation of science—of laboratory experimentation." He goes on to mention how the hermetic setting of the laboratory implicitly divested such experimentation of its potential political or ideological import. Dub, however, was composed with the sound system audience in mind; thus the experimental impulse remained connected to the general cultural climate in Jamaica. As we shall see in chapter 8, in fact, it was in many ways an important articulation of this climate.[76]

How did such a technologically dependent style develop to such an advanced extent under these circumstances, in a nation of extremely limited economic resources, within a region marked by a diversity of traditional performing ensembles? The easiest explanation would be that Jamaica's proximity to the United States provided a convenient physical and economic conduit for what Malm and Wallis have described as a "remarkable influx of electronic hardware";[77] industrious Jamaicans then used this technology to supplant the dominance of more expensive performing ensembles that the economy was incapable of supporting. But physical proximity can only be part of the answer, as dublike genres did not develop on other islands in the region with dynamic music cultures, such as Haiti, Cuba, or Trinidad. There are no definitive answers, but several likely factors. One may be the tradition of seasonal migration to the southern United States, which employed thousands of Jamaicans who purchased American records, sound equipment, and musical instruments and brought them back to Jamaica. Another might be the currents of commerce during the cold war; Cuba has an arguably more diversified music culture than Jamaica, but during the same period that sound equipment was developing in the United States, Cuba was economically alienated from the United States. Finally, there is the language factor: Jamaica is an English-speaking country, and as such had a closer economic and cultural relationship with both England and the United States, two important centers of developing musical technology.

Any other explanation for Jamaica's vigorous musical culture must lie in the elusive and unquantifiable "character" of the Jamaican people, and in the rural folk forms that were transplanted to Kingston and 'that guided Jamaica's adaptations of foreign music. Unfortunately, as Ken Bilby mentions, the class divide in Kingston meant that the rural-based cultural expressions of "downtown" culture were never considered worthy of serious study, and have gone mostly undocumented until fairly recently.[78] This indifference began to change as the music moved beyond Jamaica, and especially as foreigners became intensely interested in Jamaican reggae beginning in the late 1960s. It is in this general period that the story of dub begins.

CHAPTER TWO

"Every Spoil Is A Style"
The Evolution of Dub Music in the 1970s

In America, if Michael Jackson makes a record, the master tape is sitting there with all the orchestration, maybe it's a beautiful symphony. Nobody else ever heard it in their life! So what, the musicians don't get any feature? People are still interested to hear, "What would it sound like without all these voices on it? What were the guys actually playing?" [But] it's so low in the mix, it doesn't come across the same way. So with reggae, we don't stop there![1]
—Michael "Mikey Dread" Campbell

The history of sonic innovation in popular music is, to a large degree, a history of artists driven by necessity or accident, to push their equipment to perform unintended tasks. It might be Bo Diddley scraping his pick against the strings of his guitar or Little Walter overblowing his amplified harmonica to simulate a reed section in Chicago during the 1950s. It might be Jimi Hendrix transforming amplifier feedback into musical melody or George Martin and the Beatles stumbling upon the use of backward tape effects in London during the 1960s. It might be DJ Kool Herc and Grandmaster Flash refashioning turntables as musical instruments in New York during the 1970s, Thurston Moore using short-circuited guitar signals to create rhythmic effects in the 1990s, or electronica musicians resuscitating obsolete analog equipment for novel uses at the turn of the new century. Whatever the circumstances, the tradition of deliberately misusing or refashioning sound technology toward creative ends amounts to a shadow history of sonic innovation in popular music. These serendipitous accidents, and novel solutions have been the catalysts for new creative languages. Such holds especially true in Jamaica: that's why this chapter is titled "every spoil is a style," using a Jamaican folk phrase to evoke the way necessity, ingenuity, and accident have driven the sonic evolution of the country's popular music.[2] The first half of the chapter examines the early history of Jamaica's recording studio, identifying the economic, technical, and conceptual catalysts in the emergence of Jamaica's unique approach to the popular song. The second half is analytical, identifying the unique stylistic elements.

Producers, Studios, and the Reconfiguration of Recorded Materials

The best way to understand the evolution of Jamaican popular music is in the context of two sites: the recording labels and recording studios that were producing Jamaica's first commercial popular music, and the sound systems that played this music at public dances. Barrow and Dalton have argued that despite the international success of live performers such as Bob Marley and Jimmy Cliff, recording studios and sound systems—more than the concert stage—have been the major arenas for stylistic innovation in reggae music.[3] The studios and sound systems have continuously fed back into each other, conditioning the ongoing stylistic evolution of Jamaican popular music.

In order to understand the significance of this phenomenon, we must first establish the primacy of the *producer* in the history of Jamaican music. Dub music evolved during a period when Jamaican music was commercially ascendant internationally; as a result, the country's music industry was nourished by a fairly steady flow of foreign capital and new musical instruments and recording technologies were available to studios. In the broadest view, however, even at its most prosperous, the economy was incapable of supporting large numbers of individuals owning musical instruments, recording equipment, or other means of musical production and dissemination. The production of music thus became centralized in the hands of this small group of fiercely competitive music entrepreneurs, who came to be known as *producers*. Central to both studios and sound systems in the early years of Jamaica's music industry, the position of the producer provides important background to the emergence of dub music.

In contrast to the freelance and largely artistic function usually implied by the term *producer* in American popular music, Jamaican producers typically exercised a far greater degree of control over the means of production. These men such as Clement "Coxsone" Dodd (1932–2004) and Arthur "Duke" Reid (1915–1975) often owned their own studios, recording labels, and/or pressing facilities in the Jamaican capital of Kingston. They relied upon revolving groups of in-house studio musicians such as the Skatalites, Upsetters, Aggrovators, Revolutionaries, Roots Radics, Soul Syndicate, and others who provided instrumental accompaniment to the various singers who recorded for them. In reality, many of the studio bands were built around a relatively small nucleus of musicians, who changed their band names depending on which producer they were working for. As producer Clive Chin of Randy's studio recalls:

Now, a man say "who is *Upsetters,* who is *Aggrovators?*" You never know. But is a selective set of musicians that would play for the producers them. They [the producers] gave them that name. Same set of man them, but different name. Derrick Harriott, right? Him record and produce tune for himself and for the singers. But on the record now, they would be called the *Crystallites.* Clancy Eccles would use the same set of musicians but him don't call them the Crystallites, him call them the *Dynamics.* Beverly's now, would use the same set of musicians them, probably add one or two different [players] to the lineup—*Beverly's All Stars!* At Randy's, we called them *Impact All-Stars.*[4]

Both musicians and engineers concurred that once a session was under way, recordings were generally made under extremely efficient (some would say extremely pressured) circumstances. In bassist George "Fully" Fulwood's experience, the demand was intense for musicians to create original music on the spot: "In Jamaica those time, we might go inna the studio for about two hours, and come out with fourteen, fifteen songs! It's a challenge because you have to realize the competition that you're facing. If you don't come up with something crucial enough, that producer don't want to use you again. So you have what, three minutes, three-and-a-half minutes, four minutes to really come up with ideas, with arrangements."[5] Similarly, engineer Scientist remembered how quickly this material was turned into finished product: "All those albums, we did them like in hours. We'd come into the studio, and in eight hours we could track an album. We could track an album and the next day, it would be on the streets. None of these guys was coming into the studio for two weeks making a record or making an album. It was all done in hours. I recorded many albums that way."[6]

Some people, such as Dave Hendley, felt that such an arrangement led to problems with quality control and career longevity:

It's kind of like the guy who fixes door or windows . . . the more doors and windows you fix, the more money you're gonna make. That's why they make so many records. That's how the reggae thing is, if you're selling. You've got one Johnny Clarke record, then the public wants three or four or more, so you make them. The market gets flooded and singers get sung out, it's bound to happen. And you're thinking, "They're making too many records!" But that's what puts food on the table.

The economics of the reggae business and the Jamaican social system are [such] that Jamaican artists never had that luxury of a career plan and a record company investing in them as an artist and developing them as an artist. The rewards for making a record aren't as great as in First World countries like England and America. You haven't even got the structure of proper touring, where a band can gig a bit, make a bit of money. The whole thing is hit-and-miss and makeshift in Jamaica. It's always been like that. So if a man offers you two hundred pounds to put your tune out, and you're broke, and you've got kids who want food, you're gonna take the two hundred pounds.[7]

Given the amount of material that was being stockpiled in this way, such an arrangement certainly worked for the producer's benefit. The central point here is the degree to which these producers retained ultimate control over their recorded material—which, given the limited pool of musicians and musical resources, they recycled for additional profit as the necessary technology became gradually available. It is through this process that the reuse of generic rhythm patterns (be they reconfigured recordings or re-recorded versions by other musicians in other studios) has become a central trait of Jamaican music. The term *riddim*, initially a localizing of the English word *rhythm*, has taken on a distinctive meaning in Jamaican music over time, used to refer to these generic chord progressions and/or bass lines that have formed the basis for subsequent songs (I use the spelling *riddim* in this text when referring to these generic patterns in the Jamaican sense, and *rhythm* for the more typical usage).[8]

So although the "precise" origins of dub music are shrouded in a haze of competition, cross-pollination, and conflicting claims, the form undoubtedly grew out of these profit-driven recyclings, which became increasingly elaborate as successive forms of sound technology became available. And it is because of this vertical control of the production process by producers, that although reggae is known in the international market mainly through the work of individual artists, it is often as convenient to get an artist's most popular songs on a compilation of a given producer's (or label's) work as it is to find it under the artist's own name.

The degree of control these producers exercised over their recorded material is reflected, for example, by the fact that decades later, popular rhythm tracks continue to be associated with them even though they did not, for the most part, compose music or play musical instruments themselves. Thus, an oft-versioned rhythm track such as "Drum Song" (originally recorded as an instrumental by organist Jackie Mittoo during his years at Studio One) is still often referred to as "Coxsone's riddim" even though it was in all likelihood composed by Mittoo and the other session musicians in Dodd's employ.[9] Some Jamaicans feel that this emphasis on the producer takes credit away from the musicians who rightfully deserve it. In Clive Chin's description, for example, many producers "don't even part of the session. Them no take part in nothing. All them do is just pay the bills. To me, I can't call the man producer, I call them *executive producer*, in other words *financiers*. . . . Them can't play music, them no know it."[10]

I do not cite Chin here to vilify producers like Dodd and Duke Reid, whose contributions to Jamaican popular music are so enormous as to be virtually unquantifiable. But it remains that the implications of producers' degree of control were simultaneously hegemonic and visionary, in some ways very similar to the position of art dealers in the market for visual art-works. Jamaican producers continued to reap economic returns on music they controlled, while laboring musicians (who had only been paid on a one-off basis at the initial recording session) could only seek additional ses-sion work, creating more raw musical material to be serially reconfigured for the producer's long-term economic benefit. Nevertheless, it was this profit-driven process of reconfiguration that would revolutionize the crea-tion of popular music in Jamaica.

The Early Years of Studio Recording in Jamaica

With the exception of isolated recording attempts made at Jamaica's radio stations RJR (Radio Jamaica Rediffusion) and JBC (Jamaican Broad-casting Company), the first recording studios on the island were founded in the 1950s by entrepreneurs like Stanley Motta (who made a number of mento and calypso recordings at his studio on Hanover Street), and Ken Khouri. Khouri purchased "a disc recorder, a microphone amplifier, and blanks"[11] and began making novelty and musical recordings from the back of his home and, later, at local clubs. He went on in 1957 on to found Fed-eral (located on King Street and later on Bell Road), comprising a monau-ral recording studio and pressing plant. In 1963, Khouri upgraded Federal to a stereo facility, and later expanded to three tracks. Meanwhile, business-man and bandleader Byron Lee purchased the studio of the West Indies Records label (WIRL) from businessman (and future prime minister) Ed-ward Seaga and renamed it Dynamic Sounds, which opened as Jamaica's first multitrack recording facility.

The foundations of Jamaica's unique approach to the recording studio were laid by technicians of this generation, only some of whom are well-known. Graeme Goodall, for example, is an unsung hero of the Jamaican recording industry. Born in Australia in 1932, Goodall arrived in Jamaica from England in the late 1950s, initially to work at RJR on a three-year con-tract. After signing on with Khouri, he worked for several years as chief en-gineer at Federal, recording local music on a three-track Scully recorder. Goodall ended up living in Jamaica off and on until 1981, and was directly involved in the development of Dynamic Sounds and Studio One.[12] Bill Garnett is another important figure. Garnett began his career working with Goodall at Federal, before moving to WIRL as a technician and engineer.[13]

He was later involved in outlining and installing the electronics for several Kingston studios including Randy's, Harry J, Channel One, and Joe Gibbs's first studio in Duhaney Park.

Studio One and Treasure Isle

From the late 1950s, independent producers like Coxsone Dodd and Duke Reid had been producing records by renting time at local studios like Federal. But the "golden age" of recorded Jamaican music really began when Dodd and Reid founded their own studios. Dodd's Jamaican Recording Company (popularly known as "Studio One," after Dodd's main record label) was located on Brentford Road. The studio opened in 1963 as a one-track facility (using a board purchased from Federal when the latter upgraded to two tracks), and upgraded to two tracks (again, using Federal's two-track board when the latter upgraded to three tracks).[14] Engineering was handled by Dodd, his cousin Syd Bucknor, and occasionally, Graeme Goodall, until Sylvan Morris joined the studio as chief engineer. Reid's Treasure Isle studio, located on Bond Street, opened in 1965 as a two-track facility. Reid's engineer was Byron Smith, who had previously worked as a technician at RJR, and as an engineer at Federal alongside Goodall.[15] Both studios specialized in the recording of Jamaica's emerging popular music; by all accounts, both became the most successful and prolific studios in the mid-to-late 1960s. By the late 1960s, several other studios had emerged including, most notably, Randy's Studio on the Parade. Producer Clive Chin of Randy's recalls that by the mid-1960s, each studio had a distinctive sound:

Every studio had a sound that you could identify. Like Treasure Isle, they had a high-end sound, you could get a clarity out of the horns and their organs and stuff like that. Federal, now you get more of a quality of sound because them was into modern equipment. I think they're one of the first that went to 8-track and then 16-track. They were more into clarity. Those guys used to record uptown reggae. Studio One, you couldn't hear no midrange, you could only hear bass, and you get more weight on high end. But then again, they had their own sound.[16]

Some musicians cited differences in the musical approaches of Studio One and Treasure Isle. It is ironic that although Coxsone Dodd was known to be a passionate jazz aficionado, the Studio One sound was considered more raw and streetwise. Duke Reid, on the other hand, is remembered by everyone as a tough, streetwise man known to carry (and sometimes use) several firearms at once, but his Treasure Isle sound was considered more musically sophisticated. As Bunny Lee recalled:

Duke Reid is a great producer, *he knows what he want*. Duke Reid going inna the studio and him tell the musician, "Look bass, I want you do *this* . . ." and the bass [plays a line] and Duke say "No! *This* is what I want, play *this*." Coxsone was a good *selector*, him come a evening time when [engineer Sylvan] Morris done the work, and select the tune [that is, to be released or played on the sound system]. Duke Reid would tell [his musicians,] "When Coxsone do over our tune, him turn it to two chords." When Duke do a tune, him have him seventh chords and him different changes inna it.[17]

Dub Plates and Rhythm Versions

The link between recording studios and sound systems is a simple consequence of the fact that in the early years of the Jamaican record industry, producers owned and operated sound systems as a means of advertising their product at public dances. As mentioned in the introduction, these sound systems have been more central to musical innovation in Jamaica than live performance, and the creative practices developed in the sound systems have in turn influenced the evolution of recording conventions. During the 1960s, the increasing sophistication of imported sound processing equipment benefited both studios and sound systems. At the same time that sound system selectors began to use the simple equalization capability of their equipment (bass and treble controls) to vary the sound of prerecorded music in the dances, recording studios began to employ increasingly creative strategies of song mixing to replicate what the public heard in the sound systems. Sly Dunbar remembered King Tubby (among others) as a pioneer in this regard: "It was usually King Tubbys sound used to do that, with U-Roy on the controls, and I think Tubby's try to get that effect in the studio. So I would a say, that's where it a start from."[18]

An important early link in this process was the "dub plate." Mikey Dread defined the dub plate as "a little pre-release of the thing before it gets to the streets. Back in those days we didn't have CD burners where you could just go and get a copy. You'd have to wait months. So, the dub plate was just taking the same procedure from the mastering room [of the record manufacturing plant] and they just cut this little thing they called an *acetate*. They cut it right there [in the recording studio]."[19]

The dub plate represented a consolidation of two separate stages of the record manufacturing process into the single location of the recording studio. In most places, acetate machines are found in record mastering plants, which are devoted to a later stage of the record manufacturing process. But in Jamaica, acetate machines are often found on the premises of recording studios. In the American music industry, such acetates have generally been used as test pressings of recordings, given to music industry personnel for review in advance of commercial release. Made of a soft wax coating over a metal core, they are only meant to provide a limited number of performances before decaying. Accordingly, Dudley Sibley remembered: "What they're calling dub, we used to call it *soft wax*."[20] In Jamaica, "dub plate" referred to such acetate recordings, given on an exclusive basis to sound system operators by studios for the purpose of previewing unreleased songs.[21] But in Jamaica, the acetate also became an actual medium of public performance.

There was a reason for this novel use of the acetate. Over time, sound system operators like Ruddy Redwood discovered that they could create excitement in the sound systems by playing modified acetate versions that omitted vocals partially or entirely; the surprised audience would often sing in place of the removed vocals. The irony is that, in Bunny Lee's account, this discovery was made by accident:

When dub started it wasn't really "dub." Tubbys and myself was at Duke Reid's studio one evening, and [a sound system operator] by the name of Ruddy [Redwood] from Spanish Town was cutting some riddims, with vocal. And the engineer made a mistake and him was going stop and Ruddy said, "No man, make it run!" And then the pure riddim run because him didn't put in the voice. Ruddy said, "Now take another cut with the voice." And then, him take the cut with the voice.

[Ruddy] was playing the next Saturday and I happened to be in the dance. And they play this tune, they play the riddim and the dance get so excited that them start to sing the lyrics over the riddim part and them have to play it for about half an hour to an hour! The Monday morning when I come back into town I say, "Tubbs, boy, that little mistake we made, the people them love it!" So Tubby say, "All right, we'll try it." We try it with some Slim Smith riddim like "Ain't Too Proud To Beg." And Tubbys start it with the voice and [then] bring in the riddim. Then him play the singing, and them him play the complete riddim without voice. We start a call the thing "version."[22]

This was a seminal moment. Producers' strategy of partially or completely removing vocal tracks [or other parts] introduced an element of creativity into what was a fairly prosaic task, and was the first step in what would become one of *the* fundamental compositional strategies in dub music: dropping out of vocal and instrumental parts. There were several motivations for this dropping out of tracks. Dudley Sibley recalled that at Studio One, the initial motivation was corrective, but gradually grew into something more creative: "Punch in, punch out, experiment—a guy come inna studio, cyaan [can't] sing the song. And you have to use up the riddim. We experiment until other [producers] get involved. And when them draw out, put in, draw out, put in, is not something scientific. You had to have a *feel*. And by *feeling* it, you know where to drop in, where to put out . . . you see the people respond so you continue with it. . . . And it just evolved."[23]

Another crucial motivation was the fierce competition among the sound systems. Sylvan Morris remembered how early engineers factored into the competition, despite their limited equipment:

Now, this is how come the real dub ting started . . . the sound men, they were try-ing to compete with each other. So sometimes they come in and say "Bwoi, you have any good riddim?" And there's something that you like and you might give them a track. When you gave a man a riddim track, you give it to him in a certain style [that is, mix]. Him go away and him play it against another sound [system], 'cause them have a clash [that is, a competition between two sound systems]. And because of certain tunes that you gave him, he won the contest. The next morning he come back and him want that same music, but he no want it the same way! So you have to be innovative with these two tracks. I try to feed some likkle things, take out a thing here, put in a thing there . . . so now sometimes you'd sell the same track ten times![24]

Clive Chin remembers that at Randy's, these versions were deliberately mixed differently from the singles that were available to the general public: "The sound system, we'd give them specials, we'd give them something dif-ferent from what an average person would go out there and buy. I would give, say, a sound system like say Arrows or Emperor Faith a mix that was completely different from the way we put it out on the 45."[25] It was for similar reasons that each sound system was given a different mix. Chin con-tinued: "You would find on a given day at least two or three sound system man coming and buying. . . . I wouldn't give them the same mix. We'd have to give them something different. It would be unfair to give say, Arrows the same mix we give Ray Symbolic. That's why the dub plate start to be-come exclusive and they become very competitive and very expensive. Be-cause what you charge a sound system to cut a dub plate would be much more than if he buys it on a 7-inch 45."[26]

Because the dub plates were pressed on a softer form of vinyl, they had a very limited playing life. In Chin's opinion, this impermanency was ironic given their high price: "After a certain point they burn out and become very noisy, like a lot of popping and stuff. . . . I really didn't know the true thing behind the dub plates not standing up to its quality because if you pay so much money for it, it should have some kind of value after a period of time, but it don't."[27] But others feel that playing life wasn't a particularly important issue in the early days of the industry: the main motivation for unique music was to entice a crowd into the sound system, whose main profit was derived not from admission fees, but from alcohol sales. As Graeme Goodall described it, "usually acetates only got 10–15 plays anyway, but it was worth it for these guys to buy them because it meant people came to the dances and bought the liquor."[28]

Dub plates gradually came to be used in competitions between sound systems, who fought to present the most unique and personalized versions of popular songs. As Mikey Dread describes below, it eventually culmi-nated in the production of dub plate "specials," on which popular singers would re-record their vocal melodies, modifying the lyrics in order to praise the sound system that commissioned the special:

Another aspect of dub is for example, you can have a Dennis Brown song, which is extremely popular, right? And a sound man come and check Dennis Brown and say he want Dennis to sing that kind of lyric about *his* sound. He want Dennis to say his sound is the number one sound or the champion sound, because he gonna play a competition. The other guys don't have Dennis singing on it, they only have the regular generic one. So the other guy is gonna play the generic one, then [the first sound system] is gonna play the one with the artist singing about his sound and how he's the better sound and all that. That's another aspect of dub, the competitive thing of sound clashes. Everybody wanted the most popular singer to be singing about him on one of their popular rhythm tracks.[29]

The commercial equivalent of the dub plate was the "rhythm version," a designation indicating that the vocal track would be omitted from versions of songs that appeared on the flip side of a 45 single. The rhythm version was effectively the same as the instrumental dub plates, but could be purchased commercially instead of being exclusively available to sound systems. In fact, many commercially released rhythm versions were used by smaller sound systems that couldn't afford exclusive studio dub plates.[30] This was the impetus behind Studio One's famous "Studio One Stereo" mix, in which vocals and instruments were strictly separated into left and right channels; with this separation, the balance control on a playback system could be shifted to one side, eliminating the vocal tracks entirely and presenting a pure instrumental track. Unlike the dub plates, these commercial pressings also had a normal playing life.

It seems that in some cases, the initial impetus driving the development of both dub plates and rhythm versions was not creative, but merely a way to economize a limited amount of music. Graeme Goodall remembered that at Federal, "I used to do the vocal separate, and they said 'Let's do the B-side without the vocal.' . . . That was just a matter of 'Well, why should we give them two good songs?' An A-side, and a backing track for the B-side. . . . It was just expedient."[31]

Versioning

As Bunny Lee mentioned above, these early reconfigurations associated with dub plates were referred to as "versions." Sylvan Morris detailed the same process and agreed that the term *version* originated concurrently with dub plates and rhythm versions: "Originally, what they called "dub" was just called *version*. In other words, you'd probably take out some of the instruments and some of the voice and put [the new version] on the other side of a 45. So the dub business eventually came from that. It's just a version of the original which is done in many forms."[32] It is interesting that in

Jamaican musical parlance the noun "version" was gradually transformed into a verb; that is, "to version." The dub plate can be considered the first step in this process of "versioning," a method of serially recycling recorded material developed by producers desiring to ensure the longest commercial life for a given piece of recorded music despite economic constraints and a limited pool of musicians. The process of versioning was soon exploited to its fullest extent, as prerecorded backing tracks began to be used as a basis for a series of more distinct performances. On successive recyclings of a track, an instrumental soloist might offer a jazzy improvisation on what was termed an "instrumental" version, or a different singer might offer a new set of lyrics.[33]

The Rise of the DJ

There was another important motivation for providing instrumentals for sound systems. By the mid-1960s, the first generation of sound system operators turned record producers were increasingly devoting time to their production activities, and their roles at dances were filled by resident deejays, the most loquacious of whom began to "toast" (that is, rap) over the music to excite the crowd. The first deejays were people like Count Machuki and King Stitt (both working Coxsone's *Downbeat* system), and with the emergence of the groundbreaking U-Roy (Ewart Beckford) with King Tubby's sound system around 1970, a younger generation of DJs would go on to become recording stars in their own right: Dennis Alcapone, Big Youth, Tappa Zukie, Dillinger, Prince Jazzbo, U-Brown, Trinity, Dr. Alimantado, and I-Roy, among many others. These musicians specialized in exhorting the crowd to dance with their various styles of stream-of-consciousness vocalizing; the new dub plates, with vocals partially or completely removed, allowed the deejays the sonic space to improvise freely over the rhythm as would a jazz soloist. Clive Chin remembered the rise of the deejay as a dominant force in the sound systems, and the role the dub plate played: "Sound system become modernized now. You no have one turntable no more, you have two turntable, so you play the vocal, like Heptones' 'Tripe Girl' or 'Guiding Star,' and just about as the music finish after three minutes and change—BOOM!—the version just come in with the drum and bass and the man just pick up the mic at the same time and begin to toast, him a nice up the sound!"[34]

The dub plate thus represented a conjunction of two creative practices: the multitrack recording machines through which musical performances could now be partially disassembled, and the interruptive performance logic of the sound system deejays, who thought nothing of continuously interrupting songs with their improvised vocalizing. In fact, the process of stripping songs down to their essential components must be understood as substantially intertwined with the practice of deejaying; while studio engineers were beginning to use the mixing board to open songs up from the inside, their work was clearly prefigured by the deejays who destroyed song form from the outside. Rapping, chanting, and shouting their laconic improvisations often irrespective of harmonic or formal changes, and asking their selectors to "pull up" (stop and restart the record) at every opportunity, the deejays were rudely and creatively disrespectful of song form. Ultimately, the aesthetic of fragmented and superimposed vocalizing that would become such an important part of dub music could be thought of as at least partially inspired by the performance style of the sound system DJs and selectors.

Thus, it was no coincidence that King Tubby's later ascendance as a dub mixer would parallel the ascendance of the first full-fledged DJ, U-Roy, and that the latter was one of the DJs (and selector) on the former's *Home Town Hi-Fi* sound system; the dub impulse and the DJ impulse were almost completely intertwined. Bunny Lee described the method he developed in the studio with King Tubby:

Me just say Tubbs, I want you to mix a dub version. And then the DJ talk over the dub. Sometimes we put the singer's voice but sometime the DJs used to clash and we start doing the pure dub. If you take off the DJ voice, you have the dub LP too. So you used to take two—sometime you do three vocal/dub LPs in one night. That automatically is six albums because when you take off, put the dub aside. Take off the DJ voice, mix it off and run the pure dub, is another a three album that. So we used to take one stone and kill all three birds at the same time. You don't waste time those days![35]

Artists and producers sometimes conceived their series of versions as thematically linked, reflected in the way that retitling led to a string of B-side witticisms. So although, in Lee Perry's productions of the Wailers, "Duppy Conqueror" predictably begat "Duppy Conqueror Version 2," "Duppy Conqueror Version 3," and so on, the ghoulish-sounding "Mr. Brown" (complete with what Bunny Lee termed a "creep organ") begat "Dracula," while "Small Axe" begat "Battle Axe," "More Axe," and "Axe Man." Over time, versioning would provide an opportunity for as many wordplays and title puns as there were versions.

Besides the maximizing of profits, another motivation for versioning was the variable talent level of singers who passed through the Kingston studios. Unlike instrumentalists who worked regularly, vocalists were often "one-shot" singers with a catchy melody or lyric, but lacking the talent to translate it into a successful song formula. For example, Augustus Pablo's 1972 melodica instrumental "Java" was originally conceived as a vocal performance, but the vocal track was deemed unsatisfactory by producer Clive Chin and erased.[36] We recall Dudley Sibley's comments regarding the corrective use of the mix, and Chin recounted the process that turned "Java" into a career-launching hit for both Pablo and Chin:

it was a schoolmate of mine I took down to the studio one Friday evening while a session was going on and him say him want do a tune. So what happened now the guy couldn't sing the tune. . . . Although we tried different takes, he just couldn't handle it. So [engineer] Errol [Thompson] say, let's just rub off him voice and do something with the riddim, 'cause the riddim did wicked! . . . Pablo was there after the riddim was made . . . he heard the guy trying to sing the tune and him just ask me, him have an idea for the tune. We give him a cut off a the riddim 'pon a dub plate. Him carry it home and the next couple of days him come back. And it's two cuts we took with him. I never forget that, two cuts on the same "Java" riddim. And we use both of them cause the two of them is wicked![37]

Pablo's overdubbed melodica instrumental was just one of several subsequent versions of the riddim.[38] At this stage, then, recording technology was beginning to imply for reggae what improvisation had already implied for jazz: the notion that a "composition" must now be understood as a composite of its endlessly multiplying, mutating, and potentially infinite elaborations over time. The next phase in the development of dub would feature songs that had been stripped to their barest components.

"Drum & Bass" as a Concept in Jamaican Music

Forget 'bout pretty guitars and all that, people just wanted to hear the basic thing. So, we started making riddims with just bass and drum and people sung on it or the DJ just talk on top of it. —Philip Smart, 2003

During the early 1970s, engineers like Errol Thompson and King Tubby began to exploit a new aspect of the mixing process. Prior to this, "versions" had generally been alternate vocals, instrumentals, or rhythm versions. Around 1972, however, engineers began to produce "drum & bass" versions, as they came to be known. These minimalist mixes reflected a significant shift in several musical values in reggae.

Using the earlier "rhythm versions" as their point of departure, these new mixes stripped tracks even further, decreasing the emphasis on the horns, guitars, and keyboard instruments, while increasing the emphasis on the electric bass line and drum set, which now provided the main musical interest. A typical drum & bass mix would focus on the propulsive motion of those two instruments throughout, with the chordal instruments only occasionally filtering through. This treatment of the chordal instruments reflects what would become two central strategies of dub mixing, *fragmentation* and *incompletion*. One important result of all this was that explicit harmonic movement decreased somewhat in its importance to this type of reggae composition; chords could now be as easily used as bits of abstract color and texture to flavor the austerity of the drum & bass sound, as they could to chart harmonic movement.

As the mixes discussed below will demonstrate, the "drum & bass" tag should not be taken absolutely literally, as these mixes often included snatches of rhythm guitar, organ and piano. In essence, the term indicates the prominence accorded to the drum and bass patterns, and the gradual de-emphasis on harmony in the traditional sense. With such a de-emphasis, it makes sense that electric bass patterns became by necessity more dynamic; the new sound was crucially dependent on the inventive patterns being created by established and emerging bassists such as Errol "Bagga" Walker, Robbie Shakespeare, Fully Fulwood, Boris Gardiner, Lloyd Parks, Errol "Flabba" Holt, and Aston "Family Man" Barrett. Other musicians crucial to enlarging the stock of riddims include producer/instrumentalists Augustus Pablo, Glen Brown, and vocalist/bassist Leroy Sibbles.

Without slighting the dozens of talented session musicians who worked in ever-changing configurations around the Kingston studios, the most innovative drum & bass teams during the 1970s were the brothers Carlton and Aston "Familyman" Barrett (best known for their work with Bob Marley and the Wailers), and Sly Dunbar and Robbie Shakespeare (best known for their work with Peter Tosh and Black Uhuru). While the Barrett brothers slowed down the syncopations of rock steady to create a distinctive brand of "roots" reggae, Sly and Robbie emerged as inventive reinterpreters of old Treasure Isle and Studio One riddims, as well as masterful composers of the new generation of "militant" riddims. Musically, Sly noted the change that took place in the music once the emphasis was placed on drum and bass patterns: "Me and Robbie didn't realize what we were doing until Jamaican music went dubwise and the bass and drum would come right in your face. When the music was broken down to the raw drum & bass, we realized we had to work some magic . . . we realized this music was different from everybody playing together.[39]

It is not surprising that Barrett and Shakespeare dominated the composition of bass riddims. In Jamaica, they had been recognized for several years as premiere bassists, their lines booming out of dancehalls and sound systems across the island. It has been often discussed that the prominence of the bass line in Jamaica is at least partly attributable to the necessity of making sure low-frequency information survives in the open-air spaces in which the sound systems usually play. But we can assume that Barrett and Shakespeare's extensive touring activities must also have brought a new dimension to their craft. Playing their bass lines through huge amplification systems in the cavernous arenas and stadiums of Europe and America had clear effects on their phrasing. Lines now became longer and more suspenseful, phrased to hang in the air dramatically within the huge physical spaces in which they were now performed. This spatial component in turn fed back into the Jamaican context, these expansively phrased bass lines perfectly suited to the expansive lyrics and mixing strategies of the era.

It follows that in most musicians' opinions, the success of a dub mix is at least partially dependent upon the inventiveness of the riddim and the bass line in particular. According to Bunny Lee, "Most of the time the riddim have to be good, and the riddim unusual."[40] Bassist Fully Fulwood feels that the "bass is very important because when you have a real nice line that you can really vibe to and groove to, that's where you can find a great dub mix."[41] Adrian Sherwood similarly felt that the "performance thing is still very important; the rhythm's either good or it's not. If the bass line, the chords, the rhythm and lead melodies are good, you'll make a good record. If they're not, you can't make a piece of shit shine, as they say. If you've got good ingredients, you make a good cake. And if you're inspired because of the magic on the tape, something fantastic can happen."[42] As such, drum & bass patterns were fundamental to dub: because the most successful dub mixes transcended mere soundscaping, the atmospheric manipulations were dependent on what was happening in the rhythm section (thus, as we shall see, King Tubby and Scientist mixed differently from each other; they had different types of riddims to work with).

Karl Pitterson on the Mix
Earl "Chinna" Smith: "Satan Side" > Keith Hudson: "Black Heart"

Aston "Family Man" Barrett's bass pattern on Chinna Smith's "Satan Side" is a great example of the foregrounding of the bass line typical of roots reggae. A melodically active pattern, the line rivets the listener's attention even when stripped down by engineer Karl Pitterson into a bare drum & bass mix (titled "Black Heart"). Mixes such as "Satan Side," whether or not they also contained vocals, are best understood as a music in which engineers fused minimal sound processing with the force of the low register to articulate the atmospheric and spatial qualities of the mix, or in which the processing of texture replaces harmony in the fleshing out of a skeletal rhythm pattern.

Tracks such as "Black Heart" also demonstrate that drum & bass was more than one of the most distinctive stylistics feature of roots reggae music. It was in fact a new mixing strategy that radically altered the sound of Jamaican music and that arguably established a characteristically *Jamaican* popular music aesthetic. Over time, in fact, "drum & bass" became much more than a description of a particular mixing style: it became a musical signifier invested with the same types of resonance associated with "swing" in jazz or "clave" in Afro-Cuban music—a musical signifier of a Jamaican cultural ethos. In this case the cultural ethos was rooted in the perceived "rawness" of African roots and nature (as well as the West Kingston experience, quickly becoming a metaphor for the national condition), and encoded into musical sound via the jettisoning of Western harmony. Drum & bass was thus one of many instances in which musicians of African descent began to deconstruct and Africanize the Western popular song according to whatever ideas prevailed about which musical choices constituted "Africa" in their particular location. The irony is that studies of black power and Afrocentricity in the Caribbean have concluded that despite the Afrocentric rhetoric of the era, the popular embrace of Africa actually remained quite ambivalent.[43] Ultimately, then, the revitalization of ancestral Africa in the cultural imagination led partially to an infusion of musical Africanisms, but ultimately to a more unique form of Jamaican music.

Not all Jamaican engineers championed these developments. One such skeptic is Errol Brown, who engineered much of Bob Marley's Island-era music and whose tastes seem to reflect that he worked with several of the Jamaican artists whose work was aimed at the international market: "I work with all of the international artists, the type of people that really like *real music* [emphasis mine]. What I realized with this dub music is when you take out the middle, with the guitar, piano and organ and all of these things, it loses the life for me. I really don't like too much of that because it's like the music is missing an element with all of that drum & bass."[44] This new sound also carried certain social overtones, given that the "downtown" music coming out of West Kingston was deliberately fashioned to sound more raw and abrasive. In fact, as Scientist recalled, the sonic values of this music also posed a very literal technical challenge to both radio stations and record manufacturers, inside and outside of Jamaica: "Back before reggae got popular, you find that a lot of radio stations didn't like to play reggae because it would make the transmitters overmodulate. And when they were cutting vinyl, a lot of people didn't want to master reggae because whenever the cutting head see that amount of high frequency, it would go into protect and shut down the machine. That's one of the reason why reggae got the type of fight that it got."[45]

Philip Smart similarly recalled many instances in which he and King Tubby devised a unique mixing strategy, only to have the tape returned from the mastering plant, because it violated some convention of recording fidelity. Sylvan Morris, however, remembers that despite these various forms of resistance, "people started to recognize that drum & bass was really having a sound, [although] it was really a ting that normally people wouldn't think of that way, 'cause they were saying that that music was raw, it's not professional."[46] And Sly Dunbar felt that by the time of King Tubby's early work, drum & bass "really come in the forefront as showing people that you can just use a bass and drum and really make a hit without putting all this instrumentation on it."[47]

In purely musical terms, the most important implication of drum & bass was that it would pave the way for dub to become to reggae what modal jazz was to bebop and hip-hop was to funk and R&B: a means of disassembling the harmonic landscape to enable freer improvisation. This improvisation was by no means limited to vocalists and/or instrumentalists, however. As much as drum & bass cleared a space for inventive rhythm section composing and vocal improvisation, so did it also clear a space for the increasingly creative mixing skills of engineers. In fact, if drum & bass can be considered a distillation of the reggae structure to its most basic elements, the next stage in the evolution of the reggae remix would reanimate riddims not by reintroducing chords and melodies, but rather by a system of atmospheric remixing techniques that emphasized timbre, spatiality, and texture as primary musical values. The new spaciousness of "roots"-era reggae provided the perfect aural canvas for the increasingly spatial strategies of studio engineers who—to paraphrase Sly Dunbar—now began to work *their own* form of magic. It was the availability of increasingly sophisticated pieces of sound processing equipment that enabled engineers to elaborate drum & bass into a more radical form of improvisational engineering, one that became known as *dub*.

The Rise of the Dub Mix

Varying Definitions of the Term *Dub*

While it is possible in retrospect to delineate the evolution of these "proto-dub" practices, a visit to any Jamaican record store will reveal that even thirty years after the fact, there remain several contrasting definitions of the term *dub*. The earliest popular usage of the term "dub" in this context seems to have referred to the aforementioned "dub plates." On the other hand, some Jamaicans merely define "dub" as a style of erotically charged dancing. Max Romeo remembered "a dance which is very close, where you hold the woman and kind of rub on her, you call it *rub-a-dub*."[48] This definition spawned more explicitly sexual associations, such as those implied by The Silvertones's song title "Dub the Pum Pum" ("pum pum" being the Jamaican slang for female genitalia), Big Joe and Fay's lewd talk-over "Dub A Dawta" ("dawta" being the Rasta term for wife or girlfriend) or the deejay I-Roy's "Sister Maggie Breast," a song filled with sexual references and double-entendres:

> I man a-dub it on the side
> Say little sister you can run but you can't hide
> Slip you got to slide you got to open your crotches wide
> Peace and love abide[49]

The stylistic term *rub-a-dub* could refer either to dancing, or to the aforementioned style of deejaying. In this sense, dub is the direct forebear of what later became known from the mid-1980s as *ragga* or *dancehall*. Connected to this stylistic stream is the genre called "dub poetry," in which politicized vocalists such as Mikey Smith, Mutabaruka, or Linton Kwesi Johnson chanted and/or rapped politically conscious verses over reggae rhythms. The keyword here is *politicized;* in terms of musical delivery, the dub poets were identical to the deejays and their "rub-a-dub." The connection between the word "dub" and the practice of deejaying remains strong to this day, especially outside of Jamaica where the influence of Jamaican dancehall rapping on other regional genres is often referred to by the short-hand "dub."

Musicians often used the term on stage to indicate a particular portion of their live sets. For example, Bob Marley and the Wailers had their own definition of "dub"; when they said "dub this one," they meant to emphasize the rhythm groove and to play particularly tightly as a band.[50] Sly Dunbar related that "onstage when a man a say "dubwise!" that means bass and drums."[51] But the most obvious usage of the term relates directly to the process of recording: "dub" in this context meaning either *to record on top of* or *to make a copy of.* And the stylistic definitions offered by most musicians, engineers, and producers all cohered around the elements of rhythm (that is, drum & bass patterns), sound processing, and song re-mixing. Rather than paraphrasing them, I shall allow the following Jamaican musicians, producers, and engineers to define the term *dub* in their own words:

Engineers and producers create it. First it start out when they take out a few instruments. Then they take most of the vocals out. They get deeper and deeper until they take out everything, and just leave drum and bass. And get more and more deeper into it. The less instruments, the more effects (Clinton Fearon, member of the Gladiators and session musician at Studio One and Lee Perry's Black Ark).[52]

. . . playing around with rhythm tracks, you know like the drum & bass, the riddim set up of it (producer Clive Chin of Randy's Studio).[53]

. . . creating different type of sounds, putting different type of instruments and voices through different type of effects—the dub music is that experience (producer Winston Riley).[54]

. . . about experimenting. Let's say you make a mistake in the electronics part of it and the sound that you get out of it [makes you say] "wow, I wish I knew how to do that again." . . . There are times when those kind of impulses just happen . . . in that way you can change the whole pattern of the song (vocalist/producer Mikey Dread).[55]

. . . the fundamentals of reggae but not only is it *fundamental* music, it is *complex* in that it carries every mood, every feel, every groove that you can imagine in music, all broken down into its basic, very simple form (Bobby Vicious).

. . . [A music that] fuck up the head! It blow your mind like you dey 'pon drugs! It put you 'pon a different level, a different planet. You can feel like you's a space man, sometime you might feel like you's a deep sea diver. You can be like in an airplane in ten seconds, it make you feel anyway you want to feel (Robbie Shakespeare, producer, session bassist and touring bassist with Peter Tosh, Black Uhuru, and others).[56]

They just keep reinventing the song. That's what I feel dub does—it reinvents itself (Mikey Dread).[57]

. . . authentically Jamaican, without a doubt. There's nothing else to compare it to in the world, prior to that. [The rest of the world] might not know dub music by the name but when they hear it, it's like "Oh, that's Jamaica." It started where the emphasis was on the drums and the bass and a lot of echoes on the instruments (Computer Paul, producer and multi-instrumentalist).[58]

. . . you do as many versions as you could possibly want, emphasizing different sections, arrangements, placing the vocals here and the vocals there. And then it became a trend. . . . Some people think it's just a kind of riff-raff situation, something that was just lucky to be around. But it's where the principles [of reggae music] have been explored (Bunny Wailer, vocalist/producer).[59]

Within this constellation of meanings, "dub" implies two things overall. First, it implies the site of the recording studio, and the creative manipulations afforded by multitrack recording and sound processing. Second, it implies the site of the sound system/dancehall, in the sense that it conforms to a standard strategy of African-derived popular dance music. Like the extended vamp section of a funk composition, the montuno section of a salsa composition, or the merengue section of a merengue composition, dub serves that moment in the dancehall when excess ornamentation is stripped away to emphasize the elemental power of the rhythm pattern, to provoke more intense and erotically charged dancing, and to give an improviser free rein to excite the crowd with his or her spontaneous virtuosity—in short, the moment(s) when the dancehall "peaks." The immediate distinction here is that unlike other styles in which an instrumental improvisor steps forth to raise the intensity, the improvisation in the dub version is performed by a DJ. But more important is that another level of improvisation was performed *before* the actual moment by the engineer in his creation of the dub mix. In combination, these two understandings fuse to imply a type of music created in the recording studio through the process of remixing, functioning to service the hottest moments in the dancehall. This music gradually took on a more concrete life as a recorded genre to be judged on its own terms.

Studio Technology and Compositional Strategies of the Dub Mix

When we talk about dub, the producers take all the credit. But the people who really deserve the credit are the engineers. —Clive Chin, 1999

What made dub unique in the context of pop music both in Jamaica and worldwide was the creative and unconventional use recording engineers made of their equipment (as, for example, in using acetate as the dub plate). This enabled them to fashion a new musical language that relied as much on texture, timbre, and soundspace, as it did on the traditional musical parameters of pitch, melody, and rhythm. In general, the most important understanding of the dub mix is as a deconstructive, B-side remix of a 45 rpm single; the remix engineer draws on various strategies to manipulate the listener's anticipation of musical events, and defamiliarize the vocal song on the A-side. Over time, engineers' unconventional use of their equipment consolidated into the body of formal strategies that largely define the idiom. Following is a summary of the most frequent remix strategies and the sound processing equipment with which they were realized.

Erasure and Fragmentation of Song Lyrics: The Poetry of Dub

Although dub music is largely an instrumental medium, one of the most immediately recognizable sonic features of the dub mix is the way song lyrics are omitted and/or fragmented, on one hand, and the way successive "generations" of lyrics are juxtaposed against each other, on the other. The fragmentation of recorded material is achieved by manipulation of the *mute* switch, one of the simplest devices on the mixing console. The mute switch allows an engineer to control the audible level of an instrument or group of instruments contained on one or more tracks, placing a particular track in or out of the audible mix at the press of the button. A more gradual effect is achieved by use of the *fader* controls, sliding levers that allow the volume of an instrument to be gradually raised or lowered. These controls are central to what can be called a mixing strategy of *fragmentation*, the abrupt introduction and removal of formerly continuous musical material.

In mixing dub versions, these controls were used to create abrupt shifts in ensemble texture. In a typical dub mix, for example, the engineer might introduce the song with a snippet of the original vocal. Instead of continuing throughout as on the familiar version, however, the vocal would then drop out of the mix, appearing and disappearing in fragmentary fashion, intermittently throughout the rest of the performance. "Say So" (a remix of Paul Blackman's vocal track of the same name) from the seminal LP *King Tubbys Meets the Rockers Uptown,* is a good study of the simultaneous dissolution and distillation of meaning achieved through this subtractive textual strategy.[60] In his remix, King Tubby essentially reduces the lyrics of the original to a form of minimalist poetry in which only twelve remaining words are left to impart any textual meaning. On the first verse of the original song, Paul Blackman sang:

> You don't have to run
> away from me
> All you got to do
> is try and see
> Try and see
> if you really love me
> All that you need
> oh, I'll give to you
> All that your love needs, and all that's true
> Say so, if you love me girl
> say so . . .

Tubby's mix reduces this to:

> You don't have to run
>
>
> All that your love needs
>
>
> say so . . .

The same technique is used to strong effect on "King Tubby Meets the Rockers Uptown," Tubby's well-known remix of Jacob Miller's "Baby I Love You So."[61] On the first verse of the original track, Miller sings:

> Baby I love you so
> and this is what I really know
> and if you should ever leave
> and go away
> Baby I've been slaving every day, oh
> Night and day I pray
> that love will come my way
> Night and day I pray
> that love will come away . . .
> that you won't stay out late

Tubby's remix reduces Miller's sentiments to five bare syllables:

Baby I've . . .

that love . . .

One way of viewing such erasure is that it transformed song lyrics, after the fact, from what Curt Sachs called "logogenic" music (in which comprehensible words are the basis of the song) into what he called "pathogenic" sound (pure sound arising from the emotions).[62] It might therefore seem pointless to search for any poetic qualities in these phonemic fragments. Buttressed by sound processing, however, they often surpass the one-dimensionality of the original lyrics in their cryptically evocative power, allowing more open-ended opportunities of lyrical interpretation. As one musician muses: "Sometimes I don't even want to hear the original. It's more interesting to me to listen to the dub mix and let my imagination fill in what the original must have sounded like."[63] On the other hand, when the original lyrics addressed political, religious, or cultural themes, the remix process could sometimes distill the message into a more powerful form. King Tubby's "King Tubby's Key" remix reduces Earl Zero's entire "Shackles & Chains" to a mere four lines, but the net meaning remains equally potent, as suggestive lyrical fragments churn out of the soundscape:

The shackles and chains must be broken . . .
. . . and who still of those, that were stolen . . .
. . . what about the half, the half that never been told?

. . . there must be an end . . . [64]

As is so frequently the case in Jamaican music, there is also a competitive economic motive behind an aesthetic choice. Mikey Dread remembered that producers would ask engineers to include a snippet of the original vocal within the dub mix, in order to place an indelible identifying stamp on the music: "Back in the day people were scared of leaving the instruments alone because they know that somebody would re-release it and put a new voice on it. So they have to put something somewhere in the dub to make sure that maybe halfway through the tune the guy don't know what he's gonna do when he get to that part [with the original vocal]. You don't want a man to take your riddim and go voice it straight like it's his—you have to put your trademark in there to stop the pirates!"[65]

Collaging and Multilayering of Song Lyrics

The juxtaposition of several generations of fragmented text, on the other hand, was an additive strategy that produced an equally striking effect, through what might be called an aesthetic of *accumulation*. For example, Tony Brevett scored a hit in 1974 with "Don't Get Weary," the first two verses of which ran:

> Don't get weary, little girl
> don't get weary
> You're gettin' weary, little girl,
> don't get weary
> You pick yourself up from off the ground
> for this is no time to lie around
> If he says he love you, stick around
> Why you gonna put him down?
>
> Don't get weary, little girl
> don't get weary
> You're gettin' weary, little girl
> don't get weary
> A thousand times or more
> You told me you really love him so
> You want the whole wide world to know
> That you'll never let him go
> Don't get weary . . .

Tappa Zukie follows the "talk-over" format of the sound system on his deejay version of "Don't Get Crazy." Zukie chants in call-and-response against fragments of the prerecorded vocal performance, using Brevett's "weary" theme as a point of departure for an exhortation of Rastafarian faith, and largely transforming the romantic implications of the original lyrics (original lyrics in parentheses):

> (Don't get weary, little girl
> don't get weary . . .)
> No, no, no!
> (You're gettin' weary, little girl,
> don't get weary . . .)
> Seh! A sistah don't get weary
> I beg ya try a little theory
> Sista don't get weary
> I beg ya try a little theory
> For if ya born as a natty then you mus' be a natty
> You grow up as a natty say you mus' be a natty
> A-natty, natty, natty, natty, natty, natty . . .
> A-natty, natty, natty, natty, natty, natty . . .
> A-natty don't eat fatty
> (Thousand times or more . . .)

Thousand times I tell ya
A-natty, natty, natty, natty, natty, natty, natty
A-natty don't eat fatty
A-natty don't go a bar
A-natty dread stay far
for the baldhead go a bar
and he walk into a car
Natty dread stay far . . . [66]

The deejay I-Roy cut his own version of the track, titled "Don't Get Weary Joe Frazier." I-Roy mixes his rap with fragments of the original, reinterpreting the "weary" theme in order to console the African American boxer following his humiliating second-round loss to George Foreman in the so-called Sunshine Showdown heavyweight boxing match held in Kingston in January 1973. Frazier had a large following in Jamaica, and I-Roy's version was just one of several reggae songs consoling him:

Woah!
Tribute to the brother called Joe Frazier
"Smokin' Joe" as I would say
he lost the big fight
But I tell you people this was really out of sight as I would say
(Don't get weary . . .)
Never, never Brother Joe
Never you be late for the show
(Don't get weary . . .)
I'm beggin' you to return on the scene
There and then I know you will be keen
(Pick yourself up off from the ground . . .)
No use for lyin' around as I would tell you
Got to train harder each and every day
(Stick around, why you gonna put him down?)
No matter what certain things and folks may say
Man Joe Frazier like I tell you
was sharp like a razor
But he was no match for brother Georgie . . . [67]

Like the distinction between a thematic "head" and the improvisation in jazz music, deejaying became a fundamental method of elaborating core thematic material, via the deejay's running commentary on the original lyrics. Studio engineers took this a step further, their additive approach allowing singers, deejays, and instrumentalists to "converse" with each other over several versions, and projecting the track over virtual time into an intertextual call-and-response with its own previous incarnations.

The versions of "Don't Get Weary" demonstrate thematic continuity of a type. But the process sometimes resulted in disjunct textual meanings. It was inevitable that "hypernarratives" would eventually result, in which meaning remained suspended between two or more collaged texts, ultimately resolving to neither and inspiring novel interpretations through their juxtaposition. An example of this is Jah Woosh's deejay version of Bob Marley's "Talking Blues" as covered by the Maroons. Marley's original was a theme of personal tribulation and political challenge:

> Cold ground was my bed last night,
> and rock was my pillow too
> Cold ground was my bed last night,
> and rock was my pillow too
> I'm saying talking blues, talking blues
> Your feet is just too big for your shoes.[68]

In contrast, Jah Woosh's string of dancehall exhortations completely ignores Marley's weighty theme:

> (Cold ground was my bed last night
> and rock was my pillow too . . .)
> So mek we rub it in a Ghost Town
> And mek we sing it in a Jones Town
> Make we sing it and a dub it and a rub it
> Let we do it like we never want to do it . . .
> Cause the children dem a love it
> And so the dawta dem a scrub it
> A so the idren love it
> The walk and the talk and the singin' blues.[69]

Roland Barthes has claimed that only the act of reading itself can bring temporary unity to a text,[70] and the possibilities of interpretation clearly expand via these types of additive and subtractive strategies; both ultimately functioned to stretch the boundaries of textual meaning along the contours of evolving technology and economic necessity. More than any radical lyrical strategy, this aesthetic of accumulation reflected engineers' and producers' efforts to realize maximum commercial mileage from popular rhythm tracks.

How did vocalists feel about having their work manipulated in this way? Max Romeo, who had some of his most inventive lyrics subjected to Lee Perry's postproduction whims, claims: "It doesn't do anything negative to the song, it more enhance the song. Because then it's a matter of different version and a lot of people love that type of difference."[71] Susan Cadogan, whose most popular music was also mixed and remixed by Perry, assured me: "They put in the voice at strategic points, so it makes sense."[72] Certainly, there is something to be said for the poetic qualities inherent in the economy of expression and distillation of meaning that results from the engineer's top-down manipulations, resulting in something akin to minimalist poetry, Dadaist collage, or surrealist automatism. These additive and subtractive processes held transformative implications for conventions of textual meaning in pop songs, especially in an Afro-Caribbean culture with a strong oral bias toward oral information and a related tendency to interpret this information in a multitude of ways.[73]

An opposing stance on this issue was taken by the aforementioned "dub poets" who, although not dub artists in the sense defined by this book, were related to the deejays in terms of delivery style and production techniques (and, as such, were often implicated in the dynamic of dub remixing). Many of them resisted having their lyrics "rubbed out in the dub,"[74] feeling that the postperformance manipulations of engineers compromised the political messages they were trying to convey. The same position was taken by some of the internationally successful reggae artists like Bob Marley and Peter Tosh who occasionally released dub versions in order to remain current in Jamaica, but were ultimately invested in the sanctity of "the song" and its lyrical messages.[75] Errol Brown, the main engineer at Marley's Tuff Gong studio, remembered: "Sometime I put some delay effects on his [Marley's] voice like some outer space thing, but he had many lyrics, he didn't like it."[76] And although the "riddim twins" Sly Dunbar and Robbie Shakespeare developed an innovative approach to playing dub live in concert while touring with Peter Tosh (which they later perfected with Black Uhuru), Dunbar remembered Tosh's dismissal of their onstage dub innovations:

I remember when a lot of people used to curse dub and say "what kind of music that?" We used to get cursed on stage with Peter Tosh. Peter used to curse us, saying "what you think, Channel One and Joe Gibbs tune we a play?" But the audience used to go wild. When Peter leave me and Robbie alone on stage for a minute, the audience was saying "Jesus, this is *it!*" [Tosh] was always unwelcoming though, saying " . . . dub business deh a [belongs at] Channel One and Joe Gibbs."[77]

In England, where the idea of "dub poetry" was often directly linked to the actual technique of dub mixing, dub poet Linton Kwesi Johnson resolved this conflict through a more traditional approach, chanting his political toasts without interruption before turning the tracks over to engineer Dennis Bovell, who mixed the second half of each track as a dub background for jazz improvisations by the members of Johnson's band.[78]

Obviously, such fragmentation could also be applied to instrumental parts. In standard reggae recording procedure, the instruments—usually guitar, bass, drums, piano, organ, and percussion—were recorded together in the studio, with the band playing through an entire take to create a basic track. As reggae is a dance music of West African heritage constructed as a web of interlocking parts, the disruption of that structure by removing a part produces a striking and disorienting effect that is fundamental to the dub mix.

Spatial and Echo Effects and the Use of Reverb and Delay Devices

Another fundamental strategy of the dub mix is the use of reverberation. The reverberation unit blends a series of simulated echoes sequentially to simulate spatial dimension within a recording: by adding reverb, the music may sound as if it is being variously performed in a theater, arena, or cave when it was in fact typically recorded in the acoustically "dead" (that is, completely dampened) environment of the recording studio. The first reverberation device in Jamaica is said to have been built by Graeme Goodall around 1960, when he miked a Telefunken speaker that had been sealed off in the bathroom of Federal studios.[79] Little did Goodall know that reverberation would grow to become one of the most identifiable stylistic markers of Jamaican music. The vast majority of dub mixes are set in some degree of reverb and the effect is particularly important to the types of deconstructions dub engineers performed; it provided a unifying factor amidst all the sonic fragmentation outlined above. If fragmentation created dynamic tension in the mix, reverb (along with the listener's internalized sense of musical continuity) was the cohering agent that held the disparate sounds together; as individual parts appear and disappear from the mix, reverberating trails of their presences provide continuity between one sound and the next.

There were two basic uses of reverb in most dub mixes. In the *spatial* application, an engineer could use reverb to imply a series of spatial configurations in the mix. One important aspect of this was *panning,* which allows for a spacialized placement of an audio signal during the process of stereo mixing; sounds can then be heard as moving across a simulated soundspace. These types of spatial manipulations were best experienced at the extreme volumes of the sound system, where a listener experiencing dub at high volumes would experience the virtual sensation of being drawn into the various vortices simulated in the music.[80]

A contrasting application of reverberation can be called the *ambient* use, in which the recording is saturated with such a high amount of reverberation that a purely atmospheric dimension begins to form. Because engineers often generated these echoes by sending fragments of inaudible or barely audible tracks through the various effects processors, it can sometimes seem as if this atmospheric layer of the song is arising organically, without obvious connection to the music above which it swirls. In most cases, in fact, this processed sound actually originates from the basic tracks.

One generally overlooked effect of the heavy use of reverb in dub music is that it liberated the sound of the drum set, which had generally been buried in reggae mixes beneath the cloudy textures of the electric bass and the "shuffle" syncopations of the electric organ. The spatialized soundscapes of drum & bass pushed the funky minimalism of reggae drumming to the foreground, and gave a new weight to the jazzy fills and accents that were the trademarks of drummers like Sly Dunbar, Carlton Barrett, and Horsemouth Wallace. A syncopated bass drum, rim shot, or timbale roll suspended through reverberating, mutating space resulted in a music of charged emptiness. The combination of reverb with the minimalist drumming style also helped realize the "antigravity" of the reggae groove, which had always implied a certain "weightlessness" due to its heavy emphasis on the offbeat.

Although the effect produced by delay units is informally thought to be the same as reverb, its effects are primarily rhythmic in the sense that the delay effect is a timed replay of an audio signal, resulting in the characteristic "echo" effect. This effect was used in several different ways in dub mixes, to intensify the basic rhythm tracks or, later, to decenter them violently. The rhythmic use of delay had in fact been a part of Jamaican popular music at least since the heyday of Studio One, when Sylvan Morris had fashioned a crude slapback echo effect by using both mechanical and handmade tape loops (see chapter 3). By the 1970s, echo units were put to more radical uses. In the same way that an impressionist painter might have used a sea of repeated and modulated brushstrokes to blur or decenter a visual image, dub mixers in the 1970s often used the repeated rhythmic "strokes" of echo to alternately reinforce or decenter sonic "figures." Sometimes, as we shall see in the discussion of King Tubby in chapter 4, engineers timed the delay so that echoing fragments repeated in consonance with the underlying rhythm. Most frequently, however, delay was set to disjunct timings in order to spin jarring rhythmic tangents against the basic riddim, especially following an episode of disruption. Often, drum accents (especially the crash cymbals or timbales) would trigger the echo effect while the rest of the groove was muted out of the mix, echoing into space and creating a moment of charged tension before the rhythm section was reintroduced. This strategy, which Luke Erlich refers to as "the plunge," is one of the most recognizable strategies of dub mixing.[81]

An important element of this use of delay is that these tangents echoing in rhythmic disjunction allowed the music to be experienced as a simultaneity of sonic planes, especially when these planes project over the negative spaces created by sudden disruptions of the rhythm groove. For example, King Tubby's "Ethiopian Version" remixes Rod Taylor's "Ethiopian Kings," which moves at a tempo of quarter note = 69 beats per minute, while the delay unit is set at a completely disjunct tempo of approximately

168 bpm.[82] Consequently, disruptions of the vocal track (at 0:27), rhythm guitar track (at 0:49), and drum set track (at 1:26) are all projected against the basic rhythm, at the same delay rate. Thus, delay could be used to intensify the groove, to decenter it violently, or to elaborate it into unusual rhythmic and planar relationships.

As much as echo and delay were used to decenter rhythm, it also had the effect of decentering harmony, such as on the bridge section of King Tubby's "Heavy Duty Dub," in which the resolution of a chord progression is subverted by the use of echo.[83] A progression in A♭ major moves through the chords C minor–D♭ major–E♭7–F minor, at the rate of one chord per beat, with the resolution expected (per the original version) at the next measure in A♭ major. However, King Tubby applies delay to the piano just as it attacks the F minor chord; while the bass line modulates back to the A♭ tonic and then the E♭7 dominant, decaying chord tones of F minor remain suspended for a full measure. While this is by no means a particularly striking dissonance (being merely the juxtaposition of three diatonic chords), the effect is quite impressionistic, a sort of electronically extended harmony (comprising in this case all the pitches of the A♭ major scale) another characteristic effect in dub music. The deeper significance here is that this tendency toward a system of harmonic and/or formal resolutions subverted by sound processing would later constitute one of dub's most transformative contributions to conceptions of form in popular music in the digital age.

Timbral/Textural Effects and the Use of Equalization and Filtering Devices

The equalizer is a type of filter control that allows the engineer to accentuate or filter out specific audio frequencies, usually for the purpose of boosting an instrument's presence during the mixing process (throughout this chapter, I shall use the terms *filtering* and *equalization* more or less interchangeably). Using the equalization and filtering controls, overtones of an instrument can be manipulated until it sounds full, warm, and robust, or until it sounds thin, shrill, and eviscerated. Applied to an entire ensemble, a group can sound as if it is expanding or diminishing in size. Equalization could also be used to help craft the ambient aspects of a performance. In particular, the interplay of echo and equalization enabled engineers to make simulated soundspaces sound as if they were continually morphing in dimension and texture.

On his remix of Carl Malcolm's "Miss Wire Waist" (titled "Wire Dub"), engineer Karl Pitterson demonstrates how crucial this type of timbral manipulation was to dub.[84] While other producers worked to create an "upscale" dub sound by bringing in instrumentalists such as Jackie Mittoo and

Tommy McCook to blow jazz-styled improvisations over dubbed-up riddims, Pitterson achieved an equally striking degree of coloration by treating Jimmy Becker's simple, one-note, harmonica riff with distortion and equalization to great colorative effect. The filter would find a particularly creative application in the hands of King Tubby.

Use of Microphone "Bleed-through" and Secondary Signals

There are several other effects that dub engineers achieved through less conventional means. One striking effect is the use of microphone "bleed-through," a secondary effect of microphone placement. In some cases, a microphone placed in front of a particular instrument will pick up a bit of the sound of another instrument (usually the loud instruments of the rhythm section) in a different part of the room. The result, when combined with reverberation, is a distant-sounding "secondary" signal, exploited by many of the prominent dub mixers.

Inclusion of Extraneous Material and Nonmusical Sound

Sometimes, engineers will allow material to remain in the mix that is not part of the song itself, such as false starts, pretake studio dialogue, instruments being tuned up, or even remnants of a previous performance on the recording tape. In some cases, they will even subject this extraneous material to sound processing. On King Tubby's "Fittest of the Fittest Dub,"[85] for example, we hear the squealing sound of the master tape coming gradually coming up to playing speed, followed by the random noodling of the pianist. The beeping frequency of a test tone echoes through a delay unit amid faint studio chatter. All of this extraneous noise fades into a filtered vortext as the drummer counts the band in, after which the song proceeds as normal. On King Tubby's "Beware Dub,"[86] this tactic is even more dramatic, with nine chaotic seconds of studio dialogue and a false start by the band, all routed through echo and reverb units. The dialogue continues even after the tune has started, with Tubby and producer/vocalist Yabby U yelling instructions back and forth to each other.

Engineers also sometimes overdubbed various nonmusical sounds onto their recordings. King Tubby's dub mixes sometimes included various sound effects, while several of Lee Perry's mixes feature overdubbed excerpts of television dialogue, crying babies, telephones, and animal sounds. Perry's famous fake "cow" sound was added to so many recordings that it became a signature of his late work at the Black Ark studio. The overdubbing of sound effects was used most extensively by Errol Thompson (especially in his work with Joe Gibbs), who made use of a wide array of overdubbed sounds such as doorbells, sirens, alarm clocks, and other effects.

Backward Sound and Tape Speed Manipulation

The most frequent use of backward sound in dub mixes re-creates an effect used by sound systems, when the DJ yells to the selector (the person actually playing the records) to "lick it back to the top!" The selector would then toy with the audience's anticipation by manually rewinding the record back to the beginning after it has played for only a few seconds. This squealing sound of a record being spun rapidly in reverse was also used by dub mixers, when they rewound their amplified recording tape back to the beginning of a spool, and left this in as part of the final recording.

Engineers would also sometimes alter the playing speed of the tape. Initially, this was done to suit the vocal range of the singer, as changing the tape speed also changes the key of the song. Eventually, as Bunny Lee relates, they realized that slowing the tape speed also created a distortion that resulted in thicker sound: "Sometime the singer needs it in a different key, And you have to speed it up to change the key to suit him. Sometimes you just mix, it sound better to you in the higher key. And when you slow it down a little, the bass comes out heavier. So you just make it stay [at the slower speed]."[87]

Tape Splicing

Lee Perry's "Operation" and Prince Buster's "Big Youth" are two examples of tracks composed via the splicing together of various recorded performances, essentially creating sound collages that use reggae music as their source material.[88] In these instances, dub becomes a form of tape composition in a more literal sense, similar to musique concrète or its various offshoots in popular music (such as the early work of Frank Zappa). Particularly interesting is that some of these tracks splice together performances of completely different tempi, fundamentally subverting the music's typical function as dance music and providing the clearest parallels between Jamaica and experimental composition elsewhere. Because of the amount of time and the technical facilities needed to perform this type of composition, however, it is comparatively rare in Jamaica, given the speed at which musical product is typically turned out.

Abuse of Equipment

In general, Jamaican engineers have tended to push their equipment beyond its intended limits. Sometimes they actually damaged their equipment in order to achieve novel sounds. For example, King Tubby was famous for lifting and dropping his spring reverb unit, producing a violent and clangorous sound that was particularly jarring when heard from the giant speakers of the sound system. Lee Perry used this effect also, and did other unusual things to his equipment that will be discussed in the next chapter.

Sample Dub Mix
Horace Andy: "Mr. Bassie" (1971 Version) > Horace Andy: "Mr. Bassie" (1978 Version)

Two versions of Horace Andy's popular song "Mr. Bassie" are graphic illustrations of the gradual shift in tempo, the emergence of dub as a mixing strategy, and dub's broader implications for the sound of Jamaican music.[89] The original version had been recorded and mixed at Studio One by Sylvan Morris in 1972, composed by Andy as a tribute to the bassist Leroy Sibbles.[90] A four-bar B♭ minor blues at a tempo of quarter note = 65 bpm, the rhythm is played in a funky, syncopated one drop pattern style very similar to Lee Perry's productions of the same period. In addition to the regular roles of drum set, electric bass, and upbeat rhythm guitar and organ, an alto sax doubles the bass line an octave higher, while a second guitar embroiders the riddim with an interlocking single note line in the lower register, adding another layer of syncopation. The instruments outline the progression:

$$|| B♭- / / / | E♭- / B♭- / | B♭- / / / | F^7 / E♭- / ||$$

Around 1978, Andy revisited "Mr. Bassie," releasing a self-produced version that, while a vocal mix, is completely shaped by the production values of dub mixing. The tempo has been slowed to quarter note = 58bpm (reflecting a typical shift between reggae of the early and late 1970s), and the key dropped a half step to A minor. The more dramatic change, however, is found in the treatment of the bass line and the harmony. The bass, now more closely adapted to the generic "Stalag 17" riddim, repeats a single line, instead of modulating with the chord changes. Although the chords are mixed in so sparingly as to function more as coloration than harmony, they do change, outlining the progression:

$$|| A- / / / | A- / / / | A- / G / | A- / / / ||$$

This harmonic distillation of the minor blues results in a more modal sound that in turn allows Andy more freedom in both phrasing and melodic variation; his singing doesn't always imply the progression outlined above.

The mix, credited to Prince Jammy, constitutes a crucial part of the overall production. The slowed-down one drop arrangement is minimal, emphasizing the drums and bass, but the song acquires another level of complexity through the application of sound processing. The drummer's hi-hat, for example, is fed through a delay unit that turns his original eighth-note pattern into a stream of sixteenths. The rhythm guitar has been similarly treated, fed through the delay unit and echoing at a disjunct tempo of quarter note = 168 bpm. The de-emphasis on harmony here also opens a space for pure sound elements, the most prominent being the dissonant beeping test tone frequency which intermittently chimes in as a natural seventh (G♮) against the A minor seventh chord.

"Mr. Bassie" demonstrates that while most dub mixes could be taken on their own terms, these mixes were also used to create more interesting sonic environments for vocal songs. Sylvan Morris commented: "Even if [the song] has voices, you may just use the drum & bass alone depending on how the vibes of the drum & bass is. . . . You can add something else every now and again, make it run for awhile, or keep it low, and you can add many variations of it."[91] Such a mixing philosophy had implications for traditional vocal and instrumental performance. With all of the sound processing, Andy's own role is much different from the original. Although he sings more or less continuously throughout the song, the listener has less of a sense of him as a vocalist in the traditional sense, and more of a sense of him as a vocal presence that intermittently inhabits a fragmented and reverberating soundscape.

An Aesthetic of Surprise and Suspense, Collapse and Incompletion

The history outlined in this chapter thus far suggests that Jamaica has been crucial in the transfer of performance strategies from traditional instruments to electronic media. What makes the music so interesting is the way improvisation at each stage (performance, studio, DJ, selector) results in such an interesting song surface. In conceptual terms, the dub mix encapsulates the procedural ethos of post-1970 Jamaican popular music. As a form of real-time improvisation performed by engineers on the multitrack mixing console, dub's combination of fragmentation and its manipulation of spatiality gave a new perspective on the pop song. Like the different types of architectural sketches—plan, section, elevation—dub revealed the inner architecture of pop song constructions often understood as complete and self-contained. In a basic sense, we can understand dub as a style marked by the composition of vertical events against a relatively static horizontal background (that is, a continuously repeating rhythm pattern). One good analogy for the dub mixer is that of an "action painter" of sound. Operating upon a continuously unfolding "canvas" of drum & bass, the engineer throws up a brief snatch of piano, a few seconds of organ, a bit of guitar, and a dash of singing, modulating and blending the "colors" (frequencies) through the use of reverb, equalization, and other sound processing. Another analogy is the understanding of dub as a type of "aural fireworks;" an episodic coloration in which "explosive" sonic events take place against a static background that is nevertheless experienced as progressing through time.

Given the heavy demand for dub mixes from sound systems preparing for weekend dances, it is important to realize that these mixes were improvised on the spot, with a minimum of pre-planning. Most dub mixing was done on Friday evenings, when producers deposited their master tapes with engineers, and sound system operators gathered at the studio so that each could be given a unique mix of a currently popular tune. Under these circumstances, an engineer might create dozens of different mixes of a given tune in one remix session. Unlike the computerized mixing boards of today, engineers had no way of preparing a mix beforehand; they usually improvised their way through dozens of mixes of the same track. King Jammy's approach was typical of most engineers: "I don't plan it before I go into the mix, it just comes creatively. I don't plan like 'Okay, I'm going to take out the bass at two minutes' or whatever. It's just an instant creativity."[92] Bunny Lee felt that "it was a vibes thing, we just play with all the controls and what we get, we take. So no two dubs could sound the same."[93] Sylvan Morris offered the most procedural description: "It is a matter of feel, y'know. You might listen to the tune when you was mixing it, or you keep listening to the original version of the vocals, and you think to yourself, if you was to take out that at that moment, it would create an effect. So when you are [remixing] it now, you might feel it out first . . . try a thing here and take out this there and put a little echo on that . . . you might vary the length of the echo, or the decay time. You play along with it and see what sort of effect it give you."[94] Ultimately, the unity of engineer, mixing desk, and music is in the end no different than the unity of musician and instrument. As Sherwood describes it, "With dub, you're actually intercommunicating with the mixing desk—everything becomes one and then suddenly, magic happens. You feel it going around the room and the other people in the room feel it. It's like a buzz you can't describe when you're doing something like that."[95]

Using the mixing board as an instrument of spontaneous composition and improvisation, the effectiveness of the dub mix results from the engineer's ability to de- and reconstruct a song's original architecture while increasing the overall power of the performance through a dynamic of surprise and delayed gratification. The engineer continuously tantalizes the listener with glimpses of what they are familiar with, only to keep them out of reach, out of completion. This is what both Scientist and Adrian Sherwood seem to suggest:

What you want is the element of surprise, to keep them guessing. You have to keep the listener in suspense, they don't know what's coming next. Once you have that formula in mind—the element of surprise and suspense—then everything after that is spontaneous. (Scientist)[96]

With the dubs, you're working with a rhythm that's hanging on the verge of collapse all the time. You're putting it to pieces, holding it together with delays and adding and spinning the rhythm, taking out . . . one bar blurs into another or distorts into the end of the four-bar figure, and then you pull it back, just when you think it's gonna collapse. You soothe people by bringing back the bass when you've taken it out. There's more space in it than anything. (Adrian Sherwood)[97]

One illuminating comparison is not from an African-derived example at all, but rather from classical traditions of Japan, in which the perception of sound in time is interpreted in terms of a philosophical/aesthetic construct of *wabi* and *sabi*.[98] The former term is said to describe a listener's anticipation of a musical sound, while the latter describes the feeling of longing induced by the sound's decay. Andrew Juniper describes wabi/sabi as "suggest[ing] such qualities as impermanence, asymmetry, and imperfection" and embodying "the Zen nihilist cosmic view and seek[ing] beauty in the imperfections found as all things, in a constant state of flux, evolve from nothing and devolve back to nothing. Within this perpetual movement nature leaves arbitrary tracks for us to contemplate, and it is these random flaws and irregularities that offer a model for the modest and humble wabi sabi expression of beauty. Rooted firmly in Zen thought, wabi sabi art uses the evanescence of life to convey the sense of melancholic beauty that such an understanding brings."[99] Despite the radical difference in cultural context between Jamaica and Japan, this passage succinctly describes the way a dub mix works upon a listener's desire for completion, a desire based on their memory of a preexisting song.

This approach to pop song composition, which makes heavy use of textual fragmentation and atmospheric mixing, approximates Tony Grajeda's idea of a "feminization" of song form, marked by a dissolution of formal boundaries, the disruption of traditional cycles of (harmonic) tension and release, the embrace of negative sonic space (silence, absence) as a positive musical value, and a deliberately crude, low-fidelity production aesthetic.[100] But this gendering of musical traits presents problems in both general and specific application to Jamaica. Most obviously, it is based upon an essentialized view of gender traits that makes the masculine synonymous with presence (and, conversely, the feminine synonymous with absence). In the context of Jamaica's male-dominated music industry, moreover, the idea of any local music as a "feminizing" force would probably not go down too well, where dancehall music has been until very recently dominated by "slackness" themes of gunplay, gangsterism, and (mostly) male sexual braggadocio. Further, the gendering of Latin American and Caribbean cultures as "feminine" is a problematic by-product of the historical Euro-American political and economic exploitation of the region.[101] In light of this, it might be better to use the idea of an aesthetic of *fragmentation,* or *incompletion,* that I introduced earlier in this chapter.

The Ganja Factor: A Caribbean Psychedelia?

Psychedelia expanded not only minds but recording technology as well.[102]
—Brian Eno, 1996

Just a quarter pound of herb
Make you wiggle an' dance to the reverb.[103]
—Jah Woosh

Most Jamaican musicians and listeners agreed that ganja (marijuana) was an important factor in the slow tempi, thick textures, and bass-heavy production of roots reggae music. Given the tremendous influence of Rasta theology on roots reggae, the Rasta espousal of ganja as a religious sacrament, and the manner in which reggae was marketed as a countercultural music to Euro-American audiences in the 1970s, the stereotype of roots reggae as "ganja music" has persisted outside of Jamaica for decades. It is unsurprising that dub, the genre of roots reggae that seems to share so much with certain strands of psychedelic rock music, is a genre of Jamaican music particularly saddled with this stereotype. As one website typically describes it:

The deep rhythmic bass of reggae combined with the effects of smoking large quantities of ganja—particularly the herb's tendencies to enhance one's appreciation of tonal resonance and to distort one's perception of time—when mixed together in primitive recording studios, begat dub. It was the custom within the Jamaican music industry to fill out the flip-sides of 45rpm singles with instrumental versions of the song featured on the A side and, under the creative influence of cannabis, record producers such as Lee Perry started twiddling their knobs idiosyncratically, dropping out the treble and pumping up the bass, cutting up the vocal track and adding masses of reverb to haunting phrases that echo through the mix. No other music sounds more like the way it feels to be stoned.[104]

Among the characteristics he identifies as reflecting marijuana's influence upon artistic production, Erich Goode cites "a glorification of the irrational and seemingly nonsensical, an abandonement of traditional and 'linear' reasoning sequences, and the substitution of 'mosaic' and fragmentary lines of attack; and bursts of insight rather than chains of thought" as central.[105] Scholars have long debated the extent to which mind-altering substances can be credited with structuring aesthetic languages, but Goode's words are certainly accurate descriptions of the formal organization of many dub mixes.[106] The effects of THC (*delta-9-Tetrahydrocannabinol,* the psychoactive compound in cannabis derivations) on auditory perception are well known; when under its influence, the listener is acutely aware of changes in the perception of spatiality, movement, detail, texture, and time.[107] At the very least, then, we should not consider it surprising that an engineer would mix the music in a way that externalizes the characteristic modes of perception and sensation associated with a particular substance.

Nevertheless, the reality is more complex than the stereotype. What complicates the issue is that in Jamaica, not all studio engineers were ganja smokers. In fact, according to most of the musicians I spoke to, very few of them actually smoked. All musicians were in agreement that King Tubby—the prime exponent of dub music—was not a ganja smoker, and that smoking of any kind was forbidden inside of his studio. Mikey Dread remembered: "I never seen Tubby smoke—cigarettes, weed, nothing. Tubbys was a clean-cut man. If you wanted to smoke, you have to go in the yard, or go out in the street."[108] Bassist Robbie Shakespeare was emphatic that dub was not "ganja music," and maintained that "the engineers who mix dub music no have a spliff."[109] Sly Dunbar agreed: "Tubbys never used to smoke, Errol Thompson never smoke."[110] Mikey Dread put the issue in commonsense perspective, distinguishing between the choices of musicians and studio engineers: "Ganja is burning around the creation of most reggae. But saying that it's *all* about ganja is not true because when you mixing a song you don't want to be smoking. You have to be alert and awake—you can't be high and mixing at the board 'cause you going to mess up everything. It might sound good to you when you high but then when you wake up you might find that 'I didn't like nothing that I did yesterday.' It's not that kind of crazy atmosphere like people imagine, like the room is full of smoke."[111]

In general, musicians and producers all acknowledged that ganja played an important role in the creation and reception of dub music, while resisting the oversimplification that dub was "ganja music." Winston Riley felt that there were several things that enhanced the dub experience, ganja being only one: "Ganja is a part of it. But even if a man sit back and *drink* and listen to dub, him feel so nice because the music is so sweet. It play upon the mind and a lot of things."[112] Paul Henton felt that some of what was attributed to ganja was inherent in the sound of roots reggae itself: "[Roots] reggae music, like a Bob Marley type of reggae music, has that effect on you. I could see where it could put you in that trancelike vibe. Even if you're sober, it's kind of hypnotic."[113] Max Romeo was more explicit in his distinction. Like many Rasta-influenced musicians, he offered a more functional explanation for the mood and sound of reggae music in general: "There is a misconception among a lot of people that reggae and dub is ganja music. The thing is, dub is *meditation* music, and you can meditate on anything. The meditation can be on life, on spiritual things, or on music too. So dub is no more ganja music than rock & roll or classical is ganja music."[114] The focus on meditation allows the music to be experienced and interpreted in more varied terms than the narrow ganja stereotype. This openness was best articulated by Bobby Vicious when he reminisced: "Dub was really a revelation for the people in those times, because before that time we had mainly dealt with vocal, not really instrumental. At a Tubby's session, they might play five, ten version of the same riddim, all with a different mix. In fact they didn't call it *version*, they called it *chapter*. And each chapter opened your mind a different way."[115]

For their part, studio engineers acknowledged the role of ganja in varying ways. Philip Smart confirmed King Tubby's ban on smoking in the studio, but also acknowledged that "smoking herb, the slower the music, you can get into it more. You sit back and meditate and it's like the music is hitting you—you feel it through your whole body. So that was the revolution of the whole thing—dub, Rasta culture—and the music started to move there.[116] Probably the best-known engineer to advocate ganja smoking is Lee Perry, who has extolled the virtues of ganja throughout his career. Another advocate is Scientist, who was direct about the role of ganja in his work. "The first time I smoke a spliff, I hear music differently. And I find that some ways are more righteous and more conscious. So, yeah, what you come up with in the music is an extension of the herb. All of that is the influence of marijuana."[117]

Considering the strong ganja connection and the historical moment in which the music arose (loosely concurrent with the American counterculture), the question arises as to what extent can dub be considered a regional Caribbean variant on Euro-American psychedelic music. As Michael Hicks put it: "More than anything else, psychedelic music dynamized musical parameters previously stable in rock. Psychedelic drugs transformed fixed shapes into shifting shapes. In turn, psychedelic rock activated the music's essential form, harmony, timbre, articulation, and spatial deployment."[118] Of course, any interpretation of dub as psychedelic music rests upon (1) an unstable classification of cannabis derivations as hallucinogens;[119] (2) an admission that the question itself is only really relevant in the Euro-American zone within which psychedelic rock music exists as an established genre category; and (3) a demonstrable influence of European and American production trends in Jamaica. In the Euro-American context, drawing such a link seems deceptively easy: with the exception of transplanted sound systems serving immigrant Jamaican communities, fans of dub music in those cultural areas tend to use the music more for reflective listening than dancing—very different than the chaotically external setting of the Jamaican sound system. Further, because of the traditions of psychedelic and progressive rock, dub in England and Europe has tended to be appreciated on purely sonic terms, as opposed to Jamaica where it was largely understood to be a backdrop for deejays. With song lyrics removed, the focus on the soundscaping elements grew much stronger.

In the most literal definition, dub should not be considered a form of psychedelia; the latter is a historically and geographically specific subgenre of American rock music initially associated with San Francisco, and later more generally influential as a production style of late 1960s pop music.[120] In terms of production trends, however, it must have had some degree of influence on Jamaica although none of the engineers I spoke with mentioned psychedelia as an influence on their work (surprising, as all seemed aware of productions trends in English and American pop music). British reggae historian Dave Hendley felt that "Tubby's sound—it was really quite trippy. It was sort of like the psychedelic music that the rock guys never got 'round to making. I see the parallels with it, like the use of echo and that quite spacey sort of sound, but I don't think that had any influence on what the guys did in Jamaica. I think it's just one of those coincidental things where you could draw a parallel but certainly, I don't think there's a direct influence from that kind of music."[121] My own impression is that there must be at least some unknown history at work here. It wasn't widely known until 2006, for example, that the same British electronics whiz (Roger Mayer) who devised Jimi Hendrix's signature sound processors was a Bob Marley fan who worked with Marley and the Wailers during the 1977 recording of *Exodus*.[122] But until more information of this sort comes to light, such direct influence will remain speculative.

In broader musicological and social terms, certain comparisons might be fruitfully drawn. In general, the "term" *psychedelic* has been used to encompass two related stylistic practices. One is music characterized by long-form, open-ended song structures and extended instrumental improvisation (typified by 1960s pieces such as Iron Butterfly's "In-A-Gadda-Da-Vida" or the Grateful Dead's "Dark Star").[123] In this case, the protracted musical explorations paralleled and complemented the exploratory internal states stimulated by psychoactive substances. If we consider the "juggling" of riddims in the Jamaican sound system as a means of extending the grooves of short pop songs into long-form vehicles for (deejay) improvisation, it is possible to find a place for dub within this definition of psychedelia. The comments of Jefferson Airplane guitarist Paul Kantner, drawing a causal connection between the effects of hallucinogens and a disruption of tonality, provide another relevant point of comparison. In Kantner's experience, psychedelics were "not really conducive to acting functionally together with other people in the right key . . . because people just wander off in other keys."[124] In Jamaica, it was not uncommon for sound system deejays to wander off-key in their toasting; while this wandering reflects that they were not trained musicians (and often drew the criticism of more established vocalists), it ultimately forced a reconceptualization of harmony in Jamaican popular music. Applied to the Jamaican context, Kantner's comments imply that ganja may have been one important catalyst in this reconceptualization.

The other practice associated with psychedelic music has less to do with live performance practice, and more with studio production techniques. Specifically, I refer to a characteristic use of sound processing effects and mixing techniques such as panning, phase shifting, backward tape manipulation, double-tracking of voices, and other techniques used to approximate and/or complement the perceptual distortions of the psychedelic experience. Well-known songs that make particularly artful use of these techniques would include the Beatles's "Blue Jay Way," or the Jimi Hendrix Experience's "Are You Experienced."[125] A connection is much easier to draw between dub and psychedelic music on the basis of their common reliance on these production techniques, and a visceral connection can clearly be drawn between these performances and dub mixes created during the period of roots reggae in Jamaica, such as selected works of King Tubby, Prince Jammy, and Augustus Pablo and especially works from Lee Perry's Black Ark period (such as the Congos' *Heart of the Congos* or George Faith's *To Be A Lover*). Sheila Whiteley refers to this connection between the music and the psychedelic experience as "psychedelic coding";[126] musicologically, it was these aspects of dub that later contributed to what Michael Hicks termed a global "dynamization" of the popular song form.[127]

The broadest similarity resides in the fact that both dub and psychedelic rock were conceived—implicitly or explicitly, depending on the circumstances—as complements to the experience of mind-altering substances. Also, both were born of a period in which the use of such substances (especially in tandem with music) was considered a strategy for cultural transformation and challenge to the prevailing order. Although few of the Jamaican engineers I spoke with claimed to have been directly inspired by the studio techniques of Euro-American psychedelia, drummer Sly Dunbar did recall its surrounding counterculture as partial inspiration for the dub music he and bassist Robbie Shakespeare created as part of the group Black Uhuru in the 1980s: "We do it purposely because we come out of the age with shows like Woodstock, so we feel the same vibe. Although it's a different music, we try to do the same thing with the music."[128] Sly and Robbie purveyed ganja-inspired, low-frequency dominated music during a revolutionary period in Jamaican music and culture, and Sly's comments serve as the perfect local grounding for the observations of R. Murray Schaefer concerning the rise of low frequencies in popular music: "we will recall that the vibratory effects of high-intensity, low frequency noise, which have the power to 'touch' listeners, had first been experienced in thunder, then in the church where the bombardon of the organ had made the pews wobble under the Christians, and finally had been transferred to the cacophanies of the eighteenth-century factory . . . the 'good vibes' of the sixties promised an alternative lifestyle. What was happening was that the new counterculture . . . was actually stealing the Sacred Noise from the camp of the industrialists and setting it up in the hearts and communes of the hippies."[129]

Curiously, Murray neglects to mention the sounds of warfare, which—in addition to being one of the dominant soundscapes of the twentieth century—is certainly a dominant influence on the Jamaican sound system (itself essentially a form of low-frequency class and professional warfare). In any case, it was the revived festival ethos of rave culture and the contemporary boom in electronic dance musics that stimulated a renewed interest in dub music and its pioneers. The fusion of dub-inspired soundscaping, hip-hop production techniques, postdisco club-based dance styles, digital sound technology, and the digitally reconstituted visual iconography of 1960s psychedelia gradually fused from the 1980s to ignite the electronica boom.[130] In this light, dub might be at least partially positioned as a form of psychedelic Caribbean, proto-electronica.

In the Sound System

The Selector as Macrocomposer

Up to this point, I have largely focused on the aesthetics of the dub mix as a recorded form, a theme to which I shall return in chapters 3 through 6. But these pieces were not conceived for home listening so much as they were for play in the sound systems; as such, much of the drama of the dub mix is lost when played at the comparatively low volume levels of home audio equipment. Virtually all musicians agreed with Mikey Dread's feeling: "When you listen to a dub at your house, it sounds different than when you go to a Jamaican dance where they string up a series of maybe half a dozen double-sixteen or double-eighteen inch woofers, and you have some horns playing midrange and some tweeters playing the top end. It sounds different outdoors than you can ever imagine it indoors, listening to a headphone or listening to a little boombox or in your car. So, the dub have a different dimension that you can't get through the speakers [at home]."[131]

This commentary leads us again to the primary contexts in the dissemination of dub music, the sound system dances and dancehalls. It is these sites that provide yet another level of reconfiguration, a site in which, in the words of Norman Stolzoff, prerecorded music is given a new life.[132] By most accounts, the most popular sound systems of the early-to-mid 1970s included King Tubby's Hometown Hi-Fi, Arrows the Ambassador (also known as Arrows International), Tippatone, and Emperor Faith. Other prominent sounds of the time would include King Attorney, Black Harmony, and Ray Symbolic. It was in the dances held by these outfits, that a dub mix was usually augmented with a live deejay, and sometimes even through the manipulation of a sound system's equipment. While not nearly so elaborate as the sound processing equipment in a recording studio, sound system selectors were able to achieve fairly dramatic effects in the moment due to the immense volume and spatial control at their disposal, altering the sound of a piece by varying the equalization (bass and treble) controls on their amplifiers. For example, the Arrows sound system was known for the way its selectors would suddenly reduce the bass frequencies to a minimum while pushing the treble frequencies to the maximum setting. The result was a high-end sound that earned them the nickname "the flying sound."[133] Part of the excitement of this variance was the particularly dramatic effect created when the selector reintroduced the bass frequencies (as previously mentioned, this top-heavy mixing strategy began to be reproduced on commercial dub recordings shortly thereafter). Despite the comparative limitations of sound system equipment, even rudimentary manipulations like these caused quite a dramatic sonic effect in the dancehall.

These songs also acquire new meaning when strung together by the selector into extended "sets," comprising a string of individual songs (the local term for this process of connecting songs based on the same riddim is "juggling").[134] In this sense the selector, characterized by Stolzoff as the "musical director" of the sound system event, becomes a type of "macro-composer" creating a new metacomposition that is thematically cohesive and configured to the social dynamics of the dance. Interestingly, the strategy of disruption, previously cited as a micromusical characteristic of the dub mix, is reasserted in the selector's on-the-spot composition of a set. In most DJ cultures around the world, the DJ's ideal is to mix pieces of music seamlessly into each other, typified by concepts such as "beat matching" or "beat mixing," a skill that allows a DJ to create an imperceptible transition between two pieces of similar tempo.[135] In Jamaica, however, the opposite is often the rule. For the most part, transitions in sound systems sets are marked by abrupt transitions and interruptions typified by the DJ's command to the selector to "pull up" or "haul and come again"; that is, to interrupt the music violently and abruptly, in order to return to the beginning of the track. This disruption is such a central strategy of recent Jamaican popular music that live reggae bands have even incorporated the "pull-up" into their stage performances.

Sample Mix and Sound System Excerpt
Leo Graham: "Three Blind Mice" > King Tubby & The Upsetters: "Three Times Three" > Jah Love Sound System (Featuring Deejays Brigadier Jerry, Josey Wales & Charlie Chaplin): Set Excerpt Including "Three Times Three" (ca. early 1980s)
With its scratchy, percussive articulation and syncopation of the "one drop" rhythm pattern, Leo Graham's "Three Blind Mice" is a typical early 1970s Lee Perry production.[136] The song proceeds at a slow tempo of approximately quarter note = 63 bpm, and is mostly based on the following six-measure chord sequence in F major:

|| F C⁷ F F | F C⁷ F F | F B♭ F F | F B♭ F F | F B♭ F F | F C⁷ F F ||

The sequence underneath Graham's verses is altered to:

|| F C⁷ F F | F C⁷ F F | F B♭ F F| F C⁷ F F|
| F B♭ F F | F B♭ F F | F B♭ F F | F C⁷ F F ||

The chord sequence is anchored by a halting, 6-note bass line, doubled in octave unison by one of two guitarists; the other guitarist plays the upbeat chordal pattern. After a harmonized trumpet and saxophone theme (based on the melody of the children's song "Three Blind Mice"), Leo Graham sings a medley of children's songs adapted to Jamaican themes, as the horns play a harmonized background line of upbeat accents along with the chordal instruments. Graham's verses are separated by a second statement of the horn theme; following his second verse, the theme plays a third and final time as the song fades.

King Tubby's remix, "Three Times Three," marked by a much starker and aggressive mood, is typical of his early work. The most immediate difference here is that the vocals have been entirely removed, and the emphasis placed on the drum & bass. With the tape speed noticeably slowed, the bass is heavier in the mix, the tonality lowered approximately a quarter tone to the midpoint between the keys of E major and F major, and the tempo approximately lowered to quarter note = 58 bpm. The guitar and piano, playing the upbeat chordal pattern, are heard intermittently throughout (usually at the beginning of a chorus). In the absence of Graham's vocal, three elements define the new mix. The first is the horn theme, which remains from the vocal take and is now the song's primary organizing element. The second is King Tubby's application of filtering to the drum set, which introduces an improvised textural element into the repetitive rhythm structure. The third is the technique of drop-out, which occurs here at approximately 1:40, when the drum set drops momentarily out of the mix.

King Tubby's dub mix of "Three Blind Mice" is the point of departure at an early 1980s session of the Jah Love sound system, captured on a commercial cassette I purchased in March 2002 from Mackie's, a roadside cassette vendor at Half Way Tree in Kingston. This session features the DJ Brigadier Jerry, alternately improvising lyrics based on the "Three Blind Mice" theme and scatting nonliteral rhythmic phrases. Assuming the speed of the original recording is correct, the playback speed of the record has been lowered by an additional quarter tone, now placing the key squarely in E major. Even as captured by an inexpensive hand-held microphone in the audience, it is obvious that the bass frequencies have been emphasized by the selector to a greater degree than in the original dub mix. At 2:05, the track is abruptly interrupted, and Brigadier Jerry uses the break in the music to inform the crowd of the system's upcoming events. At 2:25, the track starts again from the beginning, with Brigadier Jerry intermittently joined by the deejays Josey Wales and Charlie Chaplin, improvising a lyrical theme based on Max Romeo's 1973 song "Every Man Ought to Know," which adapted the lyrics of a well-known hymn to a Rastafarian theme.[137]

It is interesting to note that "Everybody Should Know" is based on the four-measure chord sequence:

$$\| F\ C^7\ F\ F\ |\ F\ C^7\ F\ F\ |\ C^7\ |\ F\ C^7\ F\ F\|$$

that differs from the six-measure chord sequence underlying "Three Blind Mice." As a result, there are essentially two planes of harmony operating simultaneously here: the harmony present in the original recording and the harmony implied by the DJs' superimposed singing over the original track.

The track plays to its full conclusion this time, ending at approximately five minutes into this portion of the dance. Brigadier Jerry and the other DJs continue to chat with the crowd until the selector puts up a different record and the dance continues.

The dancehall is not the only context in which audiences can enjoy performances such as those described above. These dancehall metacompositions are often circulated on sound system cassettes sold by street vendors around Kingston, and subject to a varying combination of drop-outs, talk-overs, degenerating fidelity (as cassettes are copied and recopied over several "generations"), and sound effects overdubbed by the vendors themselves. As such, the street-sold sound system cassette can be analysed as constituting an art form within itself that in turn feeds back into studio practice. In this way, dub became vertically integrated into the musical culture of Jamaica. Robbie Shakespeare acknowledged this: "Everytime you mention dub, you have to get to so many people, you can't remember some of them often. Tubbys have to come up. Bunny Lee have to come up. Niney, Scratch, Channel One, Coxsone, Treasure Isle. You have to name the musicians. The sound operator with him dub plate. You have to name the little man who used to believe inna it and walk and sell it on the street. So much people fe get credit. You have to just give the whole music fraternity—the old school—the credit."[138]

So, as much as these songs can be analysed as individual works, they need to be understood in terms of the macroset of the sound system, and in terms of its broader role within the audio culture of Jamaica.

Economic Implications of Version-based Music

Dub appealed to human greed and spiritual need. Not only outmaneuvering the scientists and eccentrics by appealing to both body and intellect, its overground exposure and structural liberation provided the perfect recycling product for mass consumption. With the timely advent of "version," its manufactured addictiveness was guaranteed.—Kevin Martin, from the notes to Macro Dub Infection

As a remixed piece of music, the dub mix manipulates a listener's memory in several ways. Much of the genre's compositional tension is generated through subversion of the listener's expectations, based on the vocal song with which they are previously familiar. More generally, the dub mix manipulates a listener's basic expectation of the standard formal progression between verse and refrain, between tension and release, and basic continuity of groove. It is these various modes of yearning for formal "completeness" that are central to the experience of dub and I make the point here that this yearning must be at least partially satisfied in the marketplace. As Max Romeo states, the success of the dub version "has to do with how big a hit the vocal was; the people getting used to hearing the vocal and therefore they get off on the dub . . . it gets more listenership because the people dancing to the dub music also will buy the actual single to hear all the words of the song."[139] With its shards of previous vocals, the version effectively acts as an advertisement for other versions. Paul Gilroy sees the version functioning in the marketplace as "a calculated invitation to embark on an archaeological operation, tracing [a song] back to its original version."[140] Given the reality of multitrack recording, however, even this idea of an "original" version must be problematized. Where, exactly, does the "original" version of an endlessly reconfigurable form exist? Is it the material documented at the initial recording session? The first commercially-released version? The version most familiar to the public? The "archaeological operation" is potentially endless in this perpetually unfinished form.

In his discussion of postmodern arts, Frederic Jameson refers to forms that replicate and reproduce the logic of consumer capitalism, resulting in an "aesthetic of the commodity" that reflects a deep interpenetration of the aesthetic and economic.[141] We can use Jameson's observation to draw a distinction between dub as an aesthetic *process,* and its presence in the marketplace as *product.* The compositional "hyperreality" that results from the dizzying progression of versions is both a reflection of the manipulative potential of multitrack technology and an aestheticized sublimation of the profit motive.[142] The sound of dub is the sound of profit consolidation, as fiercely competitive producers do their best to maximize profits from successive reconfigurations of minimal source material. Finally, dub is, very literally, the sound of competition. As we have seen, one reason songs were deconstructed in the first place was to clear a space for the DJ's patter, itself a form of promotion meant to sell records, advertise the sound system, and lambaste competing systems. Thus, the version-encrusted song surface of the dub mix is simultaneously a signifier of the engineer's musical artistry, a visceral sonic signifier of the work's ritual history in the sound system, and (like torn layers of advertisements on a billboard) a signifier of a song's commodity history in which producers fought to sell consumers serially manipulated versions of old music with minor variations.

The process versus product distinction allows us to understand how (1) the practices of dub music work to subvert various hegemonic economic structures of the music industry, and (2) despite this, Jamaican musicians and songwriters continue to feel cheated in terms of compensation for their creative labor. The situation in Jamaica is not unique. Michael Chanan has observed that the early years of the recording industry were crucial in establishing the industry's long-term capital base: musical traditions that had previously only existed in oral form (and were thus considered "public domain" folk forms exempt from claims of individual authorship) were being concretized into commodities that could generate long-term profit.[143] Quite possibly, Jamaica is a vivid example of this integration into the world music economy taking place in a very short and intensive period of time, with the technologies of reproduction raising the stakes exponentially. Intellectual property issues began to consolidate in eighteenth-century Europe, following three centuries during which the invention and dissemination of the printing press gave rise to the need to regulate stored information. This need was also concurrent with the rise of new and significant ideas regarding the centrality of individuals and individual creators (typified by the exaltation of art music composers), and the simultaneous erection of legal structures for the protection of expanding industry.[144] Jamaican musical traditions, on the other hand, had remained orally based until the era of sound recording and never passed through the intermediate stage of printed music that was fundamental to the establishment of copyright norms in Europe and the United States. Consequently (and despite the presence of scores of talented musicians and songwriters), the idea of music as the de facto property of the "public domain" remained influential well into the 1970s and largely holds true today. The very use of a term like "dub" as a genre designation generated by the studio-based procedures of musical reproduction and reconfiguration, exists in direct subversion of the notion of "copyright" (which, in literal terms, regulates which parties have the legal *right to copy*). And certainly, this state of affairs was further complicated by the unusual nature of the music itself, which introduced ambiguity into the musical criteria upon which claims of authorship and originality could be based.[145]

This issue only became pressing when Jamaican artists such as Bob Marley began to reap large profits from their international recording activities. The entire industry entered a turbulent restructuring process; reggae prior to Marley had been merely another local island style and, as many Jamaican musicians explained to me, "no one ever thought it would get that big." It was the producers, situated as middleman between artists and foreign music corporations, who stood to benefit most from this state of affairs. Similarly to the place of resales in the market for visual artworks, the original musicians receive no proceeds from successive versions; they were only paid once at the original session. It was for this reason that all version-derived music was temporarily banned from Jamaican radio for a period in the 1970s, because of pressure from the musician's union.[146] This might seem a significant victory for musicians but, as we have seen, the radio networks could not compare to the sound systems as disseminators of popular music. Even as copyright regulations are gradually implemented, they will likely benefit producers more that artists: copyright laws ultimately benefit the *controllers* of recordings more than the actual *creators* of recordings[147] and Jamaican producers continue to maintain vertical control over the production and manufacturing of music.

There are broader consequences of this state of affairs. In Jamaica, the lack of preserving and documenting institutions (such as stable traditions of music journalism and music scholarship), the vagaries of the local market, and an international market eager to exploit this situation—all implies a common situation in the history of black musics. Instead of being recognized as an important and generative moment in the history of popular music, dub runs the risk of becoming a mere footnote to those subsequent musical movements built upon its innovations. Timothy Taylor, for example, warns that although contemporary "electronica" has strong antecedents in black dance music, historical writings tend to construct its history as based in the Western tradition of experimental/electronic music.[148] This situation is not new within the historicizing of black popular musics. In the 1950s, Ralph Ellison observed this same process taking place in the historicizing of jazz music. "Being devoted to an art which traditionally thrives on improvisation, these artists often have their most original ideas enter the public domain almost as rapidly as they are conceived to be quickly absorbed into the thought and technique of their fellows. Thus the riffs which swung the dancers and the band on some transcendent evening, and which inspired others to competitive flights of invention, become all too swiftly a part of the general style, leaving the originator as anonymous as the creators of the architecture called Gothic."[149]

The situation can be placed into broader cultural and historical perspective by Chinua Achebe's observations on the tradition of Igbo *mbari* houses in Nigeria, a fairly typical West African conceptual antecedent that recalls the fluid formal structure of some West African performance practices (and, in a more philosophical sense, the more general grounding of African arts in the demands of specific occasions, with less value placed on preservation than on the moment):

The purposeful neglect of the painstakingly and devoutly accomplished *mbari* houses with all the art objects in them as soon as the primary mandate of their creation has been served, provides a significant insight into the Igbo aesthetic value as process rather than product. Process is motion while product is rest. When the product is preserved or venerated, the impulse to repeat the process is compromised. Therefore the Igbo choose to eliminate and retain the process so that every occasion and every generation will receive its own impulse and experience of creation. Interestingly this aesthetic disposition receives powerful endorsement from the tropical climate which provides an abundance of materials for making art, such as wood, as well as formidable agencies of dissolution, such as humidity and the termite. Visitors to Igboland are shocked to see that artifacts are rarely accorded any particular value on the basis of age alone.[150]

It will probably be a while before the complicated issues surrounding version-based music in Jamaica are worked out to the satisfaction of the various parties involved. We can read in the comments of Ellison and Achebe an interpretation that dub's functional departure from Western authorial ideals was historically facilitated by certain cultural factors that survived the transition to the diaspora, and that this tendency has been reinforced in more recent history by economic factors unique to the Jamaican music industry. Ultimately, the body of social practices that make up the Jamaican music industry imply that the vanguard of Jamaican music will remain an art form in flux, ultimately configured to the improvisational dynamics of an oral culture.

The engineers who created dub in the 1970s were working within very limited technical means; Errol Thompson, Lee Perry, and the engineers at Tubby's were all initially working on four- or eight-channel mixing consoles, and had limited sound processing equipment at their disposal. Although their remix decisions were certainly predicated upon musical criteria, the fact that engineers fashioned themselves as "scientists" (that is, technicians) meant that in some ways, they were in an ideal position to guide reggae's stylistic traits beyond its traditionally "musical" norms. In this way, they might be considered important forerunners of the digital age of popular music production, in which reconfiguration has become more important as a compositional strategy than traditional conceptions of composition. The works they created are a testament to their ingenuity and creativity. Many musicians echoed the sentiments of Computer Paul:

What I know that is genius about dub music is it defied all the principles of recording. There's no way you can mix a dub song and don't have your needle, like on the mixer, going over like into the red. And American engineers say "No, no—that's distortion, pull it down!" You'll never get the sound, cause that's part of the compression and the overall vibe of it. Or, "That echo is too loud!" Jamaica's the first, I've never seen anybody who was not Jamaican do it—they'd get an echo and have the echo feeding back into itself and it keeps going and it could run for the entire song! With that tape echo that they were using and looping back in the old days, it's amazing, man—it is artistic music.[151]

The status of technological devices is never fixed; their social applications vary greatly between cultures, and they vary between social classes within the same culture.[152] In this chapter, I have demonstrated the way that the use of sound technology changed as it became embedded in a Jamaican cultural context (essentially adapted from the consumerist, domestic function it had come to serve in middle America). This different conception of what this technology represented (and the uses to which it could be put) was cultural and class-based; it also demonstrated the ways that both creative artists and consumers often devise differing applications of technological devices than those envisioned and/or intended by their creators.[153]

If reggae of the 1970s represented the cutting edge of popular cultural consciousness in the Anglophone Caribbean, then dub (and the roots rhythms upon which it was based) would become the musical cutting edge.

Under Lee Perry, Errol Thompson, King Tubby, and many others, dub became a genre and art form unto itself, with the composer acting both as de-
constructionist and soundscape architect. Virtually all reggae singles after
1972 were issued with dub versions on the flip side;[154] this practice was followed in time by both "showcase" albums (pairing both vocal and dub versions) and, eventually, entire albums consisting exclusively of dub mixes.
(The earliest such collections would include Herman Chin-Loy's 1971 collection *Aquarius Dub,* producer Clive Chin's 1973 *Java Java Dub,* and
Prince Buster's early 1970s *The Message Dubwise.*) From the early 1970s,
Perry, Tubby, and Thompson were each associated with different studios,
and would emerge as exponents of the new form. Despite their mutual ste-
wardship of the new sound, however, the dub work of these three engineers would evolve along different paths as they established their individual
studio orbits. The distinctive ways in which each would elaborate his basic
dub vision model reflected their differing, pre-dub paths through Jamaica's
studio system.

CHAPTER THREE

The "Backbone" of Studio One

⚡

Sylvan Morris's most immediate significance in the history of Jamaican studio craft is based on his role in refining the recorded sound of ska, rock steady, and reggae as chief engineer at Coxsone Dodd's Studio One, and he remains the engineer most closely associated with the studio. Given that Studio One has never been a center for dub music, however, Morris's seminal contributions have typically been overlooked in historical accounts of dub music. Among all the musicians I spoke with, his reputation is based primarily on his ability to engineer live sessions; most musicians of the roots era consider him among the country's top engineers in terms of recording live instruments. As engineer of some of the most enduring popular music ever recorded in Jamaica, however, Morris laid a crucial foundation for the dub music that followed Studio One's heyday in the 1970s. And as engineer at Harry J studio during the roots era, he also mixed many of the most influential recordings of dub music: Augustus Pablo's *East of the River Nile*, portions of Burning Spear's two-volume *Living Dub* collection, and the first volume of Bunny Wailer's *Dubd'sco*. No lesser a dub luminary than Augustus Pablo praised Morris as his preferred engineer for remixing, citing the engineer's "spiritual" sound. Morris himself defined dub music as "a different styling of the original which is done in many forms."[1] This chapter is intended to put his engineering work, which spans more than four decades, into proper perspective.

Born in Kingston in 1946, Morris had been a prodigy of sorts, working demanding electronics jobs when most of his age mates were still students. He remembered his first job:

I actually came into it in an unusual sense in that my parents had a friend. He used to come and see me fool around with wires, tryin' to make radios and all dem likkle thing. . . . I got a basic knowledge and I started to build like some little small amplifiers and things. He said to my parents that I seem to have a certain knack for this thing. So he went up by Comtech now, it's a place that he did business with and he seemed to have been a very good client there. It was on Easton Park Road and they used to repair two-way radios, VHF. At that time, that was very hi-tech in Jamaica. Because that place used to repair like the aircraft radios, the police radios and when they have any problem they would send it there. So we used to work on those things.

At that time, if you were say fifteen, sixteen, seventeen years old, they didn't really want to take you because you were a bit too young. So I told them that I was twenty. . . . To be truthful, my impression is that they were trying to get rid of me. But they wanted to do it decently. So when I arrive there, them have some old radios and they just said to me "Yeah mon, here's some radio mon, go and fix them." They think I would get frustrated . . . but all the radios fixed in about two weeks and the man mouth wide open! . . . So, them put me on staff. I started go to school at the same time—Hanover Street, Jamaica Technical High School because I had applied and got a entry. And I was working during the day, at the bench repairing two-way radios. And at the nights I was going to school. I spent about a year and a half with Comtech. So that was my training.[2]

Following a brief stint at WIRL (West Indies Records label), Morris began to work for Byron Lee's Dynamic Studios around 1965, where he assisted Graeme Goodall as chief engineer. Morris credits Goodall as his mentor in the recording industry:

Graeme Goodall was an engineer at the time, he was putting up the studio. Graeme was another person who sorta brought me into the recording field, to get familiar with the studio equipment and console and everything—he sort of schooled me there. 'Cause the field what I was leaving from was VHF, [which is] way above audio. He was quite a nice chap, I really have to give him commendation. He was one of the individuals, I suppose, who sort of kept me in the business. He showed me everything. He was like a friend to me. I mean, it was real strange to see a man of a different nation, a white man—he treated me as if I was his son or something.[3]

Morris remembers joining Dynamic and assisting Goodall during a transitional period: "I helped him put up the studio at that time. It was three tracks, can you imagine? I know that sounds weird, but it was a three track! Well, it jumped two to three, very quickly and then in a flash from three to four. Because the three wasn't feasible."[4] After a year or so at Dynamic, Morris moved to Duke Reid's studio for six months before settling in at the Brentford Road studio of Coxsone Dodd's Studio One operation around 1967, where he replaced Dodd's cousin Syd Bucknor as chief engineer.[5] While Bucknor, Dodd, and Goodall had previously handled recording duties, most Jamaican musicians and producers credit Morris with developing the distinctive sound that Studio One is known for. Morris himself considers Studio One the turning point in his career.

At Studio One, Morris was often assisted in his engineering duties by singer Larry Marshall, while at different times, Jackie Mittoo, Leroy Sibbles, Richard Ace, and Robbie Lyn arranged music, ran sessions, and functioned with Morris as de facto producers. Morris recalled: "Coxsone wasn't there when we was doing the work. Most of the times it's just me and the musicians. Jackie Mittoo, 'cause he was musical arranger at that time, and when he left, you had Leroy Sibbles."[6] Sibbles and keyboardist Jackie Mittoo are especially cited by many musicians as unsung heroes whose musical genius guided Studio One into the roots era and enriched Jamaica's bank of riddims immeasurably. Dudley Sibley echoed the sentiments of many Jamaican musicians when he explained: "You can't leave out the great Jackie Mittoo. Jackie would hardly go home. Jackie would *live* at Studio One. Night and day Jackie would be at Studio One, thinking how to evolve this music. Him really play a great part, him a the brainchild in the riddim."[7] If anything, Sibley's comments are an understatement, considering Mittoo's arrangement with Dodd, under which the keyboardist allegedly agreed to compose five new riddims per week—theoretically totalling thirteen hundred riddims during his five-year stint at Studio One![8]

When it opened in 1963, Brentford Road was configured as a monaural (one-track) studio. By the time of Morris's arrival, the studio had been upgraded to two tracks. The subsequent purchase of a second two-track recorder allowed him to "bounce" tracks back and forth; Morris remembered how his attempts to maximize the capability of this limited equipment prefigured dub music:

Coxsone had a long console. We had two two-track machines. It was like he had coupled two together, [resulting in] four tracks. And we feed it into two tracks. So we'd do the riddim [that is, rhythm guitar, rhythm piano, and organ] on one, bass & drums on one, then we'd run it from that, mix it from the same time while singing. After we did it that way, and then we'd transfer it back again. And then carry it back again. Sometimes we did that as much as four generations. We never really do the voicing at the same time, we just did rhythm tracks. It's very few occasion that we do live voices. So this is how the actual dub thing started. People couldn't really believe that's two tracks we working with.[9]

Reggae is well known for the emphasis placed on bass lines, and Studio One in particular was known for its bass-heavy sound. This was partially attributable to the many influential bassists who passed through Brentford Road during its heyday (including Boris Gardiner, Errol "Bagga" Walker, Wally Cameron, and Leroy Sibbles), and partially to the role Morris played in deliberately boosting the low end of the music:

When I used to build my sound, I noticed that the sound that I get from the back of the speakers in them days had a bassier sound than coming from the front. The front was stronger but there's a very low bass sound that you get out of the back. So I designed a box, and made two apertures at the back, right? And put a mic there. That's where I pick up my sound from actually, from the back of the speaker. It's very deep, so this is how I got a lot of those deep sounds. Plus, Coxsone had a

Pultec equalizer which sort of enhanced that sound 'cause it sorta boost the very low 40 Hz region. That's how you get the Downbeat sound.[10]

Morris also explained the ways he achieved the characteristic delay heard on Studio One recordings of the period such as Larry Marshall's "Throw Me Corn" or The Bassies "Things A Come Up to Bump":[11]

What I did on most of the recordings in those days, I used to feed back the playback head into the recorder, so you get this tape delay sound. If you notice on most of the voices, if you listen very carefully you'll hear it. This was our signature sound in those days.

There was another thing that Coxsone brought, an instrument by the name of Soundimension. It was made out of four heads. So you had a record head and you had three different playback heads that could be moved around. There was a circular tape loop about a foot and a half [long]. It was a delay, similar to what I did with the tape recorder. But that one was fixed. With this one, you could actually *move* it—you could move the playback heads. So you could get different distances and one, two, three different delay times.[12]

The Soundimension was a freestanding echo unit that was the creation of Ivor Arbiter, a British technician best known for his Fuzz Face distortion pedal and Sound City line of amplifiers, used by many leading British rock guitarists of the 1960s and 1970s. His tape-based echo unit remained popular during the late 1960s, even though tape-based echo systems were gradually being replaced by newer technologies. Arbiter advertised the Soundimension as a "compact portable device, providing echo and reverberation effects when used in conjunction with any audio amplifying system. . . . Effects possible within the Soundimension include single echo repetitions with variable delay, multiple 'flutter' echoes, and simulated reverberation giving if required, the atmosphere of a large concert hall."[13] In Sylvan Morris's hands, it was these effects that helped create the classic Studio One sound. Coxsone Dodd, in fact, was so taken by the unit that he named one of his session bands the "Sound Dimension."[14] Equally significant, as Morris recalls, the Soundimension's effects were gradually incorporated into instrumental playing techniques:

This brother named Eric Frater, them call him "Rickenbacker." He was one of the innovators of the "chenking" on the guitar [that is, the characteristic upbeat strum pattern]. So, when he played the "chenk" on the guitar we'd get it now with delay so you'd get "che–kenk." Or "che–ke–chenk," depending upon how you put it. From there, [other guitarists] were trying to create it not realizing it was a piece of equipment that we were using! So they actually played it themselves. And after the equipment broke down sometimes, Eric would start to create it himself.[15]

The Soundimension was one of the few sound processors in Studio One's setup for quite a while, although Morris relates: "There was lot of processors we used after a while. I wasn't really a specializer. I could use anything."[16] The minimal equipment resulted in a characteristic sound. Paul "Computer Paul" Henton echoed the prevalent description of the studio's sound when he opined: "If you listen to Studio One, there's no clarity. But the music was so good that it compensated for the loss of engineering quality. You just felt it."[17] Henton's comments should not be construed as deriding the engineering skills of Morris, who was cited by all the musicians and engineers I spoke with as one of Jamaica's finest engineers. More likely, it reflected the limitations of the equipment Morris had at his disposal. He described his solution to the technical limitations he encountered at Brentford Road:

What was happening down there, I'm gonna be totally frank to you—some of the mics, they had taken such a battering before I came there that they weren't really giving out the right frequencies, seen? There were some of the mics that didn't have any [high frequencies], some of them that didn't have any bottom. Their frequencies [were] all over the spectrum. I realized it because when I go and I listen to the piano, or when I put the mic on the piano, the sound that I get, I'm not getting the full range. So what I had to do was actually *create* the sound that I heard when I listened—the real sound that I thought I heard. So this is how come I came to be this type of engineer. Because I had to get the sound in my head—the sound of the actual instrument or the singer or whoever, [and reproduce it through] the electronics.[18]

However the sound was achieved, Morris's tenure coincided with Studio One's most commercially successful period. With brilliant musicians such as Mittoo, Sibbles, and many others involved, Studio One hit a second peak in the late 1960s and early 1970s as reggae developed out of rock steady. Similarly to Lee Perry's work with the Wailers from the same period, Coxsone Dodd was in tune with the changing cultural mood and had found a profitable equation between pop songcraft and Rastafarian sentiment with artists such as Horace Andy and the Gladiators.[19]

Sylvan Morris on the Mix I
Carlton and the Shoes: "Love Me Forever"
In technical terms, a facility such as Studio One was not on par with American and British studios of the time, and it is to Morris's credit as an engineer that a song like Carlton and the Shoes' 1968 "Love Me Forever"[20] achieves production values roughly on par with international standards while still reflecting a characteristically Jamaican aesthetic. The song is introduced by a harmonized saxophone and trombone theme, mixed dry and very forward in the recording. As with most rock steady songs, the unison guitar and bass line is very prominent in the mix, even overshadowing the drum set although the one drop bass drum pattern is very audible. This is not a problem for the rhythm per se, as the drum set is buttressed by a driving,

sixteenth-note tambourine pattern that blends in with the hi-hat.[21] Typically, the rhythm piano and rhythm guitar occupy the same central region of the sound space, having all been recorded onto the same track and blended together through the application of reverberation. Overall the rhythm track is best described as having a very warm, bottom-heavy sound. The harmonized vocals of Carlton Manning and the backing vocalists are positioned in the foreground, a mild delay blurring the edges of the singing very slightly, and setting them apart from the instrumental backing. A tenor sax plays interlocking syncopations between the vocals and the rhythm section. The sound Morris achieves here is not dramatically different from that which was being produced on thousands of rhythm and blues and rock and roll records of the period.

Larry Marshall, "Throw Me Corn"
Considered by many to be one of the great Studio One songs, Larry Marshall's proverbial "Throw Me Corn"[22] is mixed in a very different fashion. From the beginning, it is clear that the tracks here have been "bounced" back and forth several times to accomodate Marshall's double-tracked vocals, which are mixed far to the front of the soundscape, with a bit of flutter delay added (probably via the Soundimension). This bouncing results in a sound characteristic of Studio One; over several generations, the rhythm track becomes fairly distant-sounding and the high frequencies become progressively less audible, with Leroy Sibbles's electric bass standing out as the most audible of the rhythm instruments. The bouncing also results in an audible layer of tape hiss. The cloudy sound of white noise replicating through the delay unit (as heard during the first few seconds of this track), is actually a distinctive feature of many Studio One songs, a degeneration of fidelity that was later exploited by Lee Perry to particularly creative effect during the Black Ark period.

Morris left Brentford Road in 1972, ostensibly due to financial disagreements with Dodd. Following his departure, the bulk of the engineering work at Brentford Road was handled by Dodd himself for several years prior to the arrival of Overton "Scientist" Brown. Although Dodd was not a trained recording engineer, he did have a bit of electronics experience, having learned carpentry and built speaker cabinets in his youth.[23] Attempting to stay abreast of the latest trends, Dodd even branched out into dub mixing by the late 1970s, releasing records under the moniker "Dub Specialist." His work can be found on LPs such as *Juks Incorporation, Better Dub, Dub Store Special,* and others. The earnestness with which Dodd regarded himself as an engineer is reflected, for example, by the cover of Lone Ranger's late 1970s *Badda Dan Dem* LP, which contains a sci-fi cartoon portrait of the producer as engineer, seated at a futuristic hybrid of a mixing desk and spaceship console. The cover art was drawn by artist Jamaal Pete, who provided sci-fi illustrations for several dub albums at this time, including Scientist's seminal *Scientific Dub*. I do not cite Dodd's work here in order to make a claim for him as an engineer on par with the other engineers discussed in this chapter. Rather, I mention it to examine a mixing aesthetic that is an important feature of Studio One's 1970s output, and that also reflects indirectly on the skills of Sylvan Morris.

Dub Specialist (Clement "Coxsone" Dodd) on the mix
The Gladiators: *The Gladiators*

Studio One recordings from the early 1970s have a characteristic sound typified by, for example, several tracks from the Gladiators debut LP *Presenting the Gladiators*. Although the cover information credits Dodd as sole engineer of these sessions, several songs (such as "Hello Carol") clearly sound as if they have been engineered by Morris. Other tracks (such as "Love and Meditation") are mixed in a manner more typical of Studio One in the mid-1970s, and seem an attempt to replicate the studio's 1960s sound. The thuddy-sounding bass has been recorded directly into the console and placed very prominently in the mix. The vocals of Albert Griffiths, Clinton Fearon, and Gallimore Sutherland have been mixed flat, without any reverb or equalization, and positioned in the mix to sound as if they are being sung from a distant corner of the room. The drum set is audible, but is largely indistinct in the mix; it can be felt more than heard and its role as a timekeeper is aided by a tambourine. In standard fashion, the chordal instruments are clustered together in the mix and evidently subjected to a bit of phase shifting (although this might actually be the tape-hiss effect noted previously on "Throw Me Corn"). As raw as this mix is by professional standards, it holds its own charm as a percussion-heavy, cloudy sound typical of many Jamaican recordings of the period. Some have also attributed aspects of the Studio One sound to other factors. A number of musicians have commented that Dodd was the only producer who allowed ganja to be smoked on his premises, and cited this as an important component of a unique studio atmosphere that was in turn reflected in the sound of the music—especially during the 1970s.[24]

"Musical Science"

For the most part, Coxsone Dodd's own dub mixes were performed on particularly popular tracks that had been recorded during Sylvan Morris's tenure as engineer. "Musical Science,"[25] the title and cloudy mix of which is probably meant to evoke Obeah (Jamaica's neo-African tradition of black magic), is typical of Dodd's dub mixes. Dodd didn't possess an engineer's facility with studio equipment, and the mixing strategies on *Dub Store Special* are minimal, mostly amounting to low-fidelity drum & bass versions with passages of very basic drop-out. From a production and engineering standpoint, then, the most valuable aspect of Dodd's basic mixes is that they allow the listener a peek at the sound and quality of Studio One's rhythm tracks. Compared with the earlier vocal versions mixed by Morris, these raw mixes amount to a testament to the latter's engineering skills; he was able — with minimal equipment at hand — to bring the raw sound of these tracks to a professionally competitive standard. Bunny Lee spoke for many when he claimed: "Sylvan Morris really was the backbone of Studio One. When him leave, you don't really hear the Studio One sound again, it changed."[26]

Morris at Harry J Studio

After leaving Studio One, Sylvan Morris's next long-term engineering position was at Harry Johnson's 16-track Harry J studio on Roosevelt Avenue, which had opened in 1972 with electronics installed by Bill Garnett.[27] Here, his work took an interesting turn. As one of the latest and most advanced facilities on the island, Harry J's was heavily booked by artists such as Bob Marley and Bunny Wailer, whose work was aimed toward the international market. Johnson reportedly had a deal with Island records boss Chris Blackwell, and much of the reggae Jamaica aimed at the international market was recorded at his studio. As such, Sylvan Morris's work here represents the "mainstreaming" of dub techniques that originally had their origins in local studios that catered to the sound systems.

At Harry J, Morris earned a reputation as a talented, temperamental engineer whose work varied according to his relationship with the artist and his opinion of the music being recorded, but who could achieve a sound comparable to the most advanced American studios of the day.[28] Morris admits: "I hardly used to sit around the board. I used to stand when I'm recording. 'Cause I want to *feel* the music. If them see me not dancing, they'll probably stop playing and ask me what's wrong. I'd say I don't like the bass line, or it's too slow, or do something else, do it over . . . and they respected me a lot to that point."[29]

One of Morris's major achievements at Harry J's was his engineering of the first four albums released by Bob Marley and the Wailers on Chris Blackwell's Island Records. Along with Jimmy Cliff's soundtrack for Perry Henzell's film *The Harder They Come,* Marley's *Catch A Fire, Burnin,'* *Natty Dread,* and *Rastaman Vibration* albums were more responsible than any other for stamping Jamaican music authoritatively on the map of world popular music. Of course, it has recently become fashionable among reggae historians to emphasize Marley's distance from Jamaica's sound system culture, in order to prove their own knowledge of the full breadth of Jamaican music. This claim is partially justified; Marley's music and image *have* been disproportionately promoted as the heart and soul of reggae music, leading to the disregard of scores of talented Jamaican artists who remain virtually unknown outside of the country. But only partially: Marley's post–Lee Perry music might not have sold in as large quantities in Jamaica as it did internationally, but the Wailers composed many popular riddims during their Island years (1972–1981), a number of which were re-recorded by other artists, and which eventually entered the canon of generic riddims.

The truth of the matter is that Marley's music for Island Records broke new ground, and in no way so much as in the recorded sound of the music. The mixing of Marley's music dramatized his position at the forefront of Jamaica's musical and cultural vanguard, while simultaneously proclaiming Jamaica's important cultural presence in the postcolonial world order. The aggressive bass lines of Aston Barrett were as tough as anything being produced in Jamaica, and rank among the most celebrated riddims of the roots era. The interplay of Carlton Barrett's drum set and Bunny Wailer and/or Seeco Patterson's Nyabinghi-influenced hand percussion work brought a thick African undertone to the music. What set Marley's music apart was the clean, precise way in which the rhythm tracks were recorded, calculated to make them attractive to the international audience. This was a significant departure from the distorted, drum & bass orientation of most dancehall-oriented reggae. Comparison of Marley's recordings with cover versions of his songs by other Jamaican artists demonstrates the specific choices that were made in the production of his music.

Sylvan Morris Vs. King Tubby, On The Mix
Bob Marley & The Wailers: "Crazy Baldhead" / Johnny Clarke: "Crazy Baldhead Man"

Certainly one of Marley's most enduring riddims, "Crazy Baldhead"[30] is given a mix that pushes Aston Barrett's bluesy bass riff to the foreground. Strictly speaking, the song is not mixed in a drum & bass style, as chordal instruments can be heard. Nevertheless, they are placed very low in the mix while the bass line is doubled by the second guitar and possibly a keyboard bass as well. This bass line, along with Carlton Barrett's one drop pattern (which emphasizes a hi-hat pattern playing quarter-note triplets against the bass), is undeniably central to the song, and provides a stark foundation for

Marley's jazz-inflected vocal phrasing. Yet, as powerful as Barrett's line is on its own terms, it is given extra power by an unprecedented clarity in the recording. The final mix of "Crazy Baldhead" was not actually done by Sylvan Morris; it is credited to Chris Blackwell and Aston Barrett and was completed in England. But such a powerful mix could not have been possible without the clarity Morris achieved in recording the basic tracks at Harry J's. One relevant definition of "clarity" in this context would relate to the boosting of the high end in the mix, in a manner typical of British rock production of the period, aimed at the American market. Alex Sadkin, an engineer at Criteria Studios in Miami (who also engineered some of Marley's Island-era music), commented: "When I started at Island Records . . . the first thing I noticed about working with [Island president Chris Blackwell] was that they always had the hi-hat really bright and loud on British records, whereas it wasn't like that on American recordings. . . . So I started hearing a whole different kind of sound picture [i.e. in relation to Jamaican music]."[31]

Johnny Clarke's cover of "Crazy Baldhead," on the other hand, was produced by Bunny Lee and mixed by King Tubby; it paints a very different sound picture. Clarke's version is strong on its own terms, yet different terms than those that shaped Marley's original. Clarke retains Marley's original lyric and phrasing; sonically, however, the track forgoes the political fervor and brooding quality of Marley's version for a more uptempo interpretation driven by a dance-friendly tambourine. The rhythm track, probably recorded at Dynamic or Channel One with the Aggrovators as backing musicians, lacks the high-end clarity of the original, while the Aggrovators' articulation is a bit softer, lacking the hard edge of the Barrett brothers. With the chordal instruments playing throughout and mixed fairly frontally, Clarke's version is ironically less drum & bass–oriented than Marley's but probably more effective as a dance track in the dancehall setting.

It is worth mentioning here that in his international phase, very few of Marley's pieces were remixed into dub versions.[32] In Aston Barrett's recollections, this abstention was largely to avoid compromising the messages in the song lyrics. According to both Barrett and Marley's engineer Errol Brown, however, a dub album had been planned, but was shelved by Marley's death in 1981: "We were leaving that to do at a later time. We were just giving them the full course—breaking the message to four corner of the earth, you know? But we [would] do some local mix in Jamaica, or we mix some dub, rough mix for the sound system guys. Myself, of course, and the engineer [Errol Brown], we would put them together at our place at Hope Road. Errol Brown would come and call me and say 'It's your time now.' Come tone up that foot drum and get that hard snare and that bass."[33] Brown himself recalled that an album of Marley dubs had actually been prepared, but was never released aside from a few dub plates for Barrett's sound system: "We did a couple, I remember 'One Drop' and 'Ambush' and a couple of others from *Survival*. We did a dub LP but they never put it out. Aston Barrett had a sound [system], and we just did some dub things for his sound."[34]

So, while Marley's music departed from the drum & bass aesthetic offered in Jamaica's dancehalls, the recordings suggest that Sylvan Morris, as well as other members of Marley's production/engineering team (such as Blackwell, Sadkin, and Brown) were committed to a vision of drum & bass as the musical and conceptual cornerstone of Jamaican reggae, while simultaneously dedicated to the elevation of drum & bass to a standard comparable with work being produced in the world's most sophisticated recording studios. As Barrett's comments illustrate, this achievement was the result of several engineers' contributions over time, and culminated in the construction of Marley's own Tuff Gong studio, located in the back of his home on Hope Road:

Our first engineer was Errol Thompson [at Randy's]. He was good, still good up until today. I teach him a lot of new tricks, you know . . . to get that drum sound which is the heartbeat of the people. We did some of the early tracks at Harry J with Syl Morris. That's the main man, he do all those tracks. He's a good man because he's coming from Studio One. And we take it up in England and finish the overdubbing. Because Harry J studio was 16-track. We go over to England and transfer them to 24-track. The next engineer was Karl Pitterson. He had experience too from Dynamic Sound. We bring him into Tuff Gong and to work with us on the road too. And then the next one what come in professionally was Errol Brown. His uncle [Byron Smith] was engineer for Duke Reid. . . . We set up the best studio, not only in Jamaica but in the whole Caribbean. And the best pressing plant, Automatic. Press two 45 at once and two LP at once.[35]

Brown himself agreed that Tuff Gong represented a new era of fidelity in Jamaican music: "All the old studios, Treasure Isle and Federal, they didn't have no top end. When I got to Treasure Isle, we used the filter to bring up highs that wasn't there before. So it was just a vision from my youth, because I always like hearing the tweeter. . . . I brought that to Marley and Burning Spear—*Hail Him* and the next one, *Farover*. Plus, I like to hear separation in the instruments, where you can pick out the instruments out in the mix. Now, it started to sound normal. 'Cause we were set up for it."[36]

Similar observations can be made about Sylvan Morris's dub work; the challenge at Harry J's would be to approximate the raw, "ghetto" sound typical of dub music produced at studios like King Tubby's and Channel One, while working with tracks that had been recorded on more sophisticated equipment. Mikey Dread's position on this was representative of several Jamaican musicians, who felt that dub needs to be mixed on fairly simple equipment in order to retain a direct and authentically Jamaican feel: "It's more flexible when you have less controls to work with than when you have a big board, because it's just like you're like a kid in a candy store. You're gonna want to mess around with everything. . . . Like the foreign dub, the stuff that they do outside of Jamaica. They get too carried away."[37] Robbie Shakespeare, on the other hand, preferred the flexibility and detail made possible by more tracks: "The Tubby's days was four-track. The drum and bass would be tied to one track, the riddim to one track, and then two tracks would be for vocals. And sometimes they would put drums on one track, bass on one track, riddim on one track, and one track for just vocals. Compare that to now where every instrument is on a track by itself. You can do a lot more tightening up with it."[38]

Morris's dub mixing seems to reflect Shakespeare's position. His mixes do not challenge the capabilities of his equipment in the same edgy way as do King Tubby's, nor are they so whimsically creative as Lee Perry's. Rather, Morris's mixes tend to be restrained and finely detailed in a way that reflects a precise technical knowledge of his equipment and a methodical approach to the art of the dub mix.

Sylvan Morris on the Mix III
Augustus Pablo: "Natural Way" > Sylvan Morris: "Nature Dub";
Bunny Wailer: "Armagideon" > Sylvan Morris: "Armageddon Dub"
Although one is instrumental and the other vocal, Augustus Pablo's "Natural Way" and Bunny Wailer's "Armagideon" are both suspenseful, minor-key songs with heavy Rastafarian themes. In his dub mixes (titled "Nature Dub"[39] and "Armageddon Dub," respectively) Morris relies heavily upon delay to simulate dramatic environments that extend the lyrical themes into pure sound territory. Both mixes are crafted around the central feature of a hi-hat that has been treated with delay to stand out in starkly in the mix. Although "Nature Dub" contains remnants of Pablo's melodica, it can really be considered a feature for Morris's treatment of Leroy "Horsemouth" Wallace's drum set playing, subjected here to a series of dramatically varying delay settings, each implying a very different spatial environment. Morris's dub mix of Bunny Wailer's epochal "Armagideon" uses delay very effectively to create pools of echoing sound that well up into tremulous sonic squalls, creating a mood of foreboding and paranoid tension. The

soundscape matches Wailer's disembodied voice, which emerges from hidden corners of the mix to startle the listener with his now-fragmented narrative of biblical apocalypse:

. . . nation rising up against nation . . .

. . . and from that day on, there is trouble . . .

. . . wars and rumours of wars . . .

. . . have patience my idren, have patience . . .

CHAPTER FOUR

"Jus' Like a Volcano in Yuh Head!"

⚡

*In the beginning Dynamics and the bigger men wouldn't do it and en-
gineers such as Byron Smith and Karl Pitterson never used to mix the
dubs. Those engineers wouldn't sit down and work the board like Tubbys.
In my knowledge he was the first and that's how Tubbys got such fame.
All of them dub things used to carry on at Tubby's.*[1]
— Producer Roy Cousins

*Tubbs changed the business in that time with the dub thing. Because the
other studios weren't really into that. They were more into balancing the
songs and gettin' it a certain way. But Tubbs changed that, people start
to look at the business from the sound. This started a whole different era.*
—Philip Smart to the author, 2003

If any single figure can be considered central to the rise of dub as an influential genre, that figure would certainly be Osbourne Ruddock, professionally known as "King Tubby."[2] King Tubby, who described dub music
as "jus' like a volcano in yuh head!"[3] had a long and varied career in the Jamaican music industry: cutting dub plates for sound systems and producers, building and repairing electronic equipment for sound systems, operating his own sound system, founding two recording studios, and producing
original music. As such, he was involved in the sound of Jamaican music at
virtually every stage of the technical and creative process.

King Tubby's Home Town Hi-Fi

Osbourne "King Tubbys" Ruddock's impact on the sound of Jamaican
music was rooted in the years he worked as an electronics repairman and
sound system operator. Born in Kingston in 1941, King Tubby was an
electrician by trade, and a music lover by hobby. It was through repairing
electronic equipment for various Kingston sound systems that he eventually founded his own sound system in the mid-1960s, King Tubby's

Home Town Hi-Fi. The system was based in Tubby's neighborhood of Waterhouse, in West Kingston. He recalled to Stephen Davis that "I used to fool round [with] sound system from 1964 as a hobby. . . . We never really get famous until around May 1968. Top sound those times was Sir Mike, Sir George, Kelly, and Stereo from Spanish Town. Then we came on as Tubby's Home Town Hi-Fi. We say we wasn't going in that big, just play in we home area which was Waterhouse. But eventually we get big."[4] Although the "Hi-Fi" appelation was often used by sound systems that catered to uptown clientele,[5] Tubby's sound became strongly associated with the Waterhouse area.

By the 1970s, Jamaica's rival political parties were beginning to court locally based sound systems around Kingston. According to Bobby Vicious, however, Tubby's system largely transcended these divisions, and this was one reason for its popularity:

All the gang warfare was set up at that time [in the 1970s]. You had Emperor Faith, which was up from the Red Hills area, so they had their following. Arrows was from the East, and pretty much if Arrows played certain places it would be a big war, big trouble. But Tubby's is a sound system that could play in just about any part of the city. Even though it was from Waterhouse, it didn't carry just a local following. It wasn't a PNP [People's National Party] sound or a JLP [Jamaican Labour Party] sound. It was Tubby's, and everybody respected that sound system. Anybody from any area could come, and it would just make it neutral and those dances would be great.[6]

Another reason for the popularity of Tubby's system was that by 1970, his most popular DJ was U-Roy (Ewart Beckford), who had updated the tradition of "toasting" over prerecorded music, and almost singlehandedly sparked the DJ boom of the 1970s with his talk-over versions of popular Treasure Isle songs.[7] So, in addition to the latest hits, Tubby was playing stripped-down dub plate semi-instrumentals that U-Roy could toast over.[8]

His facility with electronics was a third factor providing King Tubby an edge over his competitors. Many Jamaicans echoed the sentiments of Bobby Vicious: "Nothing compared to Tubby's. Tubby's was the legend, you know. And I've seen a lot of sound systems, man. Even today, with all the technology we have today, you still don't hear any sound system like Tubby's. They're big and they're huge and they're heavy, but nothing compares to the sound that Tubby had."[9] Even competitors such as Duke Reid and Coxsone Dodd sometimes had their dub plates played on Tubby's system, in order to hear their product played back on optimal equipment.[10] According to Lloyd Bradley, King Tubby was the first soundman to employ separate amplifiers to boost the various frequency ranges of music he played;[11] he is also said to have been the first to employ customized sound processing (such as reverb and echo effects) in the sound system to intensify the experience for the audience.[12] Philip Smart remembered an early 1970s dance at Up Park Camp, when Tubby unveiled this latest innovation:

He unveiled delay on a sound amplifier at that dance. The first time any other sound man ever heard delay, [was] when U-Roy came and take up the mic and say "You're now entertained by the number one sound in the land-land-land-land . . ." [imitates echo]. Everybody wondering where that came from! Everybody came 'round, all the sound enthusiasts coming and looking to see what made that sound. The next day Tubbs was swamped. Every sound man want an amplifier, they're making orders. He didn't give them the delay. He kept that as a secret until people found out how he did it. It was actually a three-head cassette deck, but he had it made into the amplifier so you couldn't see it.[13]

Patrons at sound dances would even be treated to a bit of a visual spectacle, courtesy of King Tubby's customized equipment: "It was beautiful to see Tubby's sound system. . . . To give you a description, it was two boxes [amplifiers] about three feet wide. About eighteen inches high, by about another eighteen inches deep. So picture these two boxes, right? The front of them, all chrome—like a mirror, I mean chrome, both of them. And at that time they didn't use LEDs, so they used big lights, they were colored lights—red, gold, green [Rasta colors], and they're all right across the top. So now, you see these lights and front like chrome plate and the big knobs all across. And that was all built by Tubby's."[14]

The sound system context in turn influenced King Tubby's studio work: after witnessing the crowd's response in the dancehall, he would then elaborate upon these effects in the laboratory setting of his studio, and eventually use them to craft records. Smart noted that every effect released on record had first been tested on sound system audiences: "The test tone, the delay, and rewinding the tape, the crashing of the spring reverb, all of those things we do on the dub [plates] first, so that when them playing against another sound it stand out. That's where you make your engineering test. Then the producers used them on their songs afterwards."[15]

Of course, innovation in popular music has never carried a guarantee of social acceptability. As both Scientist and Sylvan Morris recalled (see chapter 2), the music coming out of West Kingston was not readily programmed by Jamaica's mainstream radio stations. The growing popularity of Tubby's sound system was one catalyst that gradually forced it above ground and onto the nation's airwaves. Bunny Lee remembered: "Tubbys used to cut the dubs for the different sound systems, including his own, that the radio never want to play—it was strictly ghetto youths. So Tubbys' sound was a kind of radio station and people start to ask for it at the record shop. Eventually the radio station have to start a play it or else them would a look stupid."[16]

Among sound system aficionados, King Tubby's Home Town Hi-Fi remains legendary in Kingston to this day. By 1970, it was among the most popular sound systems in Kingston and remained so for several years. Ultimately however, social tensions and a charged political climate doomed his enterprise, which remained strongly associated with the rough culture of Waterhouse. The DJ I-Roy claimed to Steve Barrow that King Tubby's Home Town Hi-Fi "build a name that [it] is pure bad man [who] follow the sound now,"[17] and King Tubby's equipment was reputedly destroyed on two occasions by hostile policemen. Bobby Vicious witnessed one such incident that took place in Morant Bay, to the east of Kingston:

Tubbys had played two dances there before. The first dance was right across from the Goodyear Tire factory. Very successful dance, just tons of people—half of Kingston moved to Morant Bay [for that event]! That dance went off fine, without a problem. So, they kept a second dance about a mile down the road from where the first dance was. Well, people didn't like the fact that all these people from Kingston were moving up there. . . . At that time there was a policeman named Trinity. They call him Trinity because he wore his guns in the side just like a Western—cowboy hat, boots, everything. And in the middle of the dance, Trinity came, stopped the dance [and said] "Everybody from Kingston on this side, everybody from Morant Bay on that side." If you're from Morant Bay you go home. If you're from Kingston you get locked up—all the men. Not the women. They told Tubbys, "you shouldn't play back there again."

[But] the guy who kept the second dance, did the dance again. On the same lawn. Tubbys came, they strung up the sound. They played the first record, and that's when the police guy came in. We're talking about 4 o'clock in the evening because this is how early the sound systems would come in. And [Trinity] said "I thought I warned you guys not to play in Morant Bay anymore." And he took his gun out. And he fired some shots into the speakers. And [King Tubby's famous] chrome amplifier, he went up to the amplifier—"boom!"—put a shot right into it. Right into the amplifier. And that was it, that dance never started, never went on.[18]

King Tubby's Studio

Despite this unfortunate end, the success of both King Tubby's Home Town Hi-Fi and his ongoing electronics repair operation had financed his growing home studio operation. In fact, according to Philip Smart, the electronics enterprise was Tubby's primary source of income: "He built amplifiers, that was the main thing. Building amplifiers and winding the transformers. Nobody made transformers big enough for the power amplifiers that Tubbs was building. It would be hard to get it, you have to send to England. So Tubbs say 'the hell with that, I'm going to wind my own.' So him start winding that, and the amplifier him build, him wire his own transformer for it. And he had mad orders for amplifiers, people from all over the country. So it was a wait. 'Cause it's not like he did it in a mass production. He did it by hand—he put it together himself, although he had other people working."[19]

But Tubby's reputation as an engineer was also growing at this time. In some accounts, he had actually cut some of the U-Roy/Treasure Isle dub plates used on his sound system (he had worked for a time as a mastering engineer at Duke Reid's downtown studio on Bond Street). Later, he began voicing and cutting dub plates at a small studio built into the back of his own home at 18 Dromily Avenue in Waterhouse. Bunny Lee claimed: "Tubbys and myself start that studio when U-Roy was abroad [in England], we start voicing Slim Smith and Roy Shirley [on] some specials there. And then from that, Lee Perry and myself just start voicing full-time. Some Slim Smith tunes like 'Just A Dream' was mixed there. Before Slim died, Slim do a lot of voicing there too. Tubby's make a little board himself."[20]

Philip Smart also remembered the original mixing board as being designed and built by Tubby himself: "When I first went to Tubbs, he had built his own console. This was in his bedroom. He had turned the bedroom and the bathroom into the studio, that whole half of the house. He built it from scratch, it must have been like six faders or eight faders, and then he had one four-track [tape recorder] and the two-track [tape recorder] and the dub [acetate] machine. Some of the stuff he got from Treasure Isle; I think he got the dub machine from Treasure Isle. He didn't even have the voice room yet when I started going there. He had a mic in the same control room, wired up by a curtain by the window and that's where they voiced from, right there in the same room."[21] And Dave Hendley recalled: "Tubby's did your head in because it was actually a bedroom or had been a bedroom, in the back of the house. There was furniture in there like you'd have in a normal house, and light fixings. And then one side, this crazy four-track board, a couple of four-track tape machines. So it was weird. You had all this studio stuff like it was all in your mum's back bedroom. So that was slightly surreal. But the vibes there were electrifying. Really good sound coming through two big Tannoy monitors chained to the ceiling. The sound was really heavy, crystal clear."[22]

Faders, Filters and Flying Cymbals: Enter Bunny Lee

It was after he learned of the dub plate innovations of Rudolph "Ruddy" Redwood and the proto-dub work of Errol Thompson at Randy's studio, that Tubby upgraded his studio in 1972.[23] He had been encouraged in his experiments by a number of reggae notables including Lee Perry and especially Bunny Lee, the leading reggae producer of the mid-1970s. Born in Kingston in 1941, Lee was one of the most successful of a younger generation of ghetto producers that emerged to challenge the dominance of Duke Reid and Coxsone Dodd in the late 1960s. Because of his close relationship with King Tubby and his penchant for innovation,

Lee is one of the central figures in the history of dub music. Lloyd "King Jammy" James recalled him as "a great vibes man, always boosting you up. He would make anyone work wonders."[24] Lee became Tubby's most consistent client during this period, and helped broker Tubby's purchase of a MCI 4-channel mixing console from Byron Lee's Dynamic Studio. Philip Smart referred to Lee as "the godfather of the whole thing," and recalled:

When producers like Bunny started to encourage Tubby to actually set up the studio, that's when he looked into it and then he got the board from Dynamics, and he bought the second four-track [tape recorder], so he had two, he could transfer from four track to four track.

When they put in the new console we were doing more and more work there, constantly. We were cutting maybe 200 dub [plates] a week. It was like a pressing plant. We'd actually get tons of letters from sounds all over the country, letters coming from all over Europe, and we would read them and cut what they asked for, and we mail them back. So that was a whole 'nother business.

[Tubby's] mom was living in the house with him there. He got another house across the street and move his mom over to the other side of the street. And he turned the whole house into everything—he had the sound [system] inside the house, him had an office where them work on the amplifiers and design stuff. And then him have the area where them wind the transformers.[25]

Founded by Grover C. "Jeep" Harned, Music Centers, Inc. (MCI) represented the cutting edge of American recording technology for more than two decades. Harned, who was honored by the American Recording Academy in 2002 for his contributions, was an important figure in the standardization of the American recording industry and his company eventually became the world's largest manufacturer of recording studio equipment. Prior to founding MCI, Harned had served in the U.S. Army, received a bachelor's degree in civil engineering from Mississippi State University, and opened a home electronics/record store in Fort Lauderdale, Florida. From the late 1950s, Harned worked in partnership with Mack Emerman, whose Criteria Recording Studio in Miami quickly became one of the leading recording facilities in North America. Much of Criteria's appeal was due to Harned's custom-built recording equipment; the studio was also an important catalyst in the rise of South Florida as a major recording center and the hub of a regional recording scene that included the Caribbean. Thus it was hardly surprising that as Jamaica's top recording facility, Byron Lee's Dynamic Studio took its cue from Criteria.[26]

Like many of Harned's early consoles, the four-track MCI console at Dynamics had been custom-built. Given Tubby's facility with electronics, it enjoyed a new life in at his own studio, providing Tubby a crucial edge over his competitors and leading Scientist to remark, "Dynamics sorry the day they sold it to him!"[27] One oft-repeated piece of dub lore holds that shortly after acquiring the board, Tubby customized it by replacing rotating volume knobs with sliding volume controls (faders) that could be used to slide individual tracks gradually in and out of the mix.[28] But while this is an often recounted description of King Tubby's console, it is not consistent with the types of mixing consoles actually available at that time, most of which were already equipped with sliding fader controls.[29] Philip Smart suggested that Tubby did not in fact replace rotating knobs with sliding faders, but replaced the original faders with a different type that offered less resistance to the fingers. Unlike later consoles, the MCI board was not equipped with mute buttons, so the altered faders enabled quicker manipulation of the various effects, which had to be achieved by speed of hand. King Jammy confirmed the importance of "the faders on that board, 'cause we could rout any effect to the faders and do it manually, so we could control the rhythm of it."[30]

In any case, all of the engineers at Tubby's studio are in agreement that the possibilities of the MCI board had been underexploited by Syd Bucknor, then the engineer at Dynamics. Bunny Lee remembered: "I tell Tubbys, 'Syd Bucknor didn't know how to use this board.' [Tubby] acquired the board and two four-track machines that was with it. Cause Dynamics step up their thing to eight-track now, they thought that [the other] equipment was obsolete. . . . Tubbys and myself experiment with it. And it used to have a knob on it that change the sound."[31] The "knob" that Lee refers to is almost certainly the famous high-pass filter heard on so many of the mixes from King Tubby's studio. Lloyd "King Jammy" James joined King Tubby's studio as an engineer in 1976, and also remembered this as a distinctive feature of the MCI board: "it was a very unique board because it was custom built for Dynamic Sounds. . . . it had things that the modern boards nowadays don't really have, like a high-pass filter that made some squawky sounds when you change the frequency. . . . We would put any instrument through it—drums, bass, riddim, voices. That high-pass filter is what create the unique sound at Tubby's."[32] A large, rotating knob located on the upper righthand portion of the console, this high-pass filter ranged across ten settings from 70 Hz to 7.5 kHz, and provided a wider range on the low end of the frequency spectrum than most similar circuits (which tended to shut off around 1 kHz). This broader frequency range was what enabled the "sweeping" sound heard on so many mixes from the studio.[33]

Bunny Lee's significance extends over four decades and several stylistic periods of Jamaican music, but he is probably best remembered for his string of "flying cymbal" productions in the mid-1970s. As mentioned earlier, the flying cymbal was a drum set pattern widely attributed to Carlton

"Santa" Davis, who imported the offbeat hi-hat cymbal "splash" of disco music and fused it with the one drop drumming pattern.[34] This cymbal splash provided the perfect springboard for the creative application of Tubby's high-pass filter, resulting in a corrosive, "sweeping" sound that was particularly dramatic when heard at the high volumes of the sound system. Bunny Lee remembered, "When I start this flying cymbal, is some outer space thing I come with. Man, it was magic!"[35] According to Philip Smart, however, it took some time for mastering plants to adjust to this new feature: "Bunny was recording flying cymbals, I was trying to mix some of them but it went to the mastering and it come back—they say that the highs are too high in it and all of that."[36] In time, they perfected the effect and it became the ideal medium for King Tubby's experiments with the high-pass filter. Smart also agreed that Lee's flying cymbal sound was a perfect advertisement for the studio and its unique console: "Everybody had to come there to mix their sound to get that effect, 'cause no other console had that. Everybody was saying 'Bwoi, make sure you put that sound in it!'"[37]

The most representative collections of Bunny Lee–produced tracks featuring flying cymbal drumming and creative use of the high-pass filter would include those released under Tubby's name (such as *The Roots of Dub* and *Dub From the Roots*) as well as material credited to Johnny Clarke[38] and Tubby's mixes of material produced by Winston "Niney the Observer" Holness.[39] For the most part, however, the initial mixes at Tubby's were performed on fairly limited equipment. According to King Jammy: "It was four tracks you know, it was limited. We didn't have a lot of sound processors—we had just an echo, a reverb, the mixing console and likkle one equalizer. We also have a unique way of using the 10 kHz testtone, which we turned into a form of percussion."[40] According to both Bunny Lee and King Jammy, King Tubby often improvised homemade delay units by using tape loops; even traditional musical instruments were subject to modification by King Tubby. Scientist, for example, remembered their modification of electric guitars during the early 1980s: "One of the things we did was to take a conventional guitar and each one of the strings would have its own output. So we could EQ any particular string, each string it had like its own effect on it. But that's something that you'd have to modify a guitar to do."[41]

King Tubby also relied upon less conventional procedures to realize specific effects. As with Lee Perry's, some of the uniqueness of his sound was achieved by deliberate abuse and misuse of his equipment. The most frequently used such effect was Tubby's technique of banging on his spring reverb unit to produce a jarring, clangorous sound. In a spring reverb unit, the reverberation effect is produced by passing a sound signal through a coiled metal spring. In fact, one reason these units have fallen out of favor over time is that vibrations in the environment tend to induce a ringing of the spring, resulting in an unwanted "twanging" sound that can mar a recording. But this was precisely the effect that King Tubby exploited for aesthetic purposes. Philip Smart recalled that to achieve this particular effect, "it's like you lift it up and drop it [the unit]."[42] On "A Heavy Dub" (his remix of Delroy Wilson's "Just Say Who"), the intermittent fist-attacks jar the listener violently out of the soothing, aquatic textures of Wilson's lover's mood. The technique was especially effective when applied to songs with a political or apocalyptic theme, such as "Marcus Dub" (a remix of Johnny Clarke's "Them Never Love Poor Marcus"). As Clarke castigates the local politicians who betrayed Garvey to American authorities, Tubby repeatedly pounds the reverb unit, creating a thunderous sound that implies divine retribution for their actions.[43]

Thus, the innovative sound created at King Tubby's was largely born of its founder's ingenuity. Mikey "Dread" Campbell observed: "[Tubby] would figure out an effect he wanted and then design and construct the circuit that would give him that . . . if the man don't think a sound sound like he want it, he would go into the circuitry there and then and change it to create the particular effect he want. . . . It's because he truly understood sound, in a *scientific* sense, that he was able to do what he did. He work hard, too. Even when him not at the board, he still thinking, trying things out. Like all the great musicians practice all the time, so did King Tubby."[44]

King Tubby's home studio was small in size, and not equipped for the recording of live musicians. Rather, it was used for remixing and adding vocals ("voicing") to basic rhythm tracks that had been recorded at other studios such as Dynamic and Channel One. Nevertheless, its expansion into a full-fledged remixing facility was *the* pivotal moment in the development of dub music. Unlike other engineers who worked closely with live musicians in the studio, Tubby worked with tapes that had been *musically* crafted by other producers, and deposited with him for remixing. This emphasis on remixing probably inclined Tubby to develop dub as a distinct form. "Computer Paul" Henton felt: "There's no way you can think of dub music without thinking of King Tubbys. Because when everybody else was producing a lot of other artists and doing other things, his focus was just on pioneering that dub sound."[45]

In the same light, the studio was especially conducive to the work of the younger generation of ghetto-based producers such as Bunny Lee, Vivian

"Yabby You" Jackson, Glen Brown, and Augustus Pablo who, unlike older and more established businessmen such as Coxsone Dodd and Duke Reid, didn't own their own studios. What these younger producers *did* own, however, was the recorded material on their master tapes and, as discussed in chapter 2, they found inventive ways to maximize the creative and market potential of this material. From both an engineering and production standpoint, then, dub music acquired its most strongly identified locale with the upgrading of King Tubby's studio to a full-fledged remix facility. In King Jammy's opinion, "[Tubby] developed the style that everybody took on to. He developed the style that made dub music very popular."[46]

This was a style of dub that reflected the roughness of its surroundings as well as the rapid pace of production. Dave Hendley visited Tubby's studio in 1977:

The reason why everyone went to Tubby's was because it was cheap. Cheaper than everyone else. Obviously, because you could only voice or mix. You'd go into Tubby's in the evening, and the backyard would just be full of artists and producers mingling. They'd be sitting on the old speaker boxes of Tubby's Hi-Fi. The people would wait in the backyard for their turn to go into the studio. It was pretty constant for the engineer. People would be working the whole time, virtually non-stop. As one session ends, another one starts. . . . Usually, the dub cutting was done Friday evening, because most of the big dances are at the weekend. So soundmen would come in Friday to cut the dub for the weekend dances. Or, someone like Bunny Lee would pitch up at seven o'clock in the evening with a suitcase full of tapes and that's it—Jammys would be there till like three or four in the morning. Mixing and voicing. But there's some phenomenal records in there of doing four LPs in one night. They'd just run the thing once to get the timing on the stopwatch and then just mix it. I've never seen anything mixed with more than one take at Tubby's.[47]

Although King Tubby didn't work with live musicians, his dub sound was in some ways the most organically "musical" of his contemporaries, in the sense that his knowledge of electronic circuitry enabled him to exploit the idiosyncrasies of his equipment in novel and inventive ways. It is possible that this attention to sonic detail also reflected his personal tastes in music. All of his associates attest to King Tubby's deep love of jazz, and it seems plausible that his sensitivity to jazz's labyrinth of split-second creative decisions was reflected in his refashioning of the multitrack mixing board as an improvisational instrument, as well as in his pioneering of the dub remix as an act of real-time improvisation. Thus it can be speculated that Tubby's urban-bred, jazz-mutated dub sound grew out of his electronics expertise, his sound system experience, and his personal affinity for improvised music.

The pieces mixed by King Tubby tend toward the darker side of the emotional spectrum. His early mixes were minimal in construction and often sounded stark, moody, and suspenseful. His later mixes extended this mood with corrosive-sounding passages of filtering, ominous trails of echoing voices, and jarring ruptures of the song surface. Certainly, the setting of the studio was a factor; by the 1970s, the Waterhouse area had become so violent that local residents had nicknamed the neighborhood "Firehouse," and the participants on an evening mixing session at Tubby's would often lock themselves in the studio until dawn while gunfire raged around them. Eventually, this culture found its way into Tubby's mixes, through overdubbed sounds of machine-gun fire, emergency sirens, screeching brake tires, the bracing sound of the engineer dropping his spring reverb unit, and the endless succession of gunplay-inspired "straight to the head" titles. More important, it was very evident in the structure of the sound. Whereas the work of a producer like Lee Perry was ultimately comforting in its benevolent otherworldliness, King Tubby's sound seemed much more turbulently of its world. What was most provocative was that the cutting edge of sound technology was evolving in what was rapidly becoming one of the world's roughest and most impoverished areas. Remixing the heaviest riddims crafted by the ghetto's leading producers, the engineers at King Tubby's transmuted the tension of daily existence into a style of music clearly emblematic of its social origins.

King Tubby on the Mix
Ken Boothe: "Silver Words" > King Tubby: "Silver Bullet"

"Silver Bullet" is King Tubby's remix of Ken Boothe's 1975 song "Silver Words"[48] and is typical of his early mixes, amounting to an atmospheric excursion of drum & bass with dropouts, track bleed-through, mild filtering, and echo providing compositional interest. Tubby dispenses with Boothe's vocal altogether, and reduces the musical accompaniment (played here by the Soul Syndicate band) to a staccato guitar line straddling a cloudy, compressed foundation of bass, drums, and shaker, all intermittently processed through regions of mild reverberation. The most interesting passages occur on the song's bridge, which alternates between the IV and I chords with a harmonized, legato trumpet and tenor sax line on top. King Tubby manipulates the listener's anticipation by his treatments of this horn line. The line is heard just faintly on the first pass (0:43–1:09), offering the listener the spectre of something familiar, but unattainable. The second time through the bridge (1:50–2:15), Tubby punches in the horns abruptly at full volume, then punches them out just as suddenly, again denying the listener a sense of completion. In the final analysis, "Silver Bullet" is fairly basic as dub mixes go, reflecting a fairly literal interpretation of "drum & bass." Many of King Tubby's early mixes unfold with a similarly austere sensibility. In the absence of the more sophisticated sound processing units that he would shortly acquire, he manipulates filter settings to cast different shadings above the openings he carves out of the song surface by the dropping out of tracks.

Reggae music of the early 1970s continued to reflect the strong influence of African American soul music, which had ramifications for the sound of dub music as well. Many of King Tubby's early mixes play upon the transplanted emotional dynamics of soul music: the vocal take of "Silver Words" with Boothe's soul-influenced singing; or the horn line, which is strongly reminiscent of the Memphis Stax-Volt sound and would have been perfectly at home on an Otis Redding or Sam & Dave recording. In the dub version, these inherited emotional qualities, in combination with the limited equipment at King Tubby's disposal, result in an almost blues-like sensibility in which expressiveness is realized within an economy of technical means. This economy would gradually change as the studio was upgraded, and with the emergence of more strident, "militant" rhythms later in the decade.

Johnny Clarke: "Enter His Gates With Praise" > King Tubby: "This Is The Hardest Version" / Dennis Brown: "Live After You" > King Tubby: "Dubbing With The Observer"

Tubby's use of his console's high-pass filter was the technique that most distinguished his work from the other engineers mixing dub music. In King Jammy's opinion, "That high-pass filter, that's what made Tubby's the number one, the king of dub."[49] With this particular piece of circuitry at his disposal, King Tubby established himself as dub's foremost colorist: using the filter to manipulate frequencies of sound in the same way a painter manipulates frequencies of light, he was more concerned than other engineers with the elevation of texture and timbre as primary musical values in dub music. Several of his versions are primarily studies in textural manipulation, the music ebbing, flowing, stretching, and contracting as he pulls the sound through a cycle of filtered frequencies.

King Tubby's remixes of Bunny Lee's "flying cymbal" rhythms are particularly important in this regard. "This is the Hardest Version"[50] is King Tubby's remix of Johnny Clarke's "Enter Into His Gates With Praise," a rhythm track heavily reliant on the flying cymbal sound. After Clarke's residual vocalizing sets up the groove, Tubby goes to work, using the faders to reduce a six-note bass pattern to two punchy and propulsive attacks, and the high-pass filter to gut the rhythm section, giving the bottom-heavy drum & bass mix the tinny sonority of a transistor radio. The entire performance, which violates most standards of fidelity in popular music, is ultimately a feature for King Tubby's filtered morphing of the hi-hat cymbals. Another such example is "Dubbing With the Observer," which is a remix of Dennis Brown's "Live After You."[51] The mix begins with horns filtered to produce a strangulated sound similar to what Lee Perry achieved with a phase shifter in his Black Ark productions (although much harsher), while a continuously filtered rhythm guitar is the reference point for contrasting passages of harsh ensemble accents.

Tommy McCook: "Death Trap" > King Tubby: "Living Style"
Tommy McCook's "Death Trap"[52] instrumental is built on a slow "flying cymbal" pattern typical of the rhythms produced by Bunny Lee and the Aggrovators during the mid-1970s. This version pitches the vamp in E♭ minor with a bridge section on the A♭7 chord, and McCook's multitracked flute/saxophone theme is essentially composed of two pitches harmonized a third apart but given a much bigger impact through the heavy application of reverberation. The rhythm section work is typical of roots reggae, but the tempo here is slow enough to hover between the spheres of erotic langor and ganja-inspired near-stasis. Created from fairly sparse musical resources, the original song's open-ended vamp leaves Tubby little to work against in the way of vertical events, while its minimalist horn theme provides little melodic material for development. King Tubby thus follows an atmospheric remix strategy, "softening" most of the rhythmic syncopation via the application of reverb, and crafting an atmospheric soundscape above the drum & bass foundation. His application of reverb elongates the simple phrases of Tommy McCook's saxophone and flute theme into atmospheric trails of sound that feed back through the unit until they dissolve into squalls of harmonically ambiguous white noise. Tubby sticks to this format of drum, bass, and space until the song's bridge, when he reintroduces the offbeat instruments, briefly giving the music a funkier and more syncopated rhythmic edge. But the release of this modulation is subverted at its end: just as the band modulates back to the E♭ minor chord, Tubby pulls the bottom out of the structure, and the harmonic resolution dissipates in a reverberating haze of free-time flute obbligato. Somewhat the sonic equivalent of J. M. W. Turner's late seascape canvases (but set in the Caribbean), the ambient "Living Style" seems an exercise in "liquidating" the tightness of the reggae groove while exploiting the pitch ambiguities that result when musical sounds treated with reverb bleed into each other and blur the boundaries between "music" and "noise."

Jackie Mittoo: "Sniper" > King Tubby: "Dub Fi Gwan"
If fragmentation of the song surface through the dropping out of parts was central to dub's dynamic tension, King Tubby was the master practitioner of

this strategy. In most cases, it was the console's mute switch that allowed engineers to loosen songs from their rhythm section moorings and puncture reggae's repetitive groove patterns so dramatically. This mixing technique became particularly effective when used in conjunction with delay/echo effects that gave the illusion of decentering musical time (more on this below, this chapter). As mentioned previously, however, the MCI console was not fitted with mute switches, so the dropouts are actually achieved through quick manipulation of the fader controls.

This technique is used to dramatic effect in "Dub Fi Gwan," King Tubby's remix of Jackie Mittoo's "Sniper."[53] Mittoo had recorded an original version years earlier as "Totally Together" for Studio One, reworking the groove of Santana's "Evil Ways" into a minor-key organ vamp.[54] According to Bunny Lee, this was just one of several Studio One pieces that Mittoo re-recorded while visiting Jamaica from Canada, where he had relocated: "Me and Jackie do a lot of work. I went to Canada and said 'Jackie, what's happening—nothing out man?' And Jackie was a sour man because him start these things and the people forgot him. All of what Jackie do at Studio One, we do it over. We do an album named *Keyboard King,* that's the album that brought back Jackie. *Keyboard King* album come out and tear down the place, man!"[55]

Harmonically, "Dub Fi Gwan" is shaped by Mittoo's legato organ and based on a Dorian minor modal vamp alternating between the I minor and IV[7] chords. Using reverberation, the instrument's tones are blurred by King Tubby into an ambient harmony leaving the insistent drum & bass pattern to lend form to the structure. A predictably repeating snare roll signals the oncoming cymbal crash, which sears the soundscape in a detonation of reverberation and echo, while the rest of the instruments are momentarily muted into the void. At other points in the song, Tubby allows the roll to remain audible, but punches out the cymbal crash itself while allowing reverberations of the excised sound to spill over into the soundscape. What was a fairly minor element in Mittoo's original take has been transformed here into the defining formal feature of the tune.

Vivian Jackson (Yabby You) & The Prophets: "Fire Fire" (A.K.A. "Fire Inna Kingston") > King Tubby: "Fire Fire Dub"

As mentioned earlier, the effect produced by delay units is primarily rhythmic in the sense that it is a timed replay of an audio signal that results in the characteristic "echo" effect. King Tubby tended to apply this effect in two ways, both of which exploited the rhythmic capabilities of the equipment. Most frequently, he would use the unit to spin rhythmically disjunct tangents against the basic rhythm, a strategy discussed in chapter 2. This technique was especially powerful following a disruption of the rhythm; the listener is momentarily disoriented as fragments of sound spiral into the momentary void. King Tubby's second frequent use of delay focused on the drum set, and might be described as a type of "rhythmic intensification," an effect that Sly Dunbar considers to have originated at Tubby's studio: "King Tubbys was the first person which say put on that delay and make the drums play double time."[56] The technique entailed putting certain tracks (usually the drum set) through a delay unit that is timed exactly at double-time to the basic tempo. The result is a double-speed drum track rushing alongside the basic pulse, which effectively adds a new, layer of electronically created polyrhythm. "Tickling" is the word Bunny Lee coined to describe the unique, ping-ponging sound of delay-replicated percussion rushing in double-time to the underlying rhythm. King Tubby's "Fire Fire Dub" is a remix of Yabby You and the Prophets' "Fire Inna Kingston,"[57] and an excellent example of this application of delay. After using the unit to warp the hi-hat and snare rim into double-time, King Tubby routs them through the high-pass filter, while constantly varying the settings. The result is a high-register rhythmic latticework constantly shifting in color against the basic track. The sound anticipates the frantic, double-time snare patterns of "jungle" music, leading some to speculate that the junglists were directly inspired by Tubby's rhythmic application of delay (more discussion of this in the coda).

Jacob Miller: "Baby I Love You So" > King Tubby: "King Tubby Meets the Rockers Uptown"

The 1977 release of *King Tubby Meets the Rockers Uptown* (a compilation of tracks produced by Augustus Pablo and remixed by Tubby) represented a high point in the development of dub, providing one of the enduring album-length classics of the genre. There are two likely reasons this recording has attained its classic status. The first is that by mid-decade, Tubby had fully elaborated his language of remixing, facilitated by both the natural development of his aesthetic, and the continuous upgrading of his studio equipment. The second reason is the quality of the rhythm tracks that Pablo supplied for the sessions. Sonically and thematically, the sound Pablo developed with his Rockers production outfit strongly reflected the mood of the times. Ponderous minor-key grooves and some of the most striking electric bass patterns of the decade support heavily Rastafarian lyrical themes, often augmented by liturgical Rastafarian hand drumming styles and Pablo's plaintive sounding melodica. With King Tubby, Pablo's brittle melodica improvisations were cut and stretched by into works of deeply evocative power.

The title track of *King Tubby Meets* has come to be Tubby's most recognized remix, far surpassing the popularity of its vocal incarnation as Jacob Miller's "Baby I Love You So."[58] So popular was the track, in fact, that Island Records eventually rereleased the single with the dub version placed on the A-side. One reason for its popularity was Pablo's dynamic backing rhythm, built from an insistent, eighth-note bass pattern anchoring a I minor–IV minor chord sequence very similar in structure to some of Pablo's other riddims such as the one used for Tetrack's "Look Within Yourself." "Rockers Uptown" is in fact one of Pablo's most celebrated riddims, and has remained one of the most venerated riddims of the roots era. It was multiply versioned by Pablo, used later as a vehicle for jazz improvisation by musicians such as Ernest Ranglin and Monty Alexander, and resuscitated in the digital era as well.[59] The riddim itself had a history dating to the earliest days of dub music in 1971 when it first surfaced on Herman Chin-Loy's *Aquarius Dub* collection (as "Jah Jah Dub"), credited to Pablo. Ironically, according to Philip Smart, the original backing track had been engineered that year at Dynamics by Karl Pitterson, on the very same MCI board that would later be used to transform it at King Tubby's studio.[60] Pablo had subsequently cut other versions on the riddim, including Norris Reid's "Black Force" vocal and his own melodica instrumental "Cassava Piece."[61]

The vocal side is introduced by a four-bar vamp with Miller humming in unison with remnants of the melodica line of "Cassava Piece." He then begins the lyric, essentially a four-bar verse of one-measure phrases. Miller's sentiments are simplistic, trite even, but the performance is redeemed by the force of the musical arrangement. From the first notes of the dub mix, however, it is clear that King Tubby has transformed the song into something of far greater depth than the original. The soundspace has been expanded through the use of reverb, and the snare drum accents have been routed through a delay unit, rushing along at double-time to the underlying groove. Tubby has essentially turned this into a glorified drum & bass showcase, with occasional snatches of melodica, piano, and guitar filling out the mix. He introduces a brief fragment of Miller's voice at the modulation to the bridge, which soon gives way to Pablo's melodica, and the performance continues in this fashion, with successive fragments of Miller's vocal, Pablo's melodica, and chordal instruments. The performance ends as Tubby drops the rhythm section out of the mix, leaving Miller's voice suspended on an echoing syllable. Although the disruptive elements in particular were to become more pronounced in some of his subsequent work, the song is a virtual compendium of the techniques Tubby used to de- and reconstruct vocal songs.

Other Engineers at King Tubby's Studio

Over time, King Tubby trained a series of engineers who took on increasing shares of the studio's mixing duties over time, and who would each contribute in their distinctive way to the language of dub music. The best known are "Prince" Philip Smart, Lloyd "King Jammy" James, and Overton "Scientist" Brown.[62] In general, the sound of his protégés tended to be less dense and more distilled, focusing on specific aspects of what Tubby had developed and in some cases extending his innovations into new areas.

Philip "Prince Philip" Smart

King Tubby's first assistant was "Prince" Philip Smart (b. St. Andrew, 1952), who grew up in the Harbour View area of Kingston and had attended St. George's College and Dunrobin High School. Smart described dub music as "a ghetto thing. It was like the rootsy people started to gravitate towards the dub thing and everybody going to dances want hear the dubs. They didn't want to hear no vocals after a point, it was 'Just play all dubs, we don't need fe hear no vocals!'"[63] Smart had been involved in music since his high school years, when his enthusiasm for record collecting blossomed into a neighborhood sound system enterprise: "Collecting records, I been doing that for a long time. So the natural progression—you collect records, you good at it, and you could play at parties and make the people move. We had our own equipment and a couple more friends put together a little resources and we started playing parties. Until we turned that into a business, we had our own mobile disco."[64]

It was while running this sound system that he met Errol Thompson, another Harbour View native who had recently joined Randy's studio as chief engineer, and whose family also ran a sound system. Smart credits Thompson with inspiring him to pursue a career in sound recording: "Errol was kinda the man that was instrumental in inspiring me to become an engineer. After school, we'd go to Randy's and try to get into the studio. They wouldn't let you up at first because the studio thing is under tight security. They have to know you real well. One time we all left from Harbour View and went there and got in and see it and then I start getting to go in a likkle at a time. You get in on some sessions and you just stay quiet and you watch Bob Marley recording or you watch whoever it is at the time. So it was just like in the studio you actually see how a recording is done and the whole vibe of the thing. . . . I met Clive [Chin], he went to school alongside a friend of mine, Augustus Pablo."[65]

Smart also credits the engineer Karl Pitterson as an early mentor in audio electronics, the two having worked together at a Kingston electronics store. Smart also worked in an auto repair shop for a time, until being introduced to King Tubby by his school friend Augustus Pablo: "When I first went to Tubbs, I went there with Augustus Pablo. Me and Pablo going back for a long time from school. Pablo started doing recording at Tubby's. 'Cause the word got out in the industry [about] the music Tubbys was recording. . . . It had to be probably like '70 or '71 when I was introduced to Tubbys. I used to just stand and watch while they worked. You know when Pablo did his productions he recorded tracks in like Randy's, we'd take the tape 'round to Tubbs so we could cut the dub so we could play it back at home or on our set. We started doing that frequently—anything Pablo played on, got like a cassette copy of it or two-track copy take it around to Tubbs and cut it on a dub plate and play it on the set. So that was the next step. We were there almost every day."[66]

After several years of hanging around the studio, Tubby recognized the youngster's talent and invited him to mix. Smart recalls that it was his mix of Johnny Clarke's "None Shall Escape the Judgement" which established him as a credible engineer in the eyes of many, including Bunny Lee: "When [Lee] was working on "None Shall Escape The Judgement," I voiced Johnny [Clarke] on the riddim. I think Earl Sixteen was on it before. But when Johnny voiced on it, I said, 'Bunny this tune is a *hit tune!*' And him say, 'Well, if you feel it's a hit tune, mix it off and me put it out.' So him just leave me, I mix it off, I give it to him and he put it out and it just take off. Bunny was very confident with me after that. After that song—carte blanche!"[67]

In addition to numerous single B-sides, Smart is credited with mixing Bunny Lee's *Rasta Dub '76* compilation, DJ/producer Tappa Zukie's *Tappa Zukie in Dub* LP, and portions of Brad Osbourne's *Macka Dub* collection. He also claims the seminal *Creation of Dub,* an excellent and very influential LP that had been widely attributed to King Tubby.[68] Smart's tenure at King Tubby's board was relatively brief; by 1975, he had relocated to the United States and, although he returned briefly to both Jamaica and Tubby's studio, he permanently relocated to the United States shortly afterward, founding his own HCF studio in Freeport (Long Island) New York. Nevertheless, he assumed a large share of the mixing duties while at Tubby's, as King Tubby concentrated on his lucrative electronics business: "He got more work with winding transformers so he started to give me the bulk of the studio work. He got some major contracts. When they were building this hotel, they came to him and asked him if he could make transformers to maintain the steady currents for the air conditioners. He had to build 200 transformers, or whatever it was that they ordered. . . . He left the studio part in my hands. He never really gave anybody the keys to close up the studio and anything until he gave it to me. Even if it's four o'clock in the morning, he would come back and lock up and I'd go home. He gave me a set of keys and I could open up, lock up, come in and leave when I have to. I was his right hand man at that point."[69]

Prince Philip Smart on the Mix
Johnny Clarke: "Enter into His Gates with Praise" > Prince Philip Smart: "Ja Ja In De Dub"

In general, Smart's style is more restrained and less dramatic than King Tubby's, emphasizing drum & bass in the mix and using sound processing more selectively. A good point of comparison between the two engineers is Smart's "Jah Jah in De Dub," a 1976 remix of Johnny Clarke's "Enter Into His Gates With Praise,"[70] which King Tubby had previously remixed into "This is the Hardest Version" (discussed earlier in this chapter). Smart's version completely eschews the heavy filtering of Tubby's version, relying on very selective application of reverb, dropout and relying on the momentum of the straight rhythm track to carry the tune.

Prince Alla: "Bosrah" > Prince Philip Smart: "Tapper Zukie in Dub"

In 1976, Smart remixed a batch of tracks for producer Tappa Zukie that were collectively released as *Tappa Zukie in Dub*.[71] The title track "Tapper Zukie [*sic*] in Dub," stands as one of the most remarkable dub mixes ever created at King Tubby's studio. The dub mix was versioned from Prince Alla's "Bosrah," a medium-slow one-drop vamp composed around a prominent bass riff A♭7 and minimalist drum set pattern, and moving between the A♭7 and G♭ major chords. The form is divided into a clear verse–refrain–verse–refrain structure, with a horn theme separating the song into two halves. The open form and sparse rhythm pattern sets the stage nicely for Smart, who immerses the rhythm track within streams of white noise, which dominate the soundscape, creating an ambient metanarrative to the composition.

Lloyd "King Jammy" James

King Tubby's was my teacher, so I just carry on from where he left off.
—Jammy to the author, 2000

After Smart's departure, an interim period of several months followed in which mixing duties were handled by Pat Kelly (b. Kingston, 1944), a vocalist and engineer who had studied electronics at Kingston Technical and the Massachusetts College of Technology in the United States. But Kelly's stint was only temporary; as Philip Smart recalls, "Kelly wasn't really into that heavy dub kind of thing."[72] The next major assistant at Tubby's studio was Lloyd "King Jammy" James, who began taking on some of the studio's mixing work in 1976 (*Note*: prior to the mid-1980s, James was credited in recordings as "Prince Jammy"). James defined dub music as "a roots, grass roots, hard rock riddim. That's how I take it to mean. It was developed from riddims from the vocal tracks."[73] At King Tubby's studio, it was Jammy who helped guide the sound of dub music into the era of harder "militant" rhythms in the late 1970s.

As James has been the subject of a full-length biography by Beth Lesser, my biographical sketch here will be brief.[74] Born in Montego Bay in 1947, James knew King Tubby from an early age. His family had moved to the Waterhouse area while James was in his teens, and the youngster often spent time hanging around Tubby's yard. Following primary school, James worked around Kingston as an electronic technician (at one point working at Chin's Radio Service alongside Pat Kelly),[75] and repairman for sound systems such as El Toro, Lord Kelly, and Prince Patrick. From around 1962, he also ran a small sound system that played private parties around Waterhouse. Eventually, he gravitated toward King Tubby and worked at the latter's electronics shop, repairing sound equipment and "building amplifiers and stuff."[76]

James relocated to Toronto, Canada, for several years in the early 1970s, and his time there was varied and productive. He enrolled in electronics courses at a local technical college, operated a small sound system, continued to work as an electronic technician, and built and operated his own basement demo studio, which was booked by vocalists visiting from Jamaica. James returned to Kingston at Tubby's invitation to replace Philip Smart as engineer in late 1975,[77] and it was during this period that he was renamed "Prince Jammy" by Bunny Lee.

Like Philip Smart before him, Jammy assumed much of the mixing work as King Tubby focused on more general electronics work. In time, he developed a reputation as one of the foremost engineers mixing dub music, and he remained at Tubby's through 1980. As might be expected, Jammy's early dub mixes (collected on albums such as *Kaya Dub*) sound fairly close to King Tubby in style. Eventually, however, Jammy's style of mixing dub developed into a leaner, more concise version of his mentor's. In his words, "I had my own style, I didn't want to clash with anybody's style. I created my own type of reverb that I used, like some feedback sounds and things like that."[78] In general, Jammy's work is less experimentally inclined and emotionally dark than Tubby's, refining many of the effects and strategies introduced by Tubby. This concise approach gave his mixes a unique power.

Jammy's mixing style reflected the period in which he emerged. As the 1970s progressed, the soul-influenced reggae of the early 1970s was gradually augmented by the so-called militant riddims, which themselves might be thought of as reflecting the increasingly heated political climate of the Michael Manley era. Many of these new patterns (such as the "steppers" riddim) are credited to Sly Dunbar and Robbie Shakespeare. Generally, Robbie's minor-key bass lines were anchored by Sly's pulsing bass drum and embroidered with his syncopated snare drum and timbale accents. In the same way that King Tubby made profitable use of Santa Davis's flying cymbal sound a few years earlier, Jammy crafted a dub sound that made use of these newer, harder riddims. Many of his mixes feature long stretches of drum & bass cast in an atmosphere of reverb, with the syncopated drumming used to trigger trajectories of brittle-sounding delay. Unlike much of King Tubby's work, Jammy's mixes tend not to feature extended passages of chordal instruments. He often introduced and punctuated his mixes with a characteristic roaring sound produced by sudden application of cavernous reverb and panning to the drum set.

Jammy's career as a dub mixer also benefited from the growing international popularity of dub. Thanks largely to the legacy of psychedelic and progressive rock, dub music in England and Europe was appreciated on its own terms, as opposed to in Jamaica where it was often considered a mere backdrop for DJs. Jammy frequently traveled to England in the company of Bunny Lee, and was poised to capitalize on this, developing a strong international reputation at this time; he freely admits, "I was catering mostly for Europe in those days."[79] He also kept his ears open for new sounds while abroad: "Inna the '70s and early '80s, dub music was big in Europe. I used to visit Europe, and I used to come in contact with people in the music business and listen to albums from Europe. Engineering and production angle, that's what I was looking for."[80] In addition to selling strongly on the local Jamaican market as B-sides, his mixes were also compiled onto albums aimed at the European market, such as *Jammy's in Lion Dub Style, Kamikaze Dub, Slum in Dub,* and *Uhuru in Dub.*[81]

Jammy was not only a studio engineer; around the time he returned to Jamaica, he began to branch out into record production. Following his 1978 production debut of Black Uhuru's debut album *Love Crisis,* he established himself with other Waterhouse artists such as Half Pint, Echo Minott, and Junior Reid. Like King Tubby, Jammy's first studio was set up in the front room of his family house, but eventually, as will be discussed in chapter 7, he would become one of the most important producers in the history of Jamaican music.[82]

King Jammy on the Mix
Ronnie Davis: "Sun Is Shining" > Prince Jammy: "Jammy's A Shine"

"That is the best mix I ever did! That record mash up Jamaica and England and Europe and them places completely!"[83] This was Jammy's exclamation upon hearing the delay-replicated rimshot that introduces his famous remix of Ronnie Davis's cover of the Wailers' "Sun Is Shining" (titled "Jammy's A Shine"), one of the most powerful pieces of dub music ever realized at Tubby's studio, and a textbook study in his approach to disruption.[84] Jammy remembered, "that is one of my favorite Bob riddims, so I really put my heart and soul into that mix."[85] His remix transforms a straightforward rhythm take into a canon of continuous disruption in which trails of rhythmically disjunct echoes function as the "connective tissue." The track is introduced by a lone timbale shot elongated into a stream of brittle echo. An organ melody is the next to enter (0:05), supported by the offbeat guitar and piano of Bob Marley's famous guitar riff. Against this foundation, Jammy punches in brief, teasing slivers of drums and percussion, raising the listener's expectation for the entrance of the complete groove. But when the drums do finally enter at 0:26, Jammy immediately drops the other instruments out and intensifies the drum pattern with delay. A fragment of bass at 0:35 again hints at completion of the groove, but the drums disappear at 0:48, to be replaced by the entrance of bass and guitar at 0:56. Only at just over a minute does Jammy finally allow all the instruments to play the fully orchestrated rhythm pattern.[86]

Horace Andy: "Government Land" > Prince Jammy: "Government Dub"

Jammy's mix of Horace Andy's "Government Land"[87] is an excellent example of the way a dub mix can heighten the drama of a preexisting song. In the original, Andy's singing remains at a fairly static emotional level, with the web of interlocking rhythm section parts steady and consistent, and no real dynamic variation overall. Four verses and a fade-out vamp follow a four-measure introductory vamp on a D minor chord, with an accompanying horn theme. Each verse is divided into two halves, the first being a four-measure vamp in D minor, and the second being a repeated two-measure progression with B♭ major and D minor played for one measure each. The mood is created by Andy's lyrical theme of social justice ("Give up the land, government man . . .") and a suspenseful, minor-key, one drop rhythm that creeps along at a tempo of quarter note = 124.

Jammy's dub mix, by contrast, uses sound processing to impose a level of dynamic and emotional variety that surpasses the original. The mix begins dramatically with the reverberating roar of drums that is a trademark of Jammy's mixes. This roar leads directly into the intro vamp/horn theme, in which a reverberating electric piano is now prominent in the mix. The intro section ends as Jammy applies a bit of panning to the drummer's cymbal crash, an effect he will use at the conclusion of each verse. The first verse is largely devoted to subtly filtered drum and bass, with reverberating fragments of the horn background and chordal instruments appearing intermittently, punctuated by cavernous reverberation applied to the drum set. The second and third verses continue in this fashion, each featuring lengthy trails of delay that heighten the suspense, and each concluded with passages of dropout during the final measures, building a level of tension that is resolved with the reintroduction of the rhythm section at the beginning of the subsequent verse. In the third verse, the drum and bass drop out during the two penultimate measures of the verse prefaces a fractured restatement of the horn theme in the first half of the refrain section. The second half of the refrain (on the D minor sequence) finds Andy's vocals returning briefly to haunt the mix before the song opens up to the final vamp on D minor, with fragments of the horn background intermittently audible. A final passage of dropout sets the stage for the final, repeating statement of the horn theme, over a drum & bass background colored with filtering and panning effects. The fade-out builds tension very effectively, with more frequent "bomb" effects created by applying reverb to the drum set and increasingly dramatic panning effects. The climax of the mix occurs at exactly 3:52, when Jammy pans the drummer's fill wildly across the soundspace.

In spite of my consistent claims for the "nonlinear" aspects of form in dub music, this is a dub mix with a clear buildup of dramatic tension, yielding a clear climax. The power of Jammy's dub mix is helped immeasurably by the musicians' performance on the original rhythm track. The drummer (either Horsemouth Wallace or Noel Alphonso) uses cymbal accents to heighten the drama of the slow tempo, and the bassist (either Michael Taylor or Leroy Sibbles) creates tension by varying the bass line, using foreshortening to create very effective rhythmic suspensions, especially toward the end of the tune. All of these musical effects are exploited by Jammy in his dub mix.

Prince Jammy: "Flash Gordon Meets Luke Skywalker"
Buttressed by a strong local reputation and a particularly dub-friendly audience in the United Kingdom, Jammy indulged some of his most experimental

whims on the 1980 album *Scientist & Prince Jammy Strike Back*. "Flash Gordon Meets Luke Skywalker" pushes the reggae song structure as far as it can be pushed while still maintaining a functional connection to dance music.[88] Following twelve seconds of pre-song detritus that includes studio chatter, fragments of a previous bass line, and a phantom drum roll (all routed through a delay unit), the song proper suddenly bursts forth in a haze of fragmented drum, vocal, and horn lines, all unified by Flabba Holt's repeating bass line. The most marked departure, given that this is music ostensibly mixed with the dancehall in mind, is Jammy's treatment of the drum track. On a song that lasts nearly four minutes, the drum pattern is only audible for just over a minute; the rest of the time he teases the listener with fragments of the drum and chordal tracks—a cymbal splash here, a reverberating snare hit there, a guitar or piano chord elsewhere. It is Holt's bass line, morphing through a series of filtered frequencies, that provides formal unity as Jammy works the divide between musical sound and sonic debris. Were the bass line to be removed, the listener would be left with a form of purely "ambient" music (by contemporary definitions). Jammy remembered that this particular remix "featured the bass through the high-pass filter. On some mixes I might feature specific instruments; that's why there's not much drums on that one. I was featuring the bass because it had such a dynamic line."[89]

The other fascinating feature of "Flash Gordon Meets Luke Skywalker" is that while it is, in structural terms, the polar opposite of the aforementioned "Government Dub," it can nonetheless be heard as containing a clear climax despite its radically deconstructed state, which would seem to subvert any suggestion of linear development. At 3:23, the rhythm parts (again, minus the drums) are finally allowed to coalesce underneath the fragment of a horn theme and an emphatically descending organ glissando. Despite its brevity, this seven-second sliver is the most structurally and thematically-coherent section of the mix. Unsurprisingly, the track fades out shortly thereafter, suggesting that Jammy and other engineers were not merely deconstructing vocal takes, but consciously working to create a tension with the original take.

As studio bands like Sly and Robbie and Soul Syndicate were in increasing demand to record and perform internationally, their places at Kingston sessions would often be filled by the Roots Radics, the band that would define the sound of reggae music in the 1980s. As King Tubby concerned himself with building a new studio, King Jammy became more involved with independent production work. Jammy's place at Tubby's board would be assumed by Tubby's next assistant, an engineer who defined the sound of dub as reggae music evolved into the early dancehall phase of the 1980s.

Overton "Scientist" Brown

Tubbys is somebody I saw everyday of my life for about five, six years. Not a day pass and I didn't see him. We was very close. A lot of people thought I was his son!
—Overton "Scientist" Brown to the author, 2001

Overton H. "Scientist" Brown was born in Kingston in 1960, and both Bunny Lee and King Jammy take credit for introducing him to King Tubby around 1980. Scientist defined dub as: "creation from the engineer. The engineer takes original music, adds sound effects and implements more changes to give it a type of texture. It's coming solely from the engineer."[90] Scientist's work reflected the harder mood in Kingston during the early 1980s; in production terms, it also reflected a local Jamaican variant on the "big sound" production values (especially drum sounds) of Western popular music during the 1980s. Like Philip Smart or King Jammy before him, Scientist was drawn to music through an interest in electronics:

In my early days I was a technician, building amplifiers and what I noticed is when you play regular type of music, you find that amplifiers behave normal. You use the same amplifier and you start to play reggae, you have heavy low-end and crisp highs, and that same amplifier start to freak out. So I noticed especially when a mix came from Tubby's, you have these amplifiers that tested normally, you'd start to have all these abnormal behaviors. So a friend of mine introduced me to Tubbys and me and him talked about stuff like this and he even had some of the same findings. So that's what drew me to music.[91]

As with his predecessors, Scientist was initially hired by King Tubby to help wind transformers. It is less widely known, however, that he also worked a brief stint during this time as an engineer at Studio One, and he takes credit for pushing Coxsone Dodd to expand his bare-bones approach to recording:

When I was working with Mr. Dodd, he was accustomed to doing it one way. Back in [the early days of the studio], you find that it was only two tracks. And you probably only have one or two mics on the drums, if any! So it cause a kind of a situation but when I got to 13 Brentford Road where we had more mics and more modern things, that's when you could kinda hear a difference on those records. That is where that sound kinda start changing. I came in introducing EQ into tape and to those people, it was crazy because everybody used to record flat. I tried to EQ the mix, and it [had] never really sounded that way . . . all of those first Sugar Minott, Willie Williams, Michigan & Smiley, I did those and if you note, you find that is where that sound kind a start changing.[92]

The period to which Scientist refers is well represented on compilations such as Heartbeat's *Rare Reggae Grooves from Studio One* and Soul Jazz's *Studio One Disco Mix,* which feature artists such as Lloyd Robinson, Peter Broggs, The Gaylads, and others. Scientist also mentions productions such as Sugar Minott's "Oh, Mr. D.C." as representative examples of his engineering at this time. His comment that "a lot of people don't know that Freddie McGregor played [drums] on a lot of those overdubs" is telling, as several Studio One tracks from this period seem to be older recordings (some dating as far back as the Sylvan Morris era) refashioned with later drum set overdubs.[93] A particularly tinny hi-hat cymbal is a prominent feature, and even minor alterations such as this provide more high-end information than had been the norm on Studio One recordings of the early 1970s, most of which had been engineered by Coxsone Dodd himself following the departure of Morris. Other tracks such as Michigan and Smiley's "Rub-A-Dub Style" were actually engineered by Scientist, and clearly reflect his efforts to record with more microphones and to utilize equalization. The high and midranges are much more balanced, there is clearer separation of the instruments, and the overall sound quality is significantly improved.

Scientist's stint at Brentford Road coincided with Studio One's last period of significant commercial success. This creative burst was partly attributable to the updated sound he brought to Dodd's old rhythm tracks, and partly to a new generation of vocalists such as Johnny Osbourne, Sugar Minott, and Freddie McGregor. The apprenticeship was brief, however; Scientist recalled Dodd's suspicion of his association with King Tubby,[94] as well as a lack of acknowledgment that must have been especially frustrating during a period in which many Jamaican engineers had developed international reputations: "Musically, it was good. You can't beat the music. The only problem I had with Mr. Dodd was poor documentation of the history. You work on these records and you would never see your name on it. You wouldn't get no credit. I start going 'round Tubby's because Studio One is not where you get exposure."[95]

Eventually, Scientist made his way to the mixing board at Tubby's and remained there through 1982–83, when he moved to Channel One in order to focus on live recording. His early work reflects the influence of the studio's previous engineers, and the autumnal *Scientist and Jammy Strike Back* album (1980) provides an excellent comparison, showing both engineers working out in dub's final stylistic era over a selection of Linval Thompson–produced tracks. Ultimately, Scientist developed a mixing style that was uniquely his. He remembers that initially, his innovations were not widely embraced by producers used to the styles of Tubby, Smart, and Jammy: "A lot of those sound effects that you hear on a lot of those albums, when I was first doing it I was highly criticized. And everybody in Jamaica was more hoping for it to be a failure than a success. It was something new. I was this kid that come on, and want to change things overnight, because everybody there used to it a particular way. But it eventually changed reggae."[96]

Linval Thompson, Junjo Lawes, and the Roots Radics Band

The emergence of a new generation of producers, musicians, and studios provided the professional opening for Scientist and the medium for his innovations. Just as King Tubby and Prince Jammy were best known for their work with producers like Bunny Lee, Yabby U, and Augustus Pablo, Scientist's most-recognized work was done for the leading producers of the dancehall era. Most prominent among these were Linval Thompson and especially Henry "Junjo" Lawes. He also produced several dub albums in conjunction with the British-based Jamaican producer Roy Cousins. Lawes was the most successful of these producers, known for his production of the hugely popular DJ Yellowman in the early 1980s, as well as vocalists such as Johnny Osbourne, Barrington Levy, Michael Prophet, and the Wailing Souls. He also produced a series of highly influential dub albums on the Greensleeves label, featuring Scientist's work. Thomspon remembered that Scientist's ascension as the mixer of choice at Tubby's was concurrent with Tubby and Jammy's outside activities, and that it also benefited from the growing market for dub in England: "Me and Junjo Lawes, we couldn't get Tubby to mix all the songs all the time, so Scientist was there, and Scientist used to just mess around and find a sound, and everybody been liking that sound in England. We was the ones who really make Scientist, me and Junjo—it wasn't nobody else."[97]

In the studio, both Thompson and Lawes relied on the Roots Radics, the latest studio band to shape the sound of reggae music. The Radics were built around the nucleus of Errol "Flabba Holt" Carter on bass, Eric "Bingy Bunny" Lamont, Dwight Pinkney, and Noel "Sowell" Bailey on guitars, Wycliffe "Steely" Johnson on keyboards, Lincoln "Style" Scott on drums, and Christopher "Sky Juice" Blake on percussion. Computer Paul described their ascension as Kingston's top session unit: "With every era of the music, the studio musicians evolve. Like Upsetters, with Fams [Familyman Barrett] and alla dem, they were playing for all of the hits. Then Bob Marley came in, said 'Wow, I like the sound,' work with it, took them on tour. Once they go on tour, the music has to continue surviving here, so that's when Sly & Robbie came in, as the next generation. Sly & Robbie now started working with Peter Tosh, and then they started touring with Black Uhuru after that—they went away. That's when Roots Radics slid in. And Roots Radics had about a good five-year run, and that's when Steely and Clevie came in and the music started changing to get computerized."[98]

With riddims that were sometimes almost narcoleptic in their combination of heavy downbeats and slow tempi, it was Roots Radics who ushered reggae music into the dancehall era, as the cultural dominance of Rastafari gave way to the harder-edged mood of the 1980s. Musically, the most important distinction between dancehall and the roots reggae that preceded it was in the style of drumming, as can be illustrated by a comparison of two versions of the Studio One classic "See A Man Face."[99] The song was originally recorded in the early 1970s by Horace Andy at Studio One, and the drumming on this version is a typical one drop arrangement with straight sixteenth-note time played on the hi-hat cymbal, the bass drum played on beats two and four, and interlocking syncopations improvised on the rim of the snare drum. The rest of the instruments conform to their typical functions: the bass line emphasizes strong beats, and the chordal instruments play the characteristic upbeat comping pattern. A later version of "See A Man Face" recorded by Peter Ranking for Don Mais's Roots Tradition label around 1980 finds the drumming pattern reversed in a manner more typical of American popular music, a style of drumming some refer to as "rockers." Here, the bass drum accents beats one and three, the snare is played on beats two and four, and the rest of the instrumental parts conform to the standard reggae arrangement. This change in the drumming effectively made the music less polyrhythmic in feel. Drummers such as the Roots Radics's Lincoln "Style" Scott (inspired by the innovations of Sly Dunbar and Santa Davis) had a much harder, heavier feel than more roots-oriented drummers such as Carlton Barrett or Horsemouth Wallace, who had essentially developed out of the rock steady style of drumming.

Channel One Studio

In the studio, this new style of playing gained much of its power from the work of a younger crop of engineers. In particular, it reflected the rise of the Hoo-Kim brothers' Channel One studio on Maxfield Avenue. The studio, which was owned by the brothers Ernest and Joseph "Jo-Jo" Hoo-Kim, had opened in 1972. Following a brief stint by Syd Bucknor, Stanley "Barnabas" Bryan and studio co-owner Ernest Hoo-Kim became the studio's chief engineers, working on a four-channel API console that had been installed by Bill Garnett.[100] In a few short years, Channel One became the most popular place to lay rhythm tracks for independent producers, especially after they upgraded to sixteen tracks in 1975.[101] Subsequent engineers would include Anthony "Soljie" Hamiton, Lancelot "Maxie" McKenzie, and "Crucial" Bunny "Tom Tom" Graham.

More than anything else, Channel One is remembered for its drum sound, the clarity of which was unprecedented in Jamaican music. In the opinion of Computer Paul, who began playing sessions on guitar at the studio as a teenager, "Channel One sound was fresh because everything got clear, all of a sudden you could hear the hi-hat, you could hear the snare drum, you could hear the kick drum. So it was a new sound. That within itself was pioneering."[102] Opinions are varied on who deserves credit for this sound. Scientist, who began engineering sessions at Channel One around 1983, takes some of the credit for it, claiming "That was one of the things I was known for, getting that drum sound."[103] Computer Paul credited much of it to drummer Sly Dunbar: "A lot of that had to do with Sly, because he was always into getting the best quality drum sound."[104] Clive Chin also credits Dunbar: "Sly tell them to mic every damn thing 'pon the drum! He want everything miked, I mean at least twelve mics on him drums alone!"[105]

Along with his rhythm partner Robbie Shakespeare, Dunbar anchored the studio's Revolutionaries house band and he fondly remembers Channel One as "Wicked studio man, the best! Best studio ever in Jamaica!"[106] Some of the most famous photos of the roots era feature Sly and Robbie, idling outside Channel One's famous black studio gate while on break from recording. Asked about the studio's drum sound, Dunbar acknowledges several people, including "Scientist, Bunny Tom-Tom, Maxie, Soljie, and Barnabas who was like a little whiz kid. But Ernest [Hoo-Kim] was the key man who got the sound, he say that "*This* is the sound that I want." Ernest is a man which love bass and drum, and he take great pride in getting a sound and creating a record. He would take hours and stay on a bass line. To this day when you say Channel One—drum sound and bass killing mon! It took us like probably about two years to develop that kind of sound. Before a session it take like two hours, testing the drum and getting it right."[107]

Computer Paul remembers that Channel One was also one of the earliest studios to introduce the use of electronic instruments such as synthesizers and electronic drums (Syndrums) into Jamaican music: "Channel One with Sly dem, them go put a lot of synth sounds into drumming. So it change the whole feel, 'cause we were just used to kick, snare, and hi-hat. They brought in Syndrums and synthesizers."[108] In fact, Sly and Robbie's increasing electronic work at Channel One would set the stage for their emergence as the Taxi Gang, one of Jamaica's top production teams from the early 1980s. Their experiments would culminate in their production of the vocal trio Black Uhuru, which was marked by a hard, urban and thoroughly electronic sound that expanded Channel One's vision in a manner consistent with the cutting edge of engineering and sound processing in England and America.[109]

At the time of his arrival, Scientist was poised to capitalize on the production innovations taking place at Channel One. Most of his dub albums feature tracks that had been recorded at Channel One, and given dub mixes at Tubby's. Linval Thompson felt that it was through this equation between Roots Radics, Channel One, and Scientist that early dancehall reggae hit its commercial and stylistic groove: "That was the right studio for the roots dancehall sound. We used to make the riddim at Channel One and then we take back the riddim track over to King Tubby's and mix it at King Tubby's so we kinda get a sound. Me and Junjo Lawes, we kinda conquer that sound. And that's a sound they are crazing about right now. Every echo slap, only King Tubby's could give you that mix with Scientist."[110]

Scientist on the Mix
Wailing Souls: "Bandits Taking Over" > Scientist: "The Corpse Rises" / Peter Ranking: "See A Man Face" > Scientist: "See A Dub Face" / Sammy Dread: "Follow Fashion" / Scientist: "De-Materialize"

As might be expected, Scientist's early work (featured on albums such as the Bunny Lee–produced *Scientific Dub* [1980]) sounded fairly similar to that of his predecessors at King Tubby's. It was with the heavy riddims of Roots Radics as his foundation, that he found his sound and became the remix engineer of choice in the early dancehall era. Scientist exaggerated Roots Radics' hard sound while also giving it a spacy, electronic garnish. Part of this hardness resulted from the way he blended melodic and percussive elements of the music by refashioning bleeping test-tone frequencies into pitched percussion sounds. Another key element was an emphasis on the low register, reinforcing the low end by alternately applying large amounts of reverberation to the bass and snare drums. This application of echo was one of the distinctive elements of Scientist's dub language, resulting in a violently reverberating snare drum "slap" that sounded like the cracking of a whip and a bass drum that, at sound system volume, impacted with the force of a cannon blast. As a result of this low-end emphasis, Scientist's mixes grew to sound harder, more urban, and more electronic than those of the earlier engineers at Tubby's. A particular treatment of the upright piano added to this effect. A dub remix of Freddie McGregor's "Jah Help the People" finds Scientist fashioning a unique variant of the instrument's sound by combining it with the rhythm guitar and routing both through the delay unit in a way that blended and accented their respective metallic sonorities. Chords that had previously sounded like collections of individual pitches now sounded like hardened metallic chunks (Lee Perry had achieved a similar effect on songs such as the Heptones' 1976 "Sufferer's Time").[111]

At the same time, Scientist was able to introduce several fluid elements into these stark rhythm patterns. On some tracks he would extend dub's processes of fragmentation beyond the mere dropping out of tracks such as on "De-Materialize,"[112] an aptly titled remix of Sammy Dread's "Follow Fashion."[113] The first thirty seconds feature a riddim atomized into echoing shards by sporadically muting the drum track and feeding it through a delay unit, resulting in a passage of fragmented drumming with no underlying beat audible. Similarly to King Jammy's strategy on "Flash Gordon," the bass again functions as the cohesive element as the delay unit scatters timbale accents and test tones about the soundscape. Like Tubby and (to a lesser extent) Jammy, Scientist also made use of the studio's high-pass filter, but was more likely to apply it to the electric bass than to the high-register instruments, as the former engineers had done. Dub mixes such as "The Corpse Rises"[114] (a remix of the Wailing Souls' "Bandits Taking Over")[115] were built around scalar distortions of electric bass, as Scientist funneled the instrument through the high-pass filter to bend its sonority from that of a mouth harp, to a foghorn, and finally, into the familiar soundshape of an electric bass. He also sometimes applied the filter to lead guitar lines, which made the instrument sound something like a kazoo or harmonica.

"The Corpse Rises" and "See A Dub Face"[116] also feature another of Scientist's favorite techniques, which was to build mix by building on the instrumental tracks as they "bled" through onto the vocalist's (or other instrumentalist's) track. Most often, a "bleeding" drum track was fed through a reverb unit, resulting in a spooky, alien sound that evoked images of the drums being beamed in from another planet, or the vocalist existing in another world from the musicians (and even the listeners). On "See A Dub Face," Scientist introduces the rhythm section for two measures, and then pulls them out, leaving only the bled-through drum tracks to continue with a cavernous echo. He soon reintroduces the bass, which morphs through several modes of filtering as it looms over the drums. He then builds the structure back up, only to scatter it with echo as the bass continues throughout the performance. This mixing strategy was a violation of more standard recording practice, in which the ideal was as much separation between the individual instruments as possible. But in exploiting this by-product of the spatial arrangement of instruments in the recording studio, Scientist was actually resuscitating an aesthetic practice that had been used more than fifty years earlier by engineers recording classical music. Peter Doyle has noted that as a result of improvements in recording technology in the 1920s, "recordings became capable of picking up room ambience, of carrying, in other words, significant sonic information about the spaces in which they were recorded."[117]

Scientist's sound was self-consciously futuristic, and his album covers were accordingly adorned with sci-fi imagery, especially a series of cartoon sagas depicting the engineer as hero, doing battle against a host of human, alien, and electronic life forms. Mainly designed by Greensleeves artist Tony McDermott, they provided a convenient channel for a local Jamaican consumption and reinterpretation of images and themes from global (mainly American) pop culture such as video games (*Scientist Encounters Pac Man at Channel One, Scientist Meets the Space Invaders*), horror films (*Scientist Rids the World of the Evil Curse of the Vampires*), science fiction films (*Scientist & Prince Jammy Strike Back*), and athletics (*Heavyweight Dub Champion, Scientist Wins the World Cup*). In each case, sound is the weapon with which the hero does battle. As much as this casts an eye toward the futurist iconology of dub mixers, science fiction, and cartoon superheroes, it also refers very plainly back to the battle ethos of the sound clash.

Eventually, Scientist would go on to engineer sessions at Channel One, concluding this phase of his career with a brief stint at Bob Marley's Tuff Gong studio before leaving Jamaica for the United States in 1985. He described his time within the Marley complex: "Very enjoyable. Rita Marley, Errol Brown and the rest of the staff was very professional and organized. Bob Marley and his empire was not about exploiting the music like other studios. It was a place where musicians felt at home and didn't have to worry about the gangster runnings. I wish Bob Marley was around to enjoy what he had started."[118]

CHAPTER FIVE

Tracking the "Living African Heartbeat"

☙

*Pragmatic has often been understood as being excessively attached to the
data received from reality. However, the problem is tackled in exactly the
opposite direction: how can we turn our fantasies into a certain degree
of public interest?*
—Inaki Abalos and Juan Herrera, from "End of the Century Still Lifes"

*All these records are righteous creations, you thinking only righteous
when you making music, you think in a holy mood, in a spiritual mood,
and just think righteous alone."*
—Lee Perry to the author, November 2001.

Although his most influential work was created inside of Jamaica, Lee
Perry must be considered one of the most creative popular music pro-
ducer/engineers of his generation, worldwide. Perry's innovations were
rooted in the creative currents brewing in Kingston studios during the
1960s. His career differs somewhat from that of other innovators of dub
music such as King Tubby and Errol Thompson in the sense that the former two, both being engineers, approached the art of mixing from a
fairly technicalized standpoint. Perry, on the other hand, had worked variously as a talent scout, vocalist, songwriter, producer, and conceptualist,
as well as an engineer. As such, his oeuvre operates on several simultaneous levels, and its significance transcends the mere engineering aspects of
his work. Nonetheless, Perry is probably second only to King Tubby in
the pantheon of dub music's innovators. He defined dub music as "[a
style that] make the music more understandable, and easier to dance. It's
not full of too much horns and too much keyboard. It give you more
space to dance, it's much more enjoyable, nicer, much better than when
you have all the instruments play [at] one time. It's different than the rest
of reggae music."[1]

Perry is the subject of *People Funny Boy,* a full-length biography by David Katz that stands, along with the same author's *Solid Foundation,* as a major achievement of reggae historiography.[2] My biographical sketch here will be deliberately brief. Perry was born Rainford Hugh Perry around 1936 in the town of Kendal in the northwestern rural parish of Hanover. His family was poor, and Perry quit school at an early age to work in a quarry, moving boulders with a bulldozer. Later in his career, he would identify the sounds of crashing stones he experienced at his worksite as one source of his knack for sonic experimentation.[3] He also gained a local reputation as a talented dancer, which would figure into his later work as a producer. Perry was still in his teens when he arrived in Kingston during the mid-1950s, apprenticing with Coxsone Dodd and his Downbeat sound system shortly thereafter. When Dodd established his Studio One label around 1959–60 and began recording Jamaican music, Perry stayed on, working successively as a producer, songwriter, talent scout, and auditioner for the steady stream of singing hopefuls who passed through Dodd's Jamaican Recording Studio. Vocalist Dudley Sibley remembered the close relationship between mentor and protégé: "Lee Perry was Coxsone right-hand man in the sense that Coxsone never used to travel alone. So he used to have Lee Perry who used to travel with him inna the car. Perry used to be the hands-on man who watch everything Coxsone do—both in the studio and on the road. If Coxsone is in the studio, Lee Perry is in the studio with him. Scratch learn from Coxsone, and that's how he evolved to be one of the greatest producers. Him really learned from Downbeat."[4]

In fact, it is Perry who is credited with bringing future star vocalists Delroy Wilson and Toots Hibbert to Dodd's attention.[5] Vocalist Max Romeo (later one of Perry's most successful artists) considers Perry's work for Studio One a largely underacknowledged contribution that laid the foundation for his later innovations as a producer: "Lee Perry produced most of the songs that came out on Coxsone Dodd label anyway at that time. . . . He did a lot of it, a lot of Wailers, a lot of Gaylads and all these people. So that give him the experience and expertise and in my experience he's a genius when it comes to producing."[6]

Perry also recorded a string of his own risqué ska singles for Dodd during this time (usually under the name "King Perry"), which partially placed him within Jamaica's ongoing "slackness" tradition of sexually suggestive songs. These included titles such as "Roast Duck," "Pussy Galore," and "Chicken Scratch," the last of which earned him the most enduring of uncountable nicknames.[7] From sound system to recording, the business was tough as system operators fought to establish a foothold in a volatile economy, and competition frequently boiled over into violence between followers (and hired goons) of Coxsone and those of his main rivals Duke Reid (who operated the Trojan sound system) and Vincent King Edwards (who operated the system known as King Edwards the Giant). "Little" Lee (as he was then known because of his short stature) would avoid the violence through several means, including the protection of his friend Prince Buster, a rival system DJ formerly with Coxsone and a former boxer who, like many, was captivated by Perry's quirky genius.[8] A number of Perry's song lyrics from this period strongly oppose violence and the domination of the weak by the powerful; years later as Kingston became torn between by warring political factions, Perry would occupy a similar position, decrying the street violence from the otherworld of his backyard Black Ark studio. As a vocalist, Perry possessed a soft, wistful voice that wasn't particularly effective on the driving, uptempo numbers of the ska years, but that worked well on midtempo material; as such it began to come into its own within the slower and more spacious structures of rock steady and reggae.

Although the advent of dub was still nearly a decade away during his tenure with Coxsone, Perry's dub vision grew directly from his experiences in the 1960s, as well as several other important influences. One was his ongoing fascination with the Afro-American rhythm-and-blues music played by the early systems, an interest that would manifest itself throughout every phase of his career; Perry's oeuvre is particularly rich with covered songs, riffs, dances, and catchphrases borrowed from African American music of the 1960s and 1970s. Another important inspiration was Jamaica's various forms of neo-African spritualism. Perry was fascinated by the music of Jamaica's Afro-Protestant faiths such as the *pocomania* sect, which supposedly provided the inspiration for the beat of his 1968 song "People Funny Boy." In fact, Perry once famously exclaimed, "Them poco people gettin' sweet,"[9] and can be heard getting "happy" himself at the climax of his early 1970s recording "When You Walk," as backing vocalists drone a "hallelujah" chant behind him.[10] Another influence was the aura (if not the actual practice) of Jamaica's Obeah tradition of neo-African black magic. Perry has steadfastly denied any involvement in Obeah,[11] but he nevertheless drew on much of its imagery to fashion an image for himself as a sonic spellcaster.[12] Finally, there was his fascination with the sounds and textures of Jamaica's tropical setting. Thick, cloudy, smoky, and humid, Perry's dub music sounded uncannily suffused with the sound of Jamaica's natural environment, buzzing with a tension that suggested he was receiving his inspiration directly from the island's natural forces. The black rhythms of the American mainland, the alternating frenzy and ecstasy of Jamaica's Afro-Protestant cults, the invocation of ancestral Africa via the celebration of "roots" and nature, the spell-casting power of Obeah, a savvy eye toward the international market, and successive developments in recording technology were the elements around which Perry would craft his own, hermetic sound world. In time, it would develop into a "progressive" stream of reggae, fairly independent of commercial trends. But his work developed through several stages before he realized his farthest-flung sonic visions.

Early Productions, 1966–1971

Perry eventually tired of his subordinate role under Dodd and left Studio One during 1966, working with a succession of rival producers including Clancy Eccles, Bunny Lee, Sir J.J. Johnson, and Joe Gibbs. It was his acrimonious splits with Dodd and Gibbs, respectively, that prompted several songs, including "I Am the Upsetter" and "People Funny Boy." The first became another of his most enduring nicknames, the generic name he gave all of his studio bands, as well as the name of the independent label he established in 1968. The latter was one of several hit songs credited with the introduction of the downtempo shift that gradually morphed rock steady into reggae.

Perry became a full-fledged independent producer in 1968, one of a younger crop of producers such as Eccles, Lee, and Winston "Niney" Holness, associated with the new sound that would be called "reggae." He was particularly close with Lee at this time, who remembered: "Everywhere I go I always carry Lee Perry as my spar [friend] because he and I working together for years, from West Indies Records, to Dynamic Sound, to Randy's studio. We always run the session the same day, sometime I do it first and them him do it after. So sometime you'd find that we have music on the same tape!"[13] Perry swiftly consolidated his reputation as a talented songwriter and a brilliantly eccentric producer. He scored early commercial successes during 1969: "People Funny Boy"; the Inspirations' "Tighten Up"; and, especially, a instrumental remake of Fats Domino's "Sick and Tired" titled "Return of Django," featuring veteran tenor saxophonist Val Bennett.[14] The musicians backing most of these productions were the first edition of Perry's Upsetters, and included Hux Brown on electric guitar, Winston Wright on organ, Gladstone Anderson on piano, Clifton Jackson or Jackie Jackson on electric bass, and Lloyd Adams or Hugh Malcolm on drums.[15]

Most of the early Upsetter productions were either originals, instrumentals, novelty songs, or covers of American pop hits, with production values fairly typical of British and American popular music of the period. But Perry's experimental streak was already in evidence by 1967–68. For example, he was one of the earliest producers to exploit the more creative possibilities of versioning. As early as 1967, Perry had released the song "Run For Cover," accompanied by a B-side instrumental version of the same track. He would also release "Set Them Free," an alternate spoken-word vocal over the same rhythm track, which presents a mock court case in which Perry as attorney defends the interests of the ghetto rude boys and sufferers, and the black race in general.[16] While backward tape manipulation was a new and important element of progressive rock albums such as the Beatles' *Sgt. Pepper's Lonely Hearts Club Band* and the Jimi Hendrix Experience's *Axis: Bold as Love* (both 1967), Perry used the flip side of Burt Walters's 1968 cover of the Drifters' "Honey Love" to reprise the original rhythm track, while Walters's vocals were played in reverse; the B-side version was accordingly titled "Evol Yenoh." On Walters's cover of Bob Dylan's "Blowin' in the Wind," Perry overdubs wind effects for the duration of the song, and on his own "People Funny Boy," he overdubs the sound of a baby's crying, to reinforce lyrics depicting a "crybaby" jealous of another's professional success. Perry's own "What A Botheration" vocal features a mix that foreshadows the evolution of his production style over the next ten years. He uses a rapid echo effect (different than that found on his production of other vocalists) to help distinguish his own vocal/sonic persona, and uses reverb to place the backing vocals a spooky distance behind the lead. The effect is very similar to what he would achieve with somewhat more sophisticated equipment ten years later, on his productions of artists such as the Congos.[17] These recordings demonstrate that his idiosyncratic vision of production was already in place.

African Herbsmen: Lee Perry and the Wailers

Those were dynamite sessions, man. Them deh recordings is like, speechless, timeless music. The Wailers didn't even want to record anywhere else than at Randy's because it was a sound, a particular sound that we had and they had captured it. Especially Perry had captured it and he didn't want to work anywhere else.[18]
—Producer Clive Chin to the author, 2000

They was ready to play that kinky, funny idea that I had.[19]
—Lee Perry

While he had produced several hits since striking out on his own, Perry's arrival as an independent producer was undeniably his partnership with the vocal trio of Bob Marley, Peter Tosh, and Bunny "Wailer" Livingstone—collectively known as the Wailers. The partnership lasted only from 1970 to 1971, but resulted in much of the era's most culturally conscious reggae. Inspired by the growing presences of African and Caribbean nationalism and the vision of Rastafari, the Perry/Wailers material is credited with pushing the sounds and sentiments of Rastafari to the fore of Jamaican popular music.[20] Despite the individual Wailers' subsequent international stardom, many still consider their Perry-produced work the most powerful of their careers as recording artists, and the last time their music was consistently played on Jamaica's sound systems.[21] The actual composer(s) of several of these tracks has been acrimoniously disputed by Perry and the various Wailers for years, but this likely reflects the closeness of collaboration as much as any after-the-fact skullduggery; it seems both artists and producer benefitted equally from the creative partnership.

Besides the combination of Perry's production and songwriting skills with the singing, playing, and songwriting talents of the Wailers, the partnership also resulted in Perry's pairing of the Wailers with an up-and-coming studio band created around the sibling drum & bass team of Carlton "Carlie" Barrett and his brother Aston "Familyman" Barrett (the group also included guitarists Alva Lewis and Ranford Williams, and organist Glen Adams).[22] As the second-generation Upsetters, they brought a new edge to Perry's productions. Carlton took the syncopation of rock steady drumming, slowed it down to match the tempo of his brother Aston's lumbering bass lines, funked it up via the influence of American R&B drummers like Clyde Stubblefield and Ziggy Modeliste, and drew on Rastafarian Nyabinghi drumming to give an African inflection. The signature sound of Carlie Barrett's trademark timbale roll echoing into reverberating space remains a signature sound bytes of 1970s reggae.

Most of the Perry/Wailers material was recorded at Randy's with Errol Thompson engineering; as producer, however, Perry was central in shaping the sound. The best-known material from this period includes songs like "Duppy Conqueror," "Small Axe," and "Don't Rock My Boat" — cleanly produced, clear-sounding tracks competitive according to the commercial standards of the day. But Perry pursued a less conventional sonic vision on tracks such as "It's Alright," "No Water," and Peter Tosh's "400 Years" and "No Sympathy," infusing the music with a mixture of ideas drawn from soul and Rastafarian Nyabinghi drumming.

Lee "Scratch" Perry on the Mix I
Wailers: "It's Alright," "No Sympathy"

Bob Marley sings a lonely, nocturnal theme on "It's Alright." The song is introduced by a bluesy guitar figure that settles into a midtempo, Nyabinghi-derived groove on D[7] in which the chordal instruments are played more as percussion than anything else. The foundation of the groove is layed down by Peter Tosh, whose status as a reggae icon has overshadowed his talent as one of the music's most inventive rhythm guitarists. Tosh beats quarter-note time on the muted, choked strings of his guitar while Carlton Barrett doubles him with a straight four pulse on the snare. Family Man plays an ascending R&B bass line reminiscent of James Brown's "Cold Sweat," loosely doubled by the organ, while Alva Lewis's wah-wah lead guitar noodles throughout to provide melodic counterpoint.

Tosh takes the lead on "No Sympathy," in which the listener is dropped into a groove-in-progress that comes across as a slowed and typically (for Tosh) brooding take on the rhythm pattern of Diana Ross and the Supremes' 1968 song "Reflections," refracted through the syntax of Nyabinghi percussion.[23] Tosh's voice hovers ominously over a barren soundscape, shadowed by the sorrowful voices of Marley and Livingstone. His rhythm guitar line is played through a wah-wah pedal, marking the second beat of each measure while Marley interjects a scratching pickup phrase to each measure on second guitar that exactly mirrors the role of the Nyabinghi repeater drum. Family Man's bass throbs percussively, changing its pattern to "walk" in double time on the bridge section in a style typical of Motown's James Jamerson. Departing from the typical offbeat "shuffle" pattern, the organ stitches out a straight eighth-note march that itself sounds more derived from Nyabinghi drumming than from typical reggae keyboard practice. Similarly, the drum set part is built around a two-beat pattern that replicates the role of the *funde*, the bass drum in the Nyabinghi ensemble.

Besides the structural influence of Nyabinghi drumming, what seems equally evident on these two tracks is the centrality of percussion sonorities to Perry's production aesthetic during this period. The cloudy, low end mix emphasizes the music's pulsating undercurrent, and Perry simultaneously uses the mixing board to realize the latent percussive potential of instruments like the electric guitar and electric organ. Thus, the scratchy rhythm guitar became virtually indistinguishable in the mix from the strident hand drums, the plodding bass virtually indistinguishable from the thumping bass drum, and the ringing lead guitar virtually indistinguishable from the metallic sounds of the cowbell and hi-hat cymbals. In effect, Perry fashioned a production value that evokes some sort of electrified hand drumming ensemble; in so doing, he was able to make the ensemble sound as if it were ebbing and flowing hypnotically. He described the desired effect: "When the people hear what I-man do to them, they hear a different beat, a slower beat, a waxy beat, like you stepping in glue. And dem hear a different bass, a rebel bass, coming at you like sticking a gun."[24]

Upsetting Station, 1969–1973

The first dub that really exposed, is that tune what we did for Lee "Scratch" Perry called "Clint Eastwood." And then Duke Reid send for us when him hear that vibes and we did one they called "Lock Jaw." And then dub hit the road you know, 'til it get international. —Aston "Familyman" Barrett to the author, 2003

Since his days at Studio One, Perry had his finger on the public's pulse, versioning hot rhythm tracks for their radio and dancehall potential. When he and the Wailers parted company in 1971 after two tempestuous years,

Perry lost not only his star vocalists but his star session players as well (the Barrett brothers left with the Wailers).[25] Nonetheless, Perry continued to work profitably with other vocalists, including Dave Barker and Junior Byles; this period is also notable for his cutting and versioning a sizable batch of instrumental tracks that provide important insight into his particular vision of dub music. Some of these tracks had been recorded with or prior to the Wailers team, while later tracks were recorded with the shifting cast of Upsetters who replaced the Barrett brothers.[26] David Katz cites 1969 in particular as a year of popular organ instrumentals that spotlighted the talents of sessions players such as Jackie Mittoo, Gladstone Anderson, and Winston Wright.[27] During the early 1970s Perry was leading the Upsetters, alternately featuring Anderson and Wright, through sessions at Randy's and Dynamic, producing Jamaican takes on organ-driven soul music of the type played by Booker T. and the MGs and the Meters. References to soul music abound, including riffs, licks, and songs copped from the Meters ("Sophisticated Cissy" on "Medical Operation"), the James Brown band ("The Popcorn"), and the Stax/Volt label (Eddie Floyd's "Knock on Wood").[28] Many of these tracks, such as "French Connection," "Cold Sweat," and "Live Injection," were uptempo organ features clearly aimed at the dance floor, using soul to articulate the funky side of reggae. On Perry's production of some of the Upsetters' more moody, minimalist rhythms, however, the production atmosphere is often as important as the musical structure; many of Perry's early mixes seem as much explorations of different sound atmospheres as they are distinct "songs" in any traditional sense. Also notable were Perry's crude tape compositions like "Connection" and "Kill Them All": irreverent, Frank Zappa–esque collages of several different performances in which abrupt splices violate the dance- and pop-friendly conventions of tonality, groove, tempo, and thematic continuity.[29]

Another similarity with Frank Zappa is how Perry uses the studio to insert himself as producer into the music through a variety of bizarre skits, monologues, and song introductions. Usually, his voice reverberated with silly-sinister echo suggesting he was speaking from some strange secret cave, subterranean laboratory, or tropical treehouse. Clearly, he was beginning to embrace the recording studio's potential as a creative and not merely documentary tool. Later, with the opening of his own studio, Perry's eccentric vision coalesced and he would begin to craft the particular type of sound for which he would become famous; still, his later lofty achievements as a producer and sound sculptor are rooted in the various sonic atmospheres he crafted around the Upsetters between 1968 and 1973.

Dub Revolution: 1972–1974

Tubby come to meet me, 'cause him was looking for adventure. . . . He was brilliant. I thought he was my student, maybe he thought I was his student, but it makes no matter. I'm not jealous.[30]

For obvious reasons, the collaborative work of Perry and King Tubby was a significant step in the evolution of dub music. The combination of Perry's fertile imagination, King Tubby's electronics expertise, and both men's willingness to experiment ensured that the benefit of their collaboration was mutual. The first fruits of their work, produced between 1972 and 1974, were mainly a string of B-side dub mixes recorded by Perry at Randy's and Dynamics, and remixed by Perry and Tubby at the latter's recently constructed home studio in Waterhouse. Together, they reworked productions by Perry's star vocalists such as Leo Graham, Junior Byles, and others. According to Philip Smart, Perry was also the only producer to lay down a rhythm track at Tubby's studio: "One of the innovations Scratch did at Tubbs that I don't think anyone else did, was he actually recorded a whole rhythm track at Tubbs. The drum set could barely fit in the voice room. You have the drummer out in the bedroom but the musicians in the control room and they plug in direct. The drummer only had like the kick drum, snare, and hi-hat. I don't know if it even came out, but I remember doing it and plugging in the bass directly to the board and recording it that way."[31]

The influence of King Tubby on Perry's sound during this period is reflected in the similarity between the dub sides Tubby mixed with Perry, and those released concurrently under Tubby's own name, on Bunny Lee–produced LPs such as *Dub From the Roots* and *The Roots of Dub* (both 1975). While working with Tubby, Perry's dubs conformed to a heavy drum & bass format typical of Tubby's work. Notable examples would include Tubby's mixes of Perry productions such as Jimmy Riley's "Woman's Gotta Have It" ("Woman's Dub") and Leo Graham's aforementioned "Three Blind Mice" ("Three Times Three").[32] While much of this material was actually mixed by Tubby, it still bore the unmistakable imprint of Perry and the Upsetters in the construction of the rhythms and the overall mood of the music.

Lee "Scratch" Perry on the Mix II
Lee Perry: "Bucky Skank" > Upsetters: "Black Panta"
The best-known collaboration between Perry and King Tubby is the *Blackboard Jungle Dub* LP (1973) which, while credited to the Upsetters, was actually mixed by both engineers.[33] The original mix, recently returned to circulation after having been unavailable for years, supposedly featured each engineer mixing on separate channels.[34] One of the earliest

all-dub albums to appear, *Blackboard* presented a selection of Perry's most popular rhythm tracks including those previously used for the Wailers, Junior Byles, the Gatherers, Shenley Duffus, U-Roy, and Perry himself. The album was also significant for another reason. In a genre marked by album compilations of B-side dub mixes, *Blackboard* was notable as the first self-contained, thematically consistent dub album.

In contrast to King Tubby's drum & bass aesthetic, *Blackboard* provides a contrasting example of Perry's additive tendency in mixing. The title track is built from a midtempo roots riddim in A minor that sounds derived from the Temptations' 1972 soul hit "Papa Was A Rolling Stone," and that had been previously used for Perry's "Bucky Skank" vocal. The way that Perry overhauled the basic rhythm and textures of "Bucky Skank" indicates much about his working process and its evolution. The original rhythm featured Perry vocalizing over a fairly austere rhythm track and, aside from the occasional novel effect (in this case an ascending, zipper-sounding glissando by the electric guitarist and an echo effect applied to Perry's voice), the production was fairly straightforward, with minimal sound processing.

The remix demonstrates the appropriateness of the title's "jungle" image. The soundspace has been significantly expanded through the application of reverb, and the playback speed has been slowed a bit, resulting in just enough low end distortion to give the music a greater weight without seriously compromising pitch definition. The overall rhythmic texture has also been thickened by feeding parts through a delay unit to achieve a subtle variation of the rhythmic intensification frequent in King Tubby's work. The first minute is fairly free in feel, with Lloyd "Tin Leg" Adams's distorted drum fills echoing slightly out-of-time about the soundscape, anchored by Aston Barrett's repeating bass line. A brooding flute and trumpet theme replaces the original vocal and figures prominently in the mix; the instrumental tracks have also been overlaid with prerecorded sound effects and Perry's eccentric vocalizing. The overall effect is one of a semielectronic tropical jazz-sound collage, with the engineers complementing the improvisation in the original performance through their own improvisation at the mixing console.

The probable derivation from "Papa Was a Rolling Stone" also implies "Black Panta" as a notable example of the blaxploitation influence on Jamaican music in the 1970s. Although it was never actually featured on a film soundtrack, "Papa" is, musically speaking, probably the paradigmatic blaxploitation track in terms of the way the urbanized blues impulse of James Jamerson's stark bass line has been given cinematic scope by the lush horn, string, and vocal arrangements of Paul Riser and the overall production of Norman Whitfield. In fact, the extended album version of "Papa" shares some very interesting qualities with Jamaican music, and explains in part why the rhythm groove might have been a natural for adaptation by Jamaican musicians; the episodic orchestral scoring above Jamerson's steady bass pattern closely mirrors the fragmented quality of dub mixes. [35] "Black Panta" boosts the bass presence and slows it to match the tempo of Jamaica, while the cinematic scope is provided by the wildly atmospheric mixing of Perry and King Tubby. In general, the nourish overtones of blaxploitation soundtracks and urban realist songs resonated in the tense climate of West Kingston—undoubtedly a factor in the frequent reggae adaptations of the rhythm patterns of soul songs such as War's "Slippin' Into Darkness" and Isaac Hayes's "Do Your Thing." [36]

The Black Ark Studio

Perry completed many innovative works in conjunction with other producers and engineers, but he would need his own workspace in order to realize his creative vision fully. While he would continue to work with Tubby and record at Randy's over the next year and a half, Perry began building a studio in the yard behind his home in Washington Gardens that he christened the "Black Ark." Clive Chin recalls that an upgrading of Randy's was an important catalyst for Perry's studio: "You see, Perry believe in a certain sound, and he cyaan get away from that. But we renovated the studio in '74, and we decided to get a new board and go 24-track. Perry thought that wasn't a good idea because what it meant was that we might lose the sound. He pleaded with my father . . . and my old man told him that the board was already bought and there was no way he was going to do any changes on it. So, Perry just got furious and decided not to use the studio anymore. That's why he went and opened Black Ark." [37] Speaking with me thirty years later, Perry still recalled the incident in fairly bitter terms, blaming the renovation for the eventual demise of Randy's: "Them fuck up the studio, them change it. You have something good, and because the other man have something bigger than you, you want to fuck up everything. Because of that changing the board, them have to leave Jamaica, and run away to America. [The music] was a miracle. And them want to change my miracle, so them get fucked. It's because them change the board." [38]

According to both David Katz and Lloyd Bradley, the wiring at the Black Ark was outlined by King Tubby, and installed by Errol Thompson. [39] The studio was completed in late 1973 as a four-track facility, initially with fairly rudimentary equipment. Katz details the studio as originally configured with "a quarter-inch four-track Teac 3340 for the recording of new material and a quarter-inch two-track Teac on which to mix down." The mixing desk was "a silver Alice board, a small machine with limited capabilities." The studio also contained "an electric piano and a cheap copy of [an electric] clavinet, a Marantz amplifier and speaker for guitar or keyboard use and a small drum kit placed on a riser. He also had a Grantham spring reverb and a tape-echo unit for effects."[40] Dave Hendley described the atmosphere at the Black Ark:

Quiet. Really mellow. That studio was really built for Scratch's personal use, so you've not got people passing by to hang out if they haven't got work there to do. It wasn't such a great meeting place as Tubby's was. Tubby's, everybody would pass through Tubby's at some time. Whereas Black Ark was in Scratch's back garden on Cardiff Crescent. And that was quite a posh suburb in the '70s, like the other side of the gully [from West Kingston]. It was another world, quite residential. It was quite a ways out of central Kingston, and quiet and more tranquil. Whenever we went round there, Scratch was in the studio. He was always doing something. . . . [The studio] was one of those kinds of places where you went in there, and there was bright sunlight outside, but it was quite dark in there. You stepped out of one world into Scratch's world. Once you stepped in there, you had no daylight. You had no sense geographically of where you were. And it had a kind of heavy atmosphere.[41]

The Black Ark was the final piece in the puzzle that was Lee Perry's studio genius. It allowed him a workspace tailored to his experimental whims, and it was here he that would craft what many consider his most influential work. Junior Murvin, Leo Graham, and Max Romeo stepped to the fore as Perry's main vocalists during this period, while the studio's first commercial success was Junior Byles' "Curly Locks" (1973), which was much simpler and more minimal in sound than the work he had realized earlier at studios like Dynamics, Randy's and Tubby's. A defining sound element of "Curly Locks" and other early Black Ark tracks (such as Junior Byles's "Long Way") is the offbeat keyboard pattern, played on an electric instead of an acoustic piano; the sound is consequently much dryer, and the attack softer, than the typical acoustic piano sound.[42]

Perry laid the groundwork for his Black Ark dub work with a series of atmospheric, instrumental albums during 1974 and 1975 that seem to indicate that he was gaining his bearings in his new studio before venturing back onto his sonic limb; as with "Curly Locks," the sound is much simpler and stripped down compared to profuse works such as *Blackboard Jungle Dub,* and even compared to some of the early Upsetter LPs such as *Eastwood Rides Again.* For example, *Cloak and Dagger* (1974) offers an album's worth of atmospheric, instrumental jazz-reggae of a fairly traditional format. Gradually, however, Perry's additive approach assumed the foreground on LPs such as *Kung Fu Meets the Dragon* (1975), in which rhythm tracks are reworked through the addition of electronic squeals, dissonant harmonica, incidental percussion, Augustus Pablo's melodica, and

Perry's own vocalizing. The more comfortable Perry became in his new studio, the more layered and eccentric his sound became. The same mixing style, with the aforementioned clavinet added, can be heard on many of Perry's concurrent vocal releases such as Linval Thompson's "Kung Fu Man" and Junior Byles's "Cutting Razor."[43]

Lee "Scratch" Perry on the Mix III

Leo Graham: "Black Candle" > Upsetters: "Bad Lamp" > Leo Graham: "Doctor Demand" > Upsetters: "Black Bat" > Leo Graham: "Big Tongue Buster" > Upsetters: "Bus-a-Dub"

Perry's mixing palette between 1970 and 1974 was particularly colorful: typically built around the substitution and replacing of parts rather than the soundscaping approach of King Tubby, the juxtaposition of fragments of previous versions made much of his work in this period seem like sound collages. A series of versions from the *Public Jestering* compilation demonstrates his colorful way of elaborating his rhythm tracks.[44] Known island-wide as a talented and eccentric dancer, Perry was known for favoring syncopated, "bumpity" riddims, and the following succession of versions also shows that this was accomplished not only through instrumental arrangement, but just as often through post-production. On Leo Graham's up-tempo "Black Candle," Perry punched the original rhythm guitar and organ tracks out for the first two beats of each measure, punching them back in for the second two beats; the standard, of course, was to play through the entire measure. This created a pushing-and-pulling rhythmic tension that is the most distinctive feature of the song. The second version, titled "Bad Lamp," is a dub version introduced by Perry quoting from the Bible (Psalms 1:1), after which he assumes the role of an action painter of sound: throwing random fragments of Graham's original vocal, organ, and guitar tracks upon a canvas of drum & bass. The mixing board here seemed to become an extension of Perry's own jittery nervous impulses, with him cutting in and out specific instruments after allowing them to sound for a fraction of a gesture.

Graham returns for the "Doctor Demand" vocal take, a third version to the rhythm featuring a similar lyrical theme to "Black Candle," with the clavinet playing a buzzing counter–bass line to the electric bass. The harmonic instruments have been retooled, with a wah-wah rhythm guitar replacing the previous guitar track. Nonpitched, feedback-type sounds whistle across the soundscape at intervals, while the voice of the DJ Prince Jazzbo surfaces each time Perry drops the rhythm out. The fourth version is a dub version of "Doctor Demand" titled "Black Bat": similar to the previous take but with a legato keyboard bass replacing the syncopated phrasing of the earlier keyboard part. Graham's original "Black Candle" vocal returns in fragments for "Big Tongue Buster," the fifth version and an alternate dub version of the first take, with an unidentified DJ (possibly Charlie Ace) adding overdubbed commentary. Otherwise, it is essentially the same as the first version. "Big Tongue Buster" is reprised for the sixth version, titled "Bus-A-Dub." With the previous vocals of Graham and the DJ fragmented over a drum & bass foundation, this version is closest to the standard for dub mixes.

Into the Heart of the Ark

Although Perry had parted company with the Wailers in 1971, he continued to benefit from his earlier work with Bob Marley, who had since been signed by Chris Blackwell's Island Records and transformed into an international superstar.[45] Around 1976, Perry himself signed a production deal with Island for worldwide distribution of his work. Most immediately, the new deal allowed him to upgrade his facilities. He had already replaced the Alice console with a model made by Soundcraft,[46] and this model was later augmented by the two sound processing effects that would define his Black Ark sound: Mutron's Bi-Phase phase-shifting unit, and Roland's famous Space Echo delay unit. The New Jersey–based Musitronics company was among the most adventurous manufacturers of mass-market sound processors during the 1970s and their Bi-Phase was the largest phase-shifting device offered at the time, surpassing smaller units by MXR (Phase 45, Phase 90, Phase 100) and Electro-Harmonix (Small Stone). The characteristic "swirling" sound of the phase shifter is actually a filtering effect produced by mixing a primary signal with its own delayed (out of phase) replication. The result is that specified frequencies are cancelled at a predetermined and cyclical rate. The largest phase shifter on the market, the Bi-Phase actually housed two phase shifters that could be employed separately or in tandem, and that could be triggered and adjusted by an attached foot pedal. In Jeremy Marre's 1977 film *Roots, Rock, Reggae*, Perry is seen engineering a session at the Black Ark, manipulating the Bi-Phase (on its Super Phasing setting) as if it were a musical instrument and making the kinds of facial grimaces typically reserved for lead guitarists.[47] As with most of his equipment, Perry favored the most extreme applications. The vocals on a Black Ark remix of the Inspirations' 1968 "Tighten Up" were routed through such thick phase-shifting until they sounded like a chorus of strangulated voices.[48] Perry often applied this same effect to horns; on Junior Murvin's "Tedious,"[49] Zap Pow's "River,"[50] and his own "Scratch the Dub Organizer,"[51] Perry's phase shifter reduces their majestic brassiness to the thin sonority of a kazoo. Perry's application of phase-shifting to various instruments (particularly the offbeat rhythm guitar and the hi-hat cymbals) is the most recognizable feature of his work at the Black Ark.

The Japanese Roland Company manufactured several models of their famous Space Echo unit, but the most popular remains the RE-201, introduced in 1973, and used by Perry extensively in his studio. The Space Echo was a particularly flexible device: it housed a tape delay and a spring reverb in the same unit, and as such was able to provide a unique variety of combined rhythmic (delay) and spatial (reverb) effects. Its affordable price made it a frequent choice in many studios during the 1970s, and its characteristic sound can be heard on numerous New Age recordings, popular recordings, and science fiction soundtracks of the period. Perry relied heavily upon the Roland unit for both reverb and delay effects, and its typically extreme application in his hands can be heard on reverb-saturated mixes such as Devon Iron's "Vampire,"[52] and Watty Burnett's "Open the Gate." [53] These tracks recall the spatial grandiosity of Phil Spector's "wall of sound" production concept, taken several steps further.[54]

It was the combination of these two effects that created the swirling, aquatic sound of Perry's classic Black Ark productions, and these upgradings inspired Perry to some of his greatest producing heights. By 1976, Perry had "found his sound," and his work during this period is considered the crystallization of his studio wizardry and of his keen insight into the international market. Mikey Dread remembered Perry in this period as a producer who was "a genius too in a different sense because he can visualize certain things as a man who travel over the world before most other artists. He could tell what would be worthwhile to be released in England or in Europe more than somebody who just been in Jamaica all their life. So Scratch have a edge above certain people because he was always traveling."[55]

Between 1976 and 1979, Perry would achieve his commercial apex and score international commercial successes with albums like Max Romeo's "War Inna Babylon,"[56] Junior Murvin's "Police and Thieves,"[57] and Susan Cadogan's cover of Millie Jackson's tortured 1974 soul ballad "Hurt So Good."[58] The vocalists with whom he worked most frequently and profitably during this period were Romeo, Murvin, and Leo Graham. Junior Byles was largely absent from the later phase of Perry's Black Ark work, having suffered a mental breakdown of sorts precipitated by the death of Haile Selassie in 1975, and lived in intermittent seclusion thereafter. But Perry's vision as a producer was so strong at this time that he could seemingly mold any unformed talent to his formula. Indeed, he would achieve remarkable successes—in artistic if not always commercial terms—with vocalists rarely heard of before or since: Junior Dread, Peter and Paul Lewis, Bunny and Ricky, Carlton Jackson, James

Booms, Winston Heywood, and Shaumark and Robinson, among many others. Even when Perry merely engineered sessions for outside artists who only wanted to cut basic tracks at the Black Ark, the music recorded there never lost its distinctive sound in the hands of subsequent producers or engineers at other studios. Parts of Hugh Mundell's *Africa Music Be Free By 1983*, Augustus Pablo's *East of the River Nile*, and Max Romeo's *Revelation Time* are all non-Perry productions recorded at the Black Ark that are nevertheless indelibly marked with Perry's sonic stamp. The same is true for Perry's production of foreign artists such as Robert Palmer, or Paul and Linda McCartney, for whom he produced several tracks in 1977, using the Upsetters as backing musicians.[59]

In Marre's aforementioned film, Perry is shown at the Black Ark console, dancing while engineering a session for an ad hoc vocal group (essentially a "Black Ark All-Star chorus" comprising Junior Murvin and members of the Congos and Heptones) singing an untitled song for the assembled film crew. Flinging his hands from the console to the various sound processors, Perry is doing a "live mix"; that is, applying sound processing and mixing the track directly to the master tape at the same time as it is being recorded by the musicians, instead of mixing at a later time after the performance. This live approach to the mixing process is unique to Perry's work and is recalled by many of the musicians that worked at the Black Ark, such as Sly Dunbar: "He was actually mixing the dub while it was being recorded, he wasn't waiting until after the riddim was done. He was dubbing the things in and out inside [the control room], putting on effects and all these things."[60] Susan Cadogan similarly recalled, "When he's dubbing he stands. He'd put on the tape and he'd stand in front of the machine and he'd dance and fling the things and take out and put in—right when I'm singing it. That's how he got the dub feel."[61] The habit of dancing while mixing, as well as the occasional practice of mixing the music as it was being recorded clearly demonstrates that Perry felt himself *within* the music, as opposed to doing something *to* it after the fact. More than any other engineer mixing dub, Perry's Black Ark work suggests the mood of an engineer completely absorbed within the sound world he is fashioning; this is ecstatic music created at the mixing board.

As Steve Barrow notes, as much as the early Upsetters LPs had paved the way for dub, the Black Ark never became a center for dub in the same way that Tubby's did.[62] Unlike King Tubby, whose forte was mainly versioning the music of many different producers who left their tapes to be remixed, Perry was involved in his own music at all levels, from the creation of the music itself, to the recording of it, and onto the remix stage. This is not to imply that Perry was less committed to dub as a form that the others; he merely took a different approach that probably went some way toward reconciling his creative eccentricity with commercial necessity. Where King Tubby's deconstructions were generally and pragmatically confined to B-sides of singles, Perry often produced his A-side vocal cuts as otherwordly landscapes as surreal and spaced-out as Tubby's most unconventional dub work. It was through this method of working that he created three of his most enduring contributions to dub music and earned him his legendary status as a studio innovator.

Lee "Scratch" Perry on the Mix IV
The Congos: *Heart of the Congos*

Perry's most widely-hailed work of dub-influenced mixing is probably the Congos' *Heart of the Congos* album (1977).[63] Over the rootsy rhythms of an all-star edition of the Upsetters, the ethereal vocals of Cedric Myton, Roydel Johnson, and Watty Burnett fuse echoes of Rasta chants, Afro-Protestant hymns, and 1960s soul harmonies—all given Perry's fullest studio treatment. The producer crafted a corrosive aesthetic here, in which songs swirl and rustle beneath a patina of phase-shifting, white noise, and tape hiss. The entire sound is best described as aquatic. Lead vocalist Roy Johnson's vocals are treated with a repeating echo as he trades call-and-response lines with a reverberating chorus of Cedric Myton and Watty Burnett. Heavy drum & bass patterns anchor swirling atmospheres of phase-shifted sound punctuated by dropouts both accidental and intentional. At the mixing board, Perry routes small, staccato percussion through echo units and transforms them into stuttering, legato gestures. Cymbal crashes resound across the soundscape, elongated by reverb into ambient streams of metallic sound. Distorted, offbeat piano and guitar parts are routed through echo units and transformed into scraping percussion textures that arc across spectra of phase-shifted tone color. The overall aquatic effect is heightened by an intermittent cowbell repeating with echo and ringing like a buoy, as well as by layers of phase-shifted tape noise that recall the sound of surf crashing against the shore. The juxtaposition of all these layers of sound results in a strata of ambient percussion that rustles in free-time above the soundscape.

George Faith: *To Be A Lover*

Because it has been out of print for many years, George Faith's *To Be A Lover* (1977) is one of the lesser-known works from this period of Perry's oeuvre.[64] Nonetheless, it is also one of Perry's most monumental works. Composed mainly of Faith's covers of songs by soul singers such as Wilson Pickett, Lee Dorsey, Tyrone Davis, William Bell, and others, these covers are given a particularly psychedelic treatment by Perry. The collection is assembled around Faith's 1976 hit cover of William Bell's "I Forgot to Be Your Lover." Bell's original was recorded for Stax/Volt in 1968, during the company's "second great era" following the death of Otis Redding in 1967. The song was a typically earthy Stax ballad, running a little over two minutes, and in which Bell's singing was shadowed by the gently ornamental rhythm guitar chording of guitarist Steve Cropper.[65] The body of the song is built on a chord progression of vi–I–IV–ii; like many reggae covers from the 1970s on, however, the Faith/Perry version (retitled "To Be A Lover") has been harmonically flattened so that the entire tune is now comprised of just the I and IV chords. Furthermore, the Upsetters' studio performance of the track remains dynamically static for the duration of the performance. So passive is the band track, in fact, that it approximates the aesthetic of a tape loop. What has been elaborated in the absence of the original chord sequence and dynamic variation in the band performance is the production. Throughout the entire performance, Perry constantly refigures the song surface through heavy phase shifting applied to the electric piano and rhythm guitar. With some versions running nearly ten minutes in length, "To Be A Lover" amounts to a study in timbral manipulation through phase-shifting.

"To Be A Lover" may be the album's best-known song, but not necessarily its most inventive. A hybrid lyric comprising Wilson Pickett's "In the Midnight Hour" and Lee Dorsey's "Ya-Ya" is given a similar treatment, as is Tyrone Davis's "Turn Back the Hands of Time." Besides being adapted to the reggae "steppers" rhythm, most of these performances also feature slightly altered lyrics and song arrangements, possibly for copyright reasons. The numerous and subtly interwoven layers of sound in these songs arguably tie into the spiritual ethos of the times. The romantic yearning of the originals has been transformed into something much more thematically ambiguous through sumptuous textures and undulating song surfaces that impart an erotic aura to these performances, but are simultaneously deeply psychedelic in a manner suggesting a higher devotion of some kind. At the height of his mixing wizardry in the late 1970s, in fact, Perry's work would fit partially into a stream of otherworldly sounding, "country" reggae associated with groups such as Culture, early Burning Spear, and the Wailing Souls, who evoke such a feeling through use of open vocal harmonies, repetition, and the plaintive style of singing associated with rural churches. What Perry added was his innovative use of sound mixing to evoke the otherworldly sensation.

Heart of the Congos and *To Be A Lover* are dense, surreal works in which Perry essentially offered the world his tropical vision of psychedelia. Both reflect the breadth of Perry's studio vision and, even more than his other work of the period, reflect his elevation of echo, distortion, and even tape noise as creative musical values. In fact Perry would elaborate this type of mixing on tracks such as Junior Murvin's 1977 "Cross-Over," in which he submerges the Upsetters' heavy roots rhythm in an ocean of pure ambient noise while Murvin wails on top for black cultural liberation.[66] The "ocean" metaphor is actually apt; Perry later explained to me that the mix of "Cross-Over" was meant to evoke just such an sensation: "that one makes you go walk over the ocean, you go walk on the sea."[67]

The Upsetters: *Super Ape*

In addition to producing dub-influenced vocal albums, Perry also recorded a relatively straightforward dub album. The Upsetters 1976 album *Super Ape* is often considered one of the defining statements of the genre, demonstrating the additive approach that distinguished Perry's mixing style from the deconstructive, drum & bass approach taken at studios like King Tubby's.[68] A densely layered work of mixing, *Super Ape* is essentially a collection of thematic and programmatic dubs on which Perry generally reworked tracks by adding material to preexisting backing tracks. Vocals (lead, background, and DJ) and horn lines were often added not as elements to be fragmented, but as clear and fairly linear thematic statements. "Zion's Blood" is a version of Devon Irons's "When Jah Come" with added horns. "Dub Along" is an updating of Perry's earlier "Come Along," in which Perry has fleshed out the original version by adding the vocal trio Full Experience to sing additional lyrics.[69] The track hovers between a song and a dub; the lyrics are not developed enough to constitute a "song" in the typical sense, but neither is the production approach deconstructive in a way that would typically justify the description "dub." In fact it might be argued that the retooled "Dub Along" is much neater than its earlier incarnation. Other songs like "Curly Dub" (no relation to Byles's "Curly Locks"), which offer fairly straightforward instrumental treatments of preexisting tracks, are subjected to the same additive approach, with the combination of sound processing and additional material stretching them beyond their basic jazz-derived song format of theme–solos–theme. This is not to claim that *Super Ape* lacks any of the essential elements of dub practice. On "Croaking Lizard" (Prince Jazzbo's DJ version of Max Romeo's "Chase the Devil") and "Black Vest" (Jazzbo's version of Romeo's "War Inna Babylon"), for example, Perry fragments the lyrics in typical dub fashion while using the Roland unit to reduce the remaining vocals to a stream of unintelligible, liquified exclamation.

Can the tracks on *Super Ape* actually be considered dubs? Or are they more accurately described as dubbed-up instrumentals along the lines of LPs such as Augustus Pablo's *East of the River Nile*? It is interesting to note that as much as he had focused on instrumentals during the first years of the decade, Perry's focus changed to cutting dub sides following his work with King Tubby. Possibly, the realization that a new form of electronic improvisation could be performed on the mixing console offered, for him, more interesting possibilities; he cut very few straight instrumentals during the later years at Black Ark. Perry did, however, continue to credit his dub sides to the Upsetters, seemingly implying that in his conception, the dub form had grown directly out of the instrumental form.

The Black Ark became a center for both a particularly spiritual type of reggae and for sound experimentation, and many musicians recall working with Perry during this period as the creative height of their careers. Sly Dunbar recalled his Black Ark work as "one of the greatest times in the world!"[70] Mikey Dread felt that "Scratch was ingenious in that he just do some little things in his studio and create the vibes. And in Scratch environment, herbs would be burning every day—with the people there, and he's doing his mixing."[71] Max Romeo called his period with Perry "the best moments of my life" and described the producer's approach: "He makes sounds out of stones, he would hit two stones together. If the stone didn't give him the right sound he would pick up another stone until he get the right sound. He used empty bottles with utensils for percussion sounds. He was always trying to find sounds, different weird sounds."[72] Similarly to the way he accentuated the percussive undertones in the Wailers' music years earlier, Perry also continued to draw on Nyabinghi throughout his years at the Black Ark. Tracks like Perry's own "City Too Hot"[73] and the Meditations' "Houses of Parliament"[74] feature an order of what David Katz described as "radical Nyabinghi drummers" who had taken up residence at the Black Ark in 1977.[75] Perry would later extend this mood to its logical conclusion in his production of Nyabinghi drummer Ras Michael's "Love Thy Neighbor," in which Rasta liturgical drumming and chanting is augmented by electric guitars and keyboards and smeared with a thick layer of psychedelic haze.[76] One of Perry's most fascinating projects during this period was the *African Roots* album, a collaboration between him and two stranded Congolese musicians (Seke Molenga and Kawo Kawongolo) who turned up at the Black Ark in 1977. Together, they created a hybrid of roots reggae and Congolese pop sung alternately in Lingala and Jamaican patwa, and given a wildly psychedelic Perry mix.[77]

*Anything, whether it moved or was stuck down, Scratch had written on absolutely
everything. . . . What really struck me then was the amount of time it must have
taken—like, time on your own, just writing on everything. Because some of it was
quite minute. And it wasn't just tagging something. It was quite small and deliberate lettering. None of it made any sense. The only thing I've ever seen like it is oc-
cult sort of things. I've seen some similar stuff on graves in New Orleans.*[78]
—Dave Hendley

*I think highly skilled or highly talented people have some eccentric habits, 'cause he
is strange. He writes on everything. I ask him, "Why you write up the place?" He
said, "Well, if you don't write, you wrong . . ."*
—Susan Cadogan

Over the five or so years of its operation, as Perry realized some of the
most distinctive music to come out of Jamaica, the Black Ark control room
and mixing console simultaneously grew into a virtual art installation with
photos, random objects, scrawled words, and other items that served a talis-
manic function for Perry's creative energy. He was certainly a reggae visionary: while Osbourne Ruddock and others were symbolizing their authority
by proclaiming themselves "king," "prince" and other British-derived titles
of royalty, Lee Perry was the first to rationalize his ambivalent relationship
with Western sound technology by assuming the role of the "mad" scientist
of sound. If the symbol of "science" was the Western sound technology
through which he created his art, the symbols of antiscientific madness were
inevitably drawn from stereotypes of neo-African antirationality such as the
Obeah tradition. This image of the "crazy" black sound engineer would
later be embraced by other engineers such as Scientist (Overton Brown),
Mad Professor (Neil Fraser), Peter Chemist, and others.

Of course, Perry took this type of behavior further than any of the others,
taming the technological monster through his personal brand of eccentric
mysticism and alchemy. Perry was known to run a studio microphone from
his console to a nearby palm tree, in order to record what he called the "living
African heartbeat."[79] He often "blessed" his recording equipment with mystical invocations and other icons of supernatural and spiritual power such as
burning candles and incense, whose wax and dust remnants were freely allowed to infest his electronic equipment. Perry was also known to blow
ganja smoke onto his tapes while recording, to clean the heads of his tape
machine with the sleeve of his T-shirt, to bury unprotected tapes in the soil
outside of his studio, and to spray them with a variety of fluids including
whiskey, blood, and urine, ostensibly to enhance their spiritual properties.[80]
In fact, Richard Henderson draws a direct correlation between the technical
decay of Perry's facility and the unique sounds he was able to realize from his
studio equipment.[81] In this case, Perry's "craziness" functioned to reanimate
the symbol of sound science with black personality and black spirituality,
drawn from a diverse array of ostensibly potent organic sources.

Over time, however, the "madness" became all too real, as the musical limits that Perry was pushing at this time increasingly seemed to mirror the boundaries of his sanity. As gloriously psychedelic as his Black Ark music grew during the heady days of reggae-gone-international, it nosedived into a bad trip as the decade wound down. Despite its innovative qualities, for example, the *African Roots* project, with its tremulous, frenetic soundscape and periodic "cow" sounds (later revealed to be an extremely intoxicated Perry groaning through an aluminum tube) does seem to suggest a precarious mental balance. There were several reasons for this decline. Possibly because of Perry's quirky experimenting, the Black Ark had never turned out local hits at the rate of other leading studios and producers like Channel One or Bunny Lee. Perry had resolutely resisted using old Treasure Isle or Studio One rhythms for his songs, effectively removing his music from the sound system/dancehall mainstream. Even given the mood of the times, it seems likely that his penchant for whimsical studio experimentation was at least partially at odds with the stylistic demands required of pop songs in the commercial reggae marketplace. This eccentricity probably made him more dependent on the international market and when Island Records refused four of his productions (The Congos' *Heart of the Congos*, Perry's own *Roast Fish, Collie Weed and Cornbread,* the Upsetters' *Return of the Super Ape,* and Seke Molenga and Kalo Kawongolo's *African Roots*) for reasons that remain unclear, it spelled the end of his deal with the company and the beginning of the decline of the Black Ark. The studio was basically nonfunctional after 1978, and between that year and 1983, Perry's career spiraled out of control under pressures of political violence, extortion attempts, and personal turmoil. When Dave Hendley made a return visit to the studio in 1979, he found a very different atmosphere:

> The tape machine and mixing desk still worked, but the part of the studio where the musicians played certainly didn't look in any state to be used. He had actually dug a hole in the ground, there was only about half a drum kit there. He was just doing all kinds of weird stuff. Having third-person conversations with himself or people he had made up. He had painted the whole studio—well, in fact, the whole of the building—with loads of tiny little crosses. There wasn't one surface that wasn't covered in paint or magic marker. And the name Pipecock Jackson kept coming up everywhere in different spellings. He went on about Pipecock Jackson a lot as if Pipecock Jackson was there, and you could never work out whether Scratch was Pipecock Jackson, or if he was some ghostly figure. Really strange behavior.[82]

There have been numerous accounts of these events but it seems that in several phases, Perry destroyed the Black Ark: first, by covering every surface with graffiti, and then by allowing the equipment to fall into disrepair. The building was ultimately destroyed by a fire in 1983.[83] Perry then left Jamaica for several points over the next several years: New York, London, and finally settling in Zurich, Switzerland. Although he has produced interesting work since then with producers within and outside of Jamaica (most notably Coxsone Dodd, Bullwackie Barnes, Adrian Sherwood, and Mad Professor), Perry hasn't had the same personal space in which to pursue his unique artistry. Without his own studio, he couldn't experiment with anywhere near the same freedom. He has spent the last twenty years roaming from continent to continent, reconstructing an image for himself as inspired madman—a walking, one-man art installation of reggae-inspired electronica. But his work from 1967 through 1980 remains an inspiration for musicians worldwide.

CHAPTER SIX

"Java" to "Africa"

Even had he never mixed a single dub version, Errol Thompson (1948–2004) would hold a secure place in reggae history. As chief engineer at two of the most important recording studios of the roots reggae era—Randy's and Joe Gibbs—he was responsible for committing much of the era's most significant music to tape. Thompson, who was praised by Bunny Lee as "one of the best engineers in Jamaica," was born in Kingston in 1941 and grew up in the Harbourview section of the city. His first engineering job was at Studio One where he worked as an apprentice alongside Sylvan Morris, and his first formal session was a voicing session for singer Max Romeo's controversial slackness song "Wet Dream." On this occasion, Bunny Lee had rented the studio as an independent producer:

E.T. was Morris's student at Coxsone studio. First tune that him voice, Coxsone was voicing it and Coxsone gone a bathroom and said "E.T., voice this tune here." And what E.T. voice was a tune with Maxie Romeo named "Wet Dream." That's the first tune E.T. voice and Coxsone want to wipe it off [because of the suggestive lyrics] and me said "No, you must be mad—me no wipe off tune, Jack!" Me and Coxsone was quarreling, and we had to call off the session and stop. Same "Wet Dream" go a England and stay 26 week inna the British chart![1]

Randy's Studio 17

Thompson's apprenticeship with Morris gave him a solid foundation in recording, and he was known as one of Jamaica's top engineers for live sessions. After a year at Studio One, he met producer Clive Chin at Choir School, which they both attended. Chin, who was born in 1954, is the son of Vincent and Pat Chin, owners of Randy's Studio 17, a recording facility located on the Parade in downtown Kingston. With electronics installed by Bill Garnett, Randy's opened its doors in the spring of 1968 as a two-track studio that was upgraded to four tracks after a couple of years, and eventually sixteen and twenty-four tracks by the mid-1970s. The studio rapidly became the most popular recording facility on the island, used by most of the major producers until its popularity was eclipsed by Channel One later in the decade. Chin remembers that Randy's "was *the* most prominent recording studio for a good number of years, right up until around the mid-'70s. We had guys like Lee Perry, Bunny Lee, Clancy Eccles, Derrick Harriott, Herman Chin-Loy, Sonia Pottinger. . . . I mean, we were so highly booked that we had to go 24–7 every week. We had to push our own productions to Sunday and give the producers and the artists time for themselves during the week."[2] Such was the studio's growing reputation that according to Chin, foreign artists were block-booking the facility for weeks at a time: "I can recall back around '69, when [singer-songwriter] Johnny Nash people dem came on board. That was the JAD years, when they had just signed [Bob] Marley to a songwriting contract. Them rented the studio for one month solid. And we had people like Hugh Masekela coming in from New York and Billy Price, Cissy Houston, all them big guys were coming in to record down there."[3] Chin even contends that Marley's early albums for Island Records would have been recorded at Randy's, had prior business commitments not intervened: "Bob asked me one time at 56 Hope Road: 'Clive, will your father lease me Randy's for a year to record for Island Records?' . . . Because he say Harry J has a leak, the studio had a leak. The only reason they use Harry J was because Harry was indebted to Blackwell for the studio board that they bought in England. That's the only reason why you saw *Natty Dread* and *Rastaman Vibration* recorded there. But deep down, me know say, Bob knew from Lee Perry days that the only place him could ever voice his voice was at Randy's."[4]

By 1971, Clive was making his first attempts at record production: "At that time you know I was just getting fully involved in the recording business, I was still going school at the time, coming home from school. Kids would go to like the football field, the cricket field, but I wasn't too athletic. I was more into the business aspect. . . . Errol and I was going a school call Choir School, right down 'pon North Street on South Camp Road. Choir School was a school designed for people to come there and sing. A lot of good singers pass through Choir School you know—Delroy Wilson, Tony Gregory, just to name a few. They all went to that school. That was way back about '67, somewhere between '66–'67. That's where I met Errol."[5] In time, the friendship between Chin and Thompson grew into a professional partnership, with Chin producing at Randy's and Thompson working the board as the studio's chief engineer. As such, "Errol T." worked with most of the leading Jamaican artists of his time, and was instrumental in capturing and crafting the sound of recorded reggae as the style developed through a period of rapid innovation during the early 1970s.

Thompson and Chin were part of the experimental vanguard out of which dub developed. If other engineers would pave the way for dub by omitting vocal tracks to create instrumental "rhythm versions," Thompson was reportedly among the first engineers to strip tracks further, to their drum & bass foundations. In Chin's account, "During the rock steady era, dem used to put out vocal tunes on one side, then an instrumental 'pon the B-side, whether it was organ or horns. In the early '70s now, they decide that well, we'll give them experiment on the B-side and me and Errol was one of the first."[6] In fact, Chin feels strongly that he and Thompson have yet to receive proper acknowledgment for their dub innovations:

. . . when you talk about creation of dub, you talking 'bout Errol Thompson & Clive Chin, 'cause me and Errol was one of the first . . . we throw in the rhythm every now and then, but mainly drum & bass. So, when we did that now and put it on the B-side of any vocal tune, people say "Ras!" You know, it new idea and everybody jump on the bandwagon. Including other producers like Bunny Lee and Lee Perry, Clancy and Niney, just to name a few of them. That's why when they talk about King Tubbys and how him create dub, I don't agree with that. King Tubbys *modify* dub, you know him work it and get it to perfection and have all them little effects dem pon it. But King Tubbys only come into the business *after* we . . . I might be wrong, but you always find a man jump up and say how him *create* dub, y'know. You never find a man come out clean and ever say him hear it and he just love it and he work on it to make it become perfect . . . [7]

Far East Sound

The instrument now, everyone portraying it as nothing, but the instrument itself is something because it's just like a keyboard, the same scales and notes. The only thing is that . . . it's [a] blowing instrument. And music travel within the wind and no one can hold it or catch it. It's just like the breeze—can anyone catch the breeze or touch the sun?[8]
—Augustus Pablo, 1987

Much of Thompson's early work featured his mixing of Chin's productions. One of the most significant of these is the eponymous *This Is Augustus Pablo* (1972), by a musician who would himself play a crucial role in the development of dub music. Like Vivian "Yabby You" Jackson, Horace "Augustus Pablo" Swaby was not a studio engineer, but was without doubt one of dub music's most important guiding spirits. Primarily a session musician, Pablo was born in Kingston in 1953, and from 1971 until his passing in 1999, he created a body of recorded work that reflected both his talents as an instrumentalist, producer, and arranger, and the increasingly sophisticated mixing techniques of several of Jamaica's top engineers. As an instrumentalist, Pablo was primarily a multikeyboardist (a few of his recordings also feature him on keyed percussion), but is best remembered for the plaintive sound of his melodica, the wind-blown children's keyboard instrument he used to craft brittle, haunting melodies against the heavy rhythms of his Rockers International band. His minor-key "Far Eastern" sound was inspired by the African- and Asian-themed instrumentals recorded by Don Drummond, Dizzy Moore, Jackie Mittoo, and Tommy McCook for Studio One and Treasure Isle in the 1960s.[9] Composed to evoke the locales of the Old Testament as well as the cultures stretching eastward from West Africa through East Africa and on to islands of the Indonesian archipelago, Pablo essentially created a devotional genre of reggae exotica that reflected the political and spiritual dimensions of his Rastafarian faith.

If anyone's rhythms seemed tailor-made for dub treatments, it would be Pablo's, whose rhythms were often played at slow-to-medium tempo featuring active and inventive bass lines and thickly textured Nyabinghi hand drumming. His use of unusual chord progressions such as moving between a I minor chord and a ♭VII minor provided a suitably mysterious harmonic setting for his Afro-orientalist sound paintings.

In addition to producing his own material, Pablo worked with virtually all of the major Jamaican producers over the course of his career, as well as most of the engineers associated with dub music. In fact, his most enduring work was created in collaboration with Lee Perry (various songs from Perry's Black Ark period such as "Vibrate On"), Sylvan Morris (*East of the River Nile*), and King Tubby (*King Tubbys Meets the Rockers Uptown*). Pablo's recorded legacy is particularly intertwined with King Tubby, thanks to the engineer's popular mixing board treatments of his work. But the recording that initially brought him to public attention was the 1971 instrumental "Java," produced by Clive Chin and engineered by Thompson at Randy's. Chin fondly remembers the track as "the most creative rhythm that I ever really produce."[10] Pablo and Clive Chin had known each other from their school years at Kingston College: "Pablo, you know him went to the same school with I—King's College. Him was a school mate of mine. You see the thing about musicians at the early stage, they all try to get involved in the music business. Some of dem hang around a studio, just waiting for the opportunity to be put on a recording. And Pablo was just one a dem guys where just love the music, you know? Him find music more gratifying than staying in school so him come around the studio and hang around. But I knew him from school, I didn't know him from the studio."[11]

Pablo's early work with Thompson and Chin offers an opportunity to examine how dub sprang from the intersection of two impulses: the instrumental reggae song, and the post-performance remix. *This Is* is an album of instrumentals built around "Java." In this early stage of reggae, grooves were constructed as highly syncopated, tightly interlocking rhythms, and much of the rhythmic dynamism was generated by the musicians simply *playing*. Later in the decade, as the patterns became slower and more sparse, engineers would apply more aggressive post-production techniques to elaborate instrumental tracks. But in the early 1970s when Chin and Thompson worked together, there were no elaborate studio tricks and the most frequently used post-production strategy was the dropping out of instrumental parts from the mix. This simple strategy was particularly effective, as it manipulated the rhythmic tension being generated by the funky, tightly syncopated patterns of Pablo's rhythm tracks such as the one used for Alton Ellis's cover of Cornelius Brother and Sister Rose's 1971 soul hit "It's Too Late" (Pablo's instrumental version appears on his own album as "Too Late").[12] Thompson chose to texture his mixes roughly, particularly in exploiting the scratchy sonority of the rhythm guitar as it blended with the metallic percussion, snare drum rims (in roots reggae drumming, the metal rim is played much more frequently than the open snare), cowbells, and hi-hat cymbals. He also exploited the distortion that routinely occurred as Jamaican engineers pushed tracks past standard recording and playback levels, and used this distortion to texture the percussive unison guitar and bass lines that propelled so many early reggae songs. As a result of this thick texturing, these lines often sounded like melodic drum patterns, while retaining the nuance and articulation of string instruments. Accordingly, Clive Chin distinguished his and Thompson's approach to dub mixing as "completely different from how King Tubbys would a mix. King Tubbys mix with really powerful effects, but our own now it *raw* and it very effective. Our one was like more *mature* drum and bass per se."[13]

Errol T. on the Mix I
Lloyd Parks: "Ordinary Man" > Augustus Pablo: "Assignment #1" > Errol Thompson, Bingy Bunny & General Echo: "Extraordinary Dub" > Errol Thompson: "Extraordinary Version"

Lloyd Parks croons a lament of the daily struggle for survival on "Ordinary Man" (1972),[14] built f   idtempo vamp in G minor moving between the F minor and C min   hords, with the guitar and bass playing a unison rhythm pattern. Augustus Pablo cut an instrumental melodica version of the rhythm called "Assignment No. 1"[15] that also featured his overdubbed clavinet lines, but was otherwise identical to the original in terms of production values. Two other versions of the same track, however, hinted most at Errol Thompson's experimental streak. "Extra-Ordinary Dub" dramatizes the newfound creative capabilities of the mixing console in the form of a mock conversation between an engineer (voiced by Thompson) and an aspiring engineer (voiced by guitarist Eric "Bingy Bunny" Lamont).

Attempting to convince the engineer of his talent on the mixing board, the aspirant quickly demonstrates his ineptitude: punching in bass when asked for drums, guitar when asked for bass, and so forth. The masterly engineer then steps in to correct the situation, drawing all the tracks out except from drums and gradually building the structure back, one instrument at a time. In its use of multitracking to blend music and dialogue, "Extra-Ordinary Dub" is fundamentally a document of musician friends having fun with the toys of the studio. But the inclusion of Thompson's voice also reflects the rising professional status of the recording engineer, and the fact that the engineer in Jamaica was becoming publicly recognized as an important part of the creative process.

The "Ordinary Man" series culminates in Thompson's own "Extraordinary Version,"[16] which is among the most distinctive of the early dub mixes, and often cited by Clive Chin as a high point of his work with Thompson. Thompson's approach to the remix was somewhat similar to Lee Perry's work on recordings such as *Blackboard Jungle Dub* in the sense that where the engineers at King Tubby's studio generated effects organically by applying sound processing to the recorded tracks, Thompson tended to use these tracks as a "canvas" upon which to overdub extraneous sound effects such as car horns, sirens, animal sounds, and even flushing toilets. On "Extraordinary Version," he takes a clear step from the original recording, expanding the soundscape by applying a cavernous reverb to the drum set, slowing the tape speed incrementally (resulting in a lowering of the key from G minor to F minor, a slowing of the tempo from quarter note = 70 bpm to quarter note = 64 bpm, and a more thickly textured guitar/bass unison line). On top of this, he superimposes a recording of voices played in reverse and at various speeds, interspersing their groans and squeals with various automotive sounds. This additive approach was a core element of Thompson's dub mixing style, and "Extraordinary Version" is a testament to the spirit of experimentation that he and Clive Chin contributed to reggae. Chin cited the track while summing up his work with Thompson in an interview with Brian Lindt:

Errol and myself, as two youths putting our heads together and coming up with a song like "Extraordinary Version . . ." When we finished it we looked at each other and smiled and said to each other "Could it have happened ten years ago? No, probably not. But, could it have happened twenty years in the future? Probably yes, could have—but with microphone [*sic*] chips and computerization." It's like we were ahead of our time . . .

We had a young and energetic frame of mind during the early '70s, and we would experiment for hours in the studio. You must remember that we were not paying for studio time; we were experimenting for production for the label Randy's Impact, which is my family. So we had unlimited studio time. . . . The more original we could be, the more fun it would be for us. That was the whole thing about doing music in the '70s: to be creative, to come up with fresh ideas that Studio One didn't have, Duke Reid, Derrick Harriott, or even Lee Perry for that matter.[17]

The Mighty Two

Around 1975, Thompson left Randy's to work with producer Joe Gibbs. Gibbs, who was born Joel Gibson in Montego Bay in 1945, had learned electronics through an American correspondence course and eventually worked as a technician on an islandwide electrical currency conversion project. He opened an electronics shop in Kingston in the late 1960s, and gradually ventured into music production.[18] In 1968, Gibbs opened a two-track studio on Burns Avenue in the Duhaney Park section of Kingston, the electronics having been installed by Bill Garnett.[19] Gibbs initially engineered the sessions at this studio himself until Thompson began assisting him while moonlighting from Randy's. Bunny Lee remembered this as a transitional period for Gibbs: "Joe Gibbs is an engineer too you know, when him just start. But basically, him is a businessman and him have to be out doing business. So E.T. do the work."[20] In fact, Thompson had been dividing his time between Gibbs and Randy's for some time, as Bunny Lee recalls: "Errol used to leave Randy's at night time and go a Joe Gibbs, take the tune and mix them. All them Nicky Thomas tune like "Love of the Common People" and "Have A Little Faith" that go in the British chart, they were made down at that studio at Duhaney Park."[21]

Gibbs was not a musician but, as was typical for Jamaican producers of the period, dub and instrumental sides from Gibbs's studio were credited to "Joe Gibbs and the Professionals." Drummer Sly Dunbar was a member of this unit, and remembers that Gibbs's operation was fairly haphazard during this early period: "I remember we used to go by Duhaney Park, to Joe Gibbs first studio, and we'd go there from ten o'clock to do session, and Joe Gibbs wouldn't turn up for the session. We'd be from ten to four o'clock, no money! Those sessions, we didn't work so we didn't get payed, [He'd] buy you food and bus fare, you'd catch a bus and come back [home]. . . . On and on like that sometimes two times in a week, three times a week. When he moved to Retirement Crescent now, it run much more organized."[22]

Eventually, Thompson joined Gibbs as full-time engineer once the latter opened a new sixteen-track studio on Retirement Crescent in 1975. Together, the two formed the "Mighty Two" production team. Clive Chin remembers Thompson's departure as a turning point for Randy's: "Errol left at a crucial time because the studio was at its peak. So it was really a big blow for us when we lost Errol. I felt I lost a brother when he left."[23] Thompson was replaced at Randy's by George Philpott, Pat Kelly, and Karl Pitterson, in turn. Pitterson stayed for a year and a half before moving on to work at Dynamics and later Island Records. He was at Randy's long enough to mix portions of the *Randy's Dub* collection with Chin, who remembered: "We mix some at different times, they weren't all mix one time. But it was over a period of that time that Karl was with us that those were done. You know, about four or five different set of musicians plays on it—Skin, Flesh and Bones, Wailers, Soul Syndicate, Now Generation."[24]

Errol T. on the Mix II
Clive "Lizard" Hunt: "Fight I Down" > Mighty Two: "Earthquake"
As noted by Lloyd Bradley, one major advantage Gibbs had over his competitors such as Bunny Lee was his own studio. Instead of having to rent time at other studios and keep an eye on the clock, time could now be more productively spent on experimentation and finding a signature sound.[25] The studio's sixteen-channel Sound Technique console had been purchased from Dynamics when the latter upgraded,[26] and it was on this board that Errol Thompson produced his best-known dub work.

Clive Hunt's "Fight I Down" was transformed by Thompson into "Earthquake,"[27] remixed as a "quartet" performance of drums, bass, the gentle finger-picking of guitarist Bingy Bunny Lamont, and an oscillating, gurgling low-register sound from an unidentified source. In traditional terms, Lamont's guitar line provides the main melodic material of the piece (the guitarist outlines the I and IV chords in the main section of the piece, while a six-measure bridge section follows the sequence iii–I–IV–I–V–IV). The oscillating sound, however—most likely produced by a synthesizer or sound effects record—figures prominently in the mix. This low-register sound is nearly unpitched, but hovers around scale degrees ♭7, 7, and I. Its oscillating sound intermittently alternates with what seems to be a high-pitched, reverberating test-tone frequency vaguely centered around scale degree ♭7. Because a seven-second sliver of singing is all that remains of the prior vocal version, it is in fact these three elements that constitute the melodic material of the piece. What is significant here is that Thompson's approach opened a space in which ambiguously pitched sounds generated from nontraditional (that is, electronic) sources could influence the construction of melody as Jamaican music was created through increasingly electronic means.

African Dub

Mixes such as "Earthquake" were in fact Thompson's conceptual midpoint; on his well-known series of *African Dub* albums he was given free rein by Gibbs to indulge his knack for sound collage. Having studied under Sylvan Morris, Thompson built his dub mixes around hard and very cleanly recorded rhythm section tracks, employing what many Jamaicans considered to be the most innovative drum & bass team of the day. The *African Dub* series relies heavily on sound effects over a foundation of updated Studio One and Treasure Isle riddims provided by Sly Dunbar, Robbie Shakespeare, and the rest of Gibbs's house band, The Professionals. On these recordings, Thompson didn't work inside the sound so much as around it. Like the earlier "Extraordinary Version," his later work would find him using drum & bass tracks as a sonic canvas for his arsenal of sound effects. Clive Chin remembered: "This man had such a concept of sound effects—clock alarms, car horns, sirens . . . sometimes E.T. would even take the mike into the toilet and have me stand there while the music is playing, and when he give me the signal, I just flush it on cue—not too early, not too late, but right on the beat. I mean the man was very exact about how and where he wanted it on the record.[28]

Errol T. on the Mix III
The Mighty Two: "Chapter Three," "Dub Three"
"That one deh a *killer!*" announces a voice at the beginning of the third volume in the *African Dub* series, initiating fifteen seconds of sonic mayhem unleashed by Thompson, who prefaces "Chapter Three" with a chaotic maelstrom of overdubbed earthquake and thunder sounds underpinned by Sly Dunbar's pulsing four-to-the-floor "steppers" rhythm. A reverberating tom-tom roll (similar in effect to what Lee Perry was crafting around Mikey Richards's drumming at the Black Ark studio) commences Sly and Robbie's recut of Augustus Pablo's famous "Cassava Piece" (that is, "King Tubbys Meets the Rockers Uptown") rhythm, stripped down to a drum & bass arrangement, with a driving eighth-note tambourine added for extra propulsion. If there was an original vocal track, it has been completely omitted here, and the harmony almost entirely omitted save for a few passages of guitar chopped into percussive stutters via a delay unit. On top of this prerecorded material, Thompson dubs various sound effects: jack-in-the-box noises, chiming doorbells, and the sound of jets taking off. Volume 3 closes with "Dub Three" built from the old Studio One "Rockfort Rock" rhythm. After an intro in which the drums and bass are routed through a delay unit to thunderous effect, Thompson halts the tape abruptly and rewinds it back to the top (reproducing an effect frequently used by sound system selectors), allowing a bit of space for the overdubbed sound of a doorbell to chime dissonantly against the D minor rhythm pattern. During his days at Randy's, Thompson had applied reverb to Carlton

Barrett's bass drum on tracks like Augustus Pablo's "Pablo in Dub" in such a way that the bass drum effectively orchestrated the atmospheric elements of the mix, with Barrett's low-register syncopation creating a series of atmospheric disturbances that set Pablo's melodica in stark relief.[29] On "Dub Three," he pursues a similar strategy with more advanced technology, applying so much reverb to the snare drum that its rhythmic impulses rend the soundscape with each of Sly's syncopations. Thompson further destabilizes the rhythm by adding echo effects, dropout, and various sound effects as a preface to horn solos by trombonist Vin Gordon and tenor saxophonist Tommy McCook.

As Barrow and Dalton note, some listeners criticized Thompson's penchant for overdubbed sound effects in his dub music as a vulgarization of the form (compared to, say, the subtleties of King Tubby's approach).[30] But what might be dismissed by some as a gimmick-laden approach to remixing is very successful on its own terms here, thanks in part to the power of Sly and Robbie's rhythm section performance, a tough dancehall groove that acts as a cohering agent for what is essentially a sound collage. The combined power of Thompson's mixing with Sly and Robbie's "militant" riddims ensured exciting results, and Thompson's work with Gibbs reached a wider audience than his previous efforts.[31] As such, the *African Dub* series (especially volume 3) is often cited as a high point of the genre. In tandem with the advent of digital sampling equipment a decade later, Thomspon's work ultimately laid an important foundation for the collagist approach of digital ragga music in which the overdubbing of sound effects on percussion-dominated rhythm tracks would, like Thompson's dub work, de-center harmonic practice through the use of polytonality, dissonance, and "pure" noise.

Fig. 1. Clement "Coxsone" Dodd at Studio One, late 1970s
Photo by Peter Simon

Fig 2. Dynamic studio exterior, 2000 *Photo by the author*

Fig. 3. Sylvan Morris at Dynamic studio, 2000 *Photo by the author*

Fig. 4. Harry J. studio exterior *Photo by the author*

Fig. 5. King Tubby's studio exterior, 2000 *Photo by the author*

Fig. 6. Scientist, Prince Jammy, and King Tubby, 1980
Photo courtesy of Ken "Fatman" Gordon

Fig. 7. Scientist, early 1980s *Photo by Peter Simon*

Fig. 8. Philip Smart, 2003 *Photo by the author*

Fig. 9. Bunny Lee in front of his home in Duhaney Park, 2002
Photo by the author

Fig. 10. Channel One studio exterior *Photo by the author*

Fig. 11. Sly Dunbar and Robbie Shakespeare outside of Channel One studio
Photo by Peter Simon

Fig. 12. Lee Perry at the board of the Black Ark, 1976 *Photo courtesy of urbanimage.tv/Adrian Boot*

Fig. 13. The Black Ark studio from the outside, 1976 *Photo courtesy of urbanimage.tv/Adrian Boot*

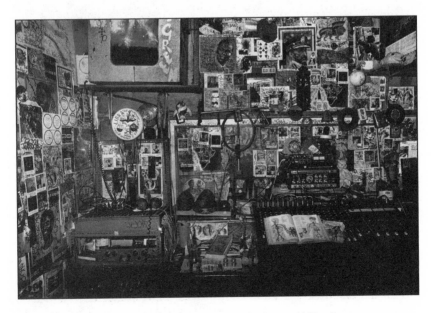

Fig. 14. The Black Ark control room *Photo courtesy of urbanimage.tv/Adrian Boot*

Fig. 15. Clive Chin and Errol Thompson
at Randy's, early 1970s
Photo courtesy of Clive Chin

Fig. 16. Augustus Pablo
Photo by Peter Simon

Fig. 17. Errol Thompson on the board at Joe Gibbs's studio, early 1980s
Photo by Peter Simon

Fig. 18. King Jammy (*left*) and a friend, 2002 *Photo by the author*

Fig. 19. King Tubby at the board of his new studio, late 1980s *Photo courtesy of Bunny Lee*

Fig. 20. Michael "Mikey Dread" Campbell
Photo by the author

Fig. 21. Neil "Mad Professor" Fraser *Photo courtesy of Neil Fraser*

Fig. 22. Mad Professor's Ariwa studio, London *Photo by the author*

Fig. 23. Adrian Sherwood, 2002 *Photo by the author*

Fig. 24. Dennis Bovell

CHAPTER SEVEN

"City Too Hot"

The End of the Roots Era and the Significance of Dub to the Digital Era of Jamaican Music[1]

In the beginning, they didn't mess with musicians. We could be standing up outside the studio on the street and you see some man running down the road with rifles and him don't trouble you. We would walk out of the area to get the bus to go home sometimes, and they won't trouble you. Them know say all you deal with is music, you just going to the studio. But I came up here [to the United States] and went to school in '75, and went back down and worked for Tubbs in '76. And it just looked different—everything looked like it get wickeder, it looked just evil. Homes burnt down everywhere, and you don't want to be outside. . . . I decided I'd have to leave again. —Philip Smart*

Speaking about snow. The kids and the children who love that part of the world so much, that is to say the igloo, is a part of the heavens, is higher than the earth. The part of the mountain that is higher than the earth is closer to heaven. So I am seeing how people act on that part of heaven that they are blessed with. 'Cause the way people act in Jamaica is not my style of life anymore. Me no want my brain to be pulled down into something too heavy and hot, because then my brain cannot fly. Me like to see children slide on ice. Me love to see the vision of the ice. Me love to see the ice making art on the mountain. Me don't see that in Jamaica. Me see guns. Me take some torturing, but from the torturing me get an education to make a positive choice 'pon a negative ice.
—Lee Perry on his life as an expatriate Jamaican in Switzerland[2]

Bob Marley died in May 1981, having lived his final years in intermittent exile following an attempt on his life in 1976. With Marley's passing, reggae lost its most powerful global spokesman. Foreign recording companies gradually abandoned their support for other Jamaican artists who had ridden to international recognition on the path opened by Marley, and the conduits for international capital began slowly drying up for all but the best-known reggae artists. This sudden shift in the priorities of the music industry remains a sore point for many roots reggae artists today, as typified by the comments of Mikey Dread: "The way the media portray reggae is like, it's Bob Marley and after Bob Marley there's no more reggae. Which is to me just like propaganda to keep the music back. Because with the death of Elvis Presley, I didn't see rock & roll dying. You know, they didn't say 'He's the king of rock & roll and the king is dead so the whole culture is dead. . . . ' Bob was the major man who break it internationally and break down all the barriers, but they want to stop it now for us to go through. We could get it but they don't want us in there!"[3]

As discussed in chapter 1, roots reggae was intimately tied to a moment of cultural nationalism in which Jamaicans of African heritage excavated the bitter past of slavery and colonization and rehabilitated it into a newfound pride in African cultural roots, a moment defined politically by Michael Manley's two-term experiment in democratic socialism. But despite Manley's efforts during his two terms in office, it was clear that hostile winds of change were in the air by 1980. Manley had antagonized the country's upper class (many of whom fled to Miami), and defied the United States by forging a close friendship with Cuba's Fidel Castro and lending support to budding socialist regimes elsewhere in the world (such as Angola). Meanwhile, the Jamaican economy had continued to dovetail throughout the 1970s, owing largely to fluctuations in world oil prices as well as fluctuating demand for bauxite, the country's most profitable export.[4]

In the months leading to the 1980 elections, the stage was set for another late–cold war intervention by the United States that, while not so direct as roughly concurrent operations in Nicaragua and El Salvador, had similarly destructive consequences for Jamaica. The elections that year—pitting Manley against his longtime rival Edward Seaga of the Jamaican Labour Party—were the most violent in the nation's history, with between eight hundred and one thousand people dying in Kingston as a result of campaign violence. Manley was routed out of office by Seaga and a resurgent JLP, who quickly signed on to the American agenda with the Reagan administration's Caribbean Basin Initiative. On the ground in Kingston, Seaga's ghetto gunmen ruthlessly subdued their People's National Party–affiliated rivals with American-made arms purchased with profits from the drug trade. To this day, the country has never fully recovered from the level of violence that was unleashed.[5]

As mentioned in the introduction, the international popularity of reggae and its Rasta component had worked together in such a way that ganja would rival reggae and bauxite as one of Jamaica's most profitable exports, but the drastic political and economic changes in the 1980s created an even more destructive context for the country's role in the global drug trade. Part of Seaga's favor with the American government resulted from his efforts at eradicating ganja production and exportation; ironically, however, the situation became much more deadly when local gunmen began trafficking in cocaine shipped from South America. The days of ganja suddenly seemed placid compared to the nightmare that cocaine unleashed on the island in this perversely ironic take on the concept of "crop substitution." Fueled by cocaine highs and the harsh reality of their ultimate disposability at the hands of their political patrons, the gangs bought their economic independence through cocaine trafficking and founded a culture of ruthless violence that detached itself from political ideals and became all-consuming.[6] The music scene could not help being affected by these changes, and a number of musicians left the island to pursue their careers in less turbulent surroundings.

At the same time, it seemed that the cultural influence of Rastafari, which had been so integral to the power of roots reggae, had run its course. While it was true that the fusion of the rude boy and the Rasta at the dawn of reggae was a potent fusion of two outsider impulses, the close relationship between the religion-ideology of Rastafari and the musical genre of roots reggae had to some degree been artificially fueled by the music's huge international popularity, the subsequent euphoria, and the corresponding influx of foreign capital. In his most insightful essay on the cultural background of the transition from reggae to the digitally produced music that became known as "ragga," Louis Chude-Sokei observed that as Kingston became mired in the politically sponsored ghetto warfare that locals dubbed "tribal war," the vision of Rastafari, centered around an African cultural referent almost extraterrestrial in its distance from local realities, was unable to provide resistance against what he called the "Reagan-Seaga-Thatcher triumvirate."[7] In an era of strong-armed American neocolonialism, protracted drug skirmishes, and harsh measures instituted by the International Monetary Fund, Jamaica's ghetto ideology collapsed from a pan-Africanist universalism to a resolutely local orientation.

As it had done in the early 1960s, Jamaica began once again to turn musically inward. Part of this retreat was a reaction against the internationalization of Jamaican music that had gradually occurred during the 1970s, and stylistic terms that seemed increasingly dictated by foreign markets.[8] What had been known as "reggae" foundered on for a few years in the early 1980s in what is usually referred to as "early dancehall," associated with such producers as Linval Thompson, Jah "Nkrumah"

Thomas and Junjo Lawes, and session bands such as Roots Radics and Soul Syndicate. But a decisive moment came in 1985 when King Tubby's former assistant engineer Prince (now King) Jammy discovered that he could use the pre-programmed patterns of a cheap Casio keyboard as riddims for songs. Wayne Smith's Jammy-produced "Under Me Sleng Teng" and the scores of versions that followed it ushered in the era of digital "ragga." [9] Inevitably (as in other parts of the world), digital studios were found to be more cost-effective than their analog counterparts, and the "Sleng Teng" craze helped put a decisive end to the era of roots reggae.[10] With Jammy and other producers shelving the accumulated remainder of their "human" riddims (as they were now called), they also ended the dominance of the performing and recording bands of the 1970s, the analog studio system in which these bands had thrived, and the era in which Jamaica's popular music had been strongly rooted in its jazz, wind-band and related traditions.[11] Most of Kingston's live studios were closed within months, and the newly crowned Jammy and his assistants Wycliffe Johnson and Cleveland Browne (known as Steely and Clevie), Squingine "Squingy" Francis and Bobby "Digital" Dixon would go on to lay the foundations for the digital age of Jamaican popular music.[12] Philip Smart considered this a natural progression of the music: "Everybody had their era of leading. Studio One had their era, Treasure Isle had their era, then Tubby's, then you have Joe Gibbs and Channel One, and then Jammys came with the computer sound. That changed the whole business."[13]

Concurrently with the decline of roots reggae, the early 1980s were also the last years of dub as a contemporary musical movement in Jamaica. By the early 1980s, Lee Perry had already destroyed the Black Ark and moved gradually into exile. King Tubby's studio continued as a center for dub during this time (mainly through the work of Scientist), while other engineers such as Phantom (Noel Gray) and Peego handled the ongoing duties of day-to-day mixing after the music went digital.[14] Tubby himself, however, had grown less interested in mixing, preferring to concentrate on building a new 24-track studio in the backyard of his house on Dromilly Avenue. He had substantial success in 1985 with Anthony Red Rose's "Tempo," an early piece of digital ragga with a moody, eccentric mix that gave at least a preliminary indication of what digital dub might have sounded like in Jamaica had Tubby lived to develop it.[15] But Tubby was murdered early one morning in February 1989 outside of his home in Duhaney Park, in an apparent robbery attempt.[16] Scientist is one of several people with whom I spoke who remain unconvinced that Tubby's still-unsolved killing was a mere robbery gone bad: "Jamaica is a place where anybody who tries to rise and help Jamaicans do something positive, is killed by the gunmen. That was no robbery. Tubby's studio—there wasn't gonna be anything else like it in Jamaica. People were afraid. It would have put a lot of other studios out of business."[17] With Lee Perry abroad, Joe Gibbs's studio closed, and King Jammy trailblazing a new era of digital music, King Tubby's murder represented the symbolic end to the era of roots dub music.

The long-term significance of dub on Jamaican music, however, cannot be adequately explained in terms of mere market popularity, a finite commercial moment, or the dominance of any particular individual. While it is true that dub music achieved a certain market presence for a time in the 1970s, most album-length recordings of dub were pressed in very limited quantities. By its very nature and setting, it was a creation of producers and engineers, with its primary market being sound system operators and reggae record collectors, as opposed to the general public, among whom it was a highly specialized taste. In Adrian Sherwood's view, "[Dub] wasn't that popular in Jamaica. It was a sound system thing. It was immensely popular with the sound system people—'version upon version,' with a live DJ chatting over it. That's how it was used in Jamaica."[18] Sound system operator Bobby Vicious concurs: "Even the average reggae lover, they can't listen to more than three or four dub mixes in a row. They need the words. You see, that's how you test a true dub lover."[19]

Many of Jamaica's musicians (including its jazz musicians), however, acknowledge dub as an important phase of the music—somewhat ironic, given the complicated authorship issues that arose as a result of versioning, as well as the distance that dub moved the music away from traditional conceptions of instrumentalism. For example, a 2004 CD of jazz instrumentals by guitarist Ernest Ranglin and pianist Monty Alexander contains several canonical songs or riddims of the roots era strongly associated with dub, including Burning Spear's "Marcus Garvey," the Congos' "Fisherman," Augustus Pablo's "East of the River Nile," and the generic "Stalag 17" riddim, which has provided the foundation for uncountable versions over the years.[20] Such developments attest to the fact that to measure dub in terms of the criteria of market "popularity" misses the point. It is more appropriate to speak of dub as a body of production techniques that, like any innovation, is gradually subsumed into the common practice of a given tradition. This is in fact the case with dub music, which is rarely produced in Jamaica today as it was in the 1970s, but the primary innovations of which can be considered core elements of Jamaican music in the digital age.

Digital Jamaica: The Birth of Ragga

Every time the outside world catches up with [Jamaican music],
the beat changes again.[21] — Prince Buster, 2000

You don't really forget the things you used to do or finish away with it, but the time
changes so you have to go with the time if you want to eat food from it. If you want
to earn a living from the music, you have to do whatever is going on today.[22]
— King Jammy to David Katz, 2005

Ragga music reflected the era of its birthing, a music of gritty survival often dominated by what Chude-Sokei called the "noirish street-level intricacies" of sexual dominance, gunplay, and gangsterism. [23] Of course, it is important to realize that such themes had always been a part of Jamaican pop, every since the downtown "rude boy" culture of Kingston helped give birth to ska shortly after independence. Roots reggae itself was always considered a ghetto music inside of Jamaica, and might still be narrowly regarded as such if Bob Marley's global success hadn't earned reggae, Rastafarians, and Jamaica so much cultural cache. During the harsh political days of the late 1970s, for example, dub music bolstered depictions of the harsh realities of the later Manley years as much as it did the utopian narratives of Rastafari; the "noirish" aspects of which Chude-Sokei speaks had been prefigured by studio engineers' sound paintings of urban strife, peppering their mixes with the sound of screeching tires, police sirens, or machine-gun fire. This same practice can even be traced back to the ska era, on tracks such as the Skatalites' 1966 "Ringo Rides," which is itself graced with the sound of intermittent gunfire.[24] The "rude-bwoi" life of Kingston had always been a core element of Jamaican popular music, and when the Afrocentric narratives of Rastafari peeled away under the weight of the new realities of the 1980s, the underlying rude boy component simply moved to the fore.

Because of the dramatic and fairly sudden shift with which roots reggae was supplanted by digitally produced music and the way this so closely paralleled sociopolitical changes in Jamaica during the 1980s, many listeners and musicians consider roots reggae and the digitally produced music that came to be variously known as *ragga* or *dancehall* music to represent two diametrically opposed musical movements. To an extent, ongoing debates on this topic have tended to focus on the issue of either methods of musical production (live bands versus digital production) or the ideology of the musicians in question (the embrace of Rastafari and Manley-era democratic socialism versus the political conservatism of the Seaga era). The music itself is then heard not only in terms of craft and aesthetics, but also as reflective of a broader social/cultural/philosophical outlook. Following are the varying opinions of several Jamaican musicians I spoke with about these issues during the course of my research:

What has Jamaica given to the world? Good music and good melodies. But some people, anytime whey someone a go do a good thing, [other people] will try and tear it down. What these youth doing today is a pure madness. A youth cyaan just grab a mic and jump 'pon the stage and call themselves making music. Them speak so fast, most times the audience don't even understand. Where is the message there? (Ras Tito, an assistant of roots reggae pioneer Burning Spear, 2000)

I will stress on one thing: live instruments are the greatest thing and computer can't stop that sound. Because the computer music is lifeless but with instruments, every song sound a bit different. Instruments makes a *moody* type of music. It can play with your mood whereas computer is something that really have no mood with it. But instruments are something that make you move and shake . . . and it's getting back because people realize how good it was. . . . It says "life" and it will always live on. (Producer Winston Riley, who ironically produced one of the canonical early ragga tracks, Tenor Saw's "Ring the Alarm," 2000)

Well, it's not the same as before but I wouldn't criticize the dancehall people, because in the rhythm and the production and things, they still have their own genius going on there. (Expatriate Jamaican sound system operator Bobby Vicious, 2000)

Most of the pickney [younger listeners] nowadays them digital anyway, so we have fe just work with it. Give the older folks whey dem want and give the younger folks whey dem want. You have fe balance it. You cyaan forget the little pickney dem you know? 'Cause when the older people buy [older] records the little pickney dem want a copy! (Seminal roots reggae bassist Robbie Shakespeare, 2002)

Digital is the future y'know. And a lot of people have to get with it. What I find a problem is not because of digital, but the music. Because you have drum machines and you have MIDI, you find that almost anybody can set up a studio inside of a basement. Even if they are only halfway musical, they will be able to come up with something with some kind of a beat because they have computers that can do all these things for you. (Overton "Scientist" Brown, 2001)

While these musicians' comments all acknowledge a perceived divide between the music of the roots and digital eras, most of them also reflect varying degrees of pragmatism and accommodation, at least now that twenty years have passed since the digital shift. In this sense, they are partially at odds with the dominant narrative of post-1980s Jamaican music held by many non-Jamaicans, which maintains that the international explosion of roots reggae associated with musicians like Bob Marley remains the golden age of Jamaican music, and that the subsequent changes in the music constitute a tragic decline. As the musicians' comments imply, the reality is actually more complex and fluid.

Of course, the most enduring musical genres must necessarily be considered organic expressions of a culture in a given period. With digital Jamaican music entering its third decade of innovation, with the verbal virtuosity of DJs now firmly established, and as Jamaican music enters a new period of global influence, it would be grossly unrealistic to dismiss the music of the digital era as a mere aberration or passing fad. On the other hand, the continued heavy reliance by younger musicians on even the most rudimentary rhythm patterns of the 1960s and 1970s seems a cause for concern. On one hand, it suggests the loss of a body of skills that in turn reflects the social and political destabilization Jamaica was subjected to in the 1980s.[25] In terms of skills and infrastructure, it can take a society decades to recover from such traumatic episodes. On the other hand, it directly reflects the legacy of dub music, in which reconfiguration has become a more central compositional ideal than the creation of "original" music. But if we ultimately accept it as axiomatic that the only constant in life is change itself, then we must acknowledge (1) the many possible modes of transformation (not all linear), and (2) the brilliant way in which musicians and producers have innovated a new form of Jamaican music from the ashes of the 1970s. In fact, the digitalization of popular music production in Jamaica was no different than anywhere else in the world; what made it seem so dramatically different was the extremely rapid pace of the transformation. But the island's economy would suggest that producers (being businesspeople above all else) would tend to be less bound by ideas of stylistic purity, and would rush to embrace any technology that minimized overhead expenses and maximized profits.

The decline of roots reggae obviously held relevance for dub music, which encapsulated the studio production values of the roots era. In this section, I shall compare the continuities and discontinuities of current Jamaican approaches to popular music production with those of the 1970s. Chude-Sokei captured up the ethos of post–1984/85 Jamaican music perfectly when he described it as a music of "raw, materialistic presence."[26] The stylistic markers of "otherworldliness" (that is, the Africa-centered narratives of Rastafari and diasporic exile) that were typified by roots-era lyrics and complemented by the reverberating aesthetic of dub were largely jettisoned (although they have made somewhat of a comeback in recent years). In fact, while the "dub" designation is still occasionally used for B-side versions, it is interesting to note that when the lyrical focus of Jamaican music shifted away from Africa-centered narratives in the 1980s, the reliance on echo and reverb seemed to decline concurrently. In the hands of Jamaica's prominent digital producers, reverb and echo have been typically used in a much more traditional manner: to achieve the desired separation of parts and occasionally, to "spice" what has become a very "dry" mixing style. Along with the differences in lyrical content discussed earlier in this chapter, contemporary Jamaican music strikes one as unmistakably of the *here and now*, as opposed to evoking the *there and then*.

The music also tends to be much faster in tempo and more aggressive in tone than its ganja-laced forebear. Some cynical observers have attributed this intensity to various sociopathologies including sociopolitical change in post-Manley Jamaica and the cocaine epidemic. The truth is that, despite its pathologies, the music is fundamentally more exuberant in spirit. Although the Rasta influence has been gradually reasserted over the last decade or so, the weighty, "voice crying in the wilderness" paradigm and the apocalyptic and patriarchal themes of the roots era seem de-emphasized overall in favor of a youthful celebration of the carnal, sensual, and irreverent. Not since the 1960s has the music spawned so many notorious dancers and dance crazes, or dynamic female performers. And despite the de-emphasis on Africa as a lyrical trope (although this also began to reverse in the early 1990s), the emphasis on dance music has allowed ragga to become arguably *more* polyrhythmic than the one drop orientation of roots reggae, drawing simultaneously on Jamaica's neo-African drumming traditions and the accumulative logics of digital sampling as influenced by hip-hop. In fact, the interaction between Jamaican music and hip-hop since the 1980s has been as dynamic as its earlier interactions with jazz, soul, rhythm and blues, and funk.

Despite the obvious shifts, however, there are also strong continuities between the roots and digital eras. In terms of Jamaican music in general, the most obvious continuity is the continued reliance on old Studio One, Treasure Isle, and other vintage riddims that provide the foundation for hundreds of songs each year. Versioning is still a central practice of Jamaican pop, with "all on the same riddim" compilations appearing today as they have since the 1970s. As in hip-hop, digital sampling of older music plays an important role in Jamaican music, with the canonized musical gestures of the 1960s and 1970s (horn riffs, the trademark drum rolls of roots-era drummers, or the exclamations of particular DJs) reappearing to provide formal punctutation, timbral variation, and de facto historical grounding.

In terms of dub music in particular, the strongest continuities can be found in the sphere of ragga music, as this is essentially the contemporary DJ style that can be considered the direct descendant of the dub and DJ music of the 1970s. Like dub, ragga is primarily focused on the sound system, where it most frequently features recording DJs like Beenie Man, Buju Banton, and Capleton. Like the early critical dismissals of rap music in the United States, many Jamaicans in the 1970s assumed DJ music was a mere fad that would fade in a few short years. In fact, the opposite is the case; the art of deejaying is not only alive, but has dominated the music in a way that (in production terms) arguably defines the cutting edge of contemporary Jamaican music. It is also the case that the strong emphasis on deejaying, dominated as it is by Jamaican patwa, has been crucial in re-orienting Jamaican music to local preferences since the mid-1980s.

The clearest connection between ragga and dub can be found in the production of the rhythm tracks. One important aspect of this connection is the continuing deconstruction of harmony. For example, although the bass motion of ragga tunes sometimes suggests the standardized chord progressions of older, generic riddims, the digital "de-tuning" of bass patterns (now created digitally instead of with electric bass) allows bass lines to be manipulated until they sound more like tuned electronic drums; in essence, texture and distortion are often emphasized over precise pitch definition. This tendency has roots in the drum & bass approach of the roots period—especially as experienced in the sound system, where distortion due to extreme volume often obscured the precise identity of pitches and made the electric bass lines sound (in Max Romeo's description) like "African drums." It was only a short step for producers to further decenter the pitch component of bass lines in the 1980s and afterward, taking advantage of the expanded range and sound design capability of digital keyboards.

This de facto decentering of tonality has allowed the music to grow increasingly polytonal, a digital hyperextension of the collage-like constructions achieved by the early versioning practices of the 1970s (in this sense, the harmonic practices of the music parallel developments in American hip-hop, which itself took a radically polytonal turn in the late 1980s with the advent of digital sampling as well as Public Enemy and their "Bomb Squad" production team).[27] Similarly to the DJ music of the roots period, we often find multiple (singing, shouting, rapping) voices in ragga organized around completely unrelated tonal centers. As in the case of bass lines, this multiplicity seems to represent a standardization of the stylistic anomalies of the 1970s; what used to seem like an inability or unwillingness to conform to chord changes has now asserted itself as a willfully aggressive disregard of common practice harmony. As discussed in chapter 2, it was dub's fragmentation of the song surface that opened up the harmonic landscape for the DJs by freeing them from the constraints of functional harmony, using chords instead as bits of incidental coloration. And it was this "sound collage" approach that was eventually extended through the overdubbing of extraneous sound material and variously keyed samples onto previously recorded rhythm tracks. The overdubbing of "pure" sound effects had been used selectively by several of the engineers discussed in the previous chapter, but was most strongly associated with Errol Thompson, particularly on his *African Dub* series with Joe Gibbs in which he essentially challenged the dominance of common practice harmony through the use of pure sound elements. Thompson passed away unexpectedly in 2004; to my knowledge, he had never gone on record regarding his influence on the production of ragga, but he deserves special acknowledgment for providing an important foundation for contemporary Jamaican music.

Fig. 25

CHAPTER EIGHT

Starship Africa
The Acoustics of Diaspora and of the Postcolony[1]

Antillean art is this restoration of our shattered histories, our shards of vocabulary, our archipelago becoming a synonym for pieces broken off from the original continent. . . . That is the basis of the Antillean experience, this shipwreck of fragments, these echoes, these shards of a huge tribal vocabulary.—Derek Walcott, 1992

First, let us imagine a time capsule loaded with various planetary music of the twentieth century, including a sample of roots reggae music of the 1970s compiled by a Jamaican producer such as Bunny Lee or Augustus Pablo. Then, let us suppose that the producer, in error, submitted King Tubby's dub remixes instead of the vocal versions that would, at the request of the project's organizers, have ostensibly addressed some representative social/cultural/political theme of the period. How might these fragmentary texts be interpreted by unknown historians at some distant future location in space and time? Might these versions ultimately offer as vivid portrayals of their culture as would the original songs with complete lyrics? Luke Erlich (paraphrasing Lee Perry) has aptly described the dub version as a type of "x-ray" music that provides glimpses at a song's inner *musical* workings (emphasis mine),[2] but what deeper resonances be gleaned from these skeletal remains of gutted pop songs with their reverberating musical language of fragmentation and erasure?[3]

For the most part, dub mixes are remixes of pieces that originally contained lyrics. In an important sense, then, the remix decisions of engineers when remixing a song into a dub version are (as discussed in chapter 2) often shaped by the original song text; consequently, the dub mix may be at least partially understood as extending the concerns of the song lyrics into (relatively) instrumental or "pure sound" territory. In this penultimate chapter, I shall draw out some of the more subtle resonances within this pure sound territory, tracing dub's reverberations by "versioning" it through the variously imagined pasts and futures animating the African diaspora (in general) and (more specifically) those animating postcolonial Jamaica.

The extensive use of reverberation/delay devices and the fragmentation of the song surface are probably the two most immediately recognizable stylistic features of dub music. As such, the idea of "echo" figures centrally in the first section of this chapter, in which I treat dub's heavy use of reverb as a sonic metaphor for the condition of diaspora. This section also explores the themes of retained Africanist aesthetics in dub, and concludes with a comparison between dub and the genre of magical realism—which I believe parallels, in literature and film, the Surrealist aspects of dub, and which I ultimately assert as an aesthetic particularly reflective of the cultural experience of (African) diaspora. The second section of the chapter builds upon ideas of musical structure introduced in chapter 2, using the formal logics of the (sound) collage to ponder a relationship between ruptures in historical narrative (the trans-Atlantic slave trade) and ruptures in musical narrative (song form). The third section of the chapter uses the trait of spatiality in the music to ponder diasporic and Afro-inflected imaginings of outer space, science fiction, and the future. In the fourth and final section of the chapter, I tie these themes together by theorizing a particular significance for dub music within the class dynamics of Jamaican society, in conjunction with the rise of the sound system DJ as a significant cultural force. Ultimately, I believe that, understood in the appropriate historical context, this strange and seemingly inscrutable music played an important role in the ongoing evolution of Jamaica's postcolonial culture.

In the opening chapter of his 1995 book *African Rhythm*, Kofi Agawu offers a richly descriptive narration of the daily soundscape in Ghana's northern Eweland.[4] In my reading, one of Agawu's goals here is to move the study of traditional African music beyond its stereotyped conceptual boundaries by demonstrating that a culture's conception of "rhythm" is not only narrowly present in their music making, but a profoundly experiential component of their total way of life. Ethnomusicologists have long spoken of the need to understand the phenomenon of music as something socially constituted; in this chapter I shall similarly discuss the characteristic treatment of song form in Jamaican dub music, not as empirical musical fact, but as something equally constituted by social and historical forces. In this light, the various stylistic processes I have referred to throughout this book are treated not merely as aspects of music, but as profoundly structural embodiments of Jamaican history and culture. And, as the final section makes clear, the musical developments also helped transform the same culture.

Reverb, Remembrance, and Reverie

The reliance on reverberation and delay devices is certainly one of the most pronounced stylistic traits of dub music, and the sensations simulated by reverb and digital delay devices—either cavernous spaces or repeated sounds, respectively—can be subsumed under the commonly used term *echo*.[5] In the sonic culture of humans, the sensation of echo is closely associated with the cognitive function of memory and the evocation of the chronological past; at the same time, it can also evoke the vastness of outer space and hence (by association), the chronological future. Most obviously, dub is about memory in the immediate sense that it is a remix, a refashioned version of an already familiar pop song; as such, it derives much of its musical and commercial power from its manipulation of the listener's prior experience of a song. In a more abstract sense, however, I am speculating that, suffusing their music with the sensation of echo during a period when the symbol of Africa was being consciously revitalized in diasporic consciousness, the creators of dub managed to evoke a cultural memory of ancestral African roots through heavy use of the reverb and echo effects and various musical strategies of African origin.

Such a "historicizing of the echo," which has also been addressed by Louis Chude-Sokei in a seminal 1997 essay, implicates dub in the diasporic tropes of exile and nostalgia shared to varying degrees by people of African descent in the New World.[6] In this interpretation, the otherworldly strain in dub music partially evokes an idealized, precolonial African utopia. It was during Michael Manley's attempt at democratic socialism in Jamaica of the 1970s, that a mood of cultural nationalism was energized by Castro's Cuba, the African American civil rights struggle, African nationalism, and the religious vision of Rastafari. All of these stimulated, in varying ways, a reevaluation of African cultural roots. Most literally, Africa was deemed by Rastas to be the site of inevitable repatriation for a people in exile—and considering the economic hardship, strife, and violence that accompanied Jamaica's attempts at social change, it was not surprising that even at the height of cultural pride, many still wished for another place to call home.

In "Reflections on Exile" (1990), Edward Said characterized exile as the "unhealable rift forced between a human being and a native place, between the self and its true home: its essential sadness can never be surmounted."[7]

James Clifford, on the other hand, has observed that "diasporism" tends to oscillate in accordance with the relationship a given [sub]culture maintains with its surrounding society, with periods of antagonism tending to inspire more intense feelings of longing for an ancestral homeland.[8] Clifford also notes that the narratives of diaspora are binary in composition, drawing upon idealized images of a past in the construction of a cultural "safe space" in a hostile present.[9] Such sentiments are echoed in the words of Jamaican poet Kwame Dawes, who surmised that in Jamaica, "the Africa that is constructed is mythic and defined in terms of the current space of exile."[10] I cite these comments in order to evoke the ethos of diaspora as experienced by those of African descent during the early independence years of the 1960s and 1970s, when the idea of Africa was being revitalized throughout the African diaspora. The condition of simultaneously yearning for and being alienated from a cultural homeland that can never be fully experienced as home, and also from the very *history* of connection to that homeland, allows us to interpret dub as a cultural sound painting of a type, vividly dramatizing the experience of diasporic exile.

At what point does culture in diaspora become normalized, ceasing to be measured in relation to some originary homeland? It may seem contradictory that I discuss diaspora and exile in terms of the use of reverberation as a stylistic trait of Jamaican music, while in chapter 7 I spoke of a music (ragga) coming out of the same diasporic context that almost completely abandoned this stylistic trait. After all, isn't digital Jamaica still part of the African diaspora? And doesn't Africa remain an important reference point in contemporary Jamaican music? The obvious answer to both of these questions is yes. My point, however, is that the music of the roots era represented the *end* of more than four centuries in which the cultures of ancestral Africa remained largely a mystery to their descendants throughout the African diaspora. This situation is quite different today, at the turn of a new millennium. While repatriation might remain a quite remote possibility for the vast majority of Jamaicans, there is a Rastafarian settlement in Ethiopia and substantial expatriate Jamaican populations in other parts of Africa (especially Ghana). Reverberation, then, only acquires this particular significance during the historical moment concerned with exploring the ancestral past. By the mid-1980s, this moment had largely passed.

If reggae in the 1970s was in many ways a musical attempt to invoke "Africa" as a newly imagined safe space in the Caribbean present, reverberation provided the cohering agent for dub's interplay of presence/absence and of completeness/incompleteness, evoking the intertwined experiences of exile and nostalgia, and reflecting Said's characterization of exile as "fundamentally a discontinuous state of being."[11] These fragments may also be interpreted as fragments of an African cultural memory under reconstruction, the building blocks being fragments of the post–World War II popular song form and fragmentary memories of Africa. The music's elasticity of form provided the perfect crucible for an elastic reimagining of history, a meditation crucial to the cultural consciousness of the new nation. As I shall mention later in this chapter, the invention of synthetic reverb had (via its capability for spatial simulation) granted new social classes of classical music listeners virtual access to the elite concert hall at the beginning of the twentieth century. However, it also granted those in the African diaspora virtual access to a new vision of the African past at the end of the same century.[12]

> *This kind of singing, coupled with the hard reggae chop of rhythm guitar, was nothing less than a setup for secular Jamaican spirit possession, trance music of the highest order.*—Stephen Davis[13]

"Africa" can also arguably be felt in much of what makes this music unique, and its effect on listeners. In his 1985 study of the relationship between music and states of altered consciousness, Gilbert Rouget distinguished between two states and their respective musical catalysts: those inducing states of *ecstatic contemplation* and those inducing states of *possession*.[14] I believe that the dub mix can, in certain respects, be seen as a catalyst for both states. By traditional definitions, reggae—notwithstanding how often and passionately it voiced Rastafarian themes—should not actually be considered a liturgical or devotional music; Rastafarians had their own Nyabinghi ceremonial music (which itself was rooted in a variety of neo-African liturgical musics such as *burru*). But, infused with the religious passion of Rastafari-influenced reggae, overtones of Euro-American psychedelia, and the political passion of the Manley years, dub nevertheless functioned in the sound system to induce states of pseudopossession and/ or contemplative ecstasy in conformity with procedures ultimately rooted in traditional African music.

Possession, marked by a violent or convulsive entry to a trance state, may be the most immediately relevant interpretation.[15] Long before the advent of recording technology, the technique of disruption was frequently used in West African and diasporic traditional musics to create a sense of momentary disorientation and heightened excitement. Rouget surveys several instances in which the sudden disruption of an insistent, repeating rhythm—through its disorienting effect on the listener's nervous system—functions to induce trance or possession.[16] This retained African strategy for creating and manipulating dynamic tension acquires new dimensions in the extreme volumes of the Jamaican sound system. Having been stoked for hours with an unending stream of bass-heavy rhythms, frenzied shouts pierce the air as the sound system peaks, rhythm parts reverberate violently in and out of the mix, and the deejay's voice exclaims above it all. As Robbie Shakespeare remembers, such intensity often resulted in extreme audience responses, such as the infamous "lickshot" (firearms fired at the ceiling or into the air in response to particularly dramatic passages of music):

When you go a dance, and you hear sound system them a play, [they have] no effects, the amplifier have just volume, bass, treble. And them used to turn off the bass, so you just get the sound through the horns; the top end a cut through, and when them put in the bass—*vroom!* People rave for that! Especially when the dub wicked, them used to go mad, man. That was one reason why a man start firing guns inna dancehall, because of dub. Ever since from way back rock steady days, when the dub part come in and them turn off the bass and then turn it back in—it sounds so *evilous* it make you fire a gun shot man! Shot used to fire in the dancehall from ever since then.[17]

With the aforementioned "inhabitability" of the dub mix in mind, the violent spatial manipulations might also be heard as functioning to liberate the body and mind from the physical rhythms of oppression by providing a convulsive glimpse of abandon; that is, "resisting the dominant disciplines of bodily reform," although not necessarily through the fits of spiritual possession that Andrew Apter suggests in his discussion of slave religion.[18] Despite the frenzied shouts that can inevitably be heard at the peak of a sound system session, the manner in which people actually dance to roots reggae is more accurately described as cool, calm, graceful, and understated. The convulsive ecstasy of possession is as often sublimated in dub into the sonic sensations of exploding and convulsing space, with its intimate psychological associations of physical movement and constraint.[19] As Lee Perry explained to Kevin Martin in 1995: "When you hear dub you fly on the music. You put your heart, your body and your spirit into the music, you gonna fly. Because if it wasn't for the music, oppression and taxes would kill you. They send taxes and oppression to hold you, a government to tell you what to do and use you like a robot. So they will torment you to death. So when you hear dub you hide from the fuckers there."[20]

That dub mixes could be described as having a "mystical" or "mysterious" feel, had as much to do with the application of reverb as it did with the Rasta-derived lyrical content. The evolution of reverberation and echo as aesthetic devices in popular music dates to the 1950s, and is largely credited to independent blues, rhythm and blues and country music recording labels such as Chess in Chicago and Sun Records in Memphis.[21] But reverb and echo had been used earlier in the recording of Western classical music, to simulate the acoustic environments of traditional performance settings such as churches and cathedrals.[22] The inevitable sonic associations that this carried—of timelessness and meditation—were equally suggested by dub mixes saturated with reverb. It was this quality that inspired Neil "Mad Professor" Fraser to launch his career as a "second wave" studio engineer creating dub music in England: "I just found that it was a music that makes you wonder and it really provides the vehicle for songs and for meditation . . . it didn't have lyrics, so there was space for incidental thought."[23] Similarly, producer Clive Chin felt that "dub music is just purely meditation,"[24] while Winston Riley considered dub "a very soothing and a relaxing music. And a meditative music too."[25] This frequent emphasis on dub as a music of meditation is significant. Rasta-influenced song texts aside for the moment, some of the more dramatic dub mixes might be considered on purely sonic terms as pseudoliturgical music of a type, invested with strong religious, magical, and psychological power deriving from the intertwined spiritual, political, and cultural tropes dominating Jamaican music during the 1970s.

When engineers slowed the tempos of their dub remixes, they eased their listeners into a sonic space conducive to more intimate and erotically charged dancing, intensified by the teasing incompleteness of the fragmented song surface and the engineer's sensuous ride across the spectrum of timbres and textures. The music became eroticized, experienced as a succession of mutating, evolving, and undulating textural/spatial sensations. But when Sasha Frere-Ellis referred to Lee Perry's Black Ark music as the "Aurora borealis of reggae,"[26] he was strongly evoking the sonic subtleties and sublimities of the mix and its contemplative effect upon the listener. Such manipulations function as a sonic catalyst for a state of what Rouget terms *ecstatic contemplation,* empowering the listener through rhythm while drawing them into contemplative states through increasingly subtle manipulations of spatial and textural elements. In this way, the engineer opens a space for the remix as a mode of experiencing more subtle and/or sublime sensations within the songscape. The psychedelic strain of Euro-American pop, the Christian emphasis on otherworldly salvation, and the Rasta emphasis on Africa fused to convey a timeless, African-inflected sense of both *otherness* and *otherworldliness.* Will Montgomery, discussing the music of Lee Perry's Black Ark era, describes how "cut after cut, stretches of otherworldly matter frame despairing social commentary . . . the intensity of the urge to transform the here-and-now in the studio adds a potent and wistful militancy to these songs."[27] The "otherworldy matter" of which he speaks is sound matter, dramatizing the Afro-Caribbean-Protestant-Rastafarian longing for political liberation–recast no longer as Christian heaven, but as African Zion.

Such artistically driven transformations of reality invite comparison with a parallel regional tradition in another artistic medium. The literary genre of *magical realism* emerged during the 1960s and 1970s as a transnational phenomenon, but remains largely associated with the work of Latin America and Caribbean authors such as Gabriel García Márquez, Alejo Carpentier, Jorge Luis Borges and others. Magical realist works characteristically rely on abrupt switches in tense and narrative mode juxtaposing realistic passages with passages of fantastic, magical, or supernatural narrative. In the words of David Mikics, these works "violat[e] the world of everyday appearances by the rich and strange world of dreams."[28] Magical realist texts have been subjected to various interpretations that tend to coalesce around two related themes. The first draws on the idea of the Caribbean as the planetary site of mixing and cultural hybridity par excellence;[29] in this interpretation, magical realism's liminal literary space between fantasy and reality functions to reconcile the diverse cultural currents flowing into the Caribbean. The reconciliation of diverse cultural histories and belief systems implies a destruction of the old in the fusion of the new; the hybrid nature of the Caribbean (especially in the context of the continued domination of Old World political, economic, and cultural structures), implies an embrace of fragmentation and juxtaposition as necessary adaptive strategies.[30]

A second interpretation of magical realism carries more political implications. Some theorists have asserted the genre as a postcolonial art form furnishing "ontological resistance" to structures of thought (including artistic forms) implicated in the colonial project. Lois Zamora and Wendy Faris have claimed that magical realism, in its subversion of colonially derived literary conventions, implicitly resists "monologic" cultural structures; as such, it is particularly useful to (and reflective of) postcolonial cultures.[31] Steven Slemon also finds magical realism "most visibly operative in cultures situated at the margins of mainstream literary traditions"[32] and considers the genre to "[have] echoes in those forms of postcolonial thought which seek to recuperate the lost voices and discarded fragments that imperialist cognitive structures push to the margins of critical consciousness. . . . [These artworks] share an interest in thematically decentering images of fixity while at the same time foregrounding the gaps and absences those fixed and monumental structures produce."[33] It was based on this particular interplay of factors that St. Lucian poet Derek Walcott could claim magical realism as "the authoritative aesthetic response to the Caribbean cultural context."[34]

What does dub share with magical realism? Its decentering of textual and musical syntax, its surreal treatment of song form, and its fragmented and/or stacked narrative voices can be thought of as a musical corollary of what Theo D'Haen describes, in magical realist literature, as the "utopian, if evanescent, promise of transfigured perception, the hypnotic reviewing of everyday existence."[35] Its reliance on practices rooted in the oral tradition—blended with the newly available technology of an emergent recording industry—strongly echoes Frederic Jameson's interpretation of magical realism (in film) as dependent on a fusion of precapitalist with nascent capitalist (especially technological) elements.[36] And, as I shall discuss toward the end of this chapter, the "gaps and absences" that populate the dub mix ultimately had a similarly political utility in Jamaica.

The Politics and Poetics of Erasure: Historical Trauma and the Jamaican Sound Collage

What better medium than collage to express the accumulation of memories? And isn't collage the emblematic medium of the century? Collagists . . . take bits of chaos to . . . investigate, organize and present evidence of the activity of a culture.
—Carrie Rickey[37]

Break a vase, and the love that reassembles the fragments is stronger than the love which took its symmetry for granted when it was whole. The glue that fits the pieces is the sealing of its original shape. It is such a love that reassembles our African and Asiatic fragments. . . . This gathering of broken pieces is the care and pain of the Antilles.—Derek Walcott

One of the historical events that continues to reverberate in cultural forms throughout the African diaspora is the transatlantic slave trade, a historical trauma characterized by forced erasures of cultural memory, and disruptions in linear conceptions of history and human progress. Much of the literature on trauma has addressed various forms of individual suffering (generally addressed through the lens of psychoanalytic theory), as well as large-scale collective traumas such as the mass tragedies suffered in the Holocaust, the nuclear attacks at Hiroshima and Nagasaki, or other recent horrors (generally addressed through the lens of medical anthropology). As Sandra Bloom (1998) has discussed, the effects of trauma seem relatively consistent between the individual and collective spheres,[38] and integral to the trauma literature is the concept of *testimony*—the various ways in which individuals or groups recount traumatic experiences that have remained suppressed.[39] There have been a number of studies tracing a connection between trauma and the formal characteristics of such narrative "testimony," including those found in artistic production. In terms of historical experience, James Clifford feels that "experiences of unsettlement, loss, and recurring terror produce discrepant temporalities—broken histories that trouble the linear, progressivist narratives."[40] Clifford is speaking in abstract terms, in relation to the construction of broadly shared historical narratives, but Shoshana Felman, in her study of the poetry of Holocaust survivors, concretizes this idea in terms of form and individual artistic creation, referring to "an [historical] accident which is materially embodied in an accidenting of the verse."[41] Might the experience of historical trauma have echoes in dub's shattering of narrative continuity?

In general, the literature on trauma has avoided the African diaspora, and the narratives produced within the cultural aftermath of the slave trade. One exception is Paul Gilroy's "Living Memory and the Slave Sublime," which directly engages the issue of historical trauma as it concerns people of African descent.[42] Another is the work of visual artist Arthur Jafa, who has sought to understand the structural and aesthetic implications of historical trauma on African American art making. Both Gilroy and Jafa perceive the legacy of the slavery experience as structurally coded within the expressive forms of the African diaspora. Gilroy finds such historical experience reflected within what he terms "radically unfinished" expressive forms that are "mark[ed] indelibly as the products of slavery."[43] In his interpretation, a legacy of unresolved psychic terror gives coded voice to the "unspeakable terrors" of black history via the narrative ruptures found in a variety of diasporic expressive forms.[44] Jafa has referenced dub music more directly in his idea of "primal sites":

those group experiences that reconfigure who we [African Americans] are as a community. One of the critical primal sites would be the Middle Passage. If you understand the level of horror directed towards a group of people, then you start getting some sense of the magnitude, impact, and level of trauma that that had on the African American community, and how it was particularly one of the earliest group experiences that reshaped an "African psyche" into the beginning of an African American psyche. . . . Now, for example, you look at Black music and see certain structural things that really are about reclaiming this whole sense of absence, loss, not knowing. One of the things I'm thinking about is dub music . . . it ends up really speaking about common experiences because the structure of the music is about things dropping out and coming back in, really reclaiming this whole sense of loss, rupture, and repair that is very common across the experience of black people in the diaspora.[45]

In this reading, an art form such as dub comes to represent a form of the "testimony" discussed by trauma theorists such as Felman. Its deconstructed song forms recalls Gilroy's "unfinished forms," while its reduction of textual meaning to nonsensical phonemes articulates his idea of "*unspeakable* (historical) terrors.*" In this line of reasoning, the privileging of rupture in dub music comes to symbolize the disruptions in cultural memory and the historical shattering of existential peace, encoded into the cultural nervous system and sublimated into musical sound.

Placed in the context of Kingston in the 1970s, these observations also come to symbolize the shattering of the *contemporary* peace, enabling an interpretation of dub as a language of musical "shock," bound closely with aesthetic values of dissonance, destruction, and decay.[46] After all, violence and (later) the overt symbols of warfare were crucial to the highly competitive sound system dances from its earliest days, and this dissonance was eventually sublimated into the very structure of the dub music created for the sound systems.[47] The overdubbed sounds of screeching tires, machine-gun fire, and police sirens in some of King Tubby's dub mixes, the rough clientele that reportedly patronized his sound system,[48] and the ultimate destruction of his system itself at the hands of Kingston police—all attest to these musicians' movement within a vortex of social "counterforces" reflecting political and cultural warfare. And this warfare was both outward (against agents of foreign neocolonialism and local class domination) and inward (in the politically driven "tribal" warfare of Kingston's ghettos). It was this last dynamic that ultimately detached itself from political ideals and became self-sustaining, a type of random violence born of social frustration that eventually claimed the life of King Tubby (and many others) and drove Lee Perry, Scientist, and Philip Smart into exile. In this interpretation, dub is the sound of a society tearing itself apart at the seams, an effect given broader context by erasures, tears, and disruptions in the seam of history itself.

In light of dub music's fragmented song structures, the tortured formal fragmentation of the sound system "macroset," the violently martial ethos of the sound clash, and even the violence sometimes inherent in the music's procedures of realization, the preceding ideas provide insight into what might have caused Jamaica to evolve a style unique in the constellation of world popular musics for such an interruptive manipulation of musical pleasure. It can be argued that in most Western musical forms, pleasure is generally constructed through a dynamic of tension and release within the system of functional harmony. Dub partially subverts this dynamic, reducing harmonic activity to an episodic coloration in which moments of harmony and melody are contrasted with segments of stark low-register relief (drum & bass). On the other hand, aesthetic pleasure in African-derived systems is often constructed around repetition of interlocking rhythmic patterns. Dub partially subverts this also, with its periodic disruption of rhythmic patterns. As such, the music essentially subverts the pleasure principles of two musical systems: aesthetic pleasure here is fundamentally predicated upon the fragmented narratives of the *sound collage,* which in this case seems to conform to the emotional pendulum of post-traumatic experience that allows pleasure to be experienced only fleetingly as it swings between sensations of harmonic fullness and starkness, and between sensations of rhythmic continuity and disruption.[49]

As a form predicated upon the de- and reconstruction of aesthetic logics, collage has often been called a quintessential form of the turbulent twentieth century, a form inviting potentially endless possibilities of invention and interpretation.[50] Cubists found in its flattening of pictorial perspective a means of portraying the simultaneity of time and space. Italian Futurists used its mechanically produced print and photographic source materials to proclaim their ideals of a machine age. Russian Constructivists used its fragmented syntax as a way to portray the class struggles of their society. Dadaists and Surrealists built collage through a variety of chance procedures and asserted the form as simultaneously the most organically poetic and potentially revolutionary.[51] But several understandings of collage seem particularly relevant in the context of the danced (and sound-engineered) cultural shifts and social turbulence of Jamaica's roots era. The Dada/Surrealist artist Jean Arp used collage to evoke processes of decay in both nature and art, while historians have also read in his collages "an attempt to express in new formats regenerative powers." A similar interpretation was offered by art historian Katherine Hoffman, who saw in collage "a sense of the possibility of connectedness but at the same time . . . a sense of alienation of individuals afloat in a world turned upside down."[52] A third interpretation can be found in the writing of jazz historian Krin Gabbard who has speculated (in relation to the deconstructive aspects of modern jazz vis-à-vis the American pop song tradition) that the aestheticization of error and chance in some forms of black music arguably "shows contempt for Western art music with its smooth, "organic" surfaces, its technical precision, and its highly-stylized set of emotional codes."[53]

In his 1996 essay "The Aesthetics of the Global Imagination," ethnomusicologist Veit Erlmann speculated that the juxtaposition of radically dissimilar or decontextualized genres in certain forms of world popular music may reflect the violent historical encounter between industrial capitalist and preindustrial societies (note how closely this echoes Jameson's aforementioned observation concerning magical realism).[54] Jamaica has been a part of the global economic order at least since the period of European colonization, but Erlmann's words are nevertheless relevant to the turbulent late–cold war dynamics of the Manley-Seaga years. Like Gilroy's "unfinished forms," dub may be one of a number of diasporic musics on which a traumatic history and turbulent present has left its structural imprint, "converting the outrage of the years into a music"[55] through an aesthetic of broken, discontinuous pleasures that may represent a synaptic adaptation to long-term historical trauma,[56] but that also fit into a broader global pattern in which collage forms join the search for new realities to define the twentieth century.

Science *and Space: Dub and Afro-futurism*

We need images of tomorrow and our people need them more than most. . . .
The historical reason we've been so impoverished in terms of future images is
because until fairly recently, as a people we've been systematically forbidden
any images of our past.[57] —Samuel Delany to Mark Dery

The machines gleam magnificently. Their newness and sophistication seems to
balance the space on the edge of the sonic future. Is this a mirror image of Apollo
and Sputnik with their cramped and awesome technical interiors?[58]
—Louise Meintjes

To the extent that Jamaican engineers relied upon the most modern sound technology to craft sonic evocations of archaic Africana, dub music has become an important musical reference point in the thematic trope often referred to as "Afro-futurism."[59] The Afro-futurist theme runs through black music, film, literature, and visual arts, often using the imagery of space travel and other advanced technology to recast the turbulent black past in terms of a liberated, technological utopia.[60] Afro-futurist ideas can be traced throughout the twentieth century, but arguably consolidated during the 1960s, when the new reality of outer space travel and the related proliferation of science fiction imagery in mass culture—in combination with the politically and culturally motivated embrace of African culture throughout the African diaspora—suggested a liberatory cultural potential for technology.

From the 1960s to the present, these ideas have seemed particularly evident in selected works by African American jazz and popular artists, the more prominent of whom would include Herbie Hancock, Jimi Hendrix, Earth Wind, and Fire, Parliament, Sun Ra, Miles Davis, Jeff Mills, and Derrick May. In the work of Hancock's electro-acoustic Mwandishi band (1969–73), for example, futuristic-sounding electronic synthesizers are used to replicate African percussion patterns, which in turn are used as the basis for jazz improvisation.[61] On Hendrix's *Electric Ladyland,* a variety of archaic, rural blues forms are electrically revamped, graced with otherworldy lyrical themes, and subjected to extensive sound processing and studio manipulation.[62] Earth, Wind and Fire fuse imagery drawn from archaic black cultural sources (Egyptian pyramids, African mysticism) with the iconography of outer space travel, while using the percussive sound of 1970s funk as a medium for the rearticulation of traditional African musical values.[63] A similar fusion is strongly evident in selected works of Sun Ra such as *Space Is the Place, Astro-Black,* and *Cosmic Tones for Mental Therapy,* in which juxtaposed themes of ancient Egypt, archaic Africana, exile, and interstellar travel are dramatized through Sun Ra's fusion of free jazz, improvised electronic textures, and African-inspired drumming.[64] Parliament's theme-driven albums such as *Mothership Connection* and *Clones of Dr. Funkenstein,* laid the foundation for their concert "funk operas," based around tropes of interstellar travel and genetic manipulation, transgressively recast through the ethos of the postindustrial urban ghetto.[65] Trumpeter Miles Davis traversed similar conceptual territory in the mid-1970s on jazz-fusion works such as *Dark Magus, Get Up With It, Agharta,* and *Pangaea,* which fused post-Coltrane free and modal jazz improvisation, abstracted rhythm and blues, psychedelic rock, African-derived percussion, pure electronic music, and extensive post-performance studio manipulation.[66] More recently, Detroit-based techno musicians such as Derrick May and Jeff Mills, working within one of the planet's most notorious postindustrial settings (and one dominated by the symbol of transport vehicles), would find resonance in the metaphor of space vessels and outer space travel on recordings such as May's *Innovator,* or Mills's *Waveform Transmissions.*[67]

Besides being a fad derived from the technological advances of the times, these images may have proliferated because they offered a novel inflection to traditional forms of African-derived mysticism, naturalism, and magic, while inspiring a rearticulation of the historical experiences of colonization, slavery, immigration, frontier, and exile. In light of the artists listed above, however, we might ask whether Afro-futurism is fundamentally an *African American* trope, reflecting a particular proximity to the apparatus of the cold war. Much of the emphasis on technology seems a likely reflection of the space race as a component of the arms race between two cold war superpowers; it is clear that many of the sonic developments during the 1960s and 1970s were by-products of military technology.[68] But to what extent is the Afro-futurist trope, or something similar to it, evident in other regions of the black world? And what is its relevance to Jamaican dub music?

It is undeniable that the sci-fi undertones of dub have garnered the music a substantial audience outside of Jamaica, among listeners from the experimental and electronic strains of Western popular music. This accounts, for example, for the cover art that was used to sell the music outside of Jamaica—a decision largely made by the English recording companies independently of the Jamaican artists.[69] Overall, however, the placement of dub within the canon of both Afro-futurist and sci-fi–influenced music has been fairly slow. Philip Hayward, for example, devotes an entire chapter to the sonic influence of science fiction on popular and experimental musics that mentions all of the above-cited examples, but fails to mention dub.[70] The likely explanation for omissions of this sort is that while the full-length album is considered the quintessential medium for post-1960s rock, dub mixes exist mainly on B-sides of singles. Dub albums tend to be mere compilations of these mixes that lack the clear thematic continuity that listeners expect of album-length works (exceptions might be thematic dub LPs such as Lee Perry's *Super Ape* and *Blackboard Jungle Dub*).

More significant, however, is the observation that in Jamaican dub, the sci-fi component has typically been more implicit than explicit. The music tends to be less concerned with images of flying saucers and interplanetary travel, and is more reflective of prominently interwoven dichotomies of nature/technology and past/future. Fundamental here is the idea of Kingston as an electronically wired urban concrete jungle set within a tropical Caribbean island. Because of an economy in which recorded music has traditionally proved more viable than performing ensembles, Jamaica has been a site of particularly interesting adaptations of successive forms of sound reproduction technology. The country's recording engineers and sound system operators have consistently pushed the envelope of what is expected of sound technology in terms of both aesthetics and performance capability, and some of their most imaginative ideas are said to have prefigured later developments in sound technology. Scientist, for example, claims: "It's been documented that me and King Tubby's joked about those things for years before they were made. . . . Even moving faders that you see come out with [the] Neve [console], it's been documented way before where me and King Tubby's been sitting around talking, joking about moving faders . . . we were talking about 64 track and all these new devices that were not invented at that time."[71] The engineer went on to claim that the manufacturers of this equipment "were listening to reggae and the problems we were finding, they run into the same problems too. . . . When you design [sound equipment] on the bench, everything work normal, you get the perfect readout you're trying to get. But when you get into the real world, that same amplifier becomes a piece of crap, especially when you playing reggae through it. So if it wasn't for reggae, they couldn't fine tune a lot of those audio equipment."[72]

So during the same period that Rasta-influenced reggae musicians were placing such emphasis on tropes of nature and the African past, foreign manufacturers of sound technology were using Jamaican music to test the durability and capabilities of their equipment, and to set a course for the future. Such dichotomies reflect a characteristic juxtaposition of "roots" and technology that has provided Jamaican popular music with its particular dynamism since the late 1960s. While conducting research on Jamaica's language and culture in 2001, Hannah Appel witnessed this juxtaposition at a party on the rural outskirts of Kingston: "I found myself at a country birthday party. We're talking *country;* no running water, as many goats and chickens at the party as people—and a man in charge of more computer equipment than I could ever hope to understand. The sound system was not a set of speakers and turntables, but two new PC computers complete with CD drives and digital amplification and sound modification equipment. And all this up in middle of the Blue Mountains!"[73]

These dichotomies also raise the issue of how cultures on the margins of the world's technological centers relate to technology as it "trickles down" to their regions, especially given the complicity of technology with Western racial/cultural/technological domination.[74] In the music culture of Jamaica it seems that technology was embraced along with its militarist baggage—hence the technomartial ethos of the sound clash.[75] Yet Jamaicans recognized its destructive and pollutive potentials: this is when it clashed against the affirming ideologies of "roots," black pride, and/or national pride, and demanded grounding via local cultural symbols and practices. Within Jamaica, this ongoing tension has shaped the local adaptation of sound technology.

In light of these juxtapositions at the heart of the music, it is not surprising that the Jamaican recording studio has often been conceptualized by its pioneers as some bizarre hybrid of laboratory, spaceship, temple, jungle, or shaman's hut. Lee Perry described his Black Ark studio to David Toop as "like a space craft. You could hear space in the tracks. Something there was like a holy vibration and a godly sensation. . . . I was getting help from God, through space, through the sky, through the firmament, through the earth, through the wind, through the fire. I got support through the weather to make space music."[76] Perry's technological ruminations were always grounded in his experience of nature; on another occasion he claimed dub was "the sound of the rain, the wind, and the water—that's the way it's mixed, that's what's in the dub. 'Cause it come from rain, thunder and lightning, breeze, and all the invisible forces."[77] Meanwhile, Scientist observed: "A lot of people don't know this, but there's a connection between music and what goes on out there in the solar system and all the universe. There is that deep, unexplained mystery that music have on the world . . . to be honest, sometime when you in the studio and you doing those mixes there, you actually feel like you're communicating with something else out there, you don't know how to explain it."[78]

Louise Meintjes has waxed insightfully about this sensation to which Scientist refers, asserting that "through the art of illusion and the capacity of the imagination, [the recording studio] seems to house a natural force that when tapped produces compelling art. . . . It is from here that music-maker's poetics travel through conversation to God, to the moon, to Mars, and back into their sound. And it is from this tape reel that the lives of music makers might spin off into new places."[79] The peculiar manner in which sound technology was adapted in Jamaica should not, at last, be surprising; as James Lastra has demonstrated, the evolution of technology has been driven as much by public and private imagination as it has by technological necessity.[80] And it is this act of public imagination that allows us to understand even the most far-flung visions in terms of postcolonial culture, predicated as it is on an intensive interrogation of future cultural possibilities.[81]

> *Some call it science*
> *Some call it necromancy*
> *Some call it plain* obeah . . .
> —Prince Buster, from "Science,"1972

The science fiction metaphor also has relevance in the irreverent way Jamaican recording engineers utilized their sound equipment (as discussed in chapter 2), which at the very least seemed to problematize the issue of Western technoscience and its network of cultural associations. The genre of dub music is populated with the trope of the "crazy" sound mixer, as well as the theme of science interwoven with madness. Lee Perry is the best-known example of this tendency, but it is also reflected in the work and imagery of engineers such as Scientist and Mad Professor.[82] Of course, it must be mentioned that the term *science* has a double resonance in Jamaica, often used colloquially to refer to the island's tradition of neo-African black magic, Obeah.[83] Derived from the Akan term *obia* (ghost), the symbol of Obeah has sometimes provided a symbolic medium for the local grounding of global sound technology. Kevin Martin has even observed that the terms *dub* (noun) and *dubby* (adjective) resonate etymologically with "duppy," the Jamaican patwa term for ghosts or malevolent spirits.[84] The diasporic project of reclaiming an African heritage was necessarily marked by an ethos of mystery that by turns reflected the exploration of a heretofore unknowable past, and an engagement with the African "other" that had historically functioned as the shadow symbol to Western modernity.[85] In the words of literary scholar Nana Wilson-Tagoe,"the [African] experience itself ha[d] been shrouded in obscurity and was the source of embarrassment and shame in a society whose unifying factor throughout its beginnings as a plantation society was the consensual acceptance of African inferiority."[86] Stated differently, dub reinserted the mystery and spookiness into reggae.

In traditional musical terms, this sense of mystery was often evoked through the use of minor keys, slow tempi, African percussion, and bottom-heavy rhythm arrangements—all key elements of 1970s roots reggae that were intensified by the sound processing of the dub mix. So it follows that when producer Coxsone Dodd remixed saxophonist Karl Bryan's minor-key "Money Generator" instrumental into a dub version, he slowed the tape speed, applied the sound processors, and retitled it "Musical Science," a moody version dominated by neo-African Nyabinghi hand drumming and a hazy, atmospheric mix.[87] Clearly, the doubly resonant image of the Jamaican engineer as a "scientist" was necessary in adapting sound technology to local priorities: it was precisely the idiosyncratic use of that technology that helped rupture stylistic norms and project diasporic Africans across space and time in order to reclaim and reinhabit a cultural heritage lost during centuries of slavery and colonization.

As such, the music actually implies several re-visionings of the concept of *space*. Dub's sonic effects, somewhat similar to what could be heard contemporaneously in the soundtracks of science fiction films, evoke the dark expanse of *outer* space. The oft-mentioned meditative quality of the music, on the other hand, resonates with a listener's *internal* space. The Africa-inspired rhythm structures evoke a mood of *historical* space, providing a soundtrack for a time when an African god-king was believed to be incarnate on Earth and the music had a ethos of grandeur that was conducive to the expansive and idealistic thinking of the era. Even the *physical* concept of space is relevant here: dub's spatialized songscapes, heard at the extreme volumes of the Jamaican sound system, simulated an actual physical space within which the "roots" African past and the utopian sci-fi future could be fleetingly experienced as one. Thus, it is not surprising that both the creators of dub music and their audiences frequently speak of the music in terms of "dimensions" and "other dimensions."

As a genre, science fiction is often considered the futurist imaginings of the technological centers of modern, industrialized nations, rather than the nostalgic, Africa-centered imaginings of a small, technologically marginal Caribbean island culture.[88] This irony in itself mirrors a broader technological-cultural-racial stereotype in which, as Alondra Nelson notes, "blackness" is typically positioned in opposition to narratives of "technology" and "progress."[89] Positioned culturally, historically, and geographically between Africa and America, Jamaican studio engineers utilized the available technology to imply a potent form of sonic Afro-futurism. And while the Africa-centered narratives of Rastafari, detached from the popular song mediums, fantasize of an uncomplicated return to ancient culture,[90] dub demonstrates that Jamaican attitudes toward technology actually contradict these oppositional distinctions between a past understood as nature-based, primitive, and stereotypically African, and a future understood as technological and stereotypically de-Africanized.

Dave Marsh characterized reggae of the 1970s as reflecting "the potential of human lives in a way peculiar to Jamaicans, living in a trap between the squalid beauties of a pre-industrial culture and the disintegrating splendors of an imperial one."[91] Dub as reggae's visionary impulse straddled a similar position between preindustrial, industrial, and information age aesthetics, reflected in the use of "roots" rhetoric in the abuse/deconstruction of the modernist/analog machine, as a precursor to a digital pop aesthetic. As a body of black science fiction gradually consolidates itself throughout the African diaspora among the poles of archaic Africana, contemporary culture, and futuristic technoimagery, the ruminative soundscapes of dub will likely continue to provide a soundtrack to the Afro-inflected transmutation of technology at the turn of the twenty-first century.[92]

Conclusion

John Cage's idea of creating a purely "ambient" music by allowing environmental sounds their rightful place within the listener's aestheticized attention was partially predicated on Eastern-influenced ideas of individual contemplation. The idea finds its Afro-inflected parallel in communally driven musics of African descent, where the formal structure of music is often partially predicated on the sounds of the surrounding society and its processes of communal composition. Dub in this sense is not so different from the mutable and modular song forms that accompany oral arts throughout West Africa, for example. This is one reason why the recorded pop song has assumed a uniquely ephemeral form in Jamaica: its structure fundamentally reflects a deep fusion of Jamaica's African-derived oral heritage (a communal process of composition) with the latent potentials of new technologies, in the context of a very raw form of profit-driven competition in the local music industry. In popular music, this ephemerality was apparent at least since the days of the early sound systems, when selectors scratched the titles off imported records to avoid detection by the spies of competing sound systems. Songs were essentially separated from their song title signifiers, leading to a multiplicity of titles for the same material, and ultimately feeding directly into (and off) the Jamaican masses' reliance on oral as opposed to written dissemination of information.

As such, the social element holds particular significance in this Afrocentric definition of the "ambient." In Jamaica, concepts such as "the individual composer" and the "integrity of the work" do not prevail to the extent that they do within American and Western European notions of authorship. As we have seen, a "song" in Jamaica must sometimes be understood as a composite of its multiple versions. One important motivation for breaking songs apart into dub mixes was to adapt them to what was essentially a communal mode of composition, with clear African roots, in which different members of the community have a voice. Many different musicians get a chance over the latest rhythm tracks; in Jamaica, as this book has chronicled, this process grew to include recording engineers. In Scientist's words, "Reggae's a very unique music on the planet. It has all these different elements where everybody gets a chance to be in the spotlight. *People even give the engineer a chance to be in the spotlight.*"[93]

We can expand the scope of this "spotlight" to encompass another class of musicians. Caribbean literary theorist Theo D'Haen once referred to language as a dominant issue in the history of colonization,[94] because of the direct relationship between the historical destruction of African culture and the forced acceptance of the colonizer's language. Simon Gikandi claims that (postcolonial) Caribbean literature as a whole is marked by the enterprise of deconstructing the colonizer's language.[95] Thus, language becomes a primary battleground during a postcolonial moment in which the formerly colonized revitalize the historical imagination while asserting an emergent national culture. In this light, another significant class of musicians to share the "spotlight" Scientist speaks of were the sound system deejays of the 1970s. The literary readings offered earlier become concrete when we consider that the musical language of dub developed side by side with the emergent virtuosity of the sound system deejays; in fact, the primary use of dub mixes was as a background for deejaying. Thus, dub's fracturing of song form did not only lead to a music that emphasized soundscape, groove, and texture. It also fractured narrative conventions in a way that broke open the logic of the colonial language, enabling the DJs to gradually move Jamaican patwa to the forefront of the country's popular music and culture. In the end, ironically, it was technological developments imported from the Euro-American context that enabled the prominence of what Kamau Brathwaite might term Jamaica's "nation language"—a localized creole tongue emerging on the deconstruction of the colonial tongue. Ultimately this allowed the Jamaican subaltern to "speak."[96]

This "speaking" was crucial in the rise of postcolonial Jamaican consciousness, and the process shares much with what Roger Fowler calls "anti-languages," described as "the special argot of subcultures which exist in an antagonistic relationship with the norm society." J. Martin Yinger describes the anti-language as an "effort to create a counter-reality, freed from the inevitable entanglement of the dominant reality—within which [certain groups] suffer—with dominant language usages."[97] Considering the cultural battle that had to be fought within Jamaica to propel roots reggae to the forefront of the country's cultural revolution, such observations are relevant internally, to Jamaica's complexion-coded class struggle, and externally, in the entire nation's relationship to its history of colonization. This idea of "anti-language" can also be applied to the very structural syntax of dub music itself: the cultural battle was not only waged on the field of language, but was also waged structurally, within the formal language of the post–World War II popular song as inherited from European and, ironically (African) American sources.

My main point here, however, is that if the sonic space opened by the dub mix liberated the musicality of "nonmusicians" such as recording engineers, it also liberated the officially marginalized, class-based social and political discourse offered by the sound system DJs. As David Katz characterizes the sound system as the "ghetto's newspaper,"[98] so does Bobby Vicious opine:

> those flip sides or dubs turned out to be a platform for people who *weren't* singers, to voice social issues in the dancehall or on their local sound systems. Many times it was a young U-Brown talking on the sound system, it was a young Big Youth, a young Dillinger, a young Brigadier Jerry, a young Charlie Chaplin, a young Josey Wales. I'm sure Tubby's didn't intend it to be a backdrop for deejays. Because at the time there weren't a lot of deejays. But that's what it evolved to be—dub music blended itself into the culture of Jamaica. Because there was a lot that needed to be said. It brought to the forefront the issues that were happening that people wouldn't address. And if you go through the history of the music you'll find that every issue that the politicians, or the social environment at the time, would fail to address, you could pick up a record and you could hear in detail what it was all about. So all the social issues were addressed in the dancehall, thanks to the fact that there was a platform created by Tubbys, or Joe Gibbs, or Studio One—dub music—that allowed that type of thing to happen.[99]

Herein lies the link between style and context, and an indication of the broader implications of dub's disruptive strategies. For the most part, the sonic fragments one hears floating throughout a dub mix are not samples drawn form external sources, but fragments of a preexisting song with which the Jamaican listening public was already familiar. The original dub engineers had to literally "break" songs apart in order to achieve their fragmentary musical language and it was this act of musical "violence," with all of its political and cultural overtones, that revolutionized Jamaican culture by creating a space for the deejays. In terms of its place *within* Jamaican culture, this is where dub acquires its deepest political significance.

From the global perspective (as we shall see in the coda), Jamaica's emphasis on versioning facilitated the transformation of formerly fixed pop songs into the more fluid, remix-based conceptions of composing typified by today's digital technology. This peculiarly Jamaican take on sound technology also had profound local implications, in terms of the nation's relationship to its own history. Michael Chanan takes the position that during the course of the twentieth century, sound media gradually replaced writing as the premier historical storage technology.[100] This shift had particularly profound implications for a (largely) African-derived Jamaican culture in which, for several reasons, aurality (and orality) had historically taken precedence over written forms.[101] The technology allowed the simultaneous consolidation and expression of an alternative Jamaican cultural history that had heretofore existed beyond the margins of official histories. Eventually, as these song histories became influential in both the local and global spheres, they forced a renegotiation of the nation's conception of itself, its history, and its relationship to the rest of the world.

Yet even this radically revised history became mere source material for the endlessly mutating remix. Like some aspects of free jazz in America, dub is a style that, by virtue of its historical moment, reified but also simultaneously subverted "blackness" as a stable signifier of cultural identity. While vocalists of the 1970s such as Bob Marley, Johnny Clarke, and Yabby U composed passionate political and religious songs rooted in their Rastafarian faith and a linear, eschatological conception of black history, the work of recording engineers such as King Tubby and Lee Perry (despite their own intentions) often disfigured these concepts into distorted catchphrases alternately rendered profoundly evocative and/or absurdly meaningless. These dub mixes at least partially foreshadow a sense of "post": "postsong," "postblackness," and especially, "posthistory." Even in Ethiopia, where Haile Selassie is remembered as a despot, it is possible to find Ethiopians who have become adherents of Rastafari at the same time that they despise the historical Selassie. As the artist Fikre Gebreyesus put it: "Their [Jamaican Rastafarians'] Selassie is not the same Selassie that we experienced. But the two can co-exist."[102] It is doubtful whether this type of historical anomaly would have occurred within such a brief historical window, without the powerful medium of Jamaican reggae music. Jamaica, then, has not only been a crucial source of unique sound concepts; it has implicitly provided in its music a template for cultural reconfiguration. With the global spread of both reggae and Rastafari, it has also offered the world one of the most potent reinterpretations of Africa, one that has in turn influenced cultural trends in Africa itself.[103] In the view of Guyanese poet David Dabydeen, such a tendency toward the cultural "remix" is central to the Caribbean cultural experience:

if you live in England where the English have a very concrete (or stone/marble) sense of their histories, and you as a Caribbean person come to a sense that your history is nebulous and shifting, it means that you have a tremendous capacity for a new kind of freedom . . . you can dream, you can surmise, you can invent. The nebulousness of one's background gives one a kind of epistemological freedom, an existential freedom . . . we were freed of certain traditions, knowledges and so on, and while we have sorrow about the loss of those, nevertheless, we are always on the threshold of originality.[104]

This dichotomy of loss and invention is at the heart of the dub mix. In cultural terms these mixes can be heard as reflecting the ruination of an idealized African past, or as the harbingers of an as-yet-unarticulated cultural formation. In existential terms, the spaces of the dub mix may be similarly perceived as either barren, monotonous craters devoid of warmth, meaning, optimism, and human presence, or as fertile, tropical wellsprings taut with anticipatory tension in which the pleasurable sensation of free-floating is periodically interrupted by glimpses of the divine. Like doomed prophet/historians who managed to leave their scriptural fragments behind, the creators of dub offered an Afro-psychedelic vision of the turbulent cultural past as well as the digital/cybernetic future—until the violence around them either consumed them, forced them to adapt to a new creative paradigm, or forced them into exile. As reggae pioneer Yabby U asserted to Steve Barrow:

Reggae music now, it suppose to teach our people. It's supposed to be the scroll, like in those days the prophets used to have scroll, wax upon stone. The words was unto them, the chief musicians. Them record history and leave it in caves, and the indivisible hand of the almighty make men discover it, and translate it to Bible. The Bible was until Revelation. When it reach Revelation, it need a new Bible. Them never know about atomic energy, them never know about digital system, computer and all them things. . . . Our Bible is music. It is wax upon record, like how theirs was wax upon stone. Everything that happened to them happened to we.[105]

A final thought about the place of technology in all this. Virtual technologies such as sound recording and film were often misunderstood in their early years as serving purely documentary functions; their creations were often dismissed as inferior simulations of reality. A more expansive take is that creative manipulations of these technologies in fact create new forms of reality (that is, new ways of "hearing" the world) within which they function as "prosthetic" devices, ultimately extending human sensory perceptions into new areas.[106] At the same time, these technologies essentially function as fantasy projection devices, containing, in their deceptively accurate simulation of "reality," the potential to disrupt human understandings of the "real." In the context of their times, this is one way to understand the creators of dub in Jamaica. As Kwame Dawes implies in his 1999 essay on

Lee Perry, the difficulty these visionary musicians experienced in the turbulence of Jamaica had a flip side. By fashioning (like Perry) idiosyncratic spaces within which they could exist as freely creative beings, they expanded the parameters of imagination within reggae music; in so doing, they provided a new cultural template as well as a fertile space for Jamaica's interaction with the wider world.[107] The terms of this interaction, which is the subject of the coda, sometimes reflected the issues raised in this chapter. Equally often, however (and in tandem with the multilayered and indeterminate nature of the music), dub fused unpredictably with other popular music traditions and their own various extramusical resonances. It was in this way that the style was gradually reimagined as both a potent musical influence and as a sonic metaphor for transatlantic culture at the end of the twentieth century.

Coda

Electronica, Remix Culture, and Jamaica as a Source of Transformative Strategies in Global Popular Music

> *We used to do a lot of experimentin'... when we were doing these things it was just a one-in-the-world thing. Everybody used to say our music is "unfinished." In America they used to say that, years ago.... And now them comin' and mixing the music just like how [Jamaicans] used to mix: heavy, the whole echo thing and drop-out.... Even the idea of rappin' and deejaying—look how long Jamaica people been deejaying![1]*
> —Augustus Pablo

> *"At six o'clock one night last month, in a midtown Manhattan recording studio that adjoins a seedy topless club, Frankie Knuckles erased everything except the vocals and string section from 'Build,' a ballad by the British pop group Innocence. Peter Schwartz, a keyboardist, booted up a network of synthesizers, samplers, and sequencers, all linked to an Atari laptop computer, and, guided by a 'shopping list' from Mr. Knuckles, began to reconstruct the song. He progressed from a persistent kick drum and staccato bass line to cymbal crescendos, cathedral-like chimes and a profusion of lush percussion. By midnight he had orchestrated 'Build' into a fireworks show, with new colors and small explosions every few seconds.... Although he hadn't touched an instrument, [Knuckles] may have transformed coal into a diamond. For someone who neither plays nor sings, he has an unusual position in the business...." For just a few thousand dollars, these audio auteurs refashion records to match changing styles. Success has made the practice rampant; one executive estimates that half the singles on the Top 100 chart are remixed.[2]*
> —Rob Tannenbaum, 1992

Directly and indirectly, the comments that open this chapter highlight several of the conceptual cornerstones of Jamaican music in the roots era, as well as their influence on the creation of popular music in the digital age. The stylistic traits of contemporary dance music cannot be solely attributed to dub, but the fact that many American and European remixes are now labeled on recordings as "dub" mixes attests that many of dub's concepts lay at the heart of what is variously referred to today as "electronic dance music," "electronica," "DJ culture," and/or "remix culture."

Louis Chude-Sokei's 1994 "Postnationalist Geographies" does an excellent job of sketching out the transnational network through which much Jamaican music has come to be produced in the digital age. He narrates a de-territorialized process of creation that benefits from the ease of circulating digital sound files, and that is situated between Kingston and the non-Jamaican cities with the largest Jamaican populations: New York City and London. While this process did intensify exponentially with the advent of digital technology, its roots have been in place for decades. In this final chapter, I shall briefly discuss some examples of the stylistic "spillages" that took place in these various locations, as Jamaican dub music interacted, in its day, with various local popular musics. I shall thus highlight the broader theme of Jamaica as the source of several transformative strategies in post–World War II popular music composition.

Dub in the English Context

If dub as a discrete genre faded away from the cutting edge of Jamaican popular music after the mid-1980s, its influence outside of Jamaica was just beginning. In England, Jamaican popular music in general had already enjoyed various phases of popularity, its geographic spread a consequence of the musical travel accompanying thousands of Caribbean workers who replenished England's labor force following World War II.[3] The music grew steadily as a presence in England from the early 1960s when the first Kingston-styled sound systems began to sprout up in London areas with sizable Jamaican populations, such as Brixton and Shepherd's Bush. The then-popular ska and rock steady styles gradually attracted the interest of working-class English youths (particularly skinheads) living adjacent to black areas. The success of infectious dance songs such as Jimmy Cliff's "Wonderful World" and Millicent Small's "My Boy Lollipop" (both 1964), and Desmond Dekker's "007" (1967) proved that Jamaican music could exist as a viable and potentially profitable genre in England.

By the time of the rise of roots reggae in the 1970s, the popularity of Jamaican music had receded a bit in the United Kingdom: the sound, ethos, and lyrical content of the music had become something quite different from that of the previous decade. Steve Barrow remembered, "The Rasta phenomenon had spread to the Jamaican communities in the UK amongst the youth. So you had a lot of guys dreading in the UK. And this really alienated the previous audience of skinheads who liked the more jump up type of reggae."[4] Dave Hendley elaborated: "Everyone in England knew what reggae was because it was so big in the skinhead era. The reggae of the late sixties had more in common with black American music, had a more poppy feel. It was accessible. We had reggae chart hits here. But by the early seventies, it kind of retreated in on itself. There wasn't much interest by white people or mainstream media. It became a really underground, almost impenetrable scene. It was the property of West Indian immigrants and their kids, a rallying thing for black youth. You've got the influence of more cultural lyrics and the whole kind of black awareness. It got more like a protest music. It didn't really appeal to anyone else. The general public just thought of it as a weird kind of music that existed underground."[5]

It was in conjunction with the experiences of these Caribbean immigrants in England, however, that this decidedly subcultural music gradually reemerged as a potent cultural symbol and factored into the consolidation of a distinct pan-Anglophone Caribbean identity in England. In fact, several incidents of racially charged conflict (including the notorious Notting Hill Carnival incident of 1976) served as catalysts for Jamaican reggae to serve as a politically charged space of cultural difference—leading in turn to an increase in song themes addressing themes of racism and police brutality, and reggae's eventual consolidation (along with punk rock) as one of England's dominant outsider musics of the 1970s.[6]

Despite reggae's marginality, then, its social urgency and stylistic innovation gradually repositioned it as a musical and social force in England. It was in conjunction with these developments that Jamaican reggae acquired a new level of cultural cachet and entered a new period of critical and popular acclaim in England, powered by the dramatic ascension of Bob Marley (as well as other artists such as Jimmy Cliff and Peter Tosh), upon whose shoulders an entire international reggae industry (largely based in England) gradually coalesced. London became the epicenter of a growing European interest in Jamaican music, and by the mid-1970s, the music was entering its first phase of broad international popularity.[7] Many seminal recordings were made in England at this time (including several live albums attesting to the importance of the British reggae audience), and recording and/or distribution arrangements were made with major British and American recording companies including Island, Virgin, EMI, and others.[8]

The Sound System in England

The spread of reggae in the United Kingdom was not limited to recordings and high-profile concert performances, however. The sound system phenomenon also became a presence in most cities with sizable Jamaican populations: Nottingham, Bristol, Liverpool, Cardiff, Birmingham, London, Doncaster, Manchester, and others. Like the popularity of reggae in general, the sound system boom of the 1970s was tied to the experiences of immigrant Caribbean populations. As Dave Hendley remembered: "In the seventies, there was a lot more racism in this country. Allegiance to your sound system gave you a kind of community. It was yours, a bit of your own culture. If you wanted to smoke ganja in there, you could smoke ganja. There was freedom in there, not living in the English system. I think that it was particularly important for that first generation of kids that was born and brought up in England. It gave them a sense of identity."[9] And British sound system pioneer Jah Shaka voiced similar sentiments about the cultural priorities of the British sound systems and the role of dub music:

The sound [system] came out of the struggle in the '70s which black people were going through in this country—we got together and decided that the sound should play a main part in black people's rights & we would work hard at it & promote some better mental purpose within the black race. I used to get a few [dub recordings] from Jamaica, and what we couldn't get we made ourselves. We had a lot of musicians creating stuff for us. . . . The spiritual concept was people remembering their past—this kept coming into the music—as people remembered their history it was repeated on record to make the rest of the nation aware what had happened.[10]

The history of which Jah Shaka speaks is in fact a dual history: an Afro-Caribbean history *and* a history of the Jamaican experience in England. In his historical survey of reggae music, Lloyd Bradley noted the "siege mentality" of immigrant Caribbeans in England and their consequent receptivity to Rastafarian-derived notions of displacement. This mentality resulted in a cultural ethos of "double exile" (or, to use Jonathan Boyarin's term, *re-diasporization*), reflecting the experience of an African diasporic population transplanted as an Anglo-Caribbean ethnic minority within the heart of the former colonial center.[11]

The British sound system eventually solidified into a viable institution and systems proliferated during the 1970s. In London alone, some of the prominent sounds of the time included those founded by Ken "Fatman" Gordon, Count Shelley, Jah Shaka, Sir Jessus, and two sound systems named in honor of Clement Dodd and Duke Reid, respectively: Lloyd Coxsone and UK Duke Reid. It was in the sound systems that dub thrived: as in Jamaica, it was typically used as a background for deejaying.

Eventually, because of the proximity of working-class communities of different ethnic origins, the music began to attract listeners from beyond local Jamaican communities. In Jamaica, as discussed earlier, definitions of the word "dub" were varied and occasionally contradictory. The style's current well-defined status is owed partly to its reception in England, where fairly discrete genre status was bestowed upon it by English pop music listeners and journalists whose ears had been (pre)conditioned by the sounds of psychedelic music of the 1960s and 1970s. Adrian Sherwood, who went on to become one of the major figures in England's neo-dub scene, speculated that among this particular audience, the popularity of dub "came down to people smoking spliffs in their houses. The UK found dub a market amongst students—a largely white crowd, but also amongst black kids. They'd sit in their houses and play dub music and it became very understandable why. We all loved taking acid and smoking weed and it was quite logical for us to do that. It's very trippy music."[12] Dave Hendley experienced the music as "very uplifting and actually pretty deep. Serious music, but you could also dance to it." He went to explain:

Something about the music really appealed to me. I think because, it was a strange music. It just sounded so radically different—I know from my point of view, when I first heard stuff like Tubby's mixes, they just sounded like no other music that I'd ever come across. It was pretty radical electronic music, that whole concept of breaking down a rhythm track and then building something totally different. It might be a completely upbeat tune, but by the time they've stripped it down and engineered it, it kind of becomes a little more threatening. . . . And it was really exotic. Even the names of people like Big Youth, U-Roy—mad names! For me, as a white kid from North London, it was totally different culture.

A few Jamaican producers, while welcoming the popularity of dub in the United Kingdom, voiced reservations about the way the fragmented lyrics allowed listeners to de-emphasize the spiritual and political messages in the songs. For example, London-based Jamaican producer Roy Cousins has released a series of well-regarded dub albums on his Tamoki Wambesi label, but nevertheless voiced a bit of ambivalence about the music's popularity outside of Jamaica: "I felt that people like[d] dub in England and on the Continent because they didn't understand what the singers were singing about. . . . If they listen to the dub and instrumental side they can appreciate it without understanding it."[13] Cousins's observations contain truth; nonetheless, the sonic innovations of dub (including its fragmented song lyrics) ultimately proved as influential in the global sphere as the more explicitly message-oriented stance of roots reggae songs.

Outside of specifically Anglo-Caribbean contexts like the sound systems, the more general influence of dub music in England owes much to the (often collaborative) work of immigrant Caribbean musicians with indigenous English musicians, producers, and engineers inspired by the developments in Kingston. The process was aided by the intermittent presence of various Jamaican musicians and producers in England, especially during the late 1970s and early 1980s. For example, Bunny Lee and King Jammy made regular trips to London to make record deals and purchase electronic equipment. Horace Andy, Prince Far-I, Keith Hudson, and Roots Radics drummer Lincoln "Style" Scott also spent increasing professional time in England from the 1980s. But there were two presences that arguably contributed most dramatically to the growth of dub in England. One was Lee Perry, who was intermittently based in London for several years following his exodus from Jamaica and who factored into the neo-dub movement through his collaborative work with the Clash, Mad Professor, and Adrian Sherwood. A similarly influential Jamaican artist in this process was the vocalist/radio deejay Mikey Dread, who also collaborated with the Clash. Such collaborations with high-profile rock musicians made dub more accessible to audiences who would not typically attend reggae concerts or patronize sound systems.

The Dub–Punk Connection

The fact that the Clash are mentioned in both of the above scenarios demonstrates the attraction of British punk musicians to reggae in general and dub in particular. Although punk music was historically rooted in the work of American rock groups of the late 1960s and 1970s (such as the Velvet Underground, New York Dolls, Patti Smith, and others), it was undeniably invested with a particular style and social stance in England during the late 1970s. In the years when punk rock was considered the cutting edge of English popular music, punk and reggae musicians were engaged in a musical and social dialogue. The Jamaican Rastaman represented an exotic and increasingly fashionable symbol of dissent, and punks responded equally to reggae's articulation of social marginality. Phil Johnson notes that by the late 1970s, punk musicians "had begun to cross the genre frontiers and seek out examples of 'otherness' to match their own mighty sense of alienation."[14] Sonically, it was the rough-hewn quality of dub that held an attraction for punk enthusiasts, who shunned the smoother black American rhythm and blues and soul styles that were popular in England at the time. As Hendley observes: "Reggae and dub were the only black musics that white kids who liked punk stuff would accept. They wouldn't accept Curtis Mayfield & the Impressions. They wouldn't understand. Because reggae sounds quite edgy and the whole structure of it is quite different from, say, an Impressions record, which is very considered and beautifully sung. They wouldn't be able to see through the gloss of it to see how deep it was. If they knew anything about it, they wouldn't be listening to Bob Marley if it hadn't been for Curtis Mayfield. But that's typical of punk rock."[15]

Several people mentioned filmmaker/club DJ Don Letts and radio disc jockey David Rodigan as key facilitators of the reggae/punk cross-influence. Steve Barrow recalled: "[Dub] was played by people like Don Letts in the punk clubs at that time. Letts was the first guy to do that. David Rodigan also got a reggae show on Radio London that time that was listened to by all kinds of people. He had a thing in it called 'Excursion on the Version.' And he played various cuts of a riddim and had all these little jingles going and all of that. A bit like Mikey Dread's style. It was very good. It was a big thing on Saturday night. People would listen to it before they went out, or when they came in, depending."[16] Clive Austen remembered Letts as "basically a film-maker at the time that the Sex Pistols were around, but he used to play at the Roxy and a lot of Jamaican dub places with Lee Perry and various other people. So there was a connection with the underground punk scene and dub."[17]

Selected examples of this musical dialogue would include the projects cited above, such as the Clash's 1977 song "Complete Control," produced by Lee Perry. Interestingly, in terms of style and production, this uptempo song shares almost nothing with any of Perry's Jamaican creations; rather, it sounds like a typical punk/new wave song of the period. The Clash subsequently covered Junior Murvin's Perry–produced "Police & Thieves" in a manner that blended reggae and punk styles more obviously; the group later collaborated with Jamaican DJ/producer Mikey "Dread" Campbell, who contributed a dub-influenced production style (as well as some deejay-ing) to portions of their 1981 LP *Sandinista*. The post-punk group A. R. Kane's music was an influential mixture of punk-derived guitar textures with an ambient dub influence.[18] A similar case is ex–Sex Pistols vocalist Johnny (Rotten) Lydon and his group Public Image, Ltd., who carved out a bleak, alien soundscape by blending dub's stark spaciness with punk-derived dissonance and minimalism on their influential 1981 recording *Second Edition* (a key element here was the thick-fingered dub-meets-punk approach of bassist Jah Wobble).[19] Lydon, in fact, is considered another important contributor to the reggae/punk dialogue. As Adrian Sherwood recalled, "a lot of people really looked up to him at that time. John really knew his reggae, he loved his reggae. I can tell you that John Lydon really helped the progress of roots and culture in Britain at that time. It was around that time . . . that he went on the radio and played Dr. Alimantado's 'Born For A Purpose.' Alimantado was immediately shot to cult status as a result!"[20] Lydon was by no means a centrist figure but he was quite influential, and it was through such conduits that the influence of reggae and dub became gradually audible in more commercial forms of popular music. In the 1980s, chart hits by artists such as Musical Youth, Eddy Grant, and Third World reflected the growing influence of reggae upon the popular music mainstream. This influence could also be felt in France, in the 1980s collaborations between Sly & Robbie and pop icon Serge Gainsbourg. Whether in the mainstream or experimental arenas of pop music, the minimalist nature of dub made it an ideal stylistic template for the mixing and matching of various genres. Its heavy textures complemented punk's stark aesthetic of alienation. Its foregrounded electronics and reconsidered human-machine relationship was compatible with the musical and philosophical questions being explored by early "Industrial" groups such as Cabaret Voltaire and Throbbing Gristle, who blended the stark textures of punk with electronic elements to reflect that industry, commerce, and mechanization had become prime determinants of human culture. As I shall discuss below, dub's blended dance-oriented and atmospheric emphases would later resonate quite strongly with composers of electronic dance music. Looking back to the 1970s and 1980s, Mark Stewart of the "trip-hop" group Massive Attack summed up this stylistic cross-fertilization when he recalled, "Buying a Prince Jammy or a Scientist dub thing was as important as buying Patti Smith or Television."[21] Robert DelNaja of the same group claimed that in England of the 1970s, "Dub was really the saviour of it all, because it brought all the different things together."[22] The seeming formlessness of dub enabled it to subvert normative notions of song composition, narrative logic, authorship, genre exclusivity, and performance context, while providing a medium for new fusions.

Neo-Dub in England and Europe

As much as England constituted a lucrative export market for Jamaican recordings, an indigenous tradition of dub music began to take root, shepherded by a younger generation of musicians, producers, and engineers who lionized (and eventually collaborated with) Jamaican legends like Perry and King Tubby. The best known of these musicians would include Adrian Sherwood, Neil "Mad Professor" Fraser, Dennis "Blackbeard" Bovell, the sound system operator Jah Shaka, and Alpha and Omega (Christine Woodbridge and John Sprosen). The work they created was inspired by Jamaican innovations, and in many cases stretched these ideas into new areas of experimentation.[23] In the following section, I shall focus on the first three of these artists, who have been the genre's best-known practitioners over the past twenty-five years.

Adrian Sherwood

Adrian Sherwood is among the most prominent creators of neo-dub music. Sherwood was born in London in 1958 and developed an early passion for reggae.[24] He was involved in England's Jamaican music industry by his late teens, working with the Pama and Trojan labels. By age twenty, Sherwood (along with various associates) had founded his own Carib Gems and Hit Run labels, which licensed various Jamaican productions for release in England, including important early music by Black Uhuru and Prince Far-I. In 1980, he founded his own On-U Sound organization that was used as an umbrella outfit for a sound system as well as his various musical productions in the sphere of neo-dub and beyond. A self-described "mixologist" (as mixing engineer, he is credited as the fourth member of the "industrial funk" group Tackhead), Sherwood tours regularly, presenting concerts and club sets of "live" dub mixing. He draws directly upon the innovations of Jamaican recording engineers and freely admits that the mixing console is his main "instrument." The core of his Jamaica-inspired work has been built around collaborative associations with musicians such as Lee Perry (with whom he produced the albums *Time Boom X De Devil Dead* [1987] and *From The Secret Laboratory* [1990]) and vocalist Bim Sherman, DJ Prince Far-I (who featured on a substantial amount of Sherwood's early work until his death in 1983), saxophonist "Deadly" Headley Bennett, and former Roots Radics drummer Lincoln "Style" Scott. He has also been central in introducing the techniques of dub into England's popular music mainstream, through his remixing work for popular groups such as the Cure, Living Colour, Depeche Mode, Simply Red, Cabaret Voltaire, and others. Sherwood recounted his early sources of inspiration: "lots of versions and DJ things, but the first identifiable albums were *The Grassroots of Dub,* produced by Winston Edwards, and also *King Tubbys Surrounded by the Dreads at the National Arena*—Winston Edwards again. I think *King Tubbys Meets the Rockers Uptown* was the first proper album. Then there's also *Ital Dub* by Augustus Pablo. Those were the ones we were listening to in heavy rotation."[25]

Sherwood tends to refer to his own dub-inspired music as "designer dub," which he defines as "music designed as a work of dub from the beginning. Which is not how it originally started. It started off as a version. What we basically started doing was making riddims and then somewhere after, adding different coloring and samples and things like that. It was a whole different way of working [than in Jamaica]."[26] What is unique about Sherwood's approach is the fusion of these dub-derived techniques with the raw aesthetics of punk (which Sherwood refers to as "the noise factor") and elements drawn from various American dance musics (especially hiphop). The result is a body of work characterized by genre-bending and sonic chance-taking that informs all of Sherwood's On-U Sound productions of artists such as Little Axe, Creation Rebel, New Age Steppers, African Head Charge, Creation Steppers, Dub Syndicate, and others.

Good introductions to Sherwood's reggae-inspired work would include the three-disc various artists compilation *On-U Sound Box* and the two-volume *Historic Moments* set by Creation Rebel. Both contain a topically and sonically inventive assortment of vocal, DJ, instrumental, and dub music in which Sherwood moves Jamaican styles beyond their established borders. Also notable are Sherwood's two collaborations with Lee Perry (*From The Secret Laboratory* and *Time Boom X De Devil Dead*), which fuse the thematic approach of Perry's late Black Ark solo albums (such as *Roast Fish, Collie Weed and Cornbread*, and *The Return of Pipecock Jackson*) with updated Jamaican rhythms and Sherwood's eclectic approach to production.[27]

Neil "Mad Professor" Fraser

Neil "Mad Professor" Fraser has been one of the major figures in neodub. Fraser described dub as "a freedom music, you know. It's a vehicle for you to ride on. At the end of the day, it invokes that feeling of freedom and creativity."[28] A native of Guyana, Fraser was born in the mid-1950s, and developed a passion for reggae music through regional radio broadcasts in the late 1960s that included Jamaican music programming. As he explained to David Katz, "you would hear Dennis Alcapone and Lizzy, a lot of Bunny Lee productions and Studio One, so I used to tune in every Saturday night."[29] Fraser was given his long-standing nickname during his school years in Guyana, thanks to an early aptitude for electronics. As he explained to Grant Smithies:

I got the "Mad Professor" name in school because I loved to experiment with wires. Instead of playing football and cricket like a normal kid, I would be messin' around with wires. When I was small, back in Guyana, the most technical thing in our house was a radio. I wanted to know where the man's voice was coming from so I opened up the back and saw all the valve lights flickering, and that started a whole curiosity about the transmission of radio frequencies. I ended up building my first radio when I was about ten years old. No books, no nothing. I just built a radio. . . . I just messed around with different diodes and transistors and picked up signals. And from then on I was hooked, from then on I was "Mad Professor."[30]

At the age of thirteen, Fraser moved with his family to England; like many of the engineers discussed in this book, he worked a variety of electronics jobs in his youth and young adulthood. Eventually he combined this fascination with electronics with his passion for music, and he found in Jamaican dub the perfect medium to pursue both interests:

I was first an electronics technician. I built my first radio when I was ten and I built all kind of devices, and then in my teens I built a mixing desk . . . it was just resistors and capacitors that I use to make it work, and then I then have some artists around to come and play around with and next thing I knew, I started a studio. . . . I was listening to *East of the River Nile, African Dub Chapter Three,* various Tubby's things . . . and Prince Buster, *The Message Dubwise.* That's the first dub album I ever bought, and I couldn't believe it. I never heard nothing like that before. It's a really haunting album. I still think it's one of the best. That one inspired me to do dub.[31]

Issued with virtually no recording information on the cover, Prince Buster's *The Message Dubwise* remains an LP of uncertain provenance. But its structure of flute soloists against a stark drum & bass background on several tracks creates a moody sensibility that has echoed throughout Fraser's dub work. By 1979, he had founded his own Ariwa label, studio, and sound system (the name is an adaptation of *ariwo,* the Yoruba language term for noise), which eventually grew from Fraser's self-built 4-track recorder to become Britain's largest black-owned studio complex, with 16-, 24-, and 48-track capability. Since that time, he has built a signature sound around a stable of Ariwa artists, including the vocalists Kofi, Pato Banton, Nolan Irie, Macka B, Rupununi Safari, and many others. He has also collaborated with several important Jamaican and non-Jamaican reggae artists, including Horace Andy, Johnny Clarke, U-Roy, Michael Prophet, Yabby U, Earl 16, and Jah Shaka.

Fraser's central role in the spread of dub music is evident on several fronts. The best-known dub recordings released under his own name are the multivolume series *Dub Me Crazy* (which commenced in the early 1980s) and *Black Liberation Dub* (which commenced in the mid-1990s). The titles of the various volumes, which blend symbols drawn from African liberation movements, mysticism, antinuclear movements, and other sources, reflect his dual commitment to dub's legacy of sonic innovation as well as reggae's broader commitment to social, political, and mystical topics. Of this, he remarked, "It's just me. I'm a political maniac. I think that people need to be reminded of certain politics. Hence I made that connection. When I make the music, I make it with that in mind."[32]

Stylistically, Fraser's work borrows from several Jamaican sources including Perry, Tubby, and Augustus Pablo. Overall, he favors a very clean soundscape with sound effects sometimes overdubbed in the manner of Errol Thompson. The *Dub Me Crazy* series mainly featured tracks recorded by live musicians, while the later *Black Liberation Dub* series features a blend of live and digital backing.

In recent years, Fraser has also been Lee Perry's most consistent post–Black Ark collaborator, producing a string of vocal and dub albums (such as *Mystic Warrior* [1990] and *Black Ark Experryments* [1995]), which feature

Perry's free-associative "word salad" vocalizing over modernized reggae beats. For several years beginning in the mid-1990s, the two toured internationally, giving concerts featuring Perry's spontaneous vocalizing, the playing of the Robotiks band (or prerecorded music), and Fraser's live dub mixing. Fraser also tours regularly on his own, giving performances of live dub (usually accompanied by a vocalist or two) across Europe, America, and Asia.

Since the 1980s, Fraser has been in demand as a remix engineer, moving dub's innovations closer to the pop music mainstream through his work with artists such as the Orb, the Ruts, UB40, Jamiroquai, the Beastie Boys, and Massive Attack. His remix of Massive Attack's 1994 *Protection* album (titled *No Protection* and released the same year), in fact, is often cited as a seminal moment in the development of what became known as *trip-hop* (more below).

Dennis Bovell

Dennis "Blackbeard" Bovell (not to be confused with Tappa Zukie's brother Dennis "Blackbeard" Sinclair) is another seminal figure in Britain's dub scene. Bovell was born in Barbados in 1953, and moved to London with his family in 1965.[33] In 1970, he formed the reggae band Matumbi who became prominent backing Jamaican artists such as I-Roy, Errol Dunkley, and Johnny Clarke on their London visits. By the late 1970s Bovell was in demand as an engineer and remix artist, working with a wide array of English and foreign artists. He solidified his international reputation as bassist, arranger, and engineer for the Dub Band, essentially a touring and recording unit for the dub poet Linton Kwesi Johnson. The pairing of Johnson and Bovell begat one of the great creative partnerships in the history of reggae. As Bovell recalled to Norman Darwen:

> this reporter came to interview us for the BBC World Service, and it was Linton. He said, "well, I write poetry." I said, "I know" because I had seen his books . . . he came to me and said "I want to make an album this weekend"—and we did. We went into the studio and by the end of the weekend we'd finished *Dread Beat & Blood,* and from there on we've been working together every since."[34]

This collaboration yielded several canonical British reggae albums released under Johnson's name including *Forces of Victory* (Island, 1979), *Bass Culture* (Island, 1980), *Tings and Times* (LKJ, 1991), and two Bovell-mixed volumes of *LKJ in Dub* (Mango, 1980s). In addition to the LKJ dub projects, Bovell also engineered a series of excellent dub albums in the late 1970s. His work evolved in the face of the dual challenges of establishing the credibility of British reggae on one hand, and adapting British studios to reggae recording practices, on the other:

they were saying that reggae couldn't be made properly in London, and I'm going "Bollocks! [Jamaicans] ain't got any better tape recorders than us—it's in the playing. . . ." Of course, there's a special way to do the engineering, with the heavy bass. I'd been fortunate enough to go to a school in South London, in Wandsworth, called Spencer Park where we built a recording studio at school and we were learning how to use this equipment—so that when we went into studios I wouldn't put up with the engineer going "Oh, you can't touch that man, you can't go over that red." I'd go "Well, I want it all in the red so put it there, will you?" [We] started finding frequencies that were what we wanted to hear.[35]

This issue of "finding the proper frequencies" is particularly resonant in the case of Bovell's work: his work with Matumbi and others artists established him as a central architect of the "Lover's Rock" genre of romantically themed reggae songs. The sound of Bovell's work suggests that there is a direct link between his lover's rock productions and his early dub work, the latter of which is best represented on collections such as *Dub Conference* (1978), *I-Wah Dub* (1980), and the retrospective 2003 compilation *Decibel*. Bovell explained to Jeb Loy Nichols that lover's rock arose "as an answer to all that hardcore man chanting business. You know, knives and guns and things. DJs shouting about this and that. I wanted to do a more ballad kind of thing. Pure soulful. Like Curtis Mayfield or William Bell. When I used to play in the sound systems I used to have a big following of women so I knew what they wanted."[36] Is there a "soulful" way of mixing? Part of the warm, sensual sound of Bovell's dub mixes on *Dub Conference* likely reflects that he is a bassist and as such can be expected to pay particularly close attention to the music's low end and the rhythm section in general. Many of his bass lines are subtly sound-processed (evidently with phase shifting or envelope filtering) and are doubled in octave unison by guitar, providing subtle nuances and resonances that can only be produced by low-register string instruments. But this warmth also reflects that many of Bovell's dub mixes were versioned from songs that were romantically themed in their vocal incarnations, with the musical backing having been crafted accordingly. The result is a warm, subtly aquatic dub sound (similar in some ways to both Lee Perry's Black Ark sound and King Tubby's filtered frequency sweeps, but much more restrained) that is quite unlike the urban, edgy sound of most British reggae.

It would seem to follow that the sound Bovell crafted for Linton Kwesi Johnson's productions would be drastically different, reflecting the often grimly realist tone of Johnson's poetry. The truth is, however, despite the graphic depictions in Johnson's lyrics ("Five Nights of Bleeding," "Song of Blood," "Sonny's Lettah, "Di Great Insoreckshun"), one of the music's prime attractions was the tone of his voice, the seeming matter-of-factness of which is belied by a melodious tone and cadence. In this context Bovell's mixes, blending deep bass, warm electric organ and bubbling hand drums, worked as a perfect counterpoint to the cadences of Johnson's patwa recitations.

Electronic Dance Music

Having opened a space for sonic experimentation and (in some cases) sociopolitical critique in popular music, the genres of punk, experimental rock, and dub can be considered important precursors in the rise of electronic dance music (often referred to as "electronica"), which evolved concurrently with the proliferation of digital sound technology from the late 1980s. The term *electronica* itself dates to the early 1990s and is generally considered to refer to several genres: ambient, house, techno, jungle/drum & bass, and trip-hop and any of innumerable subgenres. And while some performers in these genres utilize various types of mixed instrumentation, what ultimately unites them is their creation of music through digital means, their performance contexts of dance clubs and/or raves, and several broad stylistic similarities. As the digital technology upon which the electronica phenomenon is based has increased the ease with which all sorts of sound information can be manipulated, so has the creative sphere of electronica as a phenomenon been the catalyst for the consolidation of many of the creative currents in popular, improvised, and experimental music that have evolved since World War II.[37]

The influence and legacy of dub music is strongly audible in these digitally produced genres; in some the influence is fairly explicit, while in others it is more conceptual and implicit. It can be generalized, however, that in terms of musical composition, all of these aforementioned genres of electronica emphasize rhythmic complexity, fragmented lyrical and/or melodic statements, and atmospheric soundscaping. As such, all can be said to reflect the influence of dub techniques, to varying extents.

Jungle/Drum & Bass and Trip-Hop

The two electronica genres that most audibly reflect the influence of dub are *jungle/drum & bass,* and *trip-hop.* Both illustrate the way that the parallel impulses of dub (drum & bass mixing and atmospheric soundscaping) and hip-hop (excerpted breakbeats and stacked samples) merged in the 1980s and 1990s to help transform the grammar of global popular dance music. Jungle (or drum & bass, as it is also known) developed in England around 1990 as a hybrid of Jamaican dub reggae and DJ music, and English techno music. The style's practitioners are too numerous to list, but its best-known exponents have included musicians such as Goldie, LTJ Bukem, Roni Size, Photek, 4Hero, and A Guy Called Gerald.[38] The interchangeable genre names "jungle" and "drum & bass" are clearly rooted in the recent history of Jamaican music. The word "jungle" has its origins in Kingston sound systems, particularly the Jones Town area, which is commonly known as "Jungle" (or locally, "Dungle"). "Drum & bass," on the other hand, is obviously a borrowing from the parlance of roots reggae. These factors, plus the fact that jungle (especially in its early years) was/is often accompanied by Jamaican-styled DJ toasting, clearly demonstrates its partial but substantial roots in the music of Britain's immigrant Jamaican community.

Though there are several subgenres, all are structured upon three fundamental elements. First, a half-time (usually atonal) bass line that can be heard as adapted from the electric bass lines of roots reggae (but typically much lower in register to due the expanded range of digital keyboards). Second, stacked, double-time digital percussion (usually snare drum) patterns adapted partially from drastically accelerated hip-hop breakbeats, partially from the rapid tempos of techno and trance music, and partially from the double-time percussion passages that Jamaican engineers like King Tubby achieved through the use of digital delay units to intensify percussion tracks. Third, the soundscaping of the first two elements with passages of swirling, atmospheric harmonies usually produced by synthesizers, pitched in minor tonalities and treated with heavy reverberation. A good example of this fusion that refers directly back to Jamaica is Intelligent Jungalist's "Barehedd One," a 1995 jungle track built from a sample of the Techniques All-Stars canonical "Stalag 17" riddim.[39] As with Jamaican dub, the foreground of jungle tracks is typically dominated by a combination of deejaying and/or fragmented vocal texts.

Similar to the role that drummers such as Carlton Barrett and Sly Dunbar played in roots reggae, the aura of jungle rests in its foregrounding of (digital) drumming as a central structural and symbolic component: jungle pioneer A Guy Called Gerald (Gerald Simpson), whose influential 1995 album is titled *Black Secret Technology,* relies on the metaphor of the African talking drum to describe the drum-heavy sound he crafts for his music, as well as the imagistic blend of roots and technoscience.[40] Others artists such as Photek and L. T. J. Bukem would interpret this trait in more futurist or Afro-futurist terms in works such as "Rings Around Saturn" and "Earth." Writer Simon Reynolds described jungle's frantic, techno-derived drum patterns as "the metabolic pulse of a body reprogrammed and rewired to cope with an era of unimaginably intense information overload."[41] While the hyperkinetic, techno-derived traits of the genre certainly depart from dub's Caribbean langor, its juxtaposition of atmospheric soundscaping, fragmentary vocal excerpts, and ponderous bass lines is directly traceable to Jamaica. This dual legacy inspired Reynolds ultimately to describe jungle as a "postmodern dub on steroids."[42]

Trip-hop, on the other hand, takes the opposite approach. The genre can be described as a slower and dub-influenced reworking of African American hip-hop, aptly described by writer Phil Johnson as "dubbed-up hip-hop derived music . . . beats whose customary urgency is deconstructed into dreamy, erotic soundscapes."[43] The style is most strongly associated with a cluster of recording labels including Ninja Tune, Shadow, and MoWax, and is produced as both an instrumental and vocal music. As Simon Reynolds notes, differences in cultural and aesthetic sensibilities have meant that appropriations of hip-hop music in England have frequently been divested of the rapping component, which in instrumental trip-hop is often replaced by soundscape manipulations derived from dub. Trip-hop beats typically clock in at a tempo of quarter note = 60, generally too slow for couple dancing in a conventional sense, but ideally suited to the more individual, internally focused free-form dancing associated with electronica (and, historically, certain forms of psychedelic music). In its vocal variant, trip-hop is often associated with a cadre of musicians that developed out of Bristol's 1980s sound system scene, such as Portishead, Tricky, and Massive Attack (whose membership sometimes includes Jamaican reggae singer Horace Andy, himself an important figure in the development of dub owing to his work with producers like Bunny Lee and Neil "Mad Professor" Fraser).[44] The music produced by these groups, tends to be emotionally dark, moody, expansive, and spacious enough for the fragmented texts of dub to be reconciled with more accessible approaches to vocal phrasing.[45]

Conceptually, both jungle and trip-hop work according to the combined logics of hip-hop and dub. In both genres, breakbeats (accelerated in jungle and decelerated in trip-hop) anchor scratched and/or sampled melodic material (including voices) that is usually fragmented and sound-processed in dublike fashion. Harmonically, the music is typically built around smooth jazz chord progressions that are elaborated with the more abstract and collage-driven polytonality of hip-hop.

The German Context

England is among the most active arenas for neo-dub music, but it is by no means the only one. In Germany, the Jamaican influence has grown not so much through patterns of immigration, but through the currents of electronica and the investigations into its historical roots that began during the 1990s. The result is several unique streams of neo-dub that have emerged since the late 1990s, and that resuscitate dub within currents of contemporary electronica. What is interesting, as Jacob Haagsman explained, is that in Germany, this resuscitation took place in a way that "connect[ed] the stern electronic German heritage of Karlheinz Stockhausen and Kraftwerk . . . with the loose Caribbean culture that produced dub."[46] This connection can be heard in the work of dozens of artists, but is most pronounced in the work produced by the duo of Mark Ernestus and Moritz von Oswald(known by their recording name Rhythm and Sound) and of Stefan Betke (known by his recording name, Pole).

It is important to mention a particular tendency in recent European electronica as important background (to Pole and Rhythm and Sound in particular): the genre of so-called minimal techno, an aesthetic most likely rooted in earlier eras of experimental minimalism and given a uniquely contemporary slant through the more recent influence of hip-hop's use of scratched vinyl records as source material for digital samples. These so-called clicks & cuts artists have taken the anomalies of the analog-to-digital transfer process—the skips, hisses, scratches, and other glitches that have been typically sanitized by producers and engineers in the name of digital precision and fidelity—and refashioned them into new gestural and textural vocabularies.[47] In this sense they reproduce the strategies of Jamaican engineers, who themselves innovated a stylistic vocabulary partially formed from sonic anomalies and mishaps of the recording studio. What German artists such as Pole and Rhythm & Sound have done is taken this language of "clicks & cuts," and spatialized it via the soundscape techniques of dub. This combined influence of hip-hop and dub allow the German take on neo-dub to be heard in two fairly contrasting ways. Essentially it conforms to the Jamaican drum & bass aesthetic, filtered through the language of electronic minimalism. It can be heard as stark and cold because of its minimalist aesthetic, or incredibly lush and detailed, if the listener focuses on these artists' subtle manipulations of the atmopsheric elements. Ultimately, this music has provided a medium through which Germany's post–World War II heritage of electronic and experimental music could be rearticulated in a populist form.

Pole (Stefan Betke)

Working under the professional name Pole, Stefan Betke (b. Germany, 1967) is known for highly textured soundscapes that draw directly on the language of Jamaican dub while rearticulating this influence on the terms of the minimalist and conceptual tendencies of German electronic and experimental music. In this sense his work overlaps conceptually with dance music but with a more austere sensibility that seems to derive from earlier generations of electronic music practice as well as Betke's own oblique relationship to the club context. For example, when I met him in London in 2002, it was following his set that was played not at a dance club, but rather at London's Institute of Contemporary Art. Nevertheless, he cited his primary influences as "King Tubby, Lee Scratch Perry, definitely. Wayne Jarrett and Horace Andy were also really important for me. There's one [CD] out with Jarrett called *Bubble* Up, and the other, I think is *Dance Hall Style*. Those were really influential for me."[48]

These influences have been transmuted in Betke's work in a very particular way, given that his music also contains a strong conceptual streak reflecting his experimental interests. Simon Reynolds referred to Betke as "a virtuoso of monochromatic concentration";[49] visually, Betke's CD releases are only distinguishable from each other on the basis of the flat, color field cover art of each CD; this minimalism parallels Betke's musical approach, in which each disc is similarly devoted to a specific conceptual parameter. As he explained, what might be thought of as the conceptual implications of versioning inspired him to approach his own creative process in this modular manner:

When you talk about minimalism, you ask "How can I reduce a track to the main function and keep it running for 8 minutes without it getting boring at all?" It's possible to be so open-minded that you don't have to redefine [the music] every time, but bring it into a new context every time. The concept of making different work out of exactly the same tune. Like, you have a good tune in reggae music and lots of singers are singing over it with different lyrics, or the same lyrics with different music underneath. It's the same idea, transformed into different surroundings, functions, and contexts in the end, which helps it spread the word. That is something that European artists maybe learned out of Jamaican music.

I work in a very conceptual way, where everything is fulfilled in concept art. So that is why I had the blue, red, and yellow covers. It was a very strict development. Germans are really well known for analytic, intellectual ways of thinking about art. So my music tends to be very distanced, for some reason, without becoming German music, per se. That's what I like.

Rhythm & Sound *(Moritz von Oswald and Mark Ernestus)*

Moritz von Oswald and Mark Ernestus have been seminal participants in Germany's electronica scene for years, involved with both the reissue of vintage dub music as well as the creation of new dub-influenced electronica. Since 1996, they have been releasing a type of techno–house music (using the moniker Maurizio) strongly influenced by both dub and the otherwordly quality of Detroit techno.[50] Through their Basic Channel label, they have also been responsible for the reissues of the work of Lloyd "Bullwackies" Barnes. Both of these priorities have found their fullest expression in their Rhythm & Sound project in which the drum & bass template of dub functions as a medium through which the various stylistic vocabularies of electronica may be rearticulated.

Emotionally the Rhythm and Sound aesthetic is, like Pole's work, quite stark but its languid rhythms and detailed soundscaping remain fundamentally true to the mood and sound system function of dub. In rhythmic terms, Ernestus and von Oswald have found inventive ways to fuse the patterns of roots reggae with those of midtempo house and techno. For example, some of their compositions adapt the reggae rhythm "steppers," with its pulsing four-beats-to-the-measure bass drum, to the similar bass drum format at the root of house and techno music. In other compositions, they have adapted half-time bass drum of the "one drop" rhythm to the subtly mixed common-time bass drum of house and techno. With these minimal patterns as a basis, von Oswald and Ernestus can devote the foreground to the types of dub-derived atmospheric qualities they have pioneered. All of this results, as Haagsman describes it, in an aesthetic of "Jamaican hallucinations in stripped-down slow motion."[51]

In some ways, Rhythm and Sound extend the conceptual elements that were implicit in versioning as it was practiced in Jamaica, but that were of necessity balanced by elements suited to the dancehall context. Their basic stylistic template was put into place with an eponymous and largely instrumental CD released in 2000; unlike many minimal techno artists, however, they went on to fully involve vocalists into the creative process. By 2003, they had released a stunning series of rhythms featuring various vocalists from the Caribbean such as Jamaicans Cornell Campbell and Horace Andy (and other vocalists associated with "Bullwackies" Barnes), as well as vocalists from other parts of the Caribbean such as Paul St. Hilare (a.k.a. Tikiman), Walda Gabriel, Jah Walton, Ras Perez, Koki, and Ras Donovan. These vocalists sing over Ernestus and von Oswald's characteristic mixes, augmented by a version album released separately in classic Jamaican fashion.

The preceding examples make it clear that dub has been central to the soundscape of electronica, leading Steve Barrow to use the metaphor of the dub as a "virus," seen to "infect" other popular styles and facilitate their mutation into a multiplicity of new, studio-based soundscape genres.[52] A good general introduction to the dub influence on these musical genres is the two-volume compilation *Macro Dub Infection,* the title of which plays on Barrow's "virus" characterization.[53] Released in 1995 and 1996, respectively, the compilations survey dub's influence on genres as diverse as neo-dub, drum & bass, house, ambient, electronic world music, and various ensembles of traditional instrumentalists altered through post-performance sound processing. Like dub and hip-hop, the genres of electronica, taken collectively, can be simultaneously considered a musical subculture with their own audience(s), as well as the sonic "research and development" wing of popular music production, where production strategies are developed that ultimately influence production trends in the pop music mainstream.

The Postcolonial Versioned as Postimperial

The developing genres of electronica, rich with the potential of new and rapidly multiplying forms of sound technology, contained important sociopolitical resonance in Europe of the early 1990s. Jacob Haagsman has noted that in Germany, for example, the experimental and as yet nonstandardized genres of electronica were embraced for their liberatory social implications in the optimistic but ambiguous social climate of a reunited Germany.[54] Recent works such as those by Paul Gilroy and Ian Baucom suggest that a similar assertion can be made for the social resonance of styles such as jungle and trip-hop in the context of a "post-imperial" Britain alternately resisting and embracing a new national identity that alternately deconstructs and reinforces deeply held notions of race, class, and culture.[55] These electronic genres draw on Jamaican dub to varying extents; they were also nurtured in a multiethnic crucible and as such transcend (or expand) specifically black concerns. The house-techno-dub and hip-hop–dub fusions at the root of jungle and trip-hop, for example, reflect broader class strategies within English society, and the same can be said for more recent genre mutations such as *dubstep* and *grime*. In this sense, dub's more paranoid moods born of the violent Kingston climate have been recast in urban England as the hybrid electronic music of an embattled pan-ethnic working-class/cosmopolitan youth subculture reflecting the broader concerns cited above as well as what Simon Reynolds described as "late capitalist economic instability, institutionalized racism, and increased surveillance and harassment of youth by the police."[56] All resolves into what he termed the music's "bunker" imagery of alienation, surveillance, and paranoia, conveyed in song titles such as Photek's "Hidden Camera" as well as in the profusion of dialogue excerpted from radio and walkie-talkie transmissions, television crime show dialogue, and 1970s blaxploitation cinema.[57] Jungle composer Squarepusher (Tom Jenkinson) summed up the social and creative milieu in 1996 with a comment that could have easily been voiced in Kingston of the 1970s: "It's quite an aggressive, dark, and moody music, mainly because England is a fucked-up place at the moment. Everything has gone wrong; the government has fallen apart. . . . No one has any trust in the state. Their policy is to keep you scared so you stay down. That attitude breeds fear. England is a compressed country and there is loads of anger. A lot of the [jungle] coming out now is all about that."[58]

Dub in the American Context

Neo-Dub in the United States

This section has mainly been concerned with developments in England and Europe; although I shall discuss the influence of dub techniques on African American dance music later, I briefly detour to the American context to conclude this section on neo-dub music. As noted earlier, the success of musicians such as Bob Marley provided an indirect current for the influence of dub in America. The influence is most apparent in the work of expatriate Jamaican and American musicians such as Lloyd "Bullwackies" Barnes, Bill Laswell, Crooklyn Dub Consortium, and others. In this section, I shall focus on Barnes and Laswell because they represent, in a way, two contrasting tendencies of dub in the United States.

Lloyd "Bullwackies" Barnes

Lloyd "Bullwackies" Barnes (b. Jamaica, 1944) is seminal in the growth of dub outside of Jamaica, in a manner firmly rooted in the Jamaican experience. Prior to a recent reissue campaign by the Berlin-based Basic Channel label, however, his substantial body of work remained fairly obscure, even within Jamaica. During his youth in Jamaica, Barnes had worked in Duke Reid's Treasure Isle studio as a backing vocalist; he recorded sporadically for Prince Buster before relocating to New York in the early 1970s. Throughout the mid-1970s, he operated an eponymous sound system based in the Bronx (that was unfortunately plagued by the Kingston political rivalries that had been transplanted to New York). The dances promoted by Wackie's were the site of frequent outbreaks by political violence between rival Jamaican Labour Party and People's National Party supporters, and Barnes was eventually forced to disband his sound system.

It was during this same period that Barnes began releasing his own roots reggae and dancehall productions on a variety of New York–based labels, featuring the combined talents of local reggae musicians, expatriate Jamaican session players, and well-known Jamaican vocalists passing through the New York area. But although Barnes built up a sizable catalog, his work was generally pressed in very limited quantities, typically around a thousand copies per release.

The bulk of Barnes's work was created during the late 1970s and early 1980s in the Bronx at the epicenter of developing hip-hop. What is remarkable in this context is how faithful it remains to its Jamaican roots in the dynamic musical setting of New York, where a variety of powerful local influences might have influenced a change in his sound. Well into the mid-1980s, after Jamaican music had undergone its digital shift, Barnes was still stubbornly producing dubby, Rasta-influenced roots reggae at his studio. Nevertheless, the New York setting did exert a subtle influence, and the balancing act that this implied is one factor that makes Barnes music seem, in retrospect, so unique a commentary on roots reggae. The fundamental equation in his work is one in which classic Studio One and Treasure Isle riddims are subjected to dub interpretations inspired primarily by Lee Perry's Black Ark phase, and secondarily by King Tubby. Barnes explained to Jeff Chang, "I want to be roots like Downbeat, sweet like Treasure Isle, and mystic like Upsetter."[59] The Perry influence is clear in the thick aquatic textures of the mix (as with Perry, the phase shifting effect is used prominently) while the Tubby influence is clear in Barnes's overall commitment to dub as a distinct form. Working with engineers Douglas Levy and Junior Delahaye, the Wackies' outfit released several dub albums during the 1980s (*Jamaica Super Dub Session, Tribesman Assault, Creation Dub* and the multivolume *African Roots*), while most of his single releases were backed by dub mixes or mixed dubwise from the start.

On seminal recordings of artists such as Horace Andy, Wayne Jarrett, the Love Joys, the Meditations and others, the crew at Wackie's was able to capture the essence of Jamaican roots while giving the music a tight sound that was subtly reflective of its urban setting.

Bill Laswell

Bassist, producer, conceptualist, and record label founder/owner Bill Laswell represents the hybrid approach to dub. Born in 1950, Laswell has been active on the experimental fringes of various American genres since the late 1970s. His major commercial breakthrough came in 1983 when he produced keyboardist Herbie Hancock's electro-jazz-funk hit "Rockit," and he has occasionally worked with other mainstream popular artists such as Mick Jagger, Whitney Houston, and Sting. For the most part, however, his reputation has been built at the experimental intersection of jazz, funk, electronic, and a variety of world musics. It is unsurprising that Laswell would find inspiration in dub at this particular intersection, which resonates with many of the conceptual concerns explored in these various genres (and the minimalist aesthetic of which also provides a template upon which they can be recombined). Many of Laswell's recordings also reflect a mystical streak inspired by the extramusical applications of various non-Western musical traditions (for example, Moroccan Gnawa music, Indian classical music, African and Afro-Caribbean possession traditions) in which music is used for liturgical, trance, possession, or curative purposes. Rasta-derived titles such as "Ethiopia" and "Shashimani" [*sic*] reflect how dub, with its own partial roots in the mystical aspects of Rastafari, has factored into Laswell's embrace of exotic musics and provided a suitably mystical aura to his studio experiments.

Laswell's contributions to dub are varied. He has produced his own dub-influenced recordings (released mainly on his Subharmonic label), applying the strategies of dub to the collaborative work of musicians from a wide array of genres. As a remix engineer for hire, he has remixed two volumes of canonical dub recordings from the hallowed reggae vaults of England's Trojan Records and done important remix work for artists of the stature of jazz icon Miles Davis & Nigerian Afrobeat legend Fela Anikulapo-Kuti. Many, however, would consider Laswell's most significant contribution to dub to be his collection of "ambient dub" remixes of several Island-era Bob Marley and the Wailers tracks on the 1997 *Dreams of Freedom* compilation.[60] This release was quite significant in the reggae world; although, as discussed earlier, there had been selected dub mixes made of Marley's work during his lifetime (most mixed by Errol Brown or Karl Pitterson), there had never been an album-length release featuring dub versions of Marley's work.

Laswell's Marley project was met with mixed responses. He subtitled the project "ambient translations" and stated that his goal was to make the recordings sound "as if someone had dreamed them."[61] The problem, in some listeners' hearing, was that Laswell's ambient emphasis de-emphasized the rhythmic aspects of the music; it lacked the dynamic tension of Jamaican engineers, who were always sensitive to both the atmospheric and the rhythmic/structural aspects of the music. Laswell's decisions, of course, reflects that his work was not aimed at the dancing crowd of a Jamaican sound system audience, but the more reflective audience that (depending on their age) encountered dub as either a stylistic variant of American psychedelia, and/or as a cultural variant of contemporary Euro-American ambient electronica. It is among this audience that Laswell's dub music has had its most substantial impact.

In some ways, the criticisms of Laswell's Marley project echo broader criticisms of "neo-dub," or what Adrian Sherwood referred to as "designer dub": music conceived from the beginning of the creative process as dub, as opposed to the Jamaican practice of music being generally versioned from vocal songs. Whether these criticisms reflect generationally based purism or nostalgia or genuine insight varies from case to case. As previously discussed, the dub mix in Jamaica was merely one half of the vision articulated within roots reggae; it usually backed an accessible pop song on the flip side, against which it acquired its deconstructive significance. Thus, even if Jamaican pop song structure was gradually transformed in its encounter with new technology, this transformation acquired its dynamic tension within the communal imperative of the dancehall/sound system: as much as dub prefigured the fragmented aesthetics of electronica, it did so with one foot firmly rooted in the practice of communal dance musics. Without this centralizing impulse, some have claimed that "designer dub" has tended to suffocate under the weight of increasingly complex technology. Mark Sinker, for example, claims that "without a mainstream to riff off, versions have far less force,"[62] a point elaborated by Chris Sharp:

> whereas King Tubby and Prince Jammy were concerned with making people dance, with celebratory sonic audacity, with a delight in timbral novelty, these contemporary dub scientists seem more concerned with chronicling their own malaise. . . . The jouissance of 70s dub came from the sudden sense of possibility that the technical innovations of the time engendered. But the possibilities have kept multiplying, equipment and sound sources spilling endlessly into the marketplace, threatening to swamp the composer's capacity for comprehension. What was once tantalizing has become bewildering. [Neo-dub] is the sound of dub fighting for breath in the face of information overload.[63]

Simon Reynolds similarly claimed: "Where seventies roots reggae had a spiritual aura, [digital] dub evoked only the geometrically plotted grid of computer sequence programs . . . and the Jamaican dubmeisters also used supple and interactive live rhythm sections where their digital dub successors depended on inelastic programmed beats and bass lines. All of which explains why the difference between classic dub and ambient dub resembles that between a stained glass window and a computer graphic."[64]

Certainly innovation was at least partially predicated on the effort to push against technical, conceptual, or procedural boundaries or constraints. At the same time, it is probable that Jamaican dub mixes sounded cold and overtechnical to those accustomed to the norms of roots reggae in the 1970s. So, as performance contexts such as raves (discussed below) indicate, new forms of art and technology will by necessity generate new forms of spirituality that will in turn inspire creative artists to transform neutral machines into vessels of the highest inspiration.

Jamaican Music and the "Post-Soul" Era of African American Popular Music

The period of African American music that developed from the mid-1980s has sometimes been referred to as the "post-soul" era. The term was coined by writers such as Nelson George to describe an era of African American music (typified by, but not exclusive to, the New York City context) in which the sensibility of 1960s/1970s soul music and the ideals of the civil rights movement that formed its backdrop gave way to a new era of social (and correspondingly, aesthetic) values.[65] This transition is based on several significant social, musical, and technological developments in African American culture: increasing class disparity despite the material gains of the civil rights movement, the flight of the African American elite and professional classes from the urban areas, and the fiscal and infrastructural crises of the 1970s that transformed New York City during the 1970s. Musical developments would include a generational shift in musical tastes and methods, a decline in traditional musical education, and the simultaneous availability of new (especially digital) and cheaper tools for the creation of music.[66]

In one sense, the "post-soul" idea can be positioned laterally alongside ideas such as "post-blackness" and "post-nationalist," as all of these terms imply a transition away from the ethos, values, and symbols of the civil rights movement. In the realm of culture and technology, however, it also reflects the transformative role that various forms of (especially digital) technology played in stimulating fundamental changes in the nature of information, communication, and experience. This transformation leads to hip-hop, the musical genre that emerged during the mid-1970s and that was the clearest musical reflection of all these socioeconomic and music-technological transformations. The history of how this music developed out of creative currents in New York City has been fairly well documented,[67] but the emergence of hip-hop merits further contextualization here, in order to understand the role of Jamaican music in the transformation of American dance music during the 1980s.

In New York City of the mid- to late 1970s, the dominant black dance music was the party funk music of bands like Kool and the Gang, War, the Ohio Players, Mandrill, and similarly organized groups. This music was based upon a basic template that had been established by James Brown and his musicians a decade earlier, and subsequently elaborated with rock elements by musicians like Sly Stone and George Clinton.[68] Based upon a fairly Africanized conception of harmonically static vamps and the percussive hocketing of interlocking rhythm section parts, this type of funk represented a deconstruction of the (blues-, jazz-, and gospel-derived) harmonic practices of 1960s rhythm and blues and a general shift from triple to duple rhythmic structures.

The other dominant urban dance genre of the late 1970s was disco music, which emerged from a sphere defined by Euro-American gay discotheque culture, and the fusion of European dance music producers (such as Giorgio Moroder and Jean-Marc Cerrone) and African American vocal divas (such as Donna Summer and Thelma Houston).[69] What was new about disco was that it was considerably easier to produce. Unlike funk it was not, for the most part, dependent on visible "star" personalities who made personal appearances with large and highly specialized performing ensembles. Even though disco had its star performers such as Donna Summer or the Village People, it was essentially a producer's music, and its practices helped define a new age of popular musical production.[70]

As a style, disco simplified the polyrhythmic innovations of funk (and as such downplayed their implicit political resonances), leading some black pop music critics to dismiss it as a nameless, faceless, and generic music that contributed to the death of an era of innovative and socially conscious African American dance music.[71] But a deeper truth is that disco, with its emphasis on dancing for pure pleasure, simultaneously projected the aesthetics of the black body into mainstream American culture in a way that hadn't taken place since the "jazz age" of the 1930s or the birth of rock and roll in the 1950s.[72]

Beyond the ideologically charged dance floor debates, and away from the floodlit stages of concert arenas and the glitter of celebrity discotheques, funk and disco records were both put to much different use in the African American and Latino areas of New York City: there an ongoing tradition of plundering and/or reinterpreting mainstream pop music products for reconsumption and reconfiguration outside of the mainstream was intensifying because of the economic developments in New York City. By the late 1970s, further deconstruction of funk and disco music was taking place at block parties, discotheques, and house parties around New York City by a younger generation of musical aspirants who, in the absence of adequate funding for music programs in the city's public schools, turned to their parents' record collections and home playback equipment for inspiration and musical source material. Distilling the prior deconstructions of funk and disco, DJs developed the technique of mixing between two turntables to elongate brief snatches of excerpted music ("breaks" or "break beats," some as short as a few seconds) into long-form minimalist groove suites, punctuated by superimposed horn or rhythm section riffs excerpted from other recordings. As in the Jamaican sound system, these "suites" were augmented by the rapping of the MC (same role as the DJ in Jamaica), and could be prolonged indefinitely depending on the wishes of the rapper/MC or the dancers.

At the same time, a stream of new tracks began to be issued that used the criteria of the "break" as fundamental to composition, with entire songs now being composed of excerpted percussion interludes. What Kodwo Eshun memorably referred to as "isolation of the "breakbeat"[73] was a transformative compositional strategy by which, through scratching and (later) digital sampling, previously recorded music was deconstructed into minimal gestures that were then reconstructed according to the logics of the sound collage. There were harmonic implications here. Scratching and the digital sampling that supplanted it were based on the juxtaposition of sounds chosen primarily for their rhythmic and textural value. Thus scratching ultimately departed from the rules of functional harmony and resulted in a type of collage-driven polytonality characteristic of hip-hop — which in turn has shaped the harmonic tendencies of much electronically-produced popular music.

This period of stylistic transformation initiated a new conceptual epoch in black American dance music (and ultimately, popular dance music in general) that might be considered a revolution of the *songscape* over the *song*. The final catalyst in this transformation was the emergence of digital sound technology that facilitated the easy reconfiguration of sound material. The more DJs began to use finite reggae, soul, and funk songs as fodder for their long-form song suites, the more they effectively reconfigured these materials for subsequent manipulation in the digital domain.[74] In this light, the 1960s/1970s generation of musicians who invested their expression in traditional (Western) musical instruments as a means of advancing the cutting edge of black culture could be seen as the last practitioners of the old order. Henceforth, their great works would be digitally reconfigured through new forms of technology into distinctively black languages that almost entirely depart from traditionally Euro-American conceptions of songcraft. Their work was created during a period in which producers and engineers were becoming as important to musical production as singers and instrumentalists,[75] and in which dance music was in the midst of an intensive "Africanization" that gradually transformed the short song forms of midcentury popular music into longer forms more suitable for extended dancing.

What does all of this have to do with dub music? The musical evolution of hip-hop is rooted in several stylistic streams, but one of the most crucial is the innovations in Kingston's recording studios and sound systems during the 1960s and 1970s.[76] The economically driven processes described above had been foreshadowed almost a decade earlier in Jamaica, where producers recycled musical material to maximize profits in a depressed economy incapable of supporting the large-scale purchase of musical instruments and other musical technologies. More specifically, there was a strong Jamaican influence upon the formative years of hip-hop in 1970s New York City, facilitated by heavy Caribbean immigration to New York during the 1960s; as Peter Manuel notes in *Caribbean Currents*, the Jamaican population in New York City is second only to the Jamaican capital of Kingston.[77] The musical link is specifically credited to New Yorkers of Caribbean heritage like DJ Kool Herc (b. Clive Campbell, 1955) and Afrika Bambaataa

(b. Kevin Donovan, 1957) who were directly responsible for these far-reaching developments on black American popular music. What these musicians contributed to African American music were the Caribbean-derived practices of talking over pre-recorded music (toasting, referred to as "rapping" in the United States), a patchwork-collage approach to (re)composition, the appropriation and refashioning of musical technology, a tendency to strip pre-recorded music to its purely rhythmic elements, and the modular reuse and recombination of musical source materials.

Sonically and aesthetically, musicians like DJ Kool Herc essentially transplanted the Jamaican sound system model to New York City, along with the concept of mobile outdoor entertainment, which, for a brief moment in the late 1970s, was able to rearticulate urban space in a new, class-inflected way in the form of the neighborhood block party. And as with dub in Jamaica, the stylistic traits of the music grew very much out of the formal structure of the dance event in which minimalist music was used as the basis for improvised vocalizing and extended dancing. These roots remain discernible in contemporary hip-hop; the cross-cultural dialogue has continued as ragga and hip-hop continue to influence each other and as the influence of Jamaican music continues to be recognized on a global scale.[78]

The central stylistic difference, of course, was that Jamaican musicians such as DJ Kool Herc, living and working in New York City, "toasted" (rapped) over funk, soul, jazz, and rhythm-and-blues records instead of the reggae of their native country. Structurally and functionally speaking, however, the concept of the breakbeat in hip-hop closely parallels reggae's concept of drum & bass. And it is, at least in part, because of this core conceptual similarity that popular music production in Jamaica and on the American mainland has followed a similar trajectory since the 1970s. Given this similarity, a comparison of dub with hip-hop offers an important opportunity to examine the alternate evolution of a body of musical strategies that have contributed to an gradual "Africanization" of the Western popular dance song form.

Dub's primary contribution to popular music, as described earlier, can be found in the concepts of drum & bass/soundscape mixing, and the fragmenting of syntax. Hip-hop's most substantial contribution, on the other hand, has been in the aesthetics of the breakbeat, which was later formalized with the advent of digital sampling. Both are deconstructive compositional strategies that have sensitized listeners to the microaesthetics of production. Stacks of samples, all recorded at different times and places (and thus implying different sonic atmospheres), have sensitized listeners to the most subtle gestures of production. Excerpts of music that may last mere seconds are nevertheless successfully exploited for the emotional impact of their sound environment on the listener. Listeners have thus been made newly sensitive to timbre and texture in recordings. In this sense, hip-hop producers such as the Bomb Squad, DJ Red Alert, and the RZA are similar to Jamaican producers such as King Tubby and Lee Perry, in the way they have helped stretch the parameters of sound in popular music.

Of course, the two styles follow different paths. Hip-hop (at least since Public Enemy's 1988 album *It Takes A Nation of Millions to Hold Us Back*) has typically relied upon the rhythmic hocketing of sound samples to create a hypermasculinized, sonic space. Dub, on the other hand, tended toward a more implosive aesthetic. An easy comparison might be to say that while hip-hop, through its structures of stacked samples, tends to rely on a strategy of *accumulation,* dub tends much more toward a minimalist aesthetic of *incompletion.* Much has been written about both accumulation and incompletion as conceptual traits in African-derived visual art forms,[78] but to my knowledge, neither has been seriously applied in analysis of the musical forms of the African diaspora. Both were important strategies in the Africanization of the Western pop song.

I believe that certain sonic differences between the two styles also reflect the different times in which they developed. Hip-hop, born of a period in which African American culture was gradually retreating in on itself under the weight of various socioeconomic pressures, immerses the listener in a fairly hermetic sound world. Dub's atmospheric soundscaping, in contrast, may reflect its own genesis in a period of expansive thinking, optimism, historical fantasy, and hopefulness, as symbolized by the hopes of the Manley years, the ascendance of Rastafari as a new and proactive black vision of the world, and the long-term historical embrace of ancestral African culture.

Musically, hip-hop and dub meet at the intersection where carelessness, carefreeness, and alienation from the European tradition inspire a shattering of Western functional harmony into a neo-African polytonality; where sound technology facilitates a manipulation of texture and timbre according to a long-retained African predilection for thickly textured and percussive articulation; where the African-derived aesthetic strategies of accumulation and incompletion lead either to densely stratified layers of rhythmic sound, or to minimalist groove patterns; where economic circumstances dictate a reuse of previously recorded materials; where these previously recorded materials serve as the basis for real-time improvisation via the mix, the scratch/sample, and/or the voice; and where people achieve transcendence on the dance floor through the retained trance and possession logics of West African musical systems. Both styles also reflect how an emphasis on Africa as cultural motherlode gave way to and/or facilitated a period in which the ghetto was symbolically transformed into the most authentic site of black culture.

Theory and Meta-Dub: Paul D. Miller, Louis Chude-Sokei, Paul Gilroy, and the CCRU

New forms of music will of necessity generate new modes of thinking and writing about both music and culture. Such has been the case with dub. Some of the literature addresses black cultures specifically; in other instances, dub has been useful in a more abstract sense, to a wide range of thinking across various disciplines.

The work of New York–based DJ/conceptualist Paul D. Miller (a.k.a. DJ Spooky) reflects how dub has intersected in a practical way with more traditional currents of electronic and experimental music. It also demonstrates how the music has interacted with more theoretical dimensions of experimental music, generating new models that have in turn influenced practice. As a composer, Miller has been at the center of New York's Illbient movement since the mid-1990s (other artists associated with this scene would include Sub Dub, Byzar, and We).[80] An obvious play on the established term *ambient,* the illbient tag typically describes music that blends dance rhythms (usually derived from dub and decelerated hip-hop) with pure electronic textures given an ambient treatment—not in the soothing ambient sense of Brian Eno's work, for example, but in atmospheric treatments of abrasive urban, industrial, and informational sounds. This process, relying heavily on digital sampling, seems at least partially inspired by musique concrète and other late modernist tape works, such as those by Cage (for example, *Williams Mix*) or Stockhausen (for example, *Hymnen*).

A number of Miller's musical works are, like the works of his musique concrète forebears, built from found sounds (expanded to include dance music sources) to produce pure soundscape works, such as his 1995 *Necropolis* project in which he remixes the work of several of New York's underground ambient experimentalists by reaching into what he calls the "data-cloud" of "viral sonic spores and chronotopes." In practical terms, this means a host of abstracted dance music and pure experimental sources given a dense treatment that evokes the information deluge of the cybernetic age. Being for the most part derived from decelerated hip-hip and neo-dub, the beats in *Necropolis* are fairly simplistic and not nearly so engaging as the pure sound aspects of the piece. It is these ambient aspects that provide the project with a cinematic scope that most clearly presents Spooky's vision.

But although Spooky has composed a number of nondance, pure sound pieces of this type, much of his work (like the aforementioned German artists) ultimately reflects the dub influence in its reconciliation of the abstract sound emphasis of the experimental tradition with the body-oriented rhythms of dance music. The importance of Jamaican music in brokering this fusion is made explicit in song/CD titles, and other references drawn directly from Jamaica's music and culture such as *Riddim Warfare,* "Dancehall Malfunction," "Soon Forward," "Chinatown Dub," the pairing of his *Optometry* CD with a "version" set titled *Dubtometry.*

Miller is also a prolific writer and composer for whom musical composition and written theorizing are apparently complementary pursuits. Like the members of England's CCRU (discussed below), Miller has used the internal processes of dub, hip-hop, and experimental music to ponder the effects of broader phenomena (such as the information age) on aesthetics and society in general. Miller trained in philosophy and French literature in the late 1980s and early 1990s; inspired by the poststructuralist streams of these disciplines, he has found in the reconfigurative practices of dub sonic models processes he observes in society in general. His work represents an important expansion of the older conceptual model of electronic and experimental music: whereas composers like Cage and Stockhausen drew on artistic and nonartistic models (drawn from science, poetry, mathematics, visual arts) from within the high European tradition and (later) various Eastern philosophies (Taoism, Zen Buddhism) to expand their conceptual vocabularies, Miller seems to have found equally provocative models in the Africanist aesthetic and philosophical implications of dub and hip-hop.

Louis Chude-Sokei is a scholar of English specializing in postcolonial literature, literary theory, and popular culture. In his music-related work, he seems most concerned with generating what he calls a "hermeneutics of black sound" configured to the dynamics of African, Afro-diasporic and postcolonial culture. Conversely, he also cites dub as the central inspiration for his literary work. Chude-Sokei's thoughts on dub are outlined in three seminal essays authored between 1994 and 1997. In "The Sound of Culture" (1997), he interprets Jamaica's sound system culture as an embodiment of a nationalist sensibility, and roots reggae and dub as particularly vivid embodiments of Jamaica's postcolonial culture. "Post-Nationalist Geographies" (1994) offers a similar grounding of Jamaica's music in the post-1985 digital era and, within the broader contexts of the post–Michael Manley years of the 1980s, the concurrent decline of Rastafari as a dominant cultural narrative and the transnational networks of Jamaican musical production and dissemination. "Dr. Satan's Echo Chamber" (1997) grounds reggae's sonic characteristics within the broader historical sweep of Afro-diasporic cultural experience.[81] Chude-Sokei's work is a particularly notable example of a stream of Jamaicanist scholarship in which strategies of literary criticism have been brought to bear upon music. It was Africanist scholars who devised the concept of "oral literature" to account for deeply rooted traditions of verbal creativity. Similarly, the rise of deejaying in Jamaica created a space in which scholars of Jamaica's traditions of creative writing could bring literary insights to bear upon on the country's popular music. Influential work of this type has been done by Carolyn Cooper, Kwame Dawes, and others. What distinguishes Chude-Sokei's work from most of his colleagues is his interest in going beyond text and engaging the music from the perspective of its *sound*. It is dub music that inspired him to take this approach.

Dub is a similarly potent presence in the work of sociologist Paul Gilroy, albeit more obliquely articulated: while references to Jamaican music are frequent in his work, none of his major writings to date address dub exclusively. As a scholar who portrays music as one of the most reliable indexes of the history and state of black culture, however, Gilroy has included dub in several of his most pivotal hypotheses. Gilroy came of age in England in the 1970s, when black music (broadly construed) was a powerful political and moral force in global culture. And if jazz and various forms of popular music were considered musical embodiments of this force in African American culture, reggae—tied to the experiences of England's Caribbean emigrants—emerged as the most powerful embodiment of this force in England. Reggae signaled the ascension of black Britain as a newly potent cultural force in the global articulation of "blackness." As such, Gilroy could claim in 1993: "There has been no contemporary equivalent to the provocative, hermetic power of dub which supported the radical Ethiopianism of the seventies or of the anti-assimilationist unintelligibility of bebop in the forties."[82] This manner of claiming dub has, in fact, been broadly evident in England, where much of the writing of cultural studies theorists and popular music journalists invests the style with a philosophical, political, and cultural weight similar to the weight jazz carried among the more visionary theorists of African American culture in the 1960s and 1970s.

By drawing out the implications of its economic and social practices, Gilroy has found in dub a sonic model for various broader cultural and political processes. African American cultural critics (such as Albert Murray, Ralph Ellison, and Stanley Crouch) have used the communal processes of jazz improvisation as a metaphor for the democratic ideal in society. So does Gilroy find dub and its economics a potential model of subaltern politics and a challenge to the constraints of capitalism. Commenting on the communal erotics of the Jamaican sound system, for example, he noted its "Rabelaisian power to carnivalize and disperse the dominant order through an intimate yet public discourse on sexuality and the body [which] has drawn many outsiders into a dense network of black public symbols," and extends this in order to ponder "the equally distinctive *public* political character of these forms and the urban social movement they have helped to create and extend."[83] In this interpretation, an aesthetic process coded with eroticized social resistance attracts (and potentially mobilizes) listeners beyond the immediate context of its creation. In "Diaspora, Utopia and the Critique of Capitalism" (1987), Gilroy reflected on the economic and political implications of practices such as versioning, observing:

> The conflict between these traditions in black music and the constraining forms demanded by the economy of the music business is an extensive one. . . . There is a subtle dialectic between technological developments and the outcome of struggles between the priorities of black consumers and those of the record companies on which they were forced to depend. . . . The deconstructive aspects of dub . . . lay bare the anatomy of a piece and recognize in it a new order. The liberatory rationality which is spelled out in the lyrics, if there are lyrics, is thus manifest in the consumption of the musical culture. The whole dialogic process that unites performers and crowds is imported into the culture's forms. It becomes the basis of an authentic public sphere which is counterposed to the dominant alternative, from which, in any case, blacks have been excluded. The arts which, as slaves, blacks were allowed instead of freedom, have become a means to make their formal freedom tangible.[84]

The deconstruction of essentialist notions of racial identity has been a central concern of Gilroy's recent work. In *Small Acts* (1993), for example, he argued that the ostensibly stable construction of black culture had historically functioned as the "counter-culture" to Western modernity. Since World War II, however, this age has been gradually eclipsed by a global age in which a variety of factors made such stable constructions of identity far more complicated and problematic.[85] So while it is true that Gilroy has resisted the simplistic viewing of black cultures through the fashionable lens of postmodernism (preferring instead a revised definition of modernism as presented in his *Black Atlantic*), his positioning of dub as an acute commentary (in its time) on the state of black culture nevertheless implies that he has found in the fluid dynamics of the music an ideal sonic metaphor for mutable and contingent constructions of identity.[86]

Both Gilroy and Louis Chude-Sokei have also evoked the image of dub (among other musical forms) as an alternate medium of history. This type of interpretation seems to me to have grown out of two related streams. First, a fairly straightforward technological argument: a McLuhanesque understanding of new technologies for the storage of information (such as analog and digital sound media) supplanting older technologies (such as writing). Second, a rhetorical assertion of African-derived musics as, initially, a template for artistic production in other media; later, an *alternate* form of literature; and ultimately, an *alternative historical medium*.[87]

Given that music has historically been the dominant artistic medium within black culture, the notion of *sound as history* draws its conceptual grounding from the reality of sound recording technology, as well as the oral history practices of the West African societies that peopled the African diaspora; it directly challenges the modernist Western notion that history is best or most accurately preserved in written form.

Other examples of dub inspiring thought beyond the sphere of music would include Jeff Salamon's 1997 minisurvey of dub that appeared in the pages of *Artforum,* a magazine devoted to the criticism of visual arts.[88] Marina Budhos's 1999 book *Remix* examines the lives of immigrant teenagers as a microcosm of the changing contours of cultural identity in late twentieth-century America.[89] John Homiak's 1998 "Dub History" uses the remix theme to discuss the instability of oral history in the African diaspora.[90] The 2005 "Africa Remix" exhibition at the Centre Georges Pompidou in Paris used the remix theme to explore how that travel and technology have allowed migrant contemporary African artists to explode the myopic stereotype of a unitary "African art," forcing viewers to confront the kaleidoscopic reality of contemporary African cultural and artistic production.[91] Such extramusical readings are almost certainly inspired by the improvisatory nature of the music. Dub remains a dance music first and foremost, but it has proved particularly useful when its conceptual processes assume the foreground and the music suggests other parameters of thought and experience. The reality is that dub grounds the abstract, experimental impulse in the sensual experience of the body; as such, it viscerally embodies the reconciliation of "high" and "low" so valued by theorists of so-called postmodern culture.[92]

This position at the crossroads of science and sensuality has also inspired particularly imaginative ways of writing about music. Naturally, a new aesthetic form requires a new language of analysis, explanation, or criticism. Kodwo Eshun, for example, has been in the forefront of an impressionistic music criticism seemingly informed by the literary tendencies of poststructuralist writing. In the following passage, he discusses Lee Perry's use of excerpted television dialogue on the *Revolution Dub* LP:

Revolution Dub is not so much produced as reduced by Perry. The song is x-rayed into exoskeletal forms through which TV leaks. For "Woman's Dub," the distorted snares drum like needlepoint magick, but rusted, ferric. "Kojak" is an intoxicated mix, an echo chamber of moans in which space staggers and lurches dangerously. . . . By bringing the outside into the inside of The Song, Perry releases sitcom ghosts into the spectral song. Perry samples TV before the sampler, just as Holger Czukay uses radio, drawing signals down through the aerials into The Song, crackling open another timezone inside the track. Space changes places. Reality reverses itself.[93]

Dub can also be seen as an indirect influence on topics assumed to be completely unrelated to artistic production. Luciana Parisi's 2004 *Abstract Sex* uses the chaotic flows of biological and digital information to theorize the evolution of reproductive processes; here again, the transformational processes in the music can be read as having energized the rhetoric of an unrelated field. The publication of *Abstract Sex* was commemorated with a 2004 event in London titled "Bacteria in Dub," which featured audible excerpts of Parisi's text, "versioned" into musical form by a DJ.[94] In fact, both Parisi and Kodwo Eshun have been associated with the Cybernetic Culture Research Unit (CCRU), based at the University of Warwick in England. Like DJ Spooky, Parisi's use of dub in this manner reflects the CCRU's general strategy of "flipping" the interpretive "script," so to speak. Instead of using academic theory to explain music or using society to provide a context for the music, these thinkers have seized upon certain structural tendencies of the music and used them as a basis for theorizing about any number of extramusical (aesthetic, social, political, biological, technological, and so forth) processes. What makes such a link possible is technology and its transformations of both artistic and social practices. In this way, the music comes to rival the written word as a medium for theorizing, ultimately positioned as an act of theory in and of itself. This understanding of music as theory resonates with the aforementioned Africa-derived idea of music as history; simultaneously, it demonstrates the way that art is capable of energizing and/or revitalizing theory.

Parisi's use of dub in this way also typifies the music's conceptual usefulness in challenging the perceived foundations of modernism. If the modernist conception of the body, for example, is stereotypically held to be inherently stable, male, and neatly delineated, Parisi's work draws upon the "rhizomatic" and "code/flow" ideas of Gilles Deleuze and Felix Guattari, whose works *Anti-Oedipus* and *A Thousand Plateaus* reject Freudian and Lacanian ideas of various "original traumas" in favor of ideas of a (personal and/or political) "body" in a *continuous process of reconfiguration*.[95] It draws upon the poststructuralist feminism of thinkers such as Luce Irigaray, who deploys rhetorics of *absence* and *invisibility* as strategies for the subversion of "phallocentric" understandings of gender and cultural (particularly linguistic) practices.[96] Its implicit technoeroticism (in which machines are humanized, humans are mechanized, and the relationships between them eroticized) draws upon the "cyborg" feminism of Donna Haraway, whose ideas blur the dichotomy between humans and machines in the modern world and similarly contest the boundary between science fiction and social reality as an "optical illusion."[97] The dub-inspired genre mutations of electronica (that is, Barrow's idea of dub as stylistic "virus") finds a clear parallel in her use of biologist Lynn Margulis's theories of symbiotic viral and bacterial relationships between humans and nonhuman species[98] (in fact, dub's perpetual mutability strikes a resonant chord in an age in which the virus has become a dominant global metaphor). Finally, in an age when erotic desire itself has, of necessity, become more fragmented and skewed, Parisi's writing dramatizes the way dub's fragmentary construction of musical pleasure has helped articulate new strategies of eroticism. The spectres of versioning, remixing, subversion of formal development, genre-bending, and improvisation clearly haunt her ideas:

> [There is] a third way out of the binarism between embodiment and disembodiment to engage with the biodigital mutations of human sex. This third way maps the emergence of a new (but ancient) kind of sex and reproduction, linking these mutations to microcellular processes of information transmission that involve the unnatural mixtures of bodies and sexes. The speeding up of information trading, not only across sexes, but across species and between humans and machines, exposes the traits of a non-climactic (non-discharging) desire spreading through a matrix of connections that feed off each other without an ultimate apex of satisfaction. . . . The mutual feedback between biology and technology marks an unpredictable proliferation of molecular mutations that poses radical questions not only about human sex but also about what we take a body, nature and matter to be. This new approach investigates the imminent perversion of mutant species, bodies and sexes by the engineering of an altogether different conception of sex, femininity, and desire—abstract sex.[99]

Thus, it is not only musicians who have transformed dub music into a global influence. It is also writers and thinkers such as Miller, Chude-Sokei, Gilroy, Eshun, and Parisi who have grappled most creatively with the sociocultural implications of this music and shaped the metamusical resonance of dub as it relates to broader issues of culture. In their hands, dub is gradually evolving into the kind of broadly applied metaphor for early twenty-first-century culture that jazz was for the late twentieth.

It is in this global setting that the dub and the remix have come to stand as prominent metaphors of contemporary culture. The music's strategies have become a valuable existential resource for non-Jamaican, non-Caribbean artists and intellectuals whose own work reflects a crisis (or at the very least, a transformation) of certainty, authority, and meaning *within* Western culture. As discussed in the previous chapter, dub might be thought of as the electronic music of African exiles several generations removed. But its sonic symbolism has also come to resonate with a global age in which diaspora ironically represents one of the most stable examples of "community" in our transnational moment and in which exile, in the words of Edward Said, "has been transformed so easily into a potent, even enriching motif of modern culture."[100] As we have seen, dub contributed musically to articulations of the postcolonial within Jamaica and the post-imperial outside of Jamaica; the qualities of the music reflected a good amount of what has been claimed as the postmodern in music.[101] It is the structural elements of fragmentation, discontinuity, and multiple meanings that unites dub within this field of competing and complementary "posts."[102] The music's structural uncertainty resonates with an age of the refugee, the nomad, the displaced person, the de-centered inhabitant of the culturally exploding megapolis, the liminal terrorist, and a historical period in which the old seems to be giving way to an uncertain new at an unprecedented rate. As Kevin Martin surmised, "Dub proved there was an audience eager for insecurity."[103] From the perspective of this book, such insecurity reflects shifting political and cultural contours, and demonstrates how the cultural products of the (formerly) colonized ultimately exert influence upon the culture of the (former) colonizer.

This idea, of course, is nothing new. Thinkers from Fanon to Gilroy have long argued for an understanding of the experiences of colonizer and colonized as symbiotically intertwined, and this understanding inevitably implies a cross-cultural renegotiation of our understanding of modernity and modernist art. The result is that the constellation of formerly colonized cultures (including those of the African diaspora) are understood not in *opposition* to modernity, but as modernity's *many local conjugations*. The particular local conjugation I have addressed in this book differs from typical understandings of Western artistic modernism, which is often considered as either a deliberate break from the past, or a depiction of the alienation of artists from the corporate and industrial state.[104] In contrast, modernism for artists of Africa and the African diaspora often represented an opportunity to seize the reins of self-definition and to position themselves as agents in the postcolonial transformation of society.[105] Their rescuing of the definitions of black subjectivity from Eurocentric discourses was essential to the postcolonial moment and permanently altered the terms of debate on both sides. In this book, I have demonstrated the role that musical technology and local concepts of experimentation played in this redefinition. In James Lastra's thinking, the experience we describe as "modernity" has been fundamentally shaped by the technological media of the modern era.[106] Within divergent experiences of modernity, then, these technologies become implicated in various local dynamics of cultural redefinition, while ultimately remaining a complementary part of modernity, newly understood (per Gilroy) in global terms. The composite idea of technology being developed according to differing cultural priorities helps nuance the stereotypical "impact" model in which technology is seen to flow in one direction from technologically advanced to technologically marginal cultures.[107]

This same process is relevant to music. When we blend the parallel significance of dub's role within and outside of Jamaica, it becomes clear that the central artistic revolutions of the late twentieth century were not accomplished solely in the intellectual and cultural centers of Europe and America. They were also accomplished on the margins of Europe and America, where Western cultural forms mixed, mingled, or collided with a variety of non-Western forms in the creation of new aesthetic, cultural, and technological centers.

Conclusion

A lot of people now are using the word "dub," and I can understand the reason why they do it, because it sounds hip. It's trendy. But when I've gone out and done dub events around the world, and particularly in certain European cities, people say, "Play something faster." They haven't actually got a fucking clue! They don't understand at all the origins. . . . But it's very convenient for their purposes and I can understand that what we have been inspired by has inspired a whole new generation. And they've blatantly said, "We'll have that for ourselves. We'll nick that for our purposes." Which is quite healthy, it's not bad. It's just a fact of life.[108]
—Adrian Sherwood, 2001

Emerging from the multiple sites of recording studios, sound systems, discotheques and raves, remix culture has transformed the practices of popular song composition in several important ways. In the studio sphere, where production and composition have increasingly overlapped, the advent of multitrack and later digital recording technology gradually allowed studio engineers to reconfigure recorded materials in as many ways as they desired and, in so doing, to introduce an ethos of improvisation into the formerly fixed medium of the sound recording. In this coda, we have seen that Jamaican music played a central role in this shift. As Steve Barrow noted to me in 2004, "Madonna's got a *dub version,* where did she get that from? 'Drum & bass'—what's drum & bass? A new music? There's records from 1974 saying: 'Drum & bass by King Tubbys.' He was the guy who did that. That all happened because of the sound system being outside of Jamaica."[109]

This very different musical conception initially factored into currents of musical exoticism and the Western audience's need to regenerate its own musical traditions through encounter with new and novel "outsider" sounds. In the global music marketplace, dub's low-fi, densely textured aesthetic and self-consciously crude production values marked it as an "authentic" and exotic pop music to Western ears. This exoticism in turn allowed the music to factor into various sociomusical strategies outside of Jamaica, such as the use of low-fidelity aesthetics to dramatize a distance from the corporate music culture, or to dramatize a subcultural distance from what was thought to be "mainstream" society. Thus, it is unsurprising that dub production styles most influenced British popular music during the 1970s, when the dissenting stance of punk music was influential. It is equally unsurprising that although roots reggae had been popular for years, dub itself gained wider recognition in the United States during the 1990s, concurrently with the rise of the self-proclaimed marginality of corporate hip-hop, as well as the "alternative" genre of rock music, in which musicians embraced a deliberate low-fi aesthetic in order to distance themselves from the increasing standardization of corporate rock music. Most recently, the rise of electronica has enabled the music to be retrospectively constructed as a primitivist music for the incipient digital age, despite the complex technology through which it was produced.

Of course, this primitivism is a problematic construction; although Jamaica's engineers consciously and deliberately violated many conventions of studio recording, they did it with a specific aesthetic in mind and did not conceive of their work as self-consciously "low-fi." In fact, they were aspiring to just the opposite: to maximize their limited equipment to achieve the best possible sound. Scientist, for example, articulated this in competitive terms that undermine ideas of the "primitive": "If you listen to American music from the 1970s, and you listen to reggae from that time, the fidelity of reggae was higher . . . the fidelity that we was getting in Jamaica at that time, a lot of record labels [in America] just didn't have it. Motown been putting out records using much better recording equipment. They had the money that they could do it. But when you listen to Motown, the drums were weak and way in the background."[110]

I have argued that dub's sonic and formal concepts have become models for pop song composition in the digital age. If cutting edge pop music in the digital age seems to deliberately subvert the industrial and modernist narratives of mastery, the creators of dub were exemplars, creating a practice that was, to cite Houston Baker, a deliberate "deformation of mastery."[111] Inevitably, this "deformation" was merely an intermediate step in the creation of a new kind of mastery.

Not everyone hears this as mastery, of course. Linguist John McWhorter, for example, bemoans both the hyperverbosity of rap and the fragmented texts of electronica as musical legacies of the countercultural shifts of the 1960s, which he feels have contributed to a lessening of the (English) language's capability for sophisticated and nuanced expression:

We could almost predict that after the sixties, a form of pop music would emerge that is all about the performer talking over a beat. . . . Certainly we haven't tossed out melody and harmony altogether. But we can do without them if the beat is fine enough. . . . The eternal pulsations of house music, in which lyrical fragments are sprinkled thin as mere decoration, take our rhythmic fetish to its logical extreme. . . . Rhythm is deeply, elementally seductive. But it remains a less elaborated form of expression than the long, musical lines, with subtle shifting harmonies underneath that the classical musician sweats over. Mahler was complex not only within four measure units, but also in these units' constant and unpredictable transformations throughout a movement.[112]

One could, of course, make the counterargument that fragmentation is, for very concrete reasons, a central coping mechanism of our time. In an age of information overload, an aesthetic of fragmentation can be seen as a way of using art to break down the power of excess wordage. Hence the proliferation of fragmentary aesthetics in fashion, design, and advertising, an aesthetic logic that will inevitably evolve its own sophisticated modes of elaboration and abstraction. Fragmentation can also be seen as inevitable in an age in which cultural codes of all kinds are being deconstructed, reconstructed, and recombined at an unprecedented rate.[113]

Nevertheless, McWhorter raises an important point. Is it conceivable that in the future, electronic manipulations of timbre, texture, and sound space will be understood as containing emotional depth intellectual rigor equal to that of (for example) the twelve manipulated tones of the Western tradition? Only time will tell; in any case, I believe that Jamaica's influence on global pop music runs deeper than its complex of sonic influences. In America and Europe of the 1960s and 1970s, events such as countercultural music festivals were sites in which the spiritual, political, and cultural implications of new forms of sound technology (high-intensity amplification, PA systems, sound processing circuitry) could be communally explored and evaluated by musicians, audiences, and technicians alike. It is interesting to note, though, that for every high-intensity amplification system used, there was also an Indian spiritual guru, African traditional drummer, or Native American rain chant. We infer that such festivals were also sites in which the new technology was being evaluated in terms of the dominant cultural, political, and spiritual tropes of the times. The same holds true of the carnivalesque setting of the Jamaican sound system, sonically serviced by recording engineers who, by virtue of their cultural location, implicitly worked to ground the new sound technology within the critique of technology symbolized in the Rasta emphasis on "roots." As dub moved beyond Jamaica, this dichotomy was in turn an influence in the rave culture of the 1980s and 1990s, which was predicated on the juxtaposition of digital sound (and visual) technology and the countercultural ethos of the 1960s festivals. A glance through the colorful rave advertisements collected in Joel Jordan's *Searching for the Perfect Beat* (2000) makes this juxtaposition abundantly clear. Myriad forms of plant and animal life, wonders of global topography and religious iconography are juxtaposed or fused with the technological iconography of science fiction, warfare, and the computer age. In these times, when new forms of sound technology seem to proliferate faster than humans' ability to digest and adapt them to specific needs, communal settings such as concerts, raves, and festivals implicitly humanize and spiritualize these technologies.[113]

Although a thread can be drawn through these various cultural moments, my point here is not to assert a linear or causal connection. Rather, I am suggesting that such naturalist values are typically asserted in conjunction with technological advances, in the communal hope that the technology may remain accountable to social concerns and meaningful to human concerns. With endless album covers displaying tape reels, mixing consoles, and banks of sound processors, Jamaican dub music certainly helped iconicize the technology of the recording studio in the visual imagination of popular music. But its Afro-inflected humanizing, communalizing, and spiritualizing of new forms of sound technology is almost surely its most profound contribution to global popular music.

Appendix
Recommended Listening (by engineer)

SYLVAN MORRIS

AT STUDIO ONE
(Note—as Studio One's heyday predated the rise of dub, most of the Studio One recordings cited below are composed of vocal cuts.)
Horace Andy: *Mr. Bassie*
Heartbeat CD HB 88

Burning Spear: *Creation Rebel*
Hearbeat 11661=7664–2

Gladiators: *Bongo Red*
Hearbeat 11661–7662–2

Jackie Mittoo: *Tribute to Jackie Mittoo*
Heartbeat 189/190

Jackie Mittoo: *The Keyboard King at Studio One*
Universal Sound USCD 8

Various: *Best of Studio One*
Heartbeat HB 07

Various: *Studio One Classics*
Soul Jazz SJR 96

Various: *Studio One Roots*
Soul Jazz SJR 56

Various: *Studio One Rockers*
Soul Jazz SJR 48

Various: *Studio One Scorcher*
Soul Jazz 67

The Studio One Story (DVD)
Soul Jazz CD/DVD 68

Burning Spear: *Original Living Dub, Volume 1*
Burning Spear BM 316
(Winston Rodney productions; dub versions of songs from Burning Spear's *Social Living* and *Hail H.I.M.* albums)

Bunny Wailer: *Dubd'sco, Volumes 1–2*
Solomonic/RAS 3239
(Bunny Wailer productions; dub versions of tracks from Wailer's *Blackheart Man, Bunny Wailer Sings the Wailers* and *Roots, Radics, Rockers, Reggae* albums)

Augustus Pablo: *East of the River Nile*
Shanachie CD 45051
(Augustus Pablo productions; instrumental and dub versions)

KING TUBBY

King Tubbys Meets the Rockers Uptown
Shanachie 44019
(Augustus Pablo productions)

King Tubby & Soul Syndicate: *Freedom Sounds in Dub*
Blood & Fire BAFCD 011
(Bertram Brown productions)

Dub From the Roots & The Roots of Dub
(Bunny Lee productions)
Reissued together on Moll-Selekta 8

King Tubby's Special: 1973–1976
Trojan CDTRD 409
(A two-disc collection of tracks produced by Winston "Niney" Holness and Bunny Lee)

Johnny Clarke: *A Ruffer Version 1974–1978*
Trojan TJACD 025
(Bunny Lee productions. A mixture of vocal and dub versions with several tracks featuring the "flying cymbal" sound. Also contains mixes by King Jammy and Philip Smart)

Sugar Minott: *Ghetto-ology + Dub*
Easy Star ES-1004
(Sugar Minott productions. A "showcase" album containing vocal songs and their dub versions)

Yabby You: *Jesus Dread 1972–1977*
Blood & Fire BAFCD 021
(Vivian "Yabby You" Jackson productions; features many vocal songs and dub mixes)

Morwells Unlimited Meet King Tubbys: *Dub Me*
Blood & Fire BAFCD 018
(Morwells productions)

PHILIP SMART

Creation of Dub (a.k.a. King Tubby Meets the Aggrovators at the Dub Station)
Attack BSMT 015
(Bunny Lee productions)

Tappa Zukie: *Tappa Zukie in Dub*
Blood & Fire BAFCD 008
(Tappa Zukie productions)

Johnny Clarke: *A Ruffer Version*
Trojan TJACD 025
(Bunny Lee productions with several tracks featuring the "flying cymbal" sound.
Also contains mixes by King Tubby and King Jammy)

PRINCE JAMMY

Prince Jammy: *Uhuru in Dub*
CSA 2
(early Jammy productions; dub version of Black Uhuru's *Black Sounds of Freedom* album [a.k.a. *Love Crisis*])

Scientist and Prince Jammy Strike Back!
Trojan CDTRL 210
(Linval Thompson productions)

Hugh Mundell: *Africa Must Be Free by 1983 + Africa Must Be Free Dub*
Ras RASCD 3201
(Augustus Pablo productions; a "showcase" set containing vocal songs and their
dub versions)

Gregory Isaacs: *Slum in Dub*
CSA BS 1051
(Gregory Isaacs productions; dub version of Isaacs's *Slum* album)

Horace Andy: *In the Light + In the Light Dub*
Blood & Fire BAFCD 006
(Everton da Silva productions; a "showcase" set containing vocal songs and their
dub versions)

Horace Andy: *Good Vibes*
Blood & Fire BAFCD 019
(Horace Andy productions; extended vocal-dub mixes originally released on 12")

Prince Jammy Meets Crucial Bunny in Dub
Auralux LUXX CD 016
(Ken "Fatman" Gordon productions. Also contains mixes by "Crucial" Bunny
Graham)

Dub Landing, Volumes 1 and 2
Auralux LUXX CD 017
(Linval Thompson productions. Also contains mixes by Scientist)

OVERTON "SCIENTIST" BROWN

LINVAL THOMPSON PRODUCTIONS
Scientist: *Scientist Meets the Space Invaders*
Greensleeves GRELCD 019

Scientist: *Scientist Encounters Pac-Man*
Greensleeves GRELCD 46

Scientist and Prince Jammy Strike Back!
Trojan CDTRL 210
(also contains mixes by Prince Jammy)

Dub Landing, Volumes 1 and 2
Auralux LUXX CD 017
(also contains mixes by Prince Jammy)

Wailing Souls: *Wailing*
Volcano VPR 008; rereleased in resequenced form as *Face the Devil* (Trojan)
(A "showcase" set containing vocals songs and their dub versions)

Linval Thompson Sounds: *Jah Jah Dreader Than Dread*
Majestic Reggae MRCD 1005
(A mix of songs and dub versions)

HENRY "JUNJO" LAWES PRODUCTIONS
Scientist: *Heavyweight Dub Champion*
Greensleeves GRELCD 13

Scientist: *Scientist Rids the World of the Curse of the Evil Vampires*
Greensleeves GRELCD 25

Scientist: *Scientist Wins the World Cup*
Greensleeves GRELCD 37

BUNNY LEE PRODUCTIONS
Scientist: *Scientific Dub*
Clocktower/Abraham, various matrix #'s

LEE PERRY (AS BOTH PRODUCER AND ENGINEER)

EARLY YEARS THROUGH 1973–1974
Bob Marley and the Wailers: *The Complete Bob Marley & the Wailers 1967 to 1972, Volume Two*
JAD-CD-1004

Upsetters: *Return of Django*
Trojan CDTRL 19

Upsetters: *Eastwood Rides Again*
Trojan CDTRL 125

Various: *The Upsetter Box Set*
Trojan Perry 1

Upsetters: *Blackboard Jungle Dub*
Auralux LUXX CD 004

The Upsetters & Friends: *Version Like Rain*
Trojan CDTRL 278

Lee Perry & Friends: *Shocks of Mighty 1969–1974*
Trojan CDAT 104

Lee Perry & Friends: *Give Me Power*
Trojan CDTRL 254

BLACK ARK YEARS
Lee Perry: *Scratch Attack*
Ras RASCD 1415
(compilation containing an inferior version of *Blackboard Jungle Dub*, but also the
excellent *Chapter One* album)

Lee "Scratch" Perry (and various artists): *Arkology*
Island Jamaica CRNCD 6/524 379-2

Lee "Scratch" Perry and Friends: *Open the Gate*
Trojan CD PRY 2

Lee "Scratch" Perry and Friends: *Build the Ark*
Trojan CD PRY 3

Lee Perry (and various artists): *Voodooism*
Pressure Sounds PSCD 009

Lee Perry (and various artists): *Produced and Directed by the Upsetter*
Pressure Sounds PSCD 019

Congos: *Heart of the Congos*
Blood & Fire BAFCD 009

George Faith: *To Be A Lover*
Hip-O Select/Island B0001691-01

Upsetters: *Super Ape*
Hip-O Select/Island B0002430-02

Lee Perry Presents African Roots
Trojan 06076-80552-2

ERROL THOMPSON

AT RANDY'S
Various Artists: *Java Java Dub*
Impact Rebel 1

Impact All-Stars: *Forward the Bass: Dub From Randy's, 1972–1975*
Blood & Fire BAFCD 022

AT JOE GIBBS
Joe Gibbs & the Professionals: *African Dub All-Mighty, Chapters 1 & 2*
Rocky One RGCD 023
(Joe Gibbs productions)

Joe Gibbs & the Professionals: *African Dub All-Mighty, Chapters 3 & 4*
Rocky One RGCD 024
(Joe Gibbs productions)

Joe Gibbs & the Professionals: *No Bones for the Dogs*
Pressure Sounds PSCD 37
(Joe Gibbs productions)

Joe Gibbs & Errol Thompson: *The Mighty Two*
Heartbeat HB 73
(Joe Gibbs productions)

Skin Flesh & Bones Meet The Revolutionaries: *Fighting Dub, 1975–1979*
Hot Pot CKV-CD-1005
(Lloyd "Spiderman" Campbell productions)

NEIL "MAD PROFESSOR" FRASER

Any recordings from Fraser's extensive *Dub Me Crazy* or *Black Liberation Dub* series, all on the Ariwa label.

Massive Attack vs. Mad Professor: *No Protection*
Gyroscope GYR 6619–2

ADRIAN SHERWOOD

Prince Far I: *Cry Tuff Dub Encounter, Chapter 1*
Danceteria RE129CD

Lee "Scratch" Perry & Dub Syndicate: *Time Boom X De Devil Dead*
EMI 7243 5 30026 2 6

Lee "Scratch" Perry: *From My Secret Laboratory*
Island RRCD 55 842 706–2

Creation Rebel: *Historic Moments, Volume One*
On-U Sound 7 72784–2

Creation Rebel: *Historic Moments, Volume Two*
On-U Sound 7 72799–2

Various: *The On-U Sound Box*
Cleopatra CLP-0576–2

DENNIS BOVELL

Winston Edwards & Blackbeard at 10 Downing Street
Studio 16 WE 0010

Blackbeard: *I Wah Dub*
More Cut / Zonophone 7243 5 82762 2 0

Dennis Bovell: *Decibel*
Pressure Sounds PSCD 39

Linton Kwesi Johnson: *Independent Intavenshun: The Island Anthology*
Island 314 524 575–2

BILL LASWELL

Many dub projects on the Subharmonic label.

Bob Marley: *Dreams of Freedom*
Island 314–524 419–2

Various: *Mysteries of Creation*
Axiom 162–531 070–2

LLOYD "BULLWACKIES" BARNES

The Meditations: *I Love Jah*
Wackies 510

Wayne Jarrett: *Bubble Up*
Wackies 191

Horace Andy: *Dance Hall Style*
Wackies 1383

Horace Andy Meets Nago Morris / Wayne Jarrett: *Mini-Showcase*
Wackies 1716/1722

Creation Dub
Wackies 0041

Natures Dub
Wackies 306

Jamaica Super Dub
Wackies 1720

DRUM & BASS/JUNGLE

A Guy Called Gerald: *Black Secret Technology*
Juice Box (no matrix no.)

LTJ Bukem: *Mixmag Live!*
Moonshine 60003–2

Various: *Breakbeat Science*
Vital SCIN CD00

Various: *100% Drum & Bass*
Telstar TCD 2847

TRIP-HOP

Various: *Headz*
MoWax MW026CD

Portishead: *Portishead*
London/Go Beat 314–539–189–4

Massive Attack: *Protection*
Virgin 7243 8 39883 2 7

DJ SPOOKY

DJ Spooky That Subliminal Kid: *Necropolis: The Dialogic Project*
Knitting Factory Works KFW 185

DJ Spooky: *Dubtometry*
Thirsty Ear THI 57128.2

DJ Spooky: *Riddim Warfare*
Outpost-Geffen

THE GERMAN CONTEXT

Rhythm & Sound
Basic Channel BC 01042

Rhythm & Sound: *The Versions (Burial Mix)*
Asphodel ASP 2019

Rhythm & Sound: *See Mi Yah*
BCP 55872

Maurizio: *M-Series*
Indigo 23722

Pole: *1*
Matador OLE 339

Pole: *2*
Matador OLE 359

Pole: 3
Matador OLE 428

Mouse on Mars: *Instrumentals*
Thrill Jockey Sonig 01 CD

OTHER RECORDINGS OF INTEREST

Keith Hudson: *Pick A Dub*
Blood & Fire BAFCD 003
(Keith Hudson productions)

Keith Hudson and Friends: *The Hudson Affair*
Trojan 06076–80507–2
(Keith Hudson productions)

Augustus Pablo: *King David's Melody*
Shanachie 45064
(Augustus Pablo productions)

U-Roy and Various: *Version Galore*
Trojan 06076 80383–2
(Duke Reid productions)

Aquarius Dub
Black Solidarity AQCD 001
(Herman Chin-Loy productions)

Prince Buster: *The Message Dubwise*
Melodisc MS7
(Prince Buster productions)

Notes

⚡

1. McEvilley 1993.
2. Henzell quoted in Davis and Simon 1982:51.
3. For example, see "Best of the Century" in *Time* (December 31, 1999). Lee Perry was awarded a Grammy for his album *Jamaican E.T.* (Trojan/Sanctuary Records, 2002).
4. Armstrong's "King of the Zulus" features a skit midway through the performance that includes a Jamaican voice. See *The Best of Louis Armstrong: The Hot Five and Hot Seven Recordings* (Sony, 1999).
5. The terms used in the stylistic periodization of Jamaican popular music have differed in different accounts. To take two examples: Barrow and Dalton use the term *early reggae* to indicate music created between approximately 1968 and 1972, *roots reggae* to indicate music created between approximately 1973 and 1980, and *dancehall* to indicate music created between approximately 1980 and 1985 (in this account, dub music is discussed as a subgenre of the roots reggae and dancehall periods). These authors use the term *ragga* to indicate the digital music that began to be produced in 1985 (see Barrow and Dalton 1997:82–324). Norman Stolzoff (2000), on the other hand, uses the term *reggae* to indicate all of the music produced between 1968 and 1985, and uses the term *dancehall* to indicate the digital music that began to be produced in 1985 (see his chapter "Post-Independence Jamaica"). Stolzoff also uses the term *dancehall* in a broader sense, to refer to any historical site in which Jamaicans enjoyed music communally. For my purposes in this book, the most important distinction to be made is between music performed by ensembles using standard popular music instrumentation (voice, electric guitar, electric bass, drum set, keyboards, wind instruments, percussion, and so forth), and music created by digital means (digital keyboards, samplers, drum machines, computers, and so forth). Thus, I use "reggae" and "roots reggae" interchangeably to refer to the music produced between approximately 1968 and 1985, and "ragga" to refer to the digital music produced thereafter. I believe this is consistent with the general usage of these terms in Jamaica.
6. Sources for this influence of experimental music on the popular tradition would include Cope 1996; Shapiro 2000; and Prendergast 2000.
7. For sources on the musical legacy of punk, see Bennett 2001; or Laing 1997.
8. For sources on ambient music, see Bates 1997; Tamm 1989; and Mardis 2002.

9. See Tingen 2001.

10. For sources on house and disco music, see Fikentscher 2000; and Lawrence 2003.

11. Chanan 1995:48.

12. See Davis 1985 and T. White 1983 for biographies of Marley.

13. See King 1998.

14. See also Stolzoff 2000:66.

15. Michael "Mikey Dread" Campbell interviewed August 2001. Also see Bradley 2000:397 for more on the topic of Marley's gradual distance from Jamaica's dancehall culture.

16. See Alexander Weheliye, "'Feenin': Posthuman Voices in Contemporary Black Popular Music" (in Nelson 2002). The article makes the point that authenticity in soul music was constructed upon relatively direct and unmediated emotional expression.

17. Dave Hendley interviewed June 2002. Also see Bradley 2000:413 for a discussion of the negative initial perception of reggae in Britian.

18. See Malm and Wallis 1992:38.

19. Chude-Sokei 1997b:5.

20. The *Wailing* LP is currently available, in resequenced form, on Trojan Records as *Face the Devil* (Trojan CD TRL 360).

21. For an account of this performance and its background events, see Davis 1985:212–16.

22. In *The Soundscape,* sonologist R. Murray Schaefer offers a useful insight about the transformations wrought on human audio culture by radio: "Radio introduced the surrealistic soundscape. . . . The modern radio schedule, a confection of material from various sources, joined in thoughtful, funny, ironic, absurd or provocative juxtapositions, has introduced many contradictions into modern life and perhaps contributed more than anything else to the breakup of unified cultural systems and values" (Schaefer 1994:94).

23. Consult Gray 1991 for a comprehensive discussion of postindependence Jamaican politics.

24. For example, see Hendley's recollections in the notes to *The Crowning of Prince Jammy* (Pressure Sounds PSCD 25).

25. See Lesser 2002; and T. White 1983.

26. See Lesser 2002 for a full-length biography of King Jammy.

27. Perry is the subject of a full-length biography by David Katz (2000).

28. For example, see Bilby in Manuel 1995:146.

29. See Waters (1985) for an examination of Manley's use of reggae in his 1972 campaign. Also see King 1998.

30. One convenient starting point for a survey of religion in Jamaica is Morrish 1982.

31. Two comprehensive studies of Rastafari are Barrett 1997; and Chevannes 1994. See also Murrell 1999.

32. Hillman and D'Agostino 2003:291. For sources on the influence of Rastafari across social classes, see Edmonds 2003.

33. See Stolzoff 2000:7.

34. The origins and etymology of the Hindi-derived term *ganja* have been recounted in several publications; a brief introduction can be found in Shapiro 2003:210.

35. From the Wailing Souls LP *The Very Best of the Wailing Souls* (Greensleeves GREL 99).

36. From the Horace Andy LP *In the Light* (Blood & Fire BAFCD 006).

37. From the Johnny Clarke LP *Authorised Rockers* (Virgin CDFL 9014).

38. From the *Wiser Dread* compilation (Nighthawk 301).

39. From the Burning Spear LP *Marcus Garvey* (Island ILPS 9377).

40. From the Prince Far I CD *Psalms for I* (Pressure Sounds PSCD 35).

41. Manuel 1995:15.

42. See Hillman and D'Agostino 2003:291.

43. See Williams 1961:48–71.

44. Paul "Computer Paul" Henton, interviewed March 2002.

45. See Shapiro 2003:210–13.

46. Wallace as quoted in Van Pelt 2005:39.

47. Richardson 1992:130–31.

48. See Shapiro 2003:210.

49. Erlmann 1996b:49.

50. Prominent studies of hip-hop include Chang (2005), George (1998), Perkins (1996), Potter (1995), Rose (1994) and Toop (1984).

51. For example, see the chapters devoted to dub in Davis and Simon (1982), Hebdige (1987), Barrow and Dalton (1997), Potash (1997), Foster (1999), and Howard (2004).

52. See Manuel 1995:237–40.

53. I have taken this phrase from John Corbett's excellent essay "Experimental Oriental: New Music and Other Others" in Born and Hesmondhalgh (2000).

54. The recent literature on electronically produced popular music (broadly defined) would include Rose (1994), Johnson (1996), Poschardt (1995), Reynolds (1998), Fikentscher (2000), Prendergast (2000), and Shapiro (2000). The literature on the recording studio would include Eisenberg (1987), Chanan (1995), Porcello (1996), Cunningham (1998), Howard (2004), Meintjes (2003), Zak (2001), and Cogan and Clark (2003).

55. See also Meintjes 2003:9.

56. For example, see the chapter "Five Themes in the Study of Caribbean Music," in Manuel 1995; Walder 1998; and Mintz and Price 1992.

57. Obviously, this type of reference to "the music" evokes the contentious debate around gender issues in historical musicology and music theory between scholars such as Pieter Van den Toorn and Leo Treitler on one hand, and Susan McClary, Suzanne Cusick, Susan C. Cook, and Ruth Solie, on the other. Ethnomusicology, founded on both musicological and sociocultural inquiry and the axiom that music both constitutes and is constituted by sociocultural forces, has generally been less susceptible to this type of debate. See for example Solie 1995; Van den Toorn 1995; Cook and Tsou 1994; Cusick 1994; and McClary 1994.

58. See Ramsey 2003: 19–22.

59. See Everett 1999.

60. See Thompson 2005.

1. Electronic Music in Jamaica (pp. 26–44)

1. Bilby in Manuel 1995:152.

2. See Bilby in Manuel 1995 for a historical survey of Jamaican music.

3. Ibid., 145. This account of pre-reggae Jamaican music is drawn mainly from Bilby's chapter.

4. Ibid., 152.

5. Barrow and Dalton 1997:8. For additional information on mento, consult Neely (forthcoming). Also see Neely 2001.

6. Bilby in Manuel 1995:153.

7. Barrow and Dalton 1997:7. See also Neely (forthcoming).

8. See Bilby in Manuel 1995:156.

9. Barrow and Dalton 1997:11.

10. Clement "Coxsone" Dodd, as quoted in the notes to *Studio One Rockers* (Soul Jazz SJR CD48).

11. Barrow and Dalton 1997:9.

12. Bradley (2000:51) mentions Higgs and Wilson's "Manny Oh," Theophilus Beckford's "Easy Snapping," and the Fowlkes Brothers's "Oh Carolina" as typifying the shift from R&B to ska.

13. See Bradley 2000:52 for more on the mento roots of the upbeat comping style.

14. For a selection of Jamaican rhythm and blues recordings from this period, consult *Ska Boogie: Jamaican R&B, The Dawn of Ska* (Sequel NEX CD 254).

15. See the Skatalites *Foundation Ska* (Heartbeat CD HB 185/186, produced by Dodd), *The Skatalites* (Treasure Isle, produced by Reid), and/or *Ska-Boo-Da-Ba* (West Side WESM 518, produced by Yap).

16. See Bradley 2000:163.

17. Both tracks can be found on the collection *Tougher Than Tough: The Story of Jamaican Music* (Mango 162–539–935–2 518 399–2). See Bradley 2000:51 for more on ska as a reflection of Jamaica's independence.

18. There were also vocal songs with clear pro-African content, such as Lord Lebby's "Ethiopia" (see Katz 2003:34 for a discussion of this).

19. See Bradley 2000:157–58 for more on this role of the bass, and the overall significance of the introduction of the electric bass to Jamaican music.

20. See Katz 2003:67, 78, and Bradley 2000:165–66 for more on the introduction of the one drop pattern.

21. See Davis and Simon 1982:16; Bradley 2000:163.

22. Clive Chin interviewed March 1999. Pianist Gladstone Anderson makes a similar observation about the less strenuous physical demands that rock steady placed on musicians who had previously played ska (Katz 2003:69–70).

23. See Davis and Simon 1977:16–18, Katz 2003:80, and Bradley 2000:163–64.

24. Katz 2003:65.

25. See Katz 2003:76 and Bradley 2000:195. An excellent introduction to the work of Lyn Taitt is Lyn Taitt & the Jets (2005). *Hold Me Tight: Anthology 65–73* (Trojan 06076–80543–2).

26. These were the words with which Bunny Wailer opened his 1986 concert at Madison Square Garden in New York City. Brodber and Greene similarly cite a popular definition of "reggae" to be "fit for a king" (Brodber and Greene 1988:15).

27. "Toots" Hibbert in Davis and Simon 1992:17.

28. Lee Perry in *Grand Royal* #2 (1995), p. 69.

29. Drummer Leroy "Horsemouth" Wallace as quoted in Van Pelt 2005.

30. See Davis and Simon 1992:14.

31. See Bradley 2000:157 for information on Byron Lee. For an excellent profile of Jackie Jackson, see Gorney 2006.

32. For representative (and readily available) examples of the "one drop" rhythm, see Bob Marley's "One Drop" (from *Survival*, 1979), or his "One Love/People Get Ready" (from *Exodus*, 1977). The title track of *Exodus* is also a good example of the "steppers" rhythm, as is the slower "Jamming," from the same album. Several excellent examples of the "flying cymbal" pattern can be found on Johnny Clarke's CD *A Ruffer Version*, particularly on "None Shall Escape the Judgement," "Enter Into His Gates With Praise," and "Move Out of Babylon Rastaman."

33. "Do the Reggae" can be found on the Toots and the Maytals CD *The Very Best of Toots & the Maytals* (Island, 2000). "People Funny Boy" can be found on

the Lee Perry and the Upsetters CD *Some of the Best* (Heartbeat, 1990). "Nanny Goat" can be found on the Larry Marshall LP *Presenting Larry Marshall* (Heartbeat, 1990).

34. Brodber 1985:54.

35. See Katz 2003:95.

36. Philip Smart, interviewed June 2003.

37. Bradley 2000:194.

38. Jackie Jackson and Byron Lee tend to be associated with the rock steady era, but were important players in the reggae era as well.

39. Sherwood, interviewed November 2001.

40. Computer Paul Henton interviewed March 2002. Also see Bradley 2000:171, 197, for an idea of the rock steady period as a high-water mark for Jamaican music, and rock steady songs as Jamaica's "universally acceptable pop package."

41. This photo of Perry can be found in the photo section of Katz 2000, in the notes to *The Complete Upsetters Singles Collection, Volume One* (Trojan, 1998) or the notes to *The Complete Bob Marley & the Wailers, 1967–1972, Part II* (JAD, 1997).

42. This photo can be found on the back of the Lee Perry LP/CD *Megaton Dub, Volume Two* (Seven Leaves, 1992).

43. Bilby in Manuel 1995:147.

44. Bradley 2000:199.

45. See Lastra 2000:84–91.

46. Chanan 1995:59.

47. Ibid., 77.

48. Ibid., 144–45.

49. Ibid., 118. Daniel's "tapesichordist" term is cited by Matthew Malsky in his essay in Lysloff and Gay 2003. Daniel actually coined the term in relation to musique concrète, but I felt it was also useful in the context of my own discussion.

50. For background on Les Paul and the foundations of overdubbing, see the chapter "Let There Be Sound on Sound" in Cunningham 1998.

51. Chanan 1995:104.

52. For sources on these producers, consult Williams 1972; White 1994; McDermott 1992; and Martin 1979. The best source on Macero's work with Miles Davis is Tingen 2001. A good (although somewhat flawed and incomplete) general introduction to the work of these producers is Cunningham 1998.

53. See Harding 1933, esp. chap. VIII "The Musical Significance of the New Instrument."

54. See Schwartz 1973:4–5, 70.

55. Ibid., 9.

56. See Doyle 2004:32.

57. Bradley 2000:22.

58. See Malm and Wallis 1992:47.

59. These two definitions of "electronic music" are offered in Schwartz 1973:4–6. See also Chanan 1995:146.

60. For example, see Stockhausen's *Hymnen* and *Kurzwellen*, Cage's *Williams Mix*, or Ussachevsky's *Wireless Fantasy*.

61. See Schwartz 1973:253.

62. Smithies 2001.

63. See for example Lewis's essay "Improvised Music After 1950: Afrological and Eurological Perspectives," in Fischlin and Heble 2004.

64. See Witmer 1989 for a survey of the colonial-era traditions of live musical performance in Jamaica, which included jazz and blues.

65. For a discussion of the social overtones of fidelity in popular music, see Tony Grajeda's essay "The Feminization of Rock" in Beebe 2002.

66. See Kobena Mercer's essay "Romare Bearden, 1964: Collage as Kunstwollen" and Lowery Sims's essay "The Post-Modern Modernism of Wifredo Lam"; both in Mercer 2005. Another relevant source is Rubin 1984.

67. See Gilroy's essay "The Black Atlantic as a Counterculture of Modernity" in Gilroy 1993a.

68. For example, see producer Prince Buster's comments in Bradley 2000:11.

69. See Brodber and Greene 1988:15.

70. See Davis and Simon 1997:14, Manuel and Bilby 1995:156, Barrow and Dalton 1997:14–17, or Stolzoff 2000:47–48.

71. Dodd quoted in the notes to *Studio One Rockers* (Soul Jazz SJR CD 48). The information about his early equipment is taken from Barrow and Dalton 1997:15.

72. In Norman Stolzoff's account, Hedley Jones, who had learned his trade while a member of the Royal Air Force in England, is probably Jamaica's most important pioneer of sound system electronics. Jones's assistants Fred Stanford and Jacky Eastwood went on to become the main electronic technicians for the sound systems of Duke Reid and Coxsone Dodd, respectively (see Stolzoff 2000:45). See also Katz 2003:5, 47, for more information on Jones, and pp. 49–50 for more information on Lloyd Daley.

73. Bradley 2000:4.

74. Chude-Sokei 1997b:188.

75. Clarke 1980:131–32.

76. See Corbett's essay "Experimental Oriental: New Music and Other Others" in Born and Hesmondhalgh 2000.

77. Malm and Wallis 1992:39.

78. Bilby in Manuel 1995:151–59. Witmer (1989:17) also refers to "a rich and vibrant—but almost entirely undocumented—Afro-Jamaican folk or traditional music culture."

2. *"Every Spoil Is a Style"* (pp. 45–94)

1. Michael "Mikey Dread" Campbell, interviewed August 2001.

2. The correct rendering of this in Jamaican *patwa* would actually be written "every 'pwail is a style." See Cassidy and LePage 1980. Special thanks to Dr. Cecil Gutzmore for this reference.

3. Barrow and Dalton 1997:3.

4. Clive Chin, interviewed May 1998.

5. George "Fully" Fullwood, interviewed November 2001.

6. Overton H. "Scientist" Brown, interviewed September 2001.

7. Dave Hendley, interviewed June 2002.

8. Actually, the term *riddim* tends to be used in two ways that will become clear throughout this text. In terms of musical composition, it is used to refer to the aforementioned generic patterns (bass lines and/or chord progressions). In terms of recording practice, it is used to refer to the chordal instruments (guitar and keyboard instruments). When an engineer says, "We put the drum and bass on one track and the riddim on another track," he is using this second definition of the term.

9. From the Jackie Mittoo CD *The Keyboard King at Studio One* (Universal Sound USCD 8).

10. Clive Chin, interviewed March 1999.

11. Chang and Chen 1998:84. The brief studio history in the next two paragraphs is largely taken from Chang and Chen's "From Zinc Shack to 16-Track: Early Jamaican Recording Studios" (in Chang and Chen 1998), and Barrow and Dalton, chap. 1.

12. See Steve Milne's two-part interview with Goodall in *Full Watts* 3 (2 and 3).

13. Katz 2003:127.

14. See Barrow and Dalton 1997:38, and Katz 2003:47.

15. See Goodall's comments in *Full Watts* 3 (2):46.

16. Clive Chin, interviewed July 2000.

17. Bunny Lee, interviewed March 2002, Kingston, Jamaica.

18. Lowell "Sly" Dunbar, interviewed March 2002.

19. Michael "Mikey Dread" Campbell, interviewed August 2001.

20. Dudley Sibley, interviewed May 2000.

21. Barrow and Dalton 1997:200.

22. Bunny Lee, interviewed March 2002. Lee gives a slightly altered recounting of this incident in the notes to Lee Perry and the Upsetters's *Blackboard Jungle Dub* (Auralux LUXX CD 004).

23. Dudley Sibley, interviewed May 2000.

24. Sylvan Morris, interviewed May 2000.

25. Clive Chin, interviewed July 2000.

26. Ibid.

27. Ibid., both quotes.

28. Goodall as quoted in *Full Watts* 3 (2):47.

29. Michael "Mikey Dread" Campbell, interviewed August 2001. See also Stolzoff 2000:129–30 for a discussion of dub plates.

30. Barrow and Dalton 1997:205.

31. Goodall, as quoted in *Full Watts* 3 (2):46.

32. Sylvan Morris, interviewed May 2000.

33. The compilation CD *Version Like Rain* (Trojan CDTRL 278) traces Lee Perry's recycling of three of his most popular backing tracks.

34. Clive Chin, interviewed March 1999.

35. Edward "Bunny" Lee, interviewed March 2002.

36. "Java" can be found on the CD *This is Augustus Pablo* (Above Rock ARM 2001).

37. Clive Chin, interviewed March 1999.

38. Clive Chin, interviewed March 1999. For additional versions of the "Java" riddim, see "Jaro" and "Maro" from the Clive Chin–produced CD *Forward the Bass* (Blood & Fire BAFCD 022).

39. Sly Dunbar, in Stern 1998:74.

40. Bunny Lee, interviewed March 2002.

41. George "Fully" Fulwood, interviewed November 2001.

42. Adrian Sherwood, interviewed November 2001.

43. See Colin A. Palmer's "Identity, Race, and Black Power in Independent Jamaica," in Knight and Palmer 1989.

44. Errol Brown, interviewed February 2006.

45. Overton "Scientist" Brown, interviewed September 2001, Los Angeles, California.

46. Sylvan Morris, interviewed May 2000.

47. Lowell "Sly" Dunbar, interviewed March 2002. Dunbar is referring to "Watergate Rock." Larry Marshall's "I Admire You" vocal can be found on Marshall's *I Admire You* (Heartbeat CD HB 57), while the dub can be found on King Tubby and Larry Marshall's *I Admire You in Dub* (Motion FAST CD 004).

48. Max Romeo, interviewed June 2000.

49. The Silvertones's "Dub Your Pum Pum" and Big Joe and Fay's "Dub A Dawta" can be found on Trojan's 3-disc *X-Rated Box Set* (Trojan TJEDT 048), and I-Roy's "Sister Maggie Breast" can be found on the Niney the Observer compilation *Observer Station* (Heartbeat CD HB 68).

50. Bob Marley as cited in Davis and Simon 1992:44.

51. Lowell "Sly" Dunbar, interviewed March 2002.

52. Clinton Fearon, interviewed November 2001.

53. Clive Chin, interviewed July 2000.

54. Winston Riley, interviewed June 2000.

55. Michael "Mikey Dread" Campbell, interviewed August 2001.

56. Robbie Shakespeare, interviewed March 2002.

57. Michael "Mikey Dread" Campbell, interviewed August 2001.

58. Paul "Computer Paul" Henton, interviewed March 2002.

59. Bunny Wailer, in discussion with Roger Steffens, in the notes to *Dubd'sco, Volumes 1 & 2* (Ras/Solomonic RAS 3239).

60. Blackman's original vocal take can be found on the Augustus Pablo compilation CD *Classic Rockers, Volume 2* (Rockers International CD RP 012).

61. Both the vocal and dub versions can be found on the Augustus Pablo compilation CD *Classic Rockers* (Island Jamaica 162–539–953–2).

62. See Sachs 1962: chap. 2, sec. VI.

63. Jah Grant, interviewed May 1999.

64. The vocal take can be found on the Earl Zero LP *Only Jah Can Ease the Pressure* (Freedom Sounds, no label number), while the dub version can be found on the King Tubby CD *Freedom Sounds in Dub* (Blood & Fire BAFCD 011).

65. Michael "Mikey Dread" Campbell, interviewed August 2001.

66. From the Tappa Zukie CD *From the Archives* (Ras RAS CD3135).

67. From the I-Roy CD *Don't Check Me With No Lightweight Stuff* (Blood & Fire BAFCD 016).

68. From the Bob Marley and the Wailers CD *Natty Dread* (Tuff Gong CD 422–846–204–2).

69. From the compilation CD *Tribute to Bob Marley* (Trojan CDTRL 332).

70. See Barthes's essay "Death of the Author" (in Barthes 1977).

71. Max Romeo, interviewed June 2000.

72. Susan Cadogan, interviewed March 2002.

73. See a discussion of this tendency in Apter 1991.

74. Cooper 1995:68.

75. Marley, for example, seems to voice his feelings about Jamaica's profuse version culture in his song "Too Much Mix Up" (issued in 1983 on *Confrontation*, Tuff Gong 422–846–207–2).

76. Errol Brown, interviewed February 2006.

77. Lowell "Sly" Dunbar, interviewed March 2002.

78. This approach can be heard on Johnson's 1998 anthology *Independent Intavenshun: The Island Anthology* (Island 314–524–575–2).

79. See Goodall's comments in *Full Watts* 3 (2):46 (Gorney 1999).

80. This idea of a spatial experience of the dub mix has also been discussed in Ingham 1999:122–26.

81. See Erlich in Davis and Simon 1982:106.

82. I have no information on the vocal release of this song. The dub mix can be found on the King Tubby CD *Freedom Sounds in Dub* (Blood & Fire BAFCD 011).

83. From the King Tubby LP *Harry Mudie Meets King Tubby in Dub Conference, Volume One* (Moodisc HM 108).

84. From the Impact All-Stars's CD *Forward the Bass* (Blood & Fire BAFCD 022).

85. From the compilation CD *30 Years of Dub Music on the Go* (Rhino RNCD 2046).

86. From the Yabby U CD *Beware Dub* (ROIR RE 188 CD)

87. Bunny Lee, interviewed March 2002.

88. "Operation" from *The Upsetter Box Set* (Trojan PRY 1). "Big Youth" from *The Message Dubwise* (Melodisc MS 7).

89. The original version of "Mr. Bassie" can be found on Horace Andy's CD *Mr. Bassie* (Heartbeat CD HB 88). The later version can be found on Andy's CD *Good Vibes* (Blood & Fire BAFCD 019).

90. See Andy's comments in the notes to his 1997 CD *Good Vibes* (Blood & Fire BAFCD 019).

91. Sylvan Morris, interviewed May 2000.

92. Lloyd "King Jammy" James, interviewed May 2000.

93. Edward "Bunny" Lee, interviewed March 2002.

94. Sylvan Morris, interviewed May 2000.

95. Adrian Sherwood, interviewed November 2001.

96. Overton H. "Scientist" Brown, interviewed September 2001.

97. Adrian Sherwood, interviewed November 2001.

98. I would like to thank Junko Oba of Sewanee University for bringing this very useful idea to my attention.

99. Juniper 2003:2–3.

100. See Tony Grajeda's "The Feminization of Rock," in Beebe 2002. Other examples of this sort of gender-based interpretation associated with "new musicology" would include essays in McClary 1991. Also, see Sandstrom (2000) for a more specific discussion in the context of studio mixing techniques.

101. For further discussion, see Frances Aparicio, "Ethnifying Rhythms, Feminizing Cultures," in Radano and Bohlman (2000):106–10.

102. Eno 1996:293.

103. "African People" can be found on the Skin Flesh & Bones / Revolutionaries CD *Fighting Dub 1975–1979* (Hot Pot CKV-CD-1005).

104. Cronin, Russell (2005).

105. Goode in Smith 1970:174.

106. For an interesting discussion of this relationship between psychoactive experience and sound, see Whiteley 1992. Whitely uses the term *psychedelic coding*.

107. See "Cannabinoid Pharmacology" in Gold 1989.

108. Michael "Mikey Dread" Campbell, interviewed August 2001.

109. Robbie Shakespeare, interviewed March 2002.

110. Lowell "Sly" Dunbar, interviewed March 2002.

111. Michael "Mikey Dread" Campbell, interviewed August 2001.

112. Winston Riley, interviewed June 2000.

113. Paul "Computer Paul" Henton, interviewed March 2002.

114. Max Romeo, interviewed June 2000, Kingston, Jamaica.

115. Bobby Vicious, interviewed February 2000.

116. Philip Smart, interviewed June 2003, Freeport, New York.

117. Overton H. "Scientist" Brown, interviewed September 2001.

118. Hicks 1999:66.

119. Cannabis has been most often classified as a "mild hallucinogen" that exhibits both stimulant and depressant characteristics depending on a variety of chemical and environmental factors. See http://www.emedicine.com/med/topic 3407.htm.

120. The origins of psychedelic rock are generally dated to the summer of 1965, in the San Francisco music scene (associated with bands such as the Charlatans, and venues such as the Longshoreman's Hall, the Avalon Ballroom and the Fillmore Theater). It was the combination of this improvisational, long-form music with

projected light shows and the ingestion of hallucinogens that typified the style (see Whiteley 1992:119).

121. Dave Hendley, interviewed June 2002.

122. See Steffens 2006. The article features excerpts from an interview with the Wailers's lead guitarist, Junior Marvin.

123. Iron Butterfly's "In-A-Gadda-Da-Vida" can be found on the album of the same title (Elektra, 1968), and the Grateful Dead's "Dark Star" can be found on *Live Dead* (Warner Brothers, 1969)

124. Kantner quoted in Hicks 1999:69.

125. The Beatles "Blue Jay Way" can be found on *Magical Mystery Tour* (Capitol, 1967), and the Jimi Hendrix Experience's "Are You Experienced" can be found on the album of the same name (Reprise, 1967).

126. See Whiteley 1992:5.

127. In these comments, Hicks is actually paraphrasing Timothy Leary's idea of "hallucinatory art." See Leary 1966.

128. Lowell "Sly" Dunbar, interviewed March 2002.

129. Schaefer 1994:115.

130. See Reynolds 1998:41.

131. Michael "Mikey Dread" Campbell, interviewed August 2001.

132. See Stolzoff 2000:54.

133. From interview with Bobby Vicious, February 2002.

134. See Stolzoff 2000:54. Also, see pp. 126–27 for a discussion of "juggling."

135. A concise definition of the "beat mixing" concept is offered in Reynolds 1998:271–72.

136. From the Lee Perry CD *Shocks of Mighty* (Attack CDAT 104).

137. From the Max Romeo CD *Open the Iron Gate 1973–1977* (Blood & Fire BAFCD 027).

138. Robert "Robbie" Shakespeare, interviewed March 2002, Kingston, Jamaica.

139. Max Romeo, interviewed June 2000.

140. See Gilroy's essay "Diaspora, Utopia and the Critique of Capitalism," in Gilroy 1987:209.

141. Jameson in Foster 1983:125.

142. The idea of virtual technologies and the creation of "hyperreality" is obviously drawn from the ideas of Jean Baudrillard. See Baudrillard 1995.

143. Chanan 1995:47. Anthony Seeger (in Frith and Marshall 2004) has also noted that this process is currently repeating itself in the sampling of ethnographic recordings of indigenous musics.

144. See Anthony Seeger's "Traditional Music Ownership in a Commodified World," and also Martin Kretschmer and Friedemann Kawohl's "The History and Philosophy of Copyright," in Frith and Marshall 2004.

145. For an interesting precursor to this discussion in the sphere of electronic and experimental music, see Renauld 1958.

146. See Hebdige 1987:86–87.

147. See Dave Laing's essay "Copyright, Politics and the International Music Industry," in Frith and Marshall 2004.

148. Taylor 1997:67.

149. Ellison 1964:234.

150. Achebe as quoted in Clifford 1988:207.

151. Computer Paul, interviewed March 2002.

152. This idea of the fluidity of technology is a dominant theme of the fourth chapter of Sterne 2003.

153. See Sterne 2003:197.

154. Barrow and Dalton 1997:199.

3. The "Backbone" of Studio One (pp. 95–107)

1. Sylvan Morris, interviewed May 2000.
2. Ibid.
3. Ibid.
4. Ibid.
5. Katz 2003:121.
6. Sylvan Morris, interviewed May 2000. See also Bradley 2000:217–18.
7. Dudley Sibley, interviewed May 2000.
8. See Brian Keyo's comments in the notes to *Tribute to Jackie Mittoo* (Heartbeat 189/190).
9. Sylvan Morris, interviewed May 2000.
10. Ibid. Many people refer to Studio One as "Downbeat," as this was the name of Dodd's sound system.
11. "Throw Me Corn" can be found on the compilation *The Best of Studio One* (Heartbeat HB 07). "Things A Come Up To Bump" is available as a Studio One single.
12. Sylvan Morris, interviewed June 2000.
13. From a Sound City accessories advertisement, reprinted in A. Thompson 1997:45.
14. The Sound Dimension included Phil Callender and Joe Isaacs (drums), Leroy Sibbles and Boris Gardiner (bass), Eric Frater (guitar), Richard Ace (organ), Robbie Lyn (piano), and Denzel Laing (percussion).
15. Sylvan Morris, interviewed May 2000.
16. Ibid.
17. Paul "Computer Paul" Henton, interviewed March 2002.
18. Sylvan Morris, interviewed May 2000.
19. See Bradley 2000:346.
20. From the compilation *Full Up: Best of Studio One, Volume Two* (Heartbeat CD HB-14).
21. Although many Studio One recordings from the late 1960 and early 1970s contain tambourine, vocalist Freddie McGregor overdubbed additional tambourine tracks on many of these original recordings from the 1960s to the late 1970s. My analysis here is based on the assumption that the tambourine heard on "Love Me Forever" was part of the original recording.
22. From the compilation *Best of Studio One* (Heartbeat CD HB-07).
23. See Bradley 2000:28.
24. See Horace Andy's comments in Bradley 2000:222–24.
25. "Musical Science" can be found on the Studio One LP *Dub Store Special* (Studio One, no matrix number).
26. Edward "Bunny" Lee, interviewed March 2002.
27. See Katz 2003:172.
28. See Stephen Davis's comments in Davis and Simon 1982:126.
29. Sylvan Morris, interviewed May 2000.
30. Marley's "Crazy Baldhead" can be found on *Rastaman Vibration* (Island, 1976). Clarke's cover version can be found on *Tribute to Bob Marley, Vol. 1* (Crocodisc CC2–709).
31. Sadkin as quoted in Buskin 1999:214–15.
32. The various albums on the market with titles such as *Bob Marley in Dub* are typically compilations of rhythm versions the Wailers recorded with Lee Perry.
33. Aston Barrett, interviewed November 2003.
34. Errol Brown, interviewed February 2006.
35. Aston Barrett, interviewed November 2003.

36. Errol Brown, interviewed February 2006. In addition to the two Burning Spear LPs mentioned, Brown cites Marley's *Survival, Uprising,* and *Confrontation* LPs, as well as Rita Marley's *Who Feels It Knows It* and Culture's *Cumbolo* as representative examples of his roots-era work.

37. Michael "Mikey Dread" Campbell, interviewed August 2001

38. Robbie Shakespeare, interviewed March 2002.

39. "Natural Way" and "Nature Dub" can be found on the Augustus Pablo CD *East of the River Nile* (Shanachie CD 45051). Bunny Wailer's "Armagideon" can be found on *Blackheart Man* (Island 314–586–884–2) and "Armageddon Dub" can be found on the Bunny Wailer CD *Dubd'sco, Volumes 1 and 2* (Solomonic/Ras 3239).

4. *"Jus' Like a Volcano in Yuh Head!"*
(pp. 108–139)

1. Producer Roy Cousins, as quoted in the notes to *Dubbing With the Royals* (Pressure Sounds PSCD 44).

2. In Jamaica, King Tubby is often referred to (in speech and print) as "King Tubbys." This probably developed from a spoken conflation of the singular spelling of his name with the possessive spellings of his studio and sound system enterprises: *Tubby's* Home Town Hi-Fi and King *Tubby's* Studio. The name of Lloyd "King Jammy" James, Tubby's best-known protégé, is generally rendered in a similar way, as "Jammys."

3. The quote of King Tubby is from White 1983:230.

4. Tubby quoted in Davis and Simon 1982:114.

5. See Bradley 2000:6, 10, and Katz 2003:165.

6. Bobby Vicious, interviewed February 2002. For more background on the evolution of "garrison politics" in Jamaica, see Kaufman 1985.

7. Later in the decade, U-Roy and U-Brown alternated roles as selector and DJ for Tubby's system.

8. Many of U-Roy's best-known DJ versions of Treasure Isle tracks are collected on the CD compilation *Version Galore* (Trojan 06076 80383–2).

9. Bobby Vicious, interviewed February 2002, Hartford, Connecticut.

10. See Bradley 2000:295.

11. Ibid., 314.

12. See Barrow and Dalton 1997:204.

13. Philip Smart, interviewed June 2003. See also Bradley 2000:296 for an alternate account.

14. Bobby Vicious, interviewed February 2002, Hartford, Connecticut. A photo of this amplifier can be seen in the photo section of Bradley 2000.

15. Philip Smart, interviewed June 2003.

16. Edward "Bunny" Lee, interviewed March 2002, Kingston, Jamaica.

17. I-Roy, as quoted in the notes to *Don't Check Me With No Lightweight Stuff* (Blood & Fire BAFCD 016).

18. Bobby Vicious, interviewed February 2002, Hartford, Connecticut. For an account of a similar incident that took place in St. Thomas outside of Kingston, see I-Roy's recollections in the notes to his *Don't Check Me With No Lightweight Stuff* (Blood & Fire BAFCD 016).

19. Philip Smart, interviewed June 2003.

20. Edward "Bunny" Lee, interviewed March 2002.

21. Philip Smart, interviewed June 2003.

22. Dave Hendley, interviewed June 2002.

23. See Barrow and Dalton 1997:203–4, and Bradley 2000:315.

24. Lloyd "Jammy" James, as quoted in the notes to *The Crowning of King Jammy* (Pressure Sounds PSCD 25).

25. Philip Smart, interviewed June 2003.

26. For a brief biography of Jeep Harned, see "Florida Chapter to Honor Local Heroes" (http://www.grammy.org/news.academy/0410florida.html) and "'Jeep' Harned Dies at 72" (http:///www.prosoundnews.com/stories/2003/march/0327.1.shtml). For information on Mack Emerman and Criteria, see "Biograph: Mack Emerman" (http://mixonline.com/ar/audio_biograph_mack_emerman/) and "Criteria Recording Studios" (http://criteriastudios.com/html/hist.html).

27. Scientist to Steve Barrow, in the notes of *Dub in the Roots Tradition* (Blood & Fire BAFCD 012).

28. See Barrow in the notes to King Tubby 1995:29.

29. See Bradley 2000:317 for an alternate account of Tubby's customized fader controls.

30. Lloyd "King Jammy" James, interviewed May 2000.

31. Edward "Bunny" Lee, interviewed March 2002, Kingston, Jamaica.

32. Lloyd "King Jammy" James, interviewed May 2000.

33. The settings for the board's high pass filter were as follows: OFF, 70Hz, 100Hz, 150Hz, 250 Hz, 500Hz, 1 kHz, 2kHz, 3 kHz, 5kHz, 7.5 kHz.

34. Representative (and readily available) examples of the "flying cymbal" pattern can be found on Johnny Clarke's CD *A Ruffer Version: Johnny Clarke at King Tubby's 1974–1978* (Trojan TJACD 025), particularly on "None Shall Escape the Judgement," "Enter Into His Gates With Praise," and "Move Out of Babylon Rastaman."

35. Edward "Bunny" Lee, interviewed March 2002.

36. Philip Smart, interviewed June 2003.

37. Ibid.

38. See the two-disc collection *Roots of Dub and Dub From the Roots* (reissued together as Moll-Selekta 8).

39. For example, see the first disc of *King Tubby's Special* (Trojan CDTRD 409), which features his dub mixes of Holness's productions.

40. Lloyd "King Jammy" James, interviewed June 2000.

41. Overton "Scientist" Brown, interviewed September 2001, Los Angeles, California.

42. Philip Smart, interviewed June 2003.

< comp: Msp. 308 says "thin space" on either side of slash between "Tubby" and "Prince," in endnote 43.>

43. "A Heavy Dub" can be found on the King Tubby/Prince Jammy CD *Dub Gone 2 Crazy* (Blood 7 Fire BAFCD 013), while "Marcus Dub" can be found on the compilation CD *30 Years of Dub Music on the Go* (Rhino RNCD 2046).

44. Campbell, in Bradley and Maycock 1999:68–69.

45. "Computer Paul" Henton, interviewed March 2002, Kingston, Jamaica.

46. Lloyd "King Jammy" James, interviewed May 2000.

47. Dave Hendley, interviewed June 2002.

48. "Silver Words" can be found on the Niney the Observer compilation *Observer Station* (Heartbeat CD HB 68), while "Silver Bullet" can be found on the King Tubby collection *King Tubby's Special* (Trojan CDTRD 409).

49. Lloyd "King Jammy" James, interviewed May 2000.

50. Johnny Clarke's "Enter Into His Gates With Praise" and King Tubby's "This is the Hardest Version" can both be found on the CD *A Ruffer Version: Johnny Clarke at King Tubby's 1974–1978* (Trojan TJACD 025).

51. Dennis Brown's "Live After You" can be found on the compilation CD *Rock On: Greatest Hits from the Observer Label* (Heartbeat 11661-7678-2), while King

Tubby's "Dubbing With the Observer" can be found on the CD *King Tubby's Special* (Trojan CD TRD 409).

52. Tommy McCook's "Death Trap" can be found on the Yabby You CD *Jesus Dread* (Blood & Fire BAFCD 021), and King Tubby's "Living Style" can be found on the Yabby U CD *King Tubby's Prophecy of Dub* (Blood & Fire BAFCD 005).

53. "Sniper" can be found on the Jackie Mittoo CD *The Keyboard Legend* (Sonic Sounds SON CD 0073), while "Dub Fi Gwan" can be found on the compilation CD *Dub Gone Crazy* (Blood & Fire BAFCD 002).

54. "Totally Together" is available on the Jackie Mittoo recording *Now* (Studio One CD 9016).

55. Edward "Bunny" Lee, interviewed by the author, March 2002, Kingston Jamaica.

56. Lowell "Sly" Dunbar, interviewed March 2002, Kingston, Jamaica.

57. "Fire Fire" and "Fire Fire Dub" can be found on Yabby You CD *King Tubby Meets Vivian Jackson* (Yabby You) (Prophet Records (YVJ 002). This recording is also known by the title *Yabby You & King Tubby Meet: Chant Down Babylon*. Trinity's "Promise Is A Comfort to a Fool" can be found on his *Shanty Town Determination* (Blood & Fire BAFCD 031).

58. Jacob Miller's "Baby I Love You So" and King Tubby's "King Tubby's Meets the Rockers Uptown" can both be found on the Augustus Pablo CD *Classic Rockers* (Island 162–539–953–2).

59. See Ranglin's 1996 recording *Below the Bassline* (Island Jamaica Jazz 314–524–299–2) and Alexander's 2001 recording *Goin' Yard* (Telarc CD 83527).

60. Philip Smart, interviewed June 2003. Smart also remembered an early DJ version of this rhythm, featuring Big Youth.

61. "Black Force" and "Cassava Piece" are both available on the Augustus Pablo compilation *Rockers International* 2 (Greensleeves GRELCD 168). Pablo apparently sold a cut of this riddim to Linval Thompson, who would use it for a dub plate titled "Whip Them King Tubby" (accompanied by another dub version mixed by Tubby). See *Whip Them King Tubby* (Auralux LUXXCD001).

62. Other engineers at the studio included Winston "Professor" Brown and Pat Kelly.

63. Philip Smart, interviewed June 2003.

64. Ibid.

65. Ibid.

66. Ibid.

67. Ibid.

68. See also Katz 2000:216.

69. Philip Smart, interviewed June 2003.

70. Johnny Clarke's "Enter Into His Gates With Praise" is available on *A Ruffer Version* (see note 49)."Ja Ja in De Dub" is available on *Rasta Dub '76* (Attack BSMT 007).

71. Note that the DJ's name is spelled differently in the album's title, and on the title song. The vocal track can be found on the Prince Alla CD *I Can Hear the Children Singing* (Blood & Fire BAFCD 040). The dub mix can be found on the Tappa Zukie CD *Tappa Zukie in Dub* (Blood & Fire BAFCD 008).

72. Philip Smart, interviewed June 2003.

73. Lloyd "King Jammy" James, interviewed June 2000.

74. See Lesser's *King Jammy's* (Toronto: ECW, 2002).

75. See Dave Hendley's notes to *The Crowning of Prince Jammy* (Pressure Sounds PSCD 25).

76. Lloyd "King Jammy" James, interviewed May 2000.

77. These biographical details are taken from Dave Hendley's notes to *The Crowning of Prince Jammy* (Pressure Sounds PSCD 25). See also Lesser 2002.

78. Lloyd "King Jammy" James, interviewed May 2000.

79. Ibid.

80. Ibid.

81. See *Jammy's In Lion Dub Style* (Jammys, no matrix no.); *Kamikaze Dub* (Trojan TRLS 174); *Uhuru in Dub* (CSA CSLP 2); Gregory Isaacs: *Slum in Dub* (CSA BS 1051).

82. See Lesser 2002:19.

83. Lloyd "King Jammy" James, interviewed May 2000.

84. "Jammy's A Shine" can be found on the CD *Fatman Presents Prince Jammy vs. Crucial Bunny: Dub Contest* (Auralux LUXX CD 016).

85. Ibid.

86. This mix is considered the definitive dub version of this tune. An alternate mix, also by Jammy, is "Dub to the Rescue," available on the compilation *Dub Gone Crazy* (Blood & Fire BAFCD 002).

87. Both the vocal and dub versions can be found on Horace Andy's *In the Light + In the Light Dub* (Blood & Fire BAFCD 006).

88. From the Scientist/Prince Jammy CD *Scientist & Prince Jammy Strike Back* (Trojan CDTRL 210).

89. Lloyd "King Jammy" James, interviewed May 2000.

90. Overton "Scientist" Brown, interviewed September 2001.

91. Ibid.

92. Ibid.

93. Ibid.

94. See Scientist's comments in Katz 2003:310–11.

95. Overton "Scientist" Brown, interviewed September 2001.

96. Ibid.

97. Linval Thompson, as quoted in the notes to *Phoenix Dub* (Motion Records FASTCD011).

98. Paul "Computer Paul" Henton, interviewed March 2002.

99. Horace Andy's version of this song can be found on the compilation *Mr. Bassie* (Heartbeat CD HB 88), while Peter Ranking's version can be found on the compilation *Roots Tradition From the Vineyard* (Munich MRCD 1004).

100. See Katz 2003:198, and Harry Hawkes's notes to the CD compilation *Maxfield Avenue Breakdown* (Pressure Sounds PSCD031).

101. See Katz 2003:217.

102. Paul "Computer Paul" Henton, interviewed March 2002.

103. Overton "Scientist" Brown, interviewed September 2001.

104. Paul "Computer Paul" Henton, interviewed March 2002.

105. Clive Chin, interviewed March 1999.

106. Lowell "Sly" Dunbar, interviewed March 2002.

107. Ibid.

108. Paul "Computer Paul" Henton, interviewed March 2002.

109. Also see *The Dub Factor,* a collection of Black Uhuru tracks remixed into dub versions by Sly and Robbie along with engineer Paul "Groucho" Smykle (Island, 1983).

110. Thompson, as quoted in *Full Watts* 1(3):16.

111. McGregor's "Jah Help the People" from the Linval Thompson compilation *Linval Thompson Sounds: Jah Jah Dreader Than Dread* (Majestic Reggae MRCD 1005). The Heptones' "Sufferer's Time" from the Heptones 1976 album *Party Time* (Mango CCD 9456).

112. From the Scientist LP *Scientist Meets the Space Invaders* (Greensleeves GRELCD 019).

113. From the compilation CD *Linval Thompson Sounds: Jah Jah Dreader Than Dread* (Majestic Reggae MRCD 1005).

114. From the Scientist LP *Scientist Rids the World of the Evil Curse of the Vampires* (Greensleeves GRELCD 25).

115. From the Wailing Souls LP *Firehouse Rock* (Greensleeves GRELCD 21).

116. From the Scientist CD *Dub in the Roots Tradition* (Blood & Fire BAFCD 012).

117. Doyle 2004:33. The specific technological developments Doyle mentions include: the development of a fully electrical recording process, and condenser microphones "amplified by means of vacuum tubes and recorded using an electromagnetic head."

118. Scientist as quoted in *Full Watts* 3(3).

5. *Tracking the "Living African Heartbeat" (pp. 140–162)*

1. Lee Perry, interviewed November 2001.

2. Katz 2000.

3. Perry interviewed by Bruno Blum, cited in Katz 2000:8.

4. Sibley, interviewed May 2000.

5. Katz 1990: 7.

6. Romeo, interviewed June 2000.

7. Most of these singles can be found on the Lee Perry CD *Chicken Scratch* (Heartbeat CD HB 53).

8. According to David Katz, Perry joined Coxsone's organization as a partial replacement for Prince Buster (Katz 2003:41).

9. Perry, quoted in May 1977:13.

10. From the Lee Perry CD *Sounds From the Hot Line* (Heartbeat CD HB 76).

11. See Katz 2000:181–82.

12. See for example, the cover photograph of Perry's *Mystic Miracle Star* (Heartbeat, 1982), in which he is presented as a shaman of sorts, holding what appears to various talismans.

13. Edward "Bunny" Lee, interviewed March 2002. The song "Labrish" is an early collaboration between Perry and Lee. See *Lee Perry and the Upsetters: All the Hits* (Rohit RHCT 778).

14. These songs can be found on the Lee Perry CD *People Funny Boy* (Trojan CDTRL 399).

15. See the chapter "Give Me Power: The Upsetter Emerges" from Katz 2000 or Bradley 2000:227.

16. These songs can be found on the Lee Perry CD *All the Hits* (Rohit RHCT 778).

17. With the exception of "People Funny Boy," the cited songs in this paragraph can be found on the Lee Perry CD *People Funny Boy* (Trojan CDTRL 399). The version of "People Funny Boy" mentioned here can be found on the Lee Perry CD *Some of the Best* (Heartbeat CD HB 37).

18. Chin, interviewed June 2000.

19. Perry in 1994 interview with Bruno Blum, as quoted in Katz 2000:111.

20. See Bradley 2000:337. See also Dave Barker's comments in the same volume, p. 342. Bradley also cites Studio One singer Horace Andy and the self-contained Gladiators band as significant in this regard (see Bradley 2000:346).

21. See Bradley 2000:343. The Perry/Wailers collaborations can be found on *The Complete Bob Marley & the Wailers, 1967 to 1972 Part II* (JAD CD 1004), and *The Complete Bob Marley & the Wailers, 1967 to 1972, Part III* (JAD CD 1005).

22. The group had previously worked for several producers, including Lloyd Charmers (with Charmers in place of Adams on organ) as the Hippy Boys, and for Bunny Lee as the Bunny Lee All-Stars. David Katz notes that certain Perry productions dating from this period used the Soul Syndicate band (Katz 2000:114–19).

23. See Diana Ross and the Supremes' *Anthology* (Motown M9 794A3).

24. Perry quoted in Davis 1985:81.

25. The singers were alleged to have assaulted Perry following a payment dispute (Katz 2000:134–35). Perry also later claimed that the Wailers sent gunmen to his house by night to forcibly retrieve master tapes (see Terrell 1997:60).

26. The most stable edition of the later Upsetters was built around the nucleus of drummer Mikey "Boo" Richards, bassist Boris Gardiner, guitarists Ernest Ranglin and Robert Johnson, organist Winston Wright, and pianist Keith Sterling.

27. See Katz 2003:128.

28. "Medical Operation" can be found on the Upsetters CD *Return of Django* (Trojan CDTRL 19). "The Popcorn" and "Knock on Wood" can be found on the Upsetters CD *Eastwood Rides Again* (Trojan CDTBL 125).

29. "Connection" can be found on the Lee Perry CD *The Upsetter Box Set* (Trojan PRY 1). "Kill Them All" can be found on the Lee Perry CD *The Upsetter Collection* (Trojan CDTRL 195). I mention Frank Zappa here because Perry's treatment of collage work is somewhat similar to Zappa's work on recordings such as *We're Only In It For the Money* (1968).

30. Perry in Barrow and Dalton 1997:204.

31. Philip Smart, interviewed June, 2003.

32. Riley's "Woman's Gotta Have It" can be found on the Lee Perry compilation *Shocks of Mighty* (Attack CDAT 104). The Upsetters' "Woman's Dub" can be found on *Revolution Dub* (Esoldun CC2–702). Leo Graham's "Three Blind Mice" and King Tubby's "Three Times Three" can both be found on *Shocks of Mighty*.

33. "Black Panta" can be found on *Blackboard Jungle Dub* (the best available version is Auralux LUXX CD 004).

34. See the Auralux edition (Auralux LUXX CD 004).

35. The extended version of "Papa Was a Rolling Stone" can be found on the Temptations 1972 LP *All Directions* (Gordy G9621).

36. The productions of Glen Brown and Keith Hudson are particularly interesting in this regard. See the Brown-produced *Check the Winner* (Greensleeves 47007) and *Dubble Attack* (Shanachie 47005), the Hudson-produced *The Hudson Affair* (Trojan 06076–80507–2).

37. Chin, interviewed July 2000.

38. Lee Perry, interviewed November 2001.

39. See Katz 2000:181, and Bradley and Maycock 1999:69.

40. Katz 2000:180–81.

41. Dave Hendley, interviewed June 2002.

42. Both "Curly Locks" and "Long Way" can be found on the Junior Byles compilation *Curly Locks* (Heartbeat CD HB 208).

43. Thompson's "Kung Fu Man" can be found on the Lee Perry CD *The Quest* (Abraham CTCD 999).

44. These tracks can all be found on the Lee Perry LP *Public Jestering* (Attack LP 108).

45. In fact, Marley would continue to work intermittently with Perry through 1980, realizing songs and song sketches like "Punky Reggae Party," "Jah Live," "Rainbow Country," "Rastaman Live Up," "Blackman Redemption," "Who Colt the Game," "I Know A Place," an early version of "Natural Mystic," and "Revolution Dub." Perry would also contribute informally to the material that Marley and the

Wailers were recording for Island (especially on recordings such as *Rastaman Vibration* [1976]), although many of these contributions went uncredited.

46. See Katz 2000:208–209.

47. The Bi-Phase came with several placards that fit over its housing, each of which included markings for a specific effect settings. "Super Phasing" is one of these placards. See "MuTron BiPhase" (http://www.superpage.com/riffs/desc_mutron .html) and "Super Phasing" (http://homepage2.nifty.com/k-studio/K-STUDIO/ super%20phasing%sheet.htm).

48. The original track can be found on the Lee Perry CD *People Funny Boy* (Trojan CDTRL 399); the later mix can be found on the Lee Perry CD *Scratch & Company: Chapter One* (RAS CTCD 1415).

49. From the Junior Murvin CD *Police & Thieves* (Mango 162–539–499–2).

50. From the Lee Perry CD *Voodooism* (Pressure Sounds PSCD 009).

51. From the Lee Perry CD *Scratch & Company* (see note 48).

52. From the Lee Perry CD *Open the Gate* (Trojan CD PRY 2).

53. Ibid.

54. See the three-disc compilation *Phil Spector: Back to Mono (1958-1969)* (Phil Spector Records 7118).

55. Michael "Mikey Dread" Campbell, interviewed August 2001.

56. From the Max Romeo CD *War Inna Babylon* (Polygram B00025XL0).

57. From the Junior Murvin CD *Police & Thieves* (Mango 162–539–499–2).

58. From the Susan Cadogan CD *Hurts So Good* (Trojan CDTRL 122).

59. The songs can be found on Linda McCartney's CD *Wide Prairie* (Capitol CDP 7243 4 97910 2 2).

60. Lowell "Sly" Dunbar, interviewed March 2002.

61. Susan Cadogan, interviewed March 2002.

62. Barrow and Dalton 1997:204.

63. The Congos: *Heart of the Congos* (Blood & Fire BAFCD 009).

64. George Faith: *To Be A Lover* (Island/Hip-O-Select B0002693–02)

65. William Bell's "I Forgot to Be Your Lover" available on *The Best of William Bell* (Stax 8541).

66. From the Lee Perry CD *Build the Ark* (Trojan CD PRY 3).

67. Lee Perry, interviewed November 2001.

68. Upsetters: *Super Ape* (Island/Hip-O-Select B0002430–02).

69. The earlier version can be found on the Lee Perry LP *Chapter One* (RAS CTCD 1415).

70. Lowell "Sly" Dunbar, interviewed March 2002.

71. Michael "Mikey Dread" Campbell, interviewed August 2001.

72. Max Romeo, interviewed May 2000.

73. From the Lee Perry CD *Open the Gate* (Trojan CD PRY 2).

74. From the Lee Perry CD *Produced and Directed by the Upsetter* (Pressure Sounds PSCD 19).

75. Katz 1999:48.

76. From the Ras Michael and the Sons of Negus CD *Love Thy Neighbor* (Live & Learn CD 001). The sound of these tracks suggests that they were subsequently completed at Dynamic, with Sylvan Morris engineering.

77. See *Lee Perry Presents African Roots* (Trojan 06076–80552–2).

78. Dave Hendley, interviewed June 2002.

79. See Frere-Jones 1997. Also see Henk Targowski's recollections in Katz 2000:335.

80. See David Katz's recollections in Mack 1995, or Corbett 1994.

81. See Henderson 1996:60.

82. Dave Hendley, interviewed June 2002.

83. There are several conflicting accounts of the precise cause of the blaze. For background, see Katz 2000:363–65.

6. "Java" to Africa (pp. 163–184)

1. Edward "Bunny" Lee, interviewed March 2002.
2. Chin, interviewed July 2000.
3. Ibid. JAD was the company formed by Johnny Nash, Arthur Jenkins, and Danny Sims to represent Bob Marley as a songwriter outside of Jamaica.
4. Chin, as quoted in *Full Watts* 3 (1):33.
5. Chin, interviewed March 1999.
6. Chin, interviewed July 2000.
7. Chin, interviewed March 2000.
8. Pablo as quoted in Hurford and Kaski 1987:49.
9. See Pablo's comments in Hurford and Kaski 1987:36. For examples of the minor-key ska music that might have inspired him, see the Skatalites Ska-Boo-Da-Ba (West Side WESM 519), an excellent 1964 collection produced by Justin Yap.
10. Chin, as quoted in *Full Watts* 3 (1):33.
11. Chin, interviewed March 1999.
12. Ellis's original vocal can be found on the *17 North Parade* compilation. Pablo's version can be found on his CD *This Is Augustus Pablo* (Above Rock ARM 2001).
13. Chin, interviewed March 1999.
14. From the *17 North Parade* compilation (Pressure Sounds PSCD 17).
15. From the Augustus Pablo CD *This Is Augustus Pablo* (see note 12).
16. Both "Extraordinary Dub" and "Extraordinary Version" can be found on the CD compilation *Forward the Bass* (Blood & Fire BAFCD 022).
17. Chin, interviewed by Brian Lindt and William Taylor, WKCR.
18. This information taken from Harry Hawke's notes to the Mighty Two compilation *No Bones for the Dogs* (Pressure Sounds. PSCD 37).
19. Katz 2003:132.
20. Edward "Bunny" Lee, interviewed March 2002.
21. Ibid.
22. Lowell "Sly" Dunbar, interviewed March 2002.
23. Chin, interviewed March 1999.
24. Chin, interviewed July 2000. *Randy's Dub* is currently available as part of the *Forward the Bass* compilation (see note 16).
25. See Bradley 2000:352.
26. See Clive Chin's comments in the notes to the *Forward the Bass* compilation (see note 16).
27. "Earthquake" can be found on the Mighty Two compilation *No Bones for the Dogs* (see note 18).
28. Chin, interviewed May 1999.
29. From the Augustus Pablo CD *This Is Augustus Pablo* (see note 12).
30. See Barrow and Dalton 1997:214.
31. Ibid, 154.

7. "City Too Hot" (pp. 185–195)

1. This chapter takes its name from Lee Perry's song of the same name. See Lee Perry and Friends (1988). *Open the Gate*. Trojan CDPRY2.

2. See C. Taylor 1997.

3. Michael "Mikey Dread" Campbell, interviewed August 2001.

4. Gray 1991:216.

5. For a recounting of these events, see the introduction to Gunst 1995. For more detailed analysis and background, see Gray 1991:chap. 11.

6. See Gunst 1995 for a comprehensive discussion of this process.

7. Chude-Sokei in Potash 1997:216. See also Ross 1998.

8. On this theme of reaction against excessive foreign influence, also see Bradley 2000:502.

9. David Katz (2005) notes that Smith's song was not actually the first Jamaican pop song to be entirely built from electronic rhythm patterns, but it was the most distinctive and as such, had the most dramatic impact. Katz (2005) also offers a good profile of the significance of "Sleng Teng."

10. See Barrow and Dalton 1997:273–84.

11. Jammy refers to these as "human" riddims in Lesser 2002:38. For a discussion of the roots of Jamaican popular music in marching band–oriented schools such as Kingston's Alpha School for Boys, see Witmer 1987.

12. See Lesser 2002:42.

13. Philip Smart, interviewed June 2003.

14. See Phantom's recollections in Barrow and Dalton 1997:285.

15. Anthony Red Rose's "Tempo" can be found on the compilation CD *Tougher than Tough: The Story of Jamaican Music* (Island 162–539–935–2). Pressure Sounds' *Firehouse Revolution* (Pressure Sounds PSCD34) compilation chronicles some of the digital music from Tubby's second studio.

16. Although widely assumed to be a robbery, several people insisted during my trip to Kingston that Tubby's death had in fact been ordered by an unknown third party. His assailant was said to have been one of several prisoners who were killed by the police during my spring 2000 visit, as they tried to escape from a Kingston prison.

17. Scientist, interviewed November 2001.

18. Adrian Sherwood, interviewed November 2001.

19. Bobby Vicious, interviewed February 2002.

20. See Monty Alexander's 2004 CD (with Ernest Ranglin): *Rocksteady* (Telarc CD 83531). It's interesting to note that in addition to the cover of "East of the River Nile," the back cover photo shows Ringling holding a melodica, another probable reference to Augustus Pablo.

21. Prince Buster, as quoted in Bradley 2000:xvi.

22. Jammy, as quoted in Katz 2005.

23. Chude-Sokei, in Potash 1997:218.

24. "Ringo Rides" was recorded in 1966, and is collected on the Skatalites 1998 release *Ska-Boo-Da-Ba* (West Side WESM 518).

25. For further discussion on this topic of the lack of original music composition in the digital era of Jamaican music, see Bradley 2000:509.

26. Chude-Sokei, in Potash 1997:222.

27. See, for example, Public Enemy's landmark CD *It Takes a Nation of Millions to Hold Us Back* (Def Jam, 1988).

8. Starship Africa (196–219)

1. This chapter takes its name from *Starship Africa,* the Adrian Sherwood–produced album by Creation Rebel.

2. Erlich quote in Davis and Simon 1982:105.

3. The interpretation of West African *bocio* figurines (from Benin Republic) as "empowered cadavers" is introduced in the first chapter of Blier 1995, while the Surrealist nonsense word game of "exquisite corpses" is discussed in Lewis 1988:21). Both ideas interest me in the context of dub music through their suggestions of bringing something dead or used back to life, of reinvesting a spent object with a new power. Both ideas also resonate with specific interpretations of dub (discussed later in this chapter); some formal aspects of *bocio* figurines reflect a traumatic history of slavery and internecine warfare, while the Surrealist "exquisite corpse" wordplay was a group exercise in deconstructing the logic of language, reflecting a cynicism toward the Western heritage of logic and reason in the wake of World War I.

4. Agawu 1995.

5. I am using the term *echo* in this way here, despite my distinction between the effects produced by delay (echo) and reverb (spatial simulation) devices in chapter 2.

6. Chude-Sokei 1997b.

7. Said 1990:357.

8. Clifford 1994:306.

9. Ibid.:307.

10. Dawes 2001.

11. Said 1990:360.

12. Doyle (2004) relates that reverb in early recordings of classical music provided listeners "virtual access to the acoustic regime of the concert hall" (34).

13. Davis 1983:79.

14. For example, see the section titled "Trance or Ecstasy?" (Rouget 1985:3).

15. See the first two sections of Rouget 1985: "Trance and Possession" and "Music and Possession."

16. See Rouget 1985:80–81.

17. Robbie Shakespeare, interviewed March 2002.

18. Both this and the previous quotation taken from Apter 1991:255.

19. Chude-Sokei (1997b) has approached this from a slightly different angle, speculating that "individual subjectivity could be lost in the pounding volume of a sound system that was devoted to freeing the body from the oppressive imbalance of black labor and white capital" (196).

20. Perry interview in K. Martin 1995.

21. See Doyle 2004:31.

22. See Eargle 1995:283.

23. Neil Fraser, interviewed May 2000.

24. Clive Chin, interviewed July 18, 2000.

25. Winston Riley, interviewed June 5, 2000.

26. Frere-Jones 1997:67.

27. Montgomery 1997:56.

28. Mikics 1995:372.

29. For example, see the introduction to Manuel 1995.

30. David Mikics paraphrases Frederic Jameson to speculate that magical realist cinema relies on disjunctions among differing cultures and social formations that "coexist in the New World as they usually do not in Western Europe." See Mikics 1995:372, and Jameson's "On Magical Realism in Film," in Jameson 1988. See also the comments of Alondra Nelson in the introduction to Nelson 2002: "flux of identity has long been the experience of African diasporic people" (3).

31. Zamora and Faris 1995:6.

32. Slemon quote in Zamora and Faris 1995:408.

33. Ibid.:415.

34. Walcott cited in Mikics 1995:371.

35. D'Haen quote in Zamora and Faris 1995:372.

36. Jameson 1986:311.

37. Carrie Rickey [1979]. "Reviews: New York," *Artforum;* excerpted in Fine 2003.

38. Bloom states that "there is an intimate and interactive relationship between the individual and the group and our individual identity is closely tied to our "group self" . . . in fact, our group self may be the core component of our sense of personal identity. . . . Making these assumptions allows us to tentatively apply concepts rooted in individual dynamics to the psychology of the group" (quote in Tedeschi 1998:180).

39. See Felman and Laub 1992 for a comprehensive source.

40. Clifford 1994:317.

41. Felman 1995:27.

42. Gilroy 1993a:chap. 6.

43. Both quotations from Gilroy 1993a:105.

44. See Gilroy 1993a:chap. 6.

45. From Jafa 1994.

46. This idea of an aesthetic complex of "dissonance, destruction and decay" was inspired by Susan Blier's discussion of Beninoise *bocio* figurines (Blier 1995:28).

47. See Katz 2003:7–9, and "The Dancehall As A Site of Clashing" from Stolzoff 2000:8–12.

48. See I-Roy's comments in the notes to I-Roy CD 1997.

49. This particular characterization of the "emotional pendulum" of posttraumatic experience is taken from Erikson in Caruth 1995:184.

50. See Hoffman 1989:32.

51. See ibid.:7–13 for a discussion of collage in the context of these various artistic movements.

52. Ibid.:22.

53. Gabbard 1991:111.

54. Erlmann 1996a.

55. Here I am paraphrasing the words of Jorge Luis Borges as quoted in R. F. Thompson 2005:3.

56. See Glick and Bone 1990:sec. IV ("Aesthetic and Philosophic Inquiries on the Nature of Pleasure") for a discussion of *anhedonia,* or avoidance of pleasure as a symptom of trauma. The Borges reference is taken from R. F. Thompson's 2005.

57. Delany as quoted in Dery 1994:190–91.

58. Meintjes 2003:84.

59. The word "Afro-futurism" is generally considered to have been coined by Mark Dery in his essay "Black to the Future" (Dery 1994).

60. See the following for perspectives on Afro-futurist thought: Dery 1994; Corbett 1994; Eshun 1998; Lock 1999; Reynolds 2000; Greg Tate's "Ghetto in the Sky" and "Dread or Alive" (both in Tate 1992); and Nelson 2002.

61. See especially *Sextant* (Columbia/Legacy CK 64983) in this regard. The remaining work of Hancock's Mwandishi band can be found on *Mwandishi: The Complete Warner Brothers Recordings* (Warner Bros. 2–45732).

62. The Jimi Hendrix Experience, *Electric Ladyland* (MCA/Experience Hendrix MCAD 11600).

63. For example, see Earth, Wind and Fire's albums *Spirit* (1976) and *All & All* (1977).

64. Sun Ra, *Space Is the Place* (Impulse IMPD 249), *Astro-Black* (Saturn/Impulse AS 9255), and *Cosmic Tones for Mental Therapy* (Evidence ECD 22036–2). See also Sun Ra's video *Space Is the Place* (Rhapsody Films 9025).

65. See Parliament, *Mothership Connection* (Casablanca 824–502-2), *The Clones of Dr. Funkenstein* (Casablanca 842–620-2), *Parliament Live/P-Funk Earth Tour* (Casablanca 834–941-2), and the concert video George Clinton and Parliament-Funkadelic: *The Mothership Connection* (Pioneer Artists PA-98-599-D).

66. See Miles Davis, *Dark Magus* (CBS/Sony 50DP 719), *Get Up With It (CBS/* Sony50DP-712-3), *Agharta* (Columbia/Legacy C2K 46799), and *Pangaea* (Columbia/Legacy C2K 46115).

67. See May's *Innovator* (Transmat, 1986), or Mills's *Waveform Transmissions* (Caroline, 1992).

68. See Chanan 1995:chap. 3, "Polyhymnia Patent."

69. For example, see the cartoon cover illustrations of Scientist's *Heavy Metal Attack* (Clocktower CD 124), *Scientist Encounters Pac-Man* (Greensleeves GRELCD 46), *Scientist Rids the World of the Evil Curse of the Vampires* (Greensleeves GRELCD 25), *Scientist Meets the Space Invaders* (Greensleeves GRELCD 19), and Scientist and Prince Jammy's *Scientist and Jammy Strike Back* (Trojan CDTRL 210). Thanks to Adrian Sherwood for the clarification regarding Greensleeves's decision to package Scientist's music with Tony McDermotts's science fiction imagery (Adrian Sherwood, interviewed November 2001).

70. See Hayward's "Sci Fidelity—Music, Sound, and Genre History" and Nabeel Zuberi's "The Transmolecularization of [Black] Folk: *Space is the Place,* Sun Ra and Afrofuturism"; both in Hayward 2004.

71. Overton "Scientist" Brown, interviewed September 2001. His comments refer to an interview found in Davis and Simon 1982:110. "Flying" fader switches, which move automatically in tandem with an automated mixing system, are a distinctive feature of mixing consoles manufactured by the British company Neve.

72. Overton "Scientist" Brown, interviewed September 2001.

73. Hannah Appel, personal communication, September 2001.

74. See Gilroy 1993a:chap. 2, for a more philosophical grounding of this point, especially the section titled "Slavery and the Enlightenment Project."

75. See Stolzoff 2000:201–202 for a discussion of the symbolic violence of the sound clash.

76. Perry as quoted in Toop 1995:114–15.

77. Lee Perry, interviewed November 2001.

78. Overton "Scientist" Brown, interviewed September 2001.

79. Meintjes 2003:73.

80. This theme is prominently explored in Lastra's (2000) first chapter, esp. pp. 18–21.

81. Wendell Bell, for example, is a scholar of "future studies," and credits a 1956 trip to Jamaica with stimulating his interest in this area. In Bell's words, "I went to Jamaica in 1956 to do urban research, specifically intending to study the social areas of the city of Kingston to compare with work I had done in metropolitan areas of the United States. At the time, Jamaica was in transition from being a British Crown Colony to becoming a politically independent state . . . it was a heady time in Jamaica. Everyone was looking forward. All the talk was of coming independence, of what had to be done, and of what Jamaica would be like—and ought to be like—in the future, after independence. . . . Studying how the decisions of nationhood were being made in the new states of the Caribbean, I began to understand the general principles of futures thinking and the role they play in individual and collective decisions everywhere, in all settings and all situations, in both old and new states." See "On Becoming and Being a Futurist" 2005:113–24.

82. An insightful discussion of the "insanity" trope in black culture can be found in Corbett 1994.

83. I thank Hannah Appel for bringing this Jamaican resonance of the term *science* to my attention (September 2001). For another perspective on this resonance, see Bradley 2000:309.

84. Martin in notes to Martin 1995. Cassidy and LePage 1980 offers the following definition of *duppy:* "The spirit of the dead, believed to be capable of returning to aid or (more often) harm living beings, directly or indirectly; they are also believed subject to the power of OBEAH and its practitioners who can 'set' or 'put' a duppy upon a victim and 'take off' their influence" (164).

85. This is a consistent theme throughout Gilroy's work, but receives its most comprehensive treatment in *The Black Atlantic* (Gilroy 1993a).

86. Wilson-Tagoe quote in Makward 1998:293.

87. Bryan's "Money Generator" can be found on the compilation *Studio One Scorcher* (Soul Jazz SJR CD 67); "Musical Science" can be found on *Dub Store Special* (Studio One, no matrix no.).

88. I might add that another resonance of the phrase "science fiction" concerns the similarities between black popular musics and what Mark Dery (1994) describes as "the sublegitimate status of science fiction as a pulp genre in Western literature [that] mirrors the subaltern position to which blacks have been relegated throughout American history" (180).

89. Nelson 2002:4.

90. See Alondra Nelson's comments in Nelson 2002:7.

91. Marsh quote in Chang and Chen 1998:151.

92. See Thomas 2000 for a reference on this literature.

93. Overton "Scientist" Brown, interviewed September 2001.

94. D'Haen citation in Zamora and Faris 1995:202.

95. See the introduction to Gikandi 1992.

96. Obviously, I am drawing here upon the ideas of Gayatri Chakravorty Spivak's seminal "Can the Subaltern Speak?" (reprinted in Spivak 1995).

97. Yinger 1982:163.

98. See Katz 2003:5.

99. Bobby Vicious, interviewed February 2002.

100. Lastra 2000:7.

101. See Chude-Sokei 1994, as reprinted in Potash 1997:216. Chude-Sokei is drawing upon ideas of Paul Gilroy as presented in Gilroy 1993a and b.

102. Painter Fikre Gebreyesus, in conversation, August 2002.

103. It has also influenced specifically *musical* trends in Africa: see, for example, the dub-influenced work of Nigerian *juju* and *fuji* musicians such as King Sunny Ade (*Juju Music*, Mango CCD 9712) and the uncredited *Fuji Dub* (Triple Earth TRECD 116). Engineer Godwin Logie, who worked with Black Uhuru on *The Dub Factor* (as well as their concert tours), was involved in the production of both of these albums.

104. David Dabydeen, as quoted in an interview in Dawes 2001:202.

105. Yabby U as quoted in the notes to *King Tubby's Prophecy of Dub* (BAFCD 005).

106. The idea of these devices creating new sensory realities is inspired by Sterne's (2003) introduction to his fifth chapter (220–25), while the idea of these technologies as "prosthetic" devices is taken from the introduction to Lastra 2000 (esp. p. 6).

107. See Dawes's "Lee 'Scratch' Perry: Madman/Prophet/Artist" (in Dawes 1999).

1. Augustus Pablo quoted on *Disciples Boom-Shacka-Lacka Reggae and Dub Site*, http:freespace.virgin.net/russell.bell-brown/pablo2htm.

2. Rob Tannenbaum 1992.

3. For other accounts of the growth of Jamaican music in England, see deKoningh, Griffiths 2003. See also Barrow & Dalton 1997:chap. 8 ("Reggae in England"), or chaps. 11 and 18 of Bradley 2000.

4. Steve Barrow, interviewed May 2004.

5. Dave Hendley, interviewed June 2002.

6. A good source on these social tensions is Solomos 1989.

7. See Bradley 2000:145.

8. For example, see *Burning Spear Live* (Mango 9513), Toots and the Maytals *Live* (Mango 9647) or *Bob Marley and the Wailers Live* (Island 548896).

9. Dave Hendley, interviewed June 2002.

10. Jah Shaka as quoted in "Interview With Jah Shaka," http://www.jahwarrior. freeuk.com/ivshaka.htm.

11. Boyarin's term, as cited in Clifford 1994:305. For the Bradley references, see Bradley 2000:114, 431, and 434.

12. Adrian Sherwood, interviewed November 2001.

13. Cousins, as quoted in the notes to *Dubbing With the Royals* (Pressure Sounds PSCD 44).

14. Johnson 1996:6. See also Bradley 2000:447–49.

15. Dave Hendley, interviewed June 2002.

16. Steve Barrow, interviewed May 2004. Don Letts is the producer of a 2002 compilation CD titled *Dread Meets Punk Rockers Uptown* (EMI), which reconstructs the type of reggae set he might have played to an audience of punk enthusiasts at the Roxy club during the late 1970s.

17. Clive Austen, interviewed June 2002.

18. See A. R. Kane's *69* (Rough Trade US 45 CD) and *Americana* (Luaka Bop/Warner Bros. 9–26669–2).

19. Public Image, Ltd. (1981) *Second Edition* (Warner Brothers 3288–2).

20. Sherwood interviewed by Greg Whitfield, from "The Adrian Sherwood interview: the On-U Sound experience, the On-U Sound family," www.uncarved .org/dub/onu/onu.html.

21. As quoted in Johnson 1996:76.

22. Ibid.:53.

23. See Bradley 2000:121 for a discussion of the high level of experimentation in the British dub scene.

24. In addition to my own 2001 interview with him, information on Sherwood in this section is taken from the following websites: "Adrian Sherwood," www.tt.net/onusound/sherwood.html; "Adrian Sherwood," www.obsolete.com /on-u/sherwood.html; "Adrian Sherwood," www.jahsonic.com/AdrianSherwood .html; and "The Adrian Sherwood interview: the On-U Sound Experience, the On-U Sound family," www.uncarved.org/dub/onu/onu.html.

25. Adrian Sherwood interviewed November, 2001.

26. Ibid.

27. See various (1999) *On-U Sound Box* (Cleopatra CLP-0576–2); Creation Rebel's *Historic Moments Volume One* (1994, On-U Sound 7–72784–2), and *Historic Moments, Volume Two* (1995, On-U Sound 7–72799–2); Lee Perry's *From The Secret Laboratory* (Island RRCD 55 706–2, 1990); and *Time Boom X De Devil Dead* (1987, EMI 7243 5 30026 2 6).

28. Neil "Mad Professor" Fraser, interviewed May 2000.

29. Fraser interviewed by David Katz, from "The Ariwa Story," www.niceup .com/writers/david_katz/ariwastory.com. In addition to my own 2000 interview with him and the Katz article cited above, information on Fraser in this section is taken from the following websites: "More Loony Tunes: Interview With the Mad Professor," www.reggae-vibes.com/concert/madprof/madprof.htm; and "The Mad Professor—Interviewed!" www.obscure.co.nz/culture/mad_professor_interview.

30. Neil "Mad Professor" Fraser, as interviewed by Grant Smithies at http://www.obscure.co.nz/culture/mad_professor_interview.

31. Fraser, interviewed May 2000.

32. Ibid.

33. Biographical information on Bovell in this section is primarily taken from two web articles: "Dennis Bovell," www.lkjrecords.com/dennisbovell.htm, and "Dennis Bovell: The Interview," www.jovemusic.com/ewe.net/british/dbovell.htm.

34. Bovell, as interviewed by Norman Darwen (1999): "Dennis Bovell: The Interview" (see note 33).

35. Ibid.

36. Bovell, as told to Nichols in the notes to Dennis Bovell (2003), *Decibel* (Pressure Sounds PSCD 39).

37. For good sources on electronica, see Prendergast 2000. Reynolds 1998; the film *Modulations* (directed by Iara Lee), and Shapiro 2000.

38. For listening purposes, a good reference is Shapiro 1999.

39. Intelligent Jungalist (1994), "Barehedd One" from *The Best of Underground Dance*, vol. 1 (LOW CDX25).

40. A Guy Called Gerald (1995), *Black Secret Technology* (Juice Box).

41. Reynolds 1998:251–52.

42. Ibid.:257.

43. Johnson 1996:10.

44. The 2002 compilation *The Wild Bunch: Story of A Sound System* (Strut CD 019) re-creates a typical 1980s set by the Wild Bunch crew, the Bristol-based sound system who were the spark plug of hip-hop in England and several members of whom went on after 1986 to form the nucleus of the seminal trip-hop (vocal) group Massive Attack.

45. Several interesting examples of this reconciliation can be found on Massive Attack's *Protection* (1994).

46. Jacob Haagsman (2004), "Rhythm & Sound: Jamaican Hallucinations in Stripped-Down Slowmotion," http://www.reggae-vibes.com/concert/rhythm _sound.htm.

47. Two surveys of this type of work are the *Clicks & Cuts* compilation (Mille Plateaux label, 2000), and the Sound of Cologne compilation (Sound of Cologne label, 2000).

48. Betke, interviewed June 2002. The recordings he cites are both productions of Lloyd "Bullwackie's" Barnes. See Horace Andy (1980s), *Dance Hall Style* (Basic Channel/Wackie's 1383); and Wayne Jarrett (1980s), *Bubble Up* (Wackie's WRCD 191).

49. See Reynolds' "Pure Fusion: Multiculture Vs. Monoculture" (2001). Reprinted at http://members.aol.com/blissout/purefusion.htm.

50. See Maurizio (1997), *M-Series*. Basic Channel MCD.

51. See the reproduction of the label logo in Haagsman 2004 (see note 46).

52. The influence of dub on British dance music is examined in Barrow 1995.

53. See *Macro Dub Infection*, volume 1 (Caroline CAROL 1795–2: 1995) and 2 (Gyroscope GYR 6638–2: 1996).

54. Haagsman 2004 (see note 46).

55. See Gilroy 2005; and Baucom 1999.

56. Reynolds 1998:354.

57. Reynolds's chapter "Roots 'n' Future" chronicles the background factors to the emergence and popularity of drum & bass (Reynolds 1998).

58. Squarepusher (Tom Jenkinson) in Micallef 1996:28.

59. Barnes as quoted in "Wacky and Bullish," http://sfbg.com/37/14/art _music_bullwackie.html.

60. Bob Marley (1997), *Dreams of Freedom: Ambient Translations of Bob Marley in Dub* (Island 524419). The title of Laswell's remix project seems a reference to Island Records' four-disc box set of Marley material, *Songs of Freedom*.

61. See Laswell's comments in "The Island Life Interview With Bill Laswell: Dreams of Freedom," http://www.bobmarley.com/albums/dreams/session.html.

62. Sinker 1994:60.

63. Sharp 1996:60.

64. Reynolds 1998:193.

65. George 2004.

66. The sociological background to the emergence of hip-hop is thoroughly documented in Rose 1994.

67. The best source on the early years of hip-hop is Fricke and Ahearn 2002.

68. See Vincent 1996 for a history of funk music.

69. See Fikentscher 2000:chap. 2.

70. For sources on disco music, consult Shapiro 2006; Lawrence 2003; and Brewster and Broughton 1999: chap. 6. For a representative musical overview of the New York–based African American/Latin American social dialogue at the root of disco, consult the seven-disc CD compilation of 12″ releases on New York's Salsoul label (the label name says it all) spanning the late 1970s to the early 1980s. See *From the Salsoul Vault*, vols. 1–7 (Salsoul SPLK2–8048 through SPLK2–8054).

71. See George 1988: chap. 6.

72. A good background source for this theme is Talty 2003, esp. chaps. 6 and 8.

73. Eshun 1997:2.

74. Consult Brewster and Broughton 1999 and Poschardt 1995 for studies of the rise of DJ culture.

75. See Alexander G. Weheliye, "'Feenin': Posthuman Voices in Contemporary Black Popular Music" (in Nelson 2002).

76. See Hebdige 1987: chapt. 16 for an account of this influence.

77. Manuel 1995:241.

78. What has been less documented is the role that performance contexts played in the early development of hip-hop, and the way this also reflected a Jamaican cultural influence. In most early accounts, recordings have tended to be emphasized over performance contexts. I believe the reason for this has less to do with trends in scholarship and more to do with an anomaly of recent New York City history. Among the most important crucibles in the development of hip-hop music were the outdoor "block parties," summertime community events that flourished in New York City during the late 1960 and early 1970s. In addition to live bands, crews of young DJs and rappers typically provided part of the musical entertainment at these events; as such block parties became hothouses for the development of the emerging hip-hop form. From about 1980, however, New York City officials made it progressively more difficult for residents to obtain permits to hold these block parties (see chap. 4 of Rose 1994 for a discussion of the civic opposition to rap-based public events). As a result, the block party phenomenon declined from this time.

At the same time as the decline of the block parties, the rap group Sugarhill Gang released their seminal "Rapper's Delight" in 1979, generally considered to be the first significant commercial recording of rap music. Thus, the block party (as a significant social force) declined as an influence on the music at precisely the same moment that hip-hop became a commercially recorded music and began to be documented in journalistic circles. In fact, the recording of "Rapper's Delight" was itself a mere consolidation of creative currents that had been brewing around New York City for several years. Had the block party component survived for just a few more years, it would most likely have been a more prominent part of the music's history, and the Jamaican contribution to hip-hop would be more clearly evident.

79. For example, see Rush 1999.

80. A good introduction to these artists is the 1996 compilation *Incursions in Illbient* (Asphodel 0968). A good introduction to Paul D. Miller's theoretical work is *Rhythm Science* (Amsterdam/New York: COMA, 2004).

81. "Dr. Satan's Echo Chamber" takes its title from a dub track produced by Rupie Edwards. See Rupie Edwards and Friends (1997), *Let There Be Version* (Trojan CDTRL 280).

82. Gilroy 1993a:100. Many scholars would make a similar claim for hip-hop music in the 1990s.

83. Both quotations from Gilroy 1993b:35.

84. Gilroy 1987:215.

85. Gilroy's ideas on this cultural shift are neatly summarized in the introduction to *Small Acts* (Gilroy 1993b).

86. See Gilroy 2000.

87. For example, see Toni Morrison's comments on jazz as a template for creative writing (as quoted in Gilroy 1993a:78).

88. See Salamon 1997.

89. Budhos 1999.

90. See Homiak's "Dub History: Soundings on Rastafari Livity and Language," in Chevannes 1998.

91. See Njami 2005.

92. An insightful discussion of these "high-low" issues in relation to black popular culture is Potter 1994.

93. Eshun 1998:065. He refers to Holger Czukay, bassist in the influential "Krautrock" group Can.

94. See Parisi 2004. For information on the "Bacteria in Dub" event, see http://space-ape.com/bacteriaindub.html.

95. See Deleuze and Guattari 1977 and 1988. For a more immediately accessible summary of these ideas, consult Bogue 1989.

96. See Irigaray 1977 and 1985.

97. See Haraway's "A Manifesto for Cyborgs: Science, Technology, and Socialist Feminism in the 1980s" reprinted in Haraway 2004. For ideas of techno-eroticism, see Springer 1996.

98. See Margulis 1986.

99. Parisi 2004:4.

100. See Said 1990.

101. Jameson 1991 and Lyotard 1984 offer the most frequently cited characteristics of artistic production in the so-called postmodern age. Cornel West has problematized the application of these ideas to black (primarily African American) cultural production in his "Black Culture and Postmodernism," in Kruger and Marini 1989.

102. I am drawing here upon Jonathan Kramer's ideas of the postcolonial in music as presented in Kramer 1996. I am also drawing upon ideas of the linkage between the characteristics of postcolonial and postmodern music as discussed in Renee T. Coulombe's "Postmodern Polyamory or Postcolonial Challenge?" in Lochhead and Auner 2002.

103. Kevin Martin in notes to Martin 1995.

104. See Lowery Sims's "The Post-Modernism of Wifredo Lam" in Mercer 2005.

105. Ibid.

106. Lastra 2000:4.

107. See Sterne 2003:7 for a discussion of this "impact" model of technological encounter.

108. Adrian Sherwood, interviewed November 2001.

109. Steve Barrow, interviewed May 2004.

110. Overton "Scientist" Brown, interviewed September 2001.

111. Baker 1987:49.

112. See McWhorter 2003:200 and 209.

113. See also Browning 1998.

114. See Jordan 2000.

Bibliography

❧

Books and Articles

Abalos, Inaki, and Juan Herreros. 1998. "End of the Century Still Lifes." *Croquis* 90:4–23.

Adler, Peter, and Nicholas Bernard. 1992. *African Majesty: The Textile Art of the Ashanti and Ewe*. London: Thames and Hudson.

Adorno, Theodor. 1967. "Cultural Criticism and Society." In *Prisms*. London: Spearman.

Agawu, V. Kofi. 1995. *African Rhythm: A Northern Ewe Perspective*. New York: Cambridge University Press.

Alberro, Alexander. 1997. "Gerhard Richter, Marion Goodman Gallery." *Artforum* (March) 90.

Anzaldúa, Gloria. 1987. *Borderlands: La Frontera*. San Francisco, Calif.: Aunt Lute Books.

Antze, Paul, and Michael Lambek, eds. 1996. *Tense Past: Cultural Essays in Trauma and Memory*. New York: Routledge.

Appadurai, Arjun, ed. 1986. *The Social Life of Things: Commodities in Cultural Perspective*. Cambridge: Cambridge University Press.

———. 1990. "Disjuncture and Difference in the Global Cultural Economy." *Public Culture* 2(2):1–24.

———. (1996). *Modernity at Large: Cultural Dimensions of Globalization*. Minneapolis: University of Minnesota Press.

Apter, Andrew. 1991. "Herskovits's Heritage: Rethinking Syncretism in the African Diaspora." *Diaspora* 1(3):235–60.

Attali, Jacques. 1985. *Noise: The Political Economy of Music*. Minneapolis: University of Minnesota Press.

Averill, Gage. 1994. "Anraje to Angaje: Carnival Politics and Music in Haiti." *Ethnomusicology* 38(2):217–47.

———. 1997. *A Day for the Hunter, A Day for the Prey: Popular Music and Power in Haiti*. Chicago: University of Chicago Press.

Baker, Houston. 1987. *Modernism and the Harlem Renaissance*. Chicago: University of Chicago Press.

Bakhtin, Mikhail. 1981. *The Dialogic Imagination*. Austin: University of Texas Press.

Barber, Karin. 1984. "Yoruba Oriki and Deconstructive Criticism." *Research in African Literatures* 15(4):497–518.

Barrett, Leonard E. 1997. *The Rastafarians*. Boston: Beacon Press.

Barrow, Steve. 1995. "Version Therapy." *Wire* (February):28–32.

———, and Peter Dalton. 1997. *Reggae: The Rough Guide*. London: Rough Guides.

Barthes, Roland. 1977. *Image-Music-Text*. London: Fontana.

Bates, Eliot. 1997. "Ambient Music." Master's thesis, Wesleyan University.

Baucom, Ian. 1999. *Out of Place: Englishness, Empire, and the Location of Identity*. Princeton, N.J.: Princeton University Press.

Baudrillard, Jean. 1995. *Simulacra and Simulation*. Translated by Sheila Faria Glaser. Ann Arbor: University of Michigan Press.

Becker, Judith. 1981. "Hindu-Buddhist Time in Javanese Gamelan Music." In *The Study of Time*, vol. 4. New York: Springer-Verlag.

Beebe, Roger, with Denise Fulbrook and Ben Saunders. 2002. *Rock Over the Edge: Transformations in Popular Music Culture*. Durham, N.C.: Duke University Press.

Benjamin, Walter. 1968. *Illuminations*. New York: Schocken.

Bennett, Andy. 2001. "Punk and Punk Rock." In his *Cultures of Popular Music*. Philadelphia: Open University Press.

Blake, Andrew. 1999. *Living Through Pop*. London: Routledge.

Blashill, Pat. 2002. "Six Machines That Changed the Music World." *Wired* (May):104–109.

Blier, Suzanne Preston. 1995. *African Vodun: Art, Psychology, and Power*. Chicago: University of Chicago Press.

Bogue, Donald. 1989. *Deleuze and Guattari*. London: Routledge.

Bolles, Edmund Blair. 1988. *Remembering and Forgetting: An Inquiry Into the Nature of Memory*. New York: Walker.

Born, Georgina, and David Hesmondhalgh, eds. 2000. *Western Music and Its Others: Difference, Representation, and Appropriation in Music*. Berkeley and Los Angeles: University of California Press.

Bowman, Rob. 2003. *Soulsville U.S.A.: The Story of Stax Records*. New York: Schirmer.

Bradley, Lloyd. 2000. *This Is Reggae Music: The Story of Jamaica's Music*. New York: Grove.

Bradley, Lloyd, and James Maycock. 1999. "This is a Journey Into Sound." *Mojo* (April): 65–69.

Brathwaite, Edward Kamau. 1984. *History of the Voice: The Development of National Language in Anglophone Caribbean Poetry*. London: New Beacon Books.

Brewster, Bill, and Frank Broughton. 1999. *Last Night A DJ Saved My Life: The History of the Disc-Jockey*. New York: Grove.

Brodber, Erna. 1985. "Black Consciousness and Popular Music in Jamaica in the 1960s and 1970s." *Caribbean Quarterly* 31(2):53–66.

———, and J. Edward Greene. 1988. "Reggae and Cultural Identity in Jamaica." ISER Working Paper No. 35. Kingston, Jamaica: University of the West Indies Press.

Browning, Barbara. 1998. *Infectious Rhythm: Metaphors of Contagion and the Spread of African Culture*. New York: Routledge.

Budhos, Marina. 1999. *Remix: Conversations with Immigrant Teenagers*. New York: Henry Holt.

Burroughs, William, and Brion Gysin. 1978. *The Third Mind*. New York: Seaver.

Buskin, Richard. 1999. *Inside Tracks: A First-Hand History of Popular Music From the World's Greatest Producers and Engineers*. New York: Avon.

Butler, Octavia E. 1979. *Kindred*. Boston: Beacon Press.

Callen, Anthea. 1987. *Techniques of the Impressionists*. London: New Burlington.

Caruth, Cathy, ed. 1995. *Trauma: Explorations in Memory*. Baltimore: Johns Hopkins University Press.

Cassidy, F. G., and R. B. LePage, eds. 1980. *Dictionary of Jamaican English*. Cambridge: Cambridge University Press.

Chakrabarty, Dipesh. 1992. "The Death of History? Historical Consciousness and the Culture of Late Capitalism." *Public Culture* 4(2):47–65.

Chanan, Michael. 1995. *Repeated Takes: A Short History of Recording and Its Effects on Music*. London: Verso.

Chang, Jeff. 2005. *Can't Stop, Won't Stop: A History of the Hip-Hop Generation*. New York: St. Martin's.

Chang, Kevin, and Wayne Chen. 1998. *Reggae Routes: The Story of Jamaican Music*. Philadelphia: Temple University Press.

Chapman, Rob. 1999. *Never Grow Old*. N.p.:n.p.

Charlton, Katherine. 2003. *Rock Music Styles: A History*. New York: McGraw-Hill.

Chernoff, John Miller. 1979. *African Rhythm and African Sensibility*. Chicago: University of Chicago Press.

Chevannes, Barry. 1994. *Rastafari: Roots and Ideology*. Syracuse: Syracuse University Press.

———. ed. 1998. *Rastafari and other African-Caribbean Worldviews*. New Brunswick, N.J.: Rutgers University Press.

Chude-Sokei, Louis. 1994. "Postnationalist Geographies: Rasta, Ragga, and Reinventing Africa." *African Arts* (Autumn). Reprinted in *Reggae, Rasta, Revolution: Jamaican Music from Ska to Dub* (1997), by Chris Potash. New York: Simon and Schuster.

———. 1997a. "'Dr. Satan's Echo Chamber': Reggae, Technology and the Diaspora Process." Bob Marley Lecture, Reggae Studies Unit, Institute of Caribbean Studies, University of the West Indies, Mona.

———. 1997b. "The Sound of Culture: Dread Discourse and the Jamaican Sound Systems." In *Language, Rhythm, & Sound: Black Popular Cultures Into the Twenty-First Century*, edited by Joseph K. Adjaye and Adrianne R. Andrews. Pittsburgh, Pa.: University of Pittsburgh Press.

Clarke, Sebastian. 1980. *Jah Music: The Evolution of the Popular Jamaican Song*. London: Heinemann.

Cleveland, Barry. 2001. *Joe Meek's Bold Techniques*. Vallejo, Calif.: Mix Books.

Clifford, James. 1988. *The Predicament of Culture: Twentieth-Century Ethnography, Literature, and Art*. Cambridge, Mass.: Harvard University Press.

———. 1994. "Diasporas." *Cultural Anthropology* 9(3):302–38.

———, and George E. Marcus. 1986. *Writing Culture: The Poetics and Politics of Ethnography*. Berkeley and Los Angeles: University of California Press.

Cogan, Jim, and William Clark. 2003. *Temples of Sound: Inside the Great Recording Studios*. San Francisco, Calif.: Chronicle.

Connerton, Paul. 1989. *How Societies Remember*. Cambridge: Cambridge University Press.

Cook, Susan C., and Judy S. Tsou, eds. 1994. *Cecelia Reclaimed: Feminist Perspectives on Gender and Music*. With a forward by Susan McClary. Urbana: University of Illinois Press.

Cooper, Carol. 1995. *Noises in the Blood: Orality, Gender, and the "Vulgar" Body of Jamaican Popular Culture*. Durham, N.C.: Duke University Press.

———. 2004. *Sound Clash: Jamaican Dancehall Culture at Large*. New York: Palgrave Macmillan.

Cope, Julian. 1996. *Krautrock Sampler*. London: Head Heritage.

Corbett, John. 1994. *Extended Play: Sounding Off From John Cage to Dr. Funkenstein*. Durham, N.C.: Duke University Press.

Cronin, Russell. 2005. "The History of Music and Marijuana, part two." http://www.cannabisculture.com/articles/3512.html.

Crouch, Stanley. 1979. "Bringing Atlantis Up to the Top." *Village Voice* (April 16):65.

Cunningham, Mark. 1998. *Good Vibrations: A History of Record Production.* London: Sanctuary.

Cusick, Suzanne. 1994. "Feminist Theory, Music Theory, and the Mind/Body Problem." *Perspectives of New Music* 32(1):8–27.

Davis, Stephen. 1985. *Bob Marley.* Garden City, N.Y.: Doubleday.

———, and Peter Simon. 1982. *Reggae International.* New York: Rogner and Bernhard.

———. 1992. *Reggae Bloodlines: In Search of the Music and Culture of Jamaica.* New York: Da Capo.

Dawes, Kwame. 1999. *Natural Mysticism: Towards A New Reggae Aesthetic in Caribbean Writing.* Leeds, Eng.: Peepal Tree.

———. 2001. *Talk Yuh Talk: Interviews with Anglophone Caribbean Poets.* Charlottesville: University Press of Virginia.

deKoningh, Michael, and Marc Griffiths. 2003. *Tighten Up: The History of Reggae in the UK.* London: Sanctuary.

Deleuze, Gilles, and Felix Guattari. 1997. *Anti-Oedipus: Capitalism and Schizophrenia.* Translated by Robert Hurley, Mark Seem, and Helen R. Lane. New York: Viking.

———. 1988. *A Thousand Plateaus: Capitalism and Schizophrenia II.* Translated and with a foreword by Brian Massumi. London: Athlone Press.

Demby, Eric. 1998. "Original Rockers." *URB* (December): 92–93.

Dent, Gina, ed. 1992. *Black Popular Culture.* Seattle, Wash.: Bay Press.

Dery, Mark. 1994. "Black to the Future: Interviews with Samuel R. Delany, Greg Tate, and Tricia Rose." In *Flame Wars: The Discourse of Cyberculture,* edited by Mark Dery. Durham, N.C.: Duke University Press.

DiIorio, Lyn. 1997. "Laughter, Magic, and Possession in Caribbean Literature." PhD. diss. prospectus, Brown University.

Donnell, Alison, and Sarah Lawson Welsh. 1996. *The Routledge Reader in Caribbean Literature.* London: Routledge.

Douglas, Mary. 1966. *Purity and Danger: An Analysis of the Concepts of Pollution and Taboo.* New York: Routledge.

Doyle, Peter. 2004. "From 'My Blue Heaven' to 'Race With the Devil': echo, reverb and (dis)ordered space in early popular music recording." *Popular Music* 23(1):31–49.

Dr. Licks. 1989. *Standing in the Shadows of Motown: The Life and Music of Legendary Bassist James Jamerson.* Milwaukee, Wis.: Hal Leonard.

Eargle, John M. 1995. *Music, Sound, and Technology.* New York: Van Nostrand Reinhold.

Edmonds, Ennis Barrington. 2003. "Coming in from the Cold: Rastafari and the Wider Society." In *Rastafari: From Outcasts to Culture Bearers.* Oxford: Oxford University Press.

Eisenberg, Evan. 1987. *The Recording Angel: Explorations in Phonography.* New York: McGraw-Hill.

Ellison, Ralph. 1964. *Shadow and Act.* New York: Vintage.

Eno, Brian. 1996. *A Year With Swollen Appendices.* London: Faber and Faber.

Epstein, Jonathan. 1998. *Youth Culture: Identity in a Postmodern World.* Malden, Mass.: Blackwell.

Erlmann, Veit. 1996a. . "The Aesthetics of the Global Imagination: Reflections on World Music in the 1990s." *Public Culture* 8(3):467–87.

———. 1996b. *Nightsong: Performance, Power, and Practice in South Africa.* Chicago: University of Chicago Press.

Eshun, Kodwo. 1997. *Abstract Culture #2: Motion Capture* (Interview). Warwick University, Coventry: Cybernetic Culture Research Unit.
——. 1998. *More Brilliant Than the Sun: Adventures in Sonic Fiction.* London: Quartet.
Everett, Walter. 1999. *The Beatles as Musicians: From Revolver Through the Anthology.* New York: Oxford University Press.
Fanon, Frantz. 1963. *The Wretched of the Earth.* New York: Grove.
Feld, Steven. 1974. "Linguistic Models and Ethnomusicology." *Ethnomusicology* 18(2):197–217.
——. 1982. *Sound and Sentiment: Birds, Weeping, Poetics, and Song in Kaluli Expression.* Philadelphia: University of Pennsylvania Press.
——. (1984). "Sound Structure as Social Structure." *Ethnomusicology* (September): 383–409.
Felman, Shoshana. 1995. "Education and Crisis, or the Vicissitudes of Teaching." In *Trauma: Explorations in Cultural Memory,* edited by Cathy Caruth. Baltimore: Johns Hopkins University Press.
——, and Dori Laub, M.D. 1992. *Testimony: Crises of Witnessing in Literature, Psychoanalysis, and History.* New York: Routledge.
Fikentscher, Kai. 2000. *"You Better Work": Underground Dance Music in New York City.* Hanover: University Press of New England.
Fine, Ruth. 2003. *The Art of Romare Bearden.* Washington, D.C.: National Gallery of Art.
Fischlin, Daniel, and Ajay Heble. 2004. *The Other Side of Nowhere: Jazz, Improvisation, and Communities in Dialogue.* Middletown, Conn.: Wesleyan University Press.
Foster, Chuck. 1999. *Roots, Rock, Reggae: An Oral History of Reggae Music from Ska to Dancehall.* New York: Billboard.
Foster, Hal. 1983. *The Anti-Aesthetic: Essays on Postmodern Culture.* Seattle, Wash.: Bay Press.
——. 1993. *Compulsive Beauty.* Cambridge, Mass.: MIT Press.
Fowler, Roger. 1981. *Literature As Social Discourse: The Practice of Linguistic Criticism.* Bloomington: Indiana University Press.
Frere-Jones, Sasha. 1997. "Scratching the Surface." *Village Voice* (August 13–19): 67, 74.
Fricke, Jim, and Charlie Ahearn. 2002. *Yes Yes Y'all: Oral History of Hip-Hop's First Decade.* New York: Da Capo.
Frith, Simon, and Howard Horne. 1987. *Art into Pop.* London: Methuen.
Frith, Simon, and Lee Marshall, eds. 2004. *Music and Copyright.* 2nd ed. Edinburgh: Edinburgh University Press.
Full Watts: Reggae Reverberations. Vol. 1, no. 3; vol. 3, nos. 1–3. Wilton, California.
Gabbard, Krin. 1991. "The Quoter and His Culture." In *Jazz in Mind: Essays on the History and Meanings of Jazz,* edited by Reginald T. Buckner and Steven Weiland. Detroit, Mich.: Wayne State University Press.
Gates, Henry Louis, Jr., ed. 1984. *Black Literature and Literary Theory.* New York: Methuen.
George, Nelson. 1988a. *The Death of Rhythm & Blues.* New York: Methuen.
——. 1998b. *Hip-Hop America.* New York: Viking.
——. 2004. *Post-Soul Nation: The Explosive, Contradictory, Triumphant, and Tragic 1980s as Experienced by African Americans (previously known as Blacks and before that Negroes).* New York: Viking.
Gikandi, Simon. 1992. *Writing In Limbo: Modernism and Caribbean Literature.* Ithaca, N.Y.: Cornell University Press.

Gilroy, Paul. 1987. *There Ain't No Black in the Union Jack: The Cultural Politics of Race and Nation*. Chicago: University of Chicago Press.

———. 1993a. *The Black Atlantic: Modernity and Double Consciousness*. Cambridge, Mass.: Harvard University Press.

———. 1993b. *Small Acts: Thoughts on the Politics of Black Cultures*. London: Serpent's Tail.

———. 2000. *Against Race: Imagining Political Culture Beyond the Color Line*. Cambridge, Mass.: Belknap Press of Harvard University Press.

———. 2005. *Postcolonial Melancholia*. New York: Columbia University Press.

Glick, Robert, and Stanley Bone. 1990. *Pleasure Beyond the Pleasure Principle*. New Haven, Conn.: Yale University Press.

Gold, Mark S. 1989. *Marijuana*. New York: Plenum Medical Book.

Gorney, Mark. 1999. "Graeme Goodall, Part 1." *Full Watts,* vol. 3, no. 2–3: 42–49; 42–54.

———. 2006. "Heavy Hands: Jamaican Bassist Jackie Jackson Gives Birth to Rocksteady." *Wax Poetics* 15 (February–March): 90–96.

"Grand Royal Interview: Lee 'Scratch' Perry." 1995. *Grand Royal,* no. 2:67–70.

Gray, Obika. 1991. *Radicalism and Social Change in Jamaica, 1960–1972*. Knoxville: University of Tennessee Press.

Green, Paul D., and Thomas Porcello. 2005. *Wired for Sound: Engineering and Technologies in Sonic Cultures*. Middletown, Conn.: Wesleyan University Press.

Grenier, Line, and Jocelyn Guilbault. 1990. "'Authority' Revisited: The 'Other' in Anthropology and Popular Music Studies." *Ethnomusicology* 34 (3): 381–97.

Griffith, Ivelaw, ed. 2000. *The Political Economy of Drugs in the Caribbean*. New York: St. Martin's.

Grueneisen, Peter. 2003. *Soundspace: Architecture for Sound and Vision*. Basel: Birkhauser.

Gunst, Laurie. 1995. *Born Fi Dead: A Journey Through the Jamaican Posse Underworld*. New York: Henry Holt.

Guilbault, Jocelyn, with Gage Averill, Edouard Benoit, and Gregory Rabess. 1993. *Zouk: World Music in the West Indies*. Chicago: University of Chicago Press.

Hamill, James. 1990. *Ethno-Logic: The Anthropology of Human Reasoning*. Urbana: University of Illinois Press.

Haraway, Donna. 2004. *The Haraway Reader*. London: Routledge.

Harding, Rosamund. 1933. *The Piano-Forte: Its History Traced to the Great Exhibition of 1851*. Surrey, Eng.: Grisham.

Hayward, Philip, ed. 2004. *Off the Planet: Music, Sound and Science Fiction Cinema*. London: John Libbey.

Hebdige, Dick. 1979. *Subculture: The Meaning of Style*. London: Routledge.

———. 1987. *Cut 'n' Mix: Culture, Identity and Caribbean Music*. London: Routledge.

Henderson, Richard. 1996. "The Congos: *Heart of the Congos*." *The Beat* 15 (1): 60–61.

Hicks, Michael. 1999. *Sixties Rock: Garage, Psychedelic & Other Satisfactions*. Urbana: University of Illinois Press.

Hillman, Richard S., and Thomas J. D'Agostino. 2003. *Understanding the Contemporary Caribbean*. Kingston, Jamaica: Ian Randle.

Hoffman, Katherine, ed. 1989. *Collage: Critical Views*. Studies in the Fine Arts: Criticism, No. 31. Ann Arbor, Mich.: UMI Research Press.

Howard, David. 2004. *Sonic Alchemy: Visionary Music Producers and Their Maverick Recordings*. Milwaukee, Wis.: Hal Leonard.

Hurford, Ray, and Tero Kaski. 1987. *More Axe*. Helsinki: Black Star.

Hutcheon, Linda. 1988. *A Poetics of Postmodernism*. London: Routledge.

Ingham, James. 1999. "Listening Back from Blackburn: Virtual Sound Worlds and the Creation of Temporary Autonomy." In *Living Through Pop*, edited by Andrew Blake. London: Routledge

Irigaray, Luce. 1977. *This Sex Which Is Not One*. Translated by Catherine Porte with Carolyn Burke. Ithaca, N.Y.: Cornell University Press.

———. 1985. *Speculum of the Other Woman*. Translated by Gillian C. Gill. Ithaca, N.Y.: Cornell University Press.

Jafa, Arthur. 1994. Unpublished keynote address from Organization of Black Designers Conference, Chicago, Illinois.

Jahn, Brian, and Tom Weber. 1998. *Reggae Island: Jamaican Music in the Digital Age*. New York: Da Capo.

Jameson, Fredric. 1986. "On Magical Realism in Film." *Critical Inquiry* 12 (Winter): 301–325.

———. 1988. *The Ideologies of Theory: Essays 1971–1986*. vol. 1. Minneapolis: University of Minnesota Press.

———. 1991. *Postmodernism; or, The Cultural Logic of Late Capitalism*. Durham, N.C.: Duke University Press.

Jencks, Charles, ed. 1988. *Deconstruction in Architecture*. New York: St. Martin's.

Johnson, Phil. 1996. *Straight Outa Bristol: Massive Attack, Portishead, Tricky and the Roots of Trip-Hop*. London: Hodder and Stoughton.

Johnson, Philip, and Mark Wigley. 1988. *Deconstructivist Architecture*. New York: The Museum of Modern Art.

Jordan, Joel T. 2000. *Searching for the Perfect Beat: Flyer Designs of the American Rave Scene*. New York: Watson-Guptill.

Juniper, Andrew. 2003. *Wabi-Sabi: The Japanese Art of Impermanence*. Boston: Tuttle.

Katz, David. 1990. "Lee Perry at Studio One." *Upsetter* 1: 5–10.

———. 1996a. "Out of Africa Comes the Congoman: The Amazing Tale of *Heart of the Congos*." *The Beat* 15 (1) 56–61.

———. 1996b. "The Upsetter Rides Out." *Upsetter* 2: 7–14.

———. 1999a. "Original Sufferhead." *Wire* (September): 34–39.

———. 1999b. "The Primer: Lee Perry." *Wire* (November): 42–49.

———. 2000. *People Funny Boy: The Genius of Lee "Scratch" Perry*. Edinburgh: Payback Press.

———. 2003. *Solid Foundation: An Oral History of Reggae*. New York: Bloomsbury.

———. 2005. "Sleng Teng Extravaganza." *Wax Poetics* 13 (Summer): 84–90.

Kaufman, Michael. 1985. *Jamaica under Manley: Dilemmas of Socialism and Democracy*. Westport, Conn.: Lawrence Hill.

Keil, Charles. 1966. *Urban Blues*. Chicago: University of Chicago Press.

Kenner, Rob. 2002. "Melody Maker" from *Vibe* (December): 174–180.

"The King of Dub Is Gone." 1989. *The Beat* 8 (2): 15.

King, Stephen A. 1998. "International Reggae, Democratic Socialism, and the Secularization of the Rastafarian Movement, 1972–1980." *Popular Music and Society* 22 (3): 39–60.

———. 2002. *Reggae, Rastafari and the Rhetoric of Social Control*. Jackson: University of Mississippi Press.

Klanten, Robert, ed. 1995. *Localizer 1.0: The Techno House Book*. Berlin: Die Gestalten.

Knight, Franklin W., and Colin A. Palmer, eds. 1989. *The Modern Caribbean*. Chapel Hill: University of North Carolina Press.

Kozinn, Allan. 1995. *The Beatles*. London: Phaidon.

Kozul-Wright, Zeljka. 1988. *Becoming a Globally Competitive Player: The Case of the Music Industry in Jamaica*. Geneva: The Conference.

Kramer, Jonathan. 1996. "Postmodern Concepts of Musical Time." *Indiana Theory Review* 17(2):21–61.

Krauss, Lawrence M. 1995. *The Physics of Star Trek*. New York: HarperCollins.

Krims, Adam. 1998. "Disciplining Deconstruction (For Musical Analysis)." *19th Century Music* (Spring): 297–324.

Kruger, Barbara, and Phil Mariani. 1989. *Remaking History*. Seattle, Wash.: Bay Press.

Lacan, Jacques. 1977. *The Four Fundamental Concepts of Psychoanalysis*. London: Hogarth.

Laing, Dave. 1977. "Listening to Punk Rock." In *The Subcultures Reader*, edited and with introductions by Ken Gelder and Sarah Thornton. London: Routledge.

Lamming, George. 1960. *The Pleasures of Exile*. London: Allison and Busby.

Landauer, Susan. 2001. *Elmer Bischoff: The Ethics of Paint*. Berkeley and Los Angeles: University of California Press.

Lastra, James. 2000. *Sound Technology and the American Cinema: Perception, Representation, Modernity*. New York: Columbia University Press.

Lawrence, Tim. 2003. *Love Saves the Day: A History of American Dance Music Culture, 1970–1979*. Durham, N.C.: Duke University Press.

Leary, Timothy. 1996. "The Second Fine Art: Neo-Symbolic Communication of Experience." *Psychedelic Review* 8.

LeGates, Richard, and Frederic Stout, eds. 2000. *The City Reader*. 2nd ed. New York: Routledge.

Lesser, Beth. 2002. *King Jammy's*. Toronto: ECW.

Leppert, Richard, and Susan McClary, eds. 1987. *Music and Society: The Politics of Composition, Performance, and Reception*. Cambridge: Cambridge University Press.

Lewis, Helena. 1988. *The Politics of Surrealism*. New York: Paragon.

Lewisohn, Mark. 1998. *The Beatles Recording Sessions*. New York: Harmony.

Licht, Alan. 2004. "Invisible Jukebox." *Wire*, no. 204 (February):18–22.

Lipsitz, George. 1994. *Dangerous Crossroads: Popular Music, Postmodernism, and the Poetics of Place*. London: Verso.

Lochhead, Judy, and Joseph Auner, eds. 2002. *Postmodern Music/Postmodern Thought*. New York: Routledge.

Lock, Graham. 1999. *Blutopia*. Durham, N.C.: Duke University Press.

Lowenthal, David. 1985. *The Past Is A Foreign Country*. Cambridge: Cambridge University Press.

Ludlum, David. 1991. *The Audubon Society Field Guide to North American Weather*. New York: Knopf.

Lyotard, Jean-François. 1984. *The Postmodern Condition: A Report on Knowledge*. Translated by Geoff Bennington and Brian Massumi. Foreword by Fredric Jameson. Minneapolis: University of Minnesota Press.

Lysloff, Rene T. A., and Leslie Gay, Jr. 2003. *Music and Technoculture*. Middletown, Conn.: Wesleyan University Press.

Mack, Bob. 1995. "Return of the Super Ape: The Lives and Times of Lee 'Scratch' Perry." *Grand Royal* no. 2:60–66.

Makward, Edris, with Thelma Ravell-Pinto and Aliko Songolo. 1998. *The Growth of African Literature: Twenty-Five Years After Dakar and Fourah Bay*. Trenton, N.J.: Africa World Press.

Malm, Krister, and Roger Wallis. 1992. "Case Study: Jamaica." In *Media Policy and Music Activity*. London: Routledge.

Manuel, Peter. 1988. *Popular Musics of the Non-Western World*. Oxford: Oxford University Press.

———, with Kenneth Bilby and Michael Largey. 1995. *Caribbean Currents*. Philadelphia: Temple University Press.

Mardis, Catherine. 2002. "Ambient: An Exploration of Ambient Music through History, Sound Art and Theatre." Master's thesis, Yale University.

Margulis, Lynn. 1986. *Origins of Sex: Three Billion Years of Genetic Recombination*. New Haven, Conn.: Yale University Press.

Martin, George. 1979. *All You Need Is Ears*. New York: St. Martin's.

———, ed. 1983. *Making Music: The Guide to Writing, Performing and Recording*. New York: Quill.

Martin, Kevin. 1995. "Echo Chamber Odysseys." *Wire* (May):29–33.

Marx, Karl. 1887. *Capital*. London: Moore and Aveling.

May, Chris. 1977. "Starting from Scratch." *Black Music* (October):13.

Mayer, Ralph. 1969. *A Dictionary of Art Terms and Techniques*. New York: Crowell.

McClary, Susan. 1991. *Feminine Endings: Music, Gender, and Sexuality*. Minneapolis: University of Minnesota Press.

———. 1994. "Paradigm Dissonances: Music Theory, Cultural Studies, Feminist Criticism." *Perspectives of New Music* 32(1).

———, and Robert Walser. 1994. "Theorizing the Body in African-American Music." *Black Music Research Journal* 14:75–84.

McDermott, John, with Eddie Kramer. 1992. *Hendrix: Setting the Record Straight*. Edited by Mark Lewisohn. New York: Warner.

McDermott, John, with Billy Cox and Eddie Kramer. 1996. *Jimi Hendrix: Sessions: The Complete Recording Sessions, 1963–1970*. Boston: Little, Brown.

McEvilley, Thomas. 1993. "Royal Slumming: Jean-Michael Basquiat Here Below." *Artforum* (November):92–97.

McGaffey, Wyatt, and Michael Harris. 1993. *Astonishment and Power*. Washington, D.C.: National Museum of African Art.

McKay, George, ed. 1998. *DiY Culture: Party & Protest in Nineties Britain*. London: Verso.

McLuhan, Marshall. 1962. *The Gutenberg Galaxy*. Toronto: University of Toronto Press.

McWhorter, John H. 2003. *Doing Our Own Thing: The Degradation of Language and Music and why we should, like, care*. New York: Gotham Books.

Meintjes, Louise. 2003. *Sound of Africa!: Making Music Zulu in a South African Studio*. Durham, N.C.: Duke University Press.

Mercer, Kobena, ed. 2005. *Cosmopolitan Modernisms*. Cambridge, Mass.: MIT Press.

Merriam, Alan. 1964. *The Anthropology of Music*. Evanston, Ill.: Northwestern University Press.

Micallef, Ben. 1996. "Logical Percussion." *Raygun* (October).

Mikics, David. 1995. "Derek Walcott and Alejo Carpentier: Nature, History, and the Caribbean Writer." In *Magical Realism: Theory, History, Community*, edited and with an introduction by Lois Parkinson Zamora and Wendy B. Faris. Durham, N.C.: Duke University Press.

Mintz, Sidney, and Douglas Hall. 1960. "The Origins of the Jamaican Internal Marketing System." *Yale University Publications in Anthropology*, no. 57:3–26.

Mintz, Sidney, and Richard Price. 1992. *The Birth of African-American Culture: An Anthropological Perspective*. Boston: Beacon Press.

Monson, Ingrid. 1996. *Saying Something: Jazz Improvisation and Interaction*. Chicago: University of Chicago Press.

———. 1999. "Riffs, Repetition, and Theories of Globalization." *Ethnomusicology* 34(1):31–65.

Montgomery, Will. 1997. "Lee Perry: Arkology." *Wire* (May): 56–57.

Moore, Jerrold Northrup. 1999. *Sound Revolutions: A Biography of Fred Gaisberg, Founding Father of Commercial Sound Recording*. London: Sanctuary.

Morrish, Ivor. 1982. *Obeah, Christ and Rastaman*. Cambridge: James Clark.

Moser, Mary Anne, with Douglas MacLeod. 1996. *Immersed in Technology: Art and Virtual Environments*. Cambridge, Mass.: MIT Press.

Mulvaney, Rebekah Michele. 1990. *Rastafari and Reggae: A Sourcebook*. New York: Greenwood.

Murrell, Nathaniel Samuel, with William David Spencer and Adrian Anthony McFarlane. 1998. *Chanting Down Babylon: The Rastafari Reader*. Philadelphia: Temple University Press.

Nattiez, Jean-Jacques. 1990. *Music and Discourse: Toward a Semiology of Music*. Princeton, N.J.: Princeton University Press.

Neely, Daniel. 2001. "'Long Time Gal!' Mento is Back!" *The Beat* 20 no. 6 (December):38–42.

———. Forthcoming. "Mento: Jamaica's Original Folk Music." Ph.D. diss., New York University.

Nelson, Alondra, ed. 2002. *Afrofuturism*. *Social Text* 71, 20, no. 2 (Summer).

Njami, Simon. 2005. *Africa Remix: Contemporary Art of a Continent*. Ostfildern-Ruit: Hatje Cantz.

Nketia, J. H. Kwabena. 1962. "The Hocket Technique in African Music." *Journal of the International Folk Music Council* 14:44–52.

No Stone Unturned, with Jerry Davies and Organic Roots. 1999. "King David's Melodies: This is Augustus Pablo" and "Augustus Pablo: Vital Selections." *Big Daddy* (Summer):46–48, 63.

Okpewho, Isidore. 1992. *African Oral Literature: Backgrounds, Character, and Continuity*. Bloomington: Indiana University Press.

"On Becoming and Being a Futurist: An Interview with Wendell Bell." 2005. *Journal of Futures Studies* 10(2):113–24.

Osborne, Nigel, ed. 1987. "Listening." *Contemporary Music Review* 1, part 2. London: Harwood.

Ostrander, Greg. 1987. "Foucault's Disappearing Body." In *Panic Sex in America*, edited by Arthur Kroker and Marilouise Kroker. New York: St. Martin's.

Parisi, Luciana. 2004. *Abstract Sex: Philosophy, Bio-technology, and the Mutations of Desire*. New York: Continuum.

Pelzer, Birgit. 1993. "The Tragic Desire." *Parkett*, no. 35:66–72.

Perkins, William Eric, ed. 1996. *Droppin' Science: Critical Essays on Rap Music and Hip-Hop Culture*. Philadelphia: Temple University Press.

Phillips, Anghelen Arrington. 1982. *Jamaican Houses: A Vanishing Legacy*. Kingston, Jamaica: Stephensons Press.

Pinchbeck, Daniel. 1995. "Liquid Architecture." *Swing* 1 (1):26–27.

Porcello, Thomas. 1996. "Sonic Artistry: Music, Discourse, and Technology in the Recording Studio." Ph.D. diss., University of Texas, Austin.

Poschardt, Ulf. 1995. *DJ Culture*. London: Quartet.

Potash, Chris. 1997. *Reggae, Rasta, Revolution: Jamaican Music from Ska to Dub*. New York: Simon and Schuster.

Potter, Russell. 1994. "Black Modernism/Black Postmodernisms." *Postmodern Culture* 5(1).

———. 1995. *Spectacular Vernaculars: Hip-Hop and the Politics of Postmodernism*. Albany: State University of New York Press.

Prendergast, Mark J. 2000. *The Ambient Century: From Mahler to Trance: The Evolution of Sound in the Electronic Age*. New York: Bloomsbury.

Prete, Chris. 1998. "Scratch: The Mighty Upsetter, Part 2." *Let's Catch the Beat*, no. 16:22–59.

Radano, Ronald, and Philip V. Bohlman. 2000. *Music and the Racial Imagination.* Chicago: University of Chicago Press.

Ragland-Sullivan, Ellie. 1986. *Jacques Lacan and the Philosophy of Psychoanalysis.* Urbana: University of Illinois Press.

Ramsey, Guthrie P. 2003. *Race Music: Black Cultures from Bebop to Hip-Hop.* Berkely: University of California Press/Chicago: Center for Black Music Research.

Redhead, Steve, with Derek Wynne and Justin O'Connor. 1997. *The Clubcultures Reader.* Oxford: Blackwell.

Repsch, John. 1989. *The Legendary Joe Meek.* London: Cherry Red.

Reynolds, Simon. 1998. *Generation Ecstasy: Into the World of Techno and Rave Culture.* Boston: Little, Brown.

———. 2000. "Back to the Roots." *Wire,* no. 1999 (September):35–39.

———, and Joy Press. 1995. *The Sex Revolts: Gender, Rebellion, and Rock 'n' Roll.* Cambridge, Mass.: Harvard University Press.

Richardson, Bonham C. 1992. *The Caribbean in the Wider World, 1492–1992: A Regional Geography.* Cambridge, Mass.: Cambridge University Press.

Rose, Tricia. 1994. *Black Noise: Rap Music and Black Culture in Contemporary America.* Middletown, Conn.: Wesleyan University Press.

———. 1997. "Cultural Survivalisms and Marketplace Subversions: Black Popular Culture and Politics into the Twenty-First Century." In *Language, Rhythm and Sound: Black Popular Cultures Into the Twenty-First Century,* edited by Joseph K. Adjaye and Adrianne R. Andrews. Pittsburgh: University of Pittsburgh Press.

Ross, Andrew. 1996. "Wiggaz With Attitude (WWA)." *Artforum* (October):26, 136, 138.

———. 1998. "Mr. Reggae DJ, Meet the International Monetary Fund." *Black Renaissance* 1, no. 3 (Spring–Summer):208–32.

———, and Tricia Rose, eds. 1994. *Microphone Fiends: Youth Music and Youth Culture.* New York: Routledge.

Rouget, Gilbert. 1985. *Music and Trance: A Theory of the Relations Between Music and Possession.* Chicago: University of Chicago Press.

Rubin, Arnold. 1974. *African Accumulative Sculpture: Power and Display.* New York: Pace Gallery.

Rubin, William. 1984. *"Primitivism" in 20th Century Art: Affinity of the Tribal and the Modern.* New York: Museum of Modern Art.

Rush, Dana. 1999. "Eternal Potential: Chromolithographs in Vodunland." *African Arts* (Winter):61–75, 94–96.

Sachs, Curt. 1962. *The Wellsprings of Music.* The Hague: Martinus Nijhof.

Said, Edward. 1990. "Reflections on Exile." In *Out There: Marginalization and Contemporary Culture.* New York: New Museum of Contemporary Art.

Salamon, Jeff. 1997. "Dub and Dubber." *Artforum* (Summer):35.

Sandstrom, Boden. 2000. "Women Mix Engineers and the Power of Sound." In *Music and Gender,* edited by Pirkko Moisala and Beverley Diamond. Urbana: University of Illinois Press.

Schaefer, R. Murry. 1994. *The Soundscape: Our Changing Environment and the Tuning of the World.* Rochester, N.Y.: Destiny Books.

Schwartz, Elliott. 1973. *Electronic Music: A Listener's Guide.* New York: Praeger.

Segal, Ronald. 1995. *The Black Diaspora.* New York: Farrar, Straus and Giroux.

Selden, Raman. 1989. *Practicing Theory and Reading Literature: An Introduction.* Lexington: University of Kentucky Press.

Shapiro, Harry. 2003. *Waiting for the Man: The Story of Drugs and Popular Music.* London: Helter Skelter.

Shapiro, Peter. 1995. "Bass Invader." *Wire* (October):32–35.

———. 1999. *Drum & Bass: The Rough Guide.* New York: Penguin.

——. 2000. *Modulations: A History of Electronic Music: Throbbing Words on Sound.* New York: Caipirinha.

——. 2006. *Turn the Beat Around: The Secret History of Disco.* London: Faber and Faber.

Sharp, Chris. 1996. "Soundcheck: Macro Dub Infection Volume 2." *Wire,* no. 154 (December):60.

Shelemay, Kay Kaufman. 1998. *Let Jasmine Rain Down: Song and Remembrance Among Syrian Jews.* Chicago: University of Chicago Press.

Sinker, Mark. 1994. "Soundcheck: King Tubby & Friends: *Dub Gone Crazy,* New Age Steppers: *Massive Hits Volume One.*" *Wire,* no. 124 (June):60–61.

Sklair, Leslie. 1991. "The Culture-Ideology of Consumerism in the Third World." In *The Sociology of the Global System,* 129–169. Baltimore: Johns Hopkins University Press.

Slesin, Suzanne, with Stafford Cliff, Jack Berthelot, Martine Gaume, and Daniel Rozensztroch. 1985. *Caribbean Style.* New York: Crown.

Slobin, Mark. 1993. *Subcultural Sounds: Micromusics of the West.* Middletown, Conn.: Wesleyan University Press.

Smith, C. C. 1983a. "Lee Scratch Perry." *Reggae and African Beat* (July–August):17.

——. 1983b. "Scratch on the Edge." *Reggae and African Beat* (July–August):19.

Smith, David E. 1970. *The New Social Drug: Cultural, Medical, and Legal Perspectives on Marijuana.* Englewood Cliffs, N.J.: Prentice-Hall.

Smithies, Grant. 2001. "Mad Professor Interview." *Pulp magazine* (September). Reprinted www.obscure.co.nz/mad_professor_interview.

Snyder, Bob. 2000. *Music and Memory: An Introduction.* Cambridge, Mass.: MIT Press.

Solie, Ruth A., ed. 1995. *Musicology and Difference: Gender and Sexuality in Music Scholarship.* Berkeley and Los Angeles: University of California Press.

Solomos, John. 1989. *Race and Racism in Contemporary Britain.* Houndsmill, Basingstoke, Hampshire: Macmillan Education.

Southall, Brian, with Peter Vince and Allan Rouse. 2002. *Abbey Road.* London: Omnibus.

Spivak, Gayatri Chakravorty. 1985. "Can the Subaltern Speak? Speculations on Widow Sacrifice." *Wedge* (Winter–Spring):120–130.

Springer, Claudia. 1996. *Electronic Eros: Bodies and Desire in the Postindustrial Age.* Austin: University of Texas Press.

Steffens, Roger. 2006. "London Crawling." *The Beat,* vol. 25, no. 2:54–55.

Stern, Adam. 1998. "Sly Dunbar." *Seconds,* no. 47:72–75.

Sterne, Jonathan. 2003. *The Audible Past: Cultural Origins of Sound Reproduction.* Durham, N.C.: Duke University Press.

Stokes, Martin. 2003. "Talk and Text: Popular Music and Ethnomusicology." In *Analyzing Popular Music,* edited by Allan F. Moore. Cambridge: Cambridge University Press.

Stolzoff, Norman. 2000. *Wake the Town and Tell the People: Dancehall Culture in Jamaica.* Durham, N.C.: Duke University Press.

Tal, Kali. 1996. *Worlds of Hurt: Reading the Literatures of Trauma.* Cambridge: Cambridge University Press.

Talty, Stephen. 2003. *Mulatto America: At the Crossroads of Black and White Culture: A Social History.* New York: HarperColllins.

Tamm, Eric. 1989. *Brian Eno: His Music and the Vertical Color of Sound.* Boston: Faber and Faber.

Tannenbaum, Rob. 1992. "Remix, Rematch, Reprofit. Then Dance." *New York Times,* August 30, p. 23.

Tate, Greg. 1992. *Flyboy in the Buttermilk*. New York: Simon and Schuster.

Taylor, Crispin. 1997. "Return to the Ark." *Straight No Chaser*, no. 40 (Spring): 38–47.

Taylor, Timothy D. 1997. *Global Pop: World Music, World Markets*. New York: Routledge.

———. 2001. *Strange Sounds: Music, Technology & Culture*. New York: Routledge.

Tedeschi, Richard G., with Crystal L. Park and Lawrence G. Calhoun, eds. 1998. *Posttraumatic Growth: Positive Changes in the Aftermath of Crisis*. Mahwah, N.J.: Erlbaum.

Terrell, Tom. 1997. "Lee 'Scratch' Perry." *Seconds*, no. 44: 57–63.

Thomas, Sheree. 2000. *Dark Matter: A Century of Speculative Fiction from the African Diaspora*. New York: Aspect.

Thompson, Art. 1997. *Stompbox: A History of Guitar Fuzzes, Flangers, Phasers, Echoes & Wahs*. San Francisco, Calif.: Miller Freeman.

Thompson, Robert Farris. 1984. *Flash of the Spirit: African and Afro-American Art and Philosophy*. New York: Vintage.

———. 2005. *Tango: The Art History of Love*. New York: Pantheon.

Thompson, R. W. 1946. *Black Caribbean*. London: MacDonald.

Tingen, Paul. 2001. *Miles Beyond: The Electric Explorations of Miles Davis*. New York: Billboard Books.

Toop, David. 1984. *The Rap Attack: African Jive to New York Hip-Hop*. Boston: South End.

———. 1995. *Ocean of Sound: Aether Talk, Ambient Sound and Imaginary Worlds*. London: Serpent's Tale.

Van den Toorn, Pieter C. 1995. *Music, Politics, and the Academy*. Berkeley and Los Angeles: University of California Press.

Van der Merwe, Peter. 1989. *Origins of the Popular Style: The Antecedents of Twentieth-Century Popular Music*. Oxford: Clarendon Press.

Van Pelt, Carter. 2005. "Horsemouth." *Wax Poetics*, no. 12 (Spring):36–42.

Vincent, Rickey. 1996. *Funk: The Music, The People, and the Rhythm of the One*. New York: St. Martin's Griffin.

Walcott, Derek. 1973. *Another Life*. New York: Farrar, Straus and Giroux.

———. 1992. *The Antilles: Fragments of Epic Memory*. New York: Farrar, Straus and Giroux.

Walder, Dennis. 1998. *Post-Colonial Literatures in English: History, Language, Theory*. Oxford: Blackwell.

Wallis, Roger, and Krister Malm. 1984. *Big Sounds from Small Peoples: The Music Industry in Small Countries*. London: Constable.

———. 1992. *Media Policy and Music Activity*. London: Routledge.

Waterman, Christopher. 1990. *Juju: A Social History and Ethnography of an African Popular Music*. Chicago: University of Chicago Press.

Waterman, Richard. 1952. "African Influence in the Americas." In *Acculturation in the Americas*, edited by Sol Tax, 2:207–18. Chicago: University of Chicago Press.

Waters, Anita. 1985. *Race, Class, and Political Symbols: Rastafari and Reggae in Jamaican Politics*. New Brunswick, N.J.: Transaction.

Waxer, Lise. 2001. "Record Grooves and Salsa Dance Moves: The Viejoteca Phenomenon in Cali, Colombia." *Popular Music* 20, no. 2 (January):61–81.

Weber, Tom. 1992. *Reggae Island: Jamaican Music in the Digital Age*. Kingston, Jamaica: Kingston Publishers.

Wendt, Doug. 1983. "Upsetter Talking." *Reggae and African Beat* (July–August):17.

White, Garth. 1982. *The Development of Jamaican Popular Music, with Special Reference to the Music of Bob Marley*. Kingston: African-Caribbean Institute of Jamaica.

White, Hayden. 1987. *The Content of the Form: Narrative Discourse and Historical Representation*. Baltimore: Johns Hopkins University Press.

White, Paul. 1999. *The Sound On Sound Book of Creative Recording: Effects and Processors*. London: Sanctuary.

White, Timothy. 1983. *Catch A Fire: The Life of Bob Marley*. New York: Holt.

———. 1994. *The Nearest Faraway Place: Brian Wilson, The Beach Boys, and the Southern California Experience*. New York: Holt.

Whiteley, Sheila. 1992. *The Space Between the Notes: Rock and the Counter-Culture*. New York: Routledge.

Whitmont, Edward. 1969. *The Symbolic Quest: Basic Concepts of Analytical Psychology*. Princeton, N.J.: Princeton University Press.

Williams, Raymond. 1961. *The Long Revolution*. New York: Columbia University Press.

Williams, Richard. 1972. *Out of His Head: The Sound of Phil Spector*. New York: Outerbridge and Lazard.

Wilson-Tagoe, Nana. 1998. *Historical Thought and Literary Representation in West Indian Literature*. Gainesville: University of Florida Press.

Witmer, Robert. 1987. "'Local' and 'Foreign': The Popular Culture of Kingston, Jamaica, before Ska, Rock Steady, and Reggae." *Latin American Music Review* 8 (Spring–Summer):1–25.

———. 1989. "A History of Kingston's Popular Music Culture: Neo-Colonialism to Nationalism." *Jamaica Journal* 22(1):11–18.

Woods, Lebbeus. 1993. "Freespace and the Tyranny of Types." In *The End of Architecture? Documents and Manifestos*, edited by Peter Noever. Munich: Prestel-Verlag.

Woram, John M. 1982. *The Recording Studio Handbook*. Plainview: ELAR.

Yinger, J. Martin. 1982. *Countercultures: The Promise and the Peril of a World Turned Upside Down*. New York: Free Press.

Zak, Albin J. 2001. *The Poetics of Rock: Cutting Tracks, Making Records*. Berkeley and Los Angeles: University of California Press.

Zamora, Lois Parkinson, and Wendy B. Faris, eds. 1995. *Magical Realism: Theory, History, Community*. Durham, N.C.: Duke University Press.

Internet Sources

www.afrofuturism.net

www.emedicine.com/med/topic3407.htm.

"An Unfinished Melody . . . Tribute to Augustus Pablo." In *Disciples Boom-Shacka-Lacka Reggae and Dub Site*. http:freespace.virgin.net/russell.bell-brown/pablo2htm.

Discography

Aphex Twin. 1993. *Selected Ambient Works 85–92*. R & S 6002220.

Armstrong, Louis. 1988. *The Hot Fives, Volume One*. Columbia CJT 44049.

Bowie, David. 1977. *Heroes*. Rykodisc RCD 10143.

Burning Spear. 1975. *Marcus Garvey*. Island ILPS 9377.

Eno, Brian. 1975. *Another Green World*. Editions EG EGCD 21.

———. 1983. *Apollo*. Editions EG Eno 5.

Ghetto Slam. 2000. Jamdown JD 40027.

Grandmaster Flash. 2002. *The Official Adventures of Grandmaster Flash*. Strut STRUTCD 011.

Microstoria. 1995. *Init Ding*. Mille Plateux/Thrill Jockey 031.

Master Drummers of Dagbon. 1992. Rounder CD 5016.
Oval. 1996. *94 Diskont.* Thrill Jockey 36.
Ragga Ragga Ragga, Volume 12. 1998. Greensleeves 250.
Rhythms of Life, Songs of Wisdom: Akan Music from Ghana, West Africa. 1995.
    Smithsonian Folkways SF CD 40463.
Shades of Hudson. 1997. VP VPCD 2053.
Ska Boogie: Jamaican R&B, The Dawn of Ska. 1993. Sequel NEX CD 254.
Sly and the Family Stone. 1971. *There's a Riot Goin' On.* Epic EK 30986.
———. 1973. *Fresh.* Epic 32134.
Stockhausen, Karlheinz. 1966. *Hymnen.* Deutsche Grammophon 2707 039.
———. 1968. *Kurzwellen.* Deutsche Grammophon 139 451–2.
Talking Heads. 1980. *Remain in Light.* Sire 6095–2.
Tosh, Peter. 1976. *Legalize It.* Columbia PCT 34253.
Tougher Than Tough: The Story of Jamaican Music. 1993. Mango 162 539 935–2.
U2. 1987. *The Joshua Tree.* Island 90581–1.
Wiser Dread. 1981. Nighthawk 301.

Film and Video

Modulations. 1998. Directed by Lee Iara. Cipirinha Productions.
Roots, Rock, Reggae. 1988. Directed by Jeremy Marre. Shanachie Films 1202.

Interviews

Clive Austen. June 2002, London, England.
Victor Axelrod (p.k.a. Ticklah). May 2003, New York City (via telephone).
Aston "Familyman" Barrett. November 2003, New Haven, Connecticut.
Steve Barrow. May 2004, Paris, France.
Stefan Betke (p.k.a. Pole). June 2002, London, England.
Errol Brown. February 2006, Kingston, Jamaica (via telephone).
Overton H. "Scientist" Brown. September 2001, Los Angeles, California; November 2001, Seattle, Washington.
Susan Cadogan. March 2002, Kingston, Jamaica.
Michael "Mikey Dread" Campbell. August 2001, Coral Springs, Florida; November 2001, Seattle, Washington.
Clive Chin. May 1998, March 1999, July 2000, Queens, New York.
Rob Connelly. May 2003, Northampton, Massachusetts (via telephone).
Ryan Cowan. May 2003, New Haven, Connecticut.
Lowell "Sly" Dunbar. March 2002, Kingston, Jamaica.
Clinton Fearon. November 2001, Seattle, Washington.
Neil "Mad Professor" Fraser. May 2000, Hoboken, New Jersey; June 2002, London, England.
George "Fully" Fullwood. November 2001, Seattle, Washington.
Jah Grant. May 1999, New York City.
Tim Haslett. May 2001, Cambridge, Massachusetts (via telephone).
Dave Hendley. June 2002, Whitstable, England.
Paul "Computer Paul" Henton. March 2002, Kingston, Jamaica.
Lloyd "King Jammy" James. June 2000, Kingston, Jamaica.
Clive Jeffery. March 2002, Kingston, Jamaica.
Edward "Bunny" Lee. March 2002, Kingston, Jamaica.
Larry Marshall. June 2000, Kingston, Jamaica.
Jah Mike. June 2000, Kingston, Jamaica.
Sylvan Morris. May 2000, Kingston, Jamaica.

Lee "Scratch" Perry. November 2001, New Haven, Connecticut.
Winston Riley. June 2000, Kingston, Jamaica.
Max Romeo. June 2000, Kingston, Jamaica.
Robbie Shakespeare. March 2002, Kingston, Jamaica.
Adrian Sherwood. November 2001, Seattle, Washington.
Dudley Sibley. May 2000, Kingston, Jamaica.
Philip Smart. June 2003, Freeport, New York.
Bobby Vicious. February, 2002, Hartford, Connecticut.

Index of Songs and Recordings

Index of General Subjects

Auralux (record label), 25
Austen, Clive, 226
Australia, 49
Automatic (pressing plant), 105
Ayler, Albert, 40

"Bacteria in Dub" (event), 254
Bailey, Gil, 9
Bailey, Noel "Sowell," 134
Baker, Houston, 258
Ball, Philip, 24
Bambaataa, Afrika, 246–47
Banton, Buju, 193
Banton, Pato, 230
Baraka, Amiri, 41
Barbados, 231
Barker, Dave, 147
Barnes, Lloyd "Bullwackies," 9, 162, 237, 238, 240–41
Barrett, Aston "Family Man," 33, 58–59, 103, 104–5, 134, 145, 146, 147, 149
Barrett, Carlton "Carlie," 33, 58, 72, 103–4, 135, 145, 147, 171–72, 234
Barrow, Steve, 25, 46, 111, 155, 172, 218, 222, 226, 238, 254, 257
Barthes, Roland, 69
Basic Channel (record label), 237, 240
Bassies, the, 98
Baucom, Ian, 239
BBC, the, 231
Beach Boys, the, 37
Beastie Boys, the 231
Beatles, the, 24, 37, 45, 84, 144
bebop, 61, 251
Becker, Jimmy, 74
Beckford, Ewart. See U-Roy
Beenie Man, 193
Bell, William, 156–57, 232
Bennett, "Deadly" Headley, 228
Bennett, Val, 29, 143
Berklee College of Music, 8
Berlin, 240
Berry, Chuck, 28
Betke, Stefan, 236–37
Beverly's All Stars, 47
Beverly's Studio, 47
Bible, the, 152, 166
Big Joe and Fay, 61
Big Youth, 55, 216, 224
Bilby, Kenneth, 25, 27, 44
Birmingham, 223
Bishop, Maurice, 15
Black Ark (studio), 10, 13, 19, 35, 142, 159–60,

211; creation of, 150–52; decline of, 161, 188; musical style, 202; photos, 178, 179; musicians associated with, 62; sound of, 8, 74, 84, 100, 120, 155, 166, 171, 229, 232, 241; technology at, 153–54
Black Atlantic, The (book), 24, 252
Black Harmony (sound system), 86
Black Power movement, 15
Black Uhuru, 11, 58, 63, 70, 84, 128, 134, 136, 228
Blackman, Paul, 65
"blackness," 33, 35, 213, 217, 244, 251
Blackwell, Chris, 102, 104, 105, 153, 164
Blake, Christopher "Sky Juice," 134
blaxploitation, 149–50, 239
Blood & Fire (record label), 25
Bloom, Sandra, 204
blues, 28, 76, 119, 149, 201, 208, 244
Bobby Vicious, 63, 82, 109, 111, 189, 191, 216
Bomb Squad, 194, 248
Booker T. and the MGs, 147
Booms, James, 154–55
Boone, Pat, 28
Boothe, Ken, 118
Borges, Jorge Luis, 203
Boston, 8
Bovell, Dennis "Blackbeard," 70, 227, 231–33; photo, 184
Bradley, Lloyd, 25, 33, 36, 109, 150, 170, 223
Brad's Record Shack, 9
Bradshaw, Sonny, 29
Brathwaite, Kamau, 215
breakbeats, 3, 233, 234, 235, 245, 247
Brevett, Tony, 67
Brigadier Jerry, 87, 88, 216
Bright Earth: Art and the Invention of Color (book), 24
Bristol, 223, 235
Britz, Chuck, 37
Brixton, 221
Broadber, Erna, 33
Broggs, Peter, 132
Bronx, the, 9, 240
Brooklyn, 9
Brown, Charles, 28
Brown, Cleveland "Clevie," 134, 188
Brown, Dennis, 5, 11, 54, 119, 120
Brown, Errol, 60, 70, 104–5, 139, 242
Brown, Glen, 33, 58, 117
Brown, Hux, 143
Brown, James, 28, 145, 147, 244
Brown, Overton H. "Scientist." See Scientist

Culture, 11, 17, 157
Cure, the, 228
Cybernetic Culture Research Unit (CCRU), 250, 254
Czukay, Holger, 253

Dabydeen, David, 217–18
Dadaists, 207
Daley, Lloyd "Matador," 42
Dalton, Peter, 46, 172
dancehall music, 11–12, 62, 79, 131, 134–35, 137, 172, 187–88, 190–91, 240. *See also* ragga
dancehalls, 4–5, 42, 146; in New York, 12; role in addressing social issues, 216; role in the creation of dub, 63–64, 86, 88, 110, 161, 243; role in the dissemination of Rastafari, 15; sound quality of music in, 103, 104, 105, 131, 201, 238. *See also* sound systems
Daniel, Oliver, 37
Darwen, Norman, 231
Davidowsky, Mario, 39
Davis, Carlton "Santa," 33–34, 114–15, 128, 135
Davis, Miles, 3, 37, 208, 209, 242
Davis, Ronnie, 129
Davis, Stephen, 25, 29, 31, 109, 200
Davis, Tyrone, 156, 157
Dawes, Kwame, 199, 218–19, 251
deejaying, 70, 220, 232; as component of dub, 62, 63, 68–69, 86–87, 90, 189, 201, 215–16, 223; as component of other musics, 191, 193–94, 234, 245; by specific deejays, 88, 109; comparison with psychedelia, 83–84; rise of, 55–56, 197, 251. *See also* sound systems
Dekker, Desmond, 221
Delahaye, Junior, 241
Delany, Samuel, 208
Deleuze, Gilles, 254
DelNaja, Robert, 227
Dennis, Rudolph "Garth," 7
Depeche Mode, 228
Detroit, 209, 237
D'Haen, Theo, 204, 215
diaspora, 20, 199, 207, 212, 255. *See also* African diaspora
"Diaspora, Utopia and the Critique of Capitalism" (essay), 252
Diddley, Bo, 28, 45
Dillinger, 55, 216
disco, 3, 32, 85, 115, 244–45

Dixon, Bobby "Digital," 188
DJ Kool Herc, 45, 246, 247
DJ Red Alert, 248
DJ Spooky, 41, 249–50, 254, 255
Dodd, Clement "Coxsone," 89, 97–98, 99, 112, 117, 223; as producer, 29, 30, 33, 34, 49, 50–51, 96, 100–102, 132, 133, 163, 213; as sound system operator, 28, 29, 42, 109, 142; as studio owner, 46, 50; collaboration with Lee "Scratch" Perry, 141–43, 162; photo, 173. *See also* Sir Coxsone's Downbeat; Studio One
Doncaster, 223
Donovan, Kevin, 247
Donovan, Ras, 238
Dorsey, Lee, 156, 157
Dowd, Tom, 37
Doyle, Peter, 138
Dr. Alimantado, 55, 226
"Dr. Satan's Echo Chamber" (essay), 250
Dread, Junior, 154
Dread, Mikey. *See* Mikey Dread
Drifters, the, 144
drum and bass: as aesthetic, 36, 103, 104, 105, 149, 158, 167, 194, 236, 247; as components of dub, 62, 77, 87, 118, 119, 120, 121, 126, 128, 130, 152, 153, 156, 165, 206; as distinct genre, 57–61, 72, 102, 123, 148, 233–34, 238, 257; influence on modern electronic music, 230, 237; musicians associated with, 145, 171. *See also* jungle music
Drummond, Don, 30, 35, 41, 166
dub: aesthetics of, 77–80; as African-derived music, 63, 214; as communal art form, 88–89, 214–15; as electronic music, 38–41; as product of the African diaspora, 198–99, 205–6; as reflective of Jamaican history, 197–202, 204–8, 218; comparison to hip-hop, 20, 61, 245–48; comparison to psychedelia, 82–85; comparison to ragga, 193–94; compositional strategies of, 52–55, 64–76, 197–98; decline of, 188–89; definition of, 61–64, 127; economics of, 89–93; forerunners of, 26–34, 36–38, 57–61; influence on global popular music, 2, 3, 10, 20, 41, 221, 225–27, 255–60; influence on scholarship, 249–55; intellectual property issues in, 90–91, 189; neo-dub, 13, 224, 225, 227–43, 249; relationship to reggae, 34, 63, 140, 212, 224, 243–44; relationship to ganja, 80–82; role of the deejay, 55–56, 62, 63, 68–69, 86–87, 90, 189, 201, 215–16, 223; role of

the producer, 46–49; role of the sound system, 42–44, 51–55, 63–64, 85–89, 110, 161, 243. *See also* reggae

Dub Band, the, 231

"Dub History" (essay), 253

dub plates, 51–55, 61, 64, 89, 105, 108, 109, 110, 112, 113, 125

dub poets, 62, 70, 231

Dub Specialist, 100, 101. *See also* Dodd, Clement "Coxsone"

Dub Syndicate, 229

dubstep, 239

Duffus, Shenley, 149

Duhaney Park, 50, 169, 188; photo, 177

Dunbar, Lowell "Sly," 34, 72, 128, 135, 136, 171, 234; comments and interviews, 51, 58, 61, 62, 70, 81, 84–85, 122, 136, 155, 159, 169; photo, 178. *See also* Sly & Robbie

Dunkley, Errol, 231

Dunrobin High School, 124

Dylan, Bob, 144

Dynamic Studio, 10, 96, 105, 108, 143, 151, 170; music recorded at, 104, 116, 123, 147, 148; photos, 173, 174; technology at, 49, 113–14, 123, 170

Dynamics, the, 47

Earth, Wind and Fire, 208

Eastwood, Jacky, 42

Eccles, Clancy, 47, 143, 164, 165

Echo Minott, 128

Eckstine, Billy, 28

ecstatic contemplation, 200, 202

Edison, Thomas, 36

Edwards, Vincent "King," 42, 142

Edwards, Winston, 228

Eek-A-Mouse, 11

Egypt, 208, 209

El Salvador, 186

El Toro (sound system), 127

Electric Lady (studio), 37

Electro-Harmonix (sound processor manufacturer), 153

electronic music, 3, 2, 8, 19, 38–41, 92, 209, 236, 238, 241, 249, 250

electronica, 45, 85, 92, 162, 221, 227, 233–39, 242, 243, 254, 258

Ellington, Duke, 35

Ellis, Alton, 167

Ellison, Ralph, 92, 251

Emerick, Geoff, 37

Emerman, Mack, 113

EMI (record label), 37, 222

Emperor Faith (sound system), 53, 86, 109

England. *See* United Kingdom

Eno, Brian, 3, 80, 249

Erlich, Luke, 72, 196

Erlmann, Veit, 20, 207

Ernestus, Mark, 236, 237–38

Eshun, Kodwo, 41, 245, 253, 254, 255

Ethiopia, 15, 199, 217

Etu (folk genre), 26

Everett, Walter, 24

"Excursion on the Version" (radio segment), 226

experimental music, 2–3, 19, 40–41, 75, 92, 209, 233, 236, 249, 250

Faith, George, 84, 156–57

Fanon, Frantz, 15, 256

Faris, Wendy, 203

Fats Domino, 143

Fearon, Clinton, 62, 101

Federal (studio), 49, 50, 54, 71, 105

Felman, Shoshana, 205

"feminization" of song form, 79–80

Fender bass, 32

Flesh and Bones, 170

Floyd, Eddie, 147

"flying cymbal" (drumming pattern), 32, 114–15, 119, 120, 128

Foreman, George, 68

Fort Lauderdale, 113

Fowler, Robert, 215

France, 227

Francis, Squingine "Squingy," 188

Frankie Knuckles, 220

Fraser, Neil "Mad Professor." *See* Mad Professor

Frater, Eric, 98

Frazier, Joe, 68

Freeport, 125

Frere-Jones, Sasha, 202

Full Experience, 158

Fulwood, George "Fully," 33, 47, 58, 59

funk, 61, 63, 193, 208, 241, 244–45, 246, 247

Futurists, 207

Gabbard, Krin, 207

Gabriel, Walda, 238

Gainsbourg, Serge, 227

Gaisberg, Fred, 36

ganja, 5, 16, 17–18, 31, 35, 80–82, 120, 160, 186–87, 193, 223, 224

García Márquez, Gabriel, 203

Gardiner, Boris, 33, 58, 97

Garnett, Bill, 49–50, 102, 135, 163, 169
Garvey, Marcus, 5, 15, 16, 116
Gatherers, the, 149
Gaylads, the, 132, 141
Gebreyesus, Fikre, 217
General Echo, 167
George, Nelson, 243
Germany, 235–38, 239
Ghana, 197, 199
Giant (sound system), 42
Gibbs, Joe, 5, 33, 74, 143, 169–71, 172, 188, 194, 216. *See also* Joe Gibbs's Studio
Gikandi, Simon, 215
Gillespie, Dizzy, 30
Gilroy, Paul, 24, 41–42, 89, 205, 207, 239, 251–52, 255, 256
Gladiators, the, 62, 99, 101
Glass, Philip, 39
Gnawa (Moroccan folk genre), 241
Gold Star (studios), 37
Goldie, 233
Gombe (folk genre), 26
Goodall, Graeme, 49, 50, 53, 54, 71, 96
Goode, Erich, 80
Gordon, Ken "Fatman," 223
Gordon, Vin, 172
gospel music, 28, 244
Graham, "Crucial" Bunny "Tom Tom," 135, 136
Graham, Leo, 87–88, 148, 151, 152–53, 154
Grajeda, Tony, 79
Grandmaster Flash, 45
Grant, Eddy, 227
Grateful Dead, the, 83
Gray, Noel, 188
Greensleeves (record label), 134, 139
Gregory, Tony, 164
Griffiths, Albert, 101
grime, 239
Guattari, Felix, 254
Guy Called Gerald, A, 233, 234
Guyana, 229

Haagsman, Jacob, 235, 238, 239
Haiti, 26, 44
Half Pint, 128
Hamilton, Anthony "Soljie," 135, 136
Hancock, Herbie, 208, 241
hand drums, 28
Haraway, Donna, 254
Harbour View, 124, 163
Harder They Come, The (film), 102
Harned, Grover C. "Jeep," 113

Harriott, Derrick, 47, 164, 169
Harriott, Joe, 41
Harry J Studio, 10, 19, 50, 95, 102, 104, 105–6, 164; photo, 174
Harvard Stadium, 8
Hayes, George "Buddy," 7
Hayes, Isaac, 150
Hayward, Philip, 209–10
HCF (studio), 125
Heartbeat (record label), 25, 132
Henderson, Richard, 160
Hendley, Dave, 11, 25; comments about the Black Ark, 151, 160, 161; comments about King Tubby's studio, 112, 117; comments about reggae in Jamaica, 47–48, 83; comments about reggae in the U.K., 6, 222, 223, 224, 225–26
Hendrix, Jimi, 37, 45, 83, 208. *See also* Jimi Hendrix Experience, the
Henri, Pierre, 38, 39
Henton, "Computer Paul." *See* Computer Paul
Henzell, Perry, 1, 102
Heptones, the, 13, 55, 137, 155
Herrera, Juan, 140
Heywood, Winston, 155
Hibbert, Toots, 141. *See also* Toots and the Maytals
Hicks, Michael, 84
highlife, 30
hip-hop, 2, 238, 240, 258; comparison to dub and ragga, 20, 61, 194, 245, 247–48; history of, 3, 29, 244–46; influence on modern electronic music, 85, 193, 229, 233–35, 236, 239, 247, 249; scholarship on, 41, 250
Hiroshima, 204
Hit Run (record label), 228
Hoffman, Katherine, 207
Hollywood, 36, 37
Holness, Winston "Niney the Observer," 89, 115, 143, 165
Holocaust, the, 204, 205
Holt, Errol "Flabba," 33, 58, 131, 134
Homiak, John, 253
Hoo-Kim, Ernest, 5, 10, 135, 136
Hoo-Kim, Joseph "Jo-Jo," 5, 10, 135
house music, 2, 3, 233, 237, 238, 239
Houston, Cissy, 164
Houston, Thelma, 244
Houston, Whitney, 241
Hudson, Clive, 9
Hudson, Keith, 59, 225

Hugh, Sang, 16
Hunt, Clive "Lizard," 170
Hynes Auditorium, 8

Illbient movement, 249
Impact All-Stars, the, 47
Impressions, the, 225–26
Indian classical music, 241
industrial music, 227
Innocence, 220
Inspirations, the, 143, 153
Institute of Contemporary Art, 237
Intelligent Jungalist, 234
International Monetary Fund, 187
Irie, Nolan, 230
Irigaray, Luce, 254
Iron, Devon, 154, 158
Iron Butterfly, 83
I-Roy, 55, 62, 68, 111, 231
Isaacs, Gregory, 5, 11
Island (record label), 60, 102–3, 104, 123, 153,
    161, 164, 170, 222, 231, 242
I-Tones, the, 8

Jackson, Carlton, 154
Jackson, Clifton, 143
Jackson, Jackie, 31, 32, 143
Jackson, Michael, 45
Jackson, Millie, 154
Jackson, Vivian "Yabby You." See Yabby You
JAD Records, 164
Jafa, Arthur, 205
Jagger, Mick, 241
Jah Love (sound system), 87, 88
Jah Shaka, 223, 227, 230
Jah Walton, 238
Jah Wobble, 226
Jah Woosh, 69, 80
Jamaica: African legacy in, 26–27; as re-
    flected in its music, 23, 30, 31, 190, 192,
    193, 197–98, 204, 206, 256; copyright is-
    sues in, 90–92; culture in, 41, 103, 216,
    219, 250; decline of dub in, 188–89; de-
    cline of reggae in, 185–88; development
    of ragga in, 188; development of reggae
    in, 31–34; development of rock steady in,
    30–31; development of ska in, 29–30;
    drugs in, 17–18, 81, 186–87, 193; early mu-
    sical developments in, 26–28; history of,
    14, 26, 186–87, 207; images of Africa in,
    199; influence on global popular music,
    1–2, 4–7, 21, 24, 38, 217, 221, 259; musical
    legacy of, 34, 40; political struggles in,

10, 11–12, 31, 109; Rastafari influence in,
    15–17, 187; relationship to the United
    Kingdom, 26, 30, 35, 44; relationship to
    the United States, 14, 17, 18, 36, 44, 186,
    213; "roots" era in, 21, 35, 95, 192, 193,
    207, 220. See also Kingston
Jamaica Technical High School, 96
Jamaican Broadcasting Corporation (JBC),
    4, 49
Jamaican Labour Party (JLP), 10, 109, 186,
    240
Jamaican Recording Studio. See Studio One
Jamerson, James, 146, 149, 150
James, C. L. R., 15
James, Lloyd "King Jammy." See King
    Jammy
Jameson, Frederic, 90, 204
Jamiroquai, 231
Japan, 79
Jarrett, Wayne, 237, 241
jazz, 19, 30, 35, 50, 251, 255; avant-garde, 40–
    41; comparison to dub, 8, 57, 61, 68, 217;
    history of, 3, 37, 208–9, 245; in Jamaica,
    28, 188, 189; influence on dub, 55, 74, 104,
    117, 158; influence on other musics, 34,
    39, 235; interaction with Jamaican music,
    70, 123, 151, 193; interaction with other
    musics, 241, 242, 244, 247; scholarship
    on, 92, 207
Jefferson Airplane, 83
Jenkinson, Tom, 239
Jerry, Jah, 29
Jets, the, 31
Jimi Hendrix Experience, the, 84, 144
Joe Gibbs's Studio, 10, 19, 50, 70, 163, 169,
    170, 189; photo, 181
Johnson, Harry, 10, 102, 164
Johnson, Linton Kwesi, 11, 62, 70, 231, 232–33
Johnson, Phil, 225, 235
Johnson, Roydel, 156
Johnson, Sir J. J., 143
Johnson, Wycliffe "Steely," 134, 188
Jones, Hedley, 42
Jones Town, 234
Jordan, Joel, 260
Jordan, Louis, 28
jungle music, 2, 122, 233–34, 235, 239. See also
    drum and bass
Juniper, Andrew, 79

Kantner, Paul, 83–84
Katz, David, 25, 31, 141, 147, 150–51, 159, 190,
    216, 229

Kawongolo, Kawo, 159, 161
Kelly, Pat, 126–27, 170
Kendal, 141
Kenner, Rob, 42
Kete (folk drumming genre), 27
Khouri, Ken, 27, 49
King Attorney (sound system), 86
King, Bertie, 29
King Edwards the Giant (sound system), 142
King Jammy, 19, 132, 133, 134, 189, 225, 227, 243; comments and interviews, 78, 113, 114, 115, 117, 119, 127, 128, 129, 131, 190; photos, 175, 181; relationship with King Tubby, 12, 124, 126–31; works by, 76, 84, 129–31, 138, 188
King Jammy's Studio, 12–13
King Stitt, 55
King Tubby, 43, 196; as major figure in dub, 2, 8, 35, 38, 61, 84, 89, 94, 108–33, 210, 216, 217, 227, 234, 243, 257; attitude toward ganja, 81, 82; collaboration with Augustus Pablo, 33, 134, 166; collaboration with Bunny Lee, 33, 52, 56, 134; collaboration with Lee "Scratch" Perry, 148–50, 159; comparisons with, 59, 138, 140, 152, 167, 172, 232, 248, 155–56, 160; death of, 11, 12, 188–89; influence on King Jammy, 12–13, 124, 126–29; influence on others, 230, 237, 241; influence on "Prince" Philip Smart, 124–26, 185; influence on Scientist, 8, 132–33; innovations by, 9, 51, 52, 56, 57, 60, 74, 75–76, 165; photos, 175, 182; style of, 83, 206, 224; works by, 65–66, 72–73, 74, 87–88, 103–4, 118–23
King Tubby's Home Town Hi Fi (sound system), 55, 56, 86, 108–11
King Tubby's Studio, 10, 11, 12–13, 19, 93, 106, 112–18, 131, 134, 137, 151, 155, 158, 188, 189; photo, 175
Kingston, 68, 88, 124, 125, 127, 141, 211, 221; as birthplace, 95, 108, 112, 126, 132, 163, 165; as location of musical innovations, 2, 18, 44, 225, 246; audiences in, 28, 42; images of, 210; musicians in, 131, 134; political rivalries of, 109, 240; Rastafari in, 15; social conditions in, 14, 27, 132, 190; sound systems of, 5, 42, 108–9, 111, 234; studios in, 10, 12–13, 46, 50, 56, 58, 140, 163, 169, 188; violence in, 10–11, 43, 142, 186, 187, 206, 239
Kingston College, 166
Kingston Technical, 127

Kofi, 230
Koki, 238
Kool and the Gang, 244
Kraftwerk, 236
Kramer, Eddie, 37
Kumina (Afro-Jamaican liturgical genre), 26–27, 35

Lamont, Eric "Bingy Bunny," 134, 167–68, 170
lancer, 27
Lastra, James, 24, 212, 256
Laswell, Bill, 240, 241–43
Lawes, Henry "Junjo," 5, 33, 134, 137, 188
Lee, Byron, 10, 32, 49, 96, 113
Lee, Bunny, 127, 128, 132, 225; as major figure in dub, 5, 33, 89, 112–13, 114–15, 116–17, 119, 120, 125, 134, 143, 161, 164, 165, 170, 196, 229, 235; comments and interviews, 50–51, 52, 54, 56, 59, 75, 78, 102, 110, 114, 115, 121, 122, 143, 163, 169; photo, 177; works by, 104, 125, 137, 148
Legge, Walter, 36
Lesser, Beth, 12, 127
Letts, Don, 226
Levine, Larry, 37
Levy, Barrington, 134
Levy, Douglas, 241
Lewis, Alva, 145
Lewis, George, 40
Lewis, Hopeton, 31
Lewis, Peter and Paul, 154
"lickshot," 201
Lindt, Brian, 168
Lingala, 159
Little Axe, 229
Little Richard, 28, 35
Little Walter, 45
Liverpool, 223
Living Color, 228
"Living Memory and the Slave Sublime" (essay), 205
Livingstone, Bunny "Wailer." See Wailer, Bunny
LKJ Records, 231
Lloyd Coxsone (sound system), 223
London, 161, 225, 228, 231, 232, 236, 254; Jamaican music in, 6, 221, 222, 223, 224; musical innovations in, 37, 45; photo, 183
Lone Ranger, 101
Lord Kelly (sound system), 109, 127
Love Joys, the, 241
lover's rock, 5, 232
LTJ Bukem, 233, 234

Motown (record label), 28, 34, 146, 258
Motta, Stanley, 27, 49
MoWax (record label), 235
Mundell, Hugh, 155
Murray, Albert, 251
Murvin, Junior, 151, 153, 154, 155, 158, 226
Music Centers, Inc. (MCI), 113
Musical Youth, 227
musique concrète, 38, 39, 75, 249
Musitronics, 153
Mutabaruka, 62
Mwandishi, 208
Myton, Cedric, 156

Nagasaki, 204
Nash, Johnny, 164
Nelson, Alondra, 213
New Age Steppers, 229
New Jersey, 153
New Orleans, 28, 30, 160
New York City, 7, 10, 40, 161, 221, 240; Ja-
    maican music in, 9, 12, 246; other musics
    in, 3, 37, 45, 220, 240–41, 243–45, 246–
    47, 249
New York Dolls, the, 225
Nicaragua, 186
Nichols, Jeb Loy, 232
Nigeria, 92
Ninja Tune (record label), 235
Nordwestdeutscher Rundfunk (studio), 40
Notting Hill Carnival, 222
Nottingham, 223
Now Generation, 170
Nyabinghi (Rastafarian liturgical genre), 27,
    103, 145, 146, 159, 166, 200, 213

Obeah, 102, 142, 160, 212
Ohio Players, the, 244
Olympic Studios, 37
One People, 8
"one-drop" (drumming pattern), 31, 32, 76,
    87, 99, 103, 115, 126, 130, 135, 193, 238
On-U Sound, 228, 229
oral culture, 18, 22, 70, 90, 91, 93, 204, 214,
    217, 250–51, 253
Orb, the, 231
Orientalism, 43
Osaka, 40
Osbourne, Brad, 125
Osbourne, Johnny, 133, 134

Pablo, Augustus, 151, 165–67; as major fig-
    ure in dub, 9, 58, 84, 117, 134, 196, 230;

collaboration with King Tubby, 33; collab-
oration with Lee "Scratch" Perry, 13; com-
ments and interviews, [...], 220; friend-
ship with "Prince" Philip Smart, 124, 125;
photo, 180; works by, 16, 56–57, 95, 106,
122–23, 155, 159, 166–67, 171, 172, 189, 228
Palmer, Robert, 155
palo (Afro-Cuban liturgical genre), 26
Pama (record label), 228
Parade, the, 10, 50, 163
Paris, 40, 253
Parisi, Luciana, 254–55
Parker, Charlie, 30
Parks, Lloyd, 33, 58, 167
Parliament, 208, 209
Patterson, Seeco, 103
patwa, 7, 159, 194, 212, 215, 233
Paul, Les, 37, 38
Peego (engineer), 188
People Funny Boy (book), 141
People's National Party (PNP), 10, 14, 109,
    186, 240
Perry, Lee "Scratch," 8, 196; as major figure
    in dub, 1, 2, 9, 19, 33, 34–35, 38, 69, 93,
    94, 112, 140–62, 164, 165, 217, 219, 227; as
    studio owner, 10, 13, 62, 150–51, 153–55,
    159–61, 188; attitude toward ganja, 82;
    collaboration with Adrian Sherwood,
    228, 229; collaboration with Augustus
    Pablo, 166; collaboration with Bob Mar-
    ley and the Wailers, 56, 99, 103, 144–46;
    collaboration with Mad Professor, 230–
    31; comments and interviews, 185, 201,
    211; comparisons with, 106, 115, 120, 168,
    169, 171, 230, 232, 248; influence on oth-
    ers, 237, 241; life abroad, 13, 188, 189, 206,
    225; mental state of, 160–61, 212; musical
    innovations by, 74, 76, 80, 100; photo,
    178; sound of, 202; works by, 17, 33, 75,
    84, 87, 137, 141–50, 151–54, 156–59, 210,
    226, 253. *See also* Black Ark
Pete, Jamaal, 101
Peter Chemist, 41, 160
Perez, Ras, 238
Petty, Norman, 38
Phantom (engineer), 188
Philips, Sam, 38
Philpott, George, 170
Photek, 233, 234, 239
Pickett, Wilson, 156, 157
Pinkney, Dwight, 134
Pitterson, Karl, 59, 73–74, 105, 108, 123, 125,
    170, 242

Pocomania (folk genre), 26–27, 142
Pole, 236–37, 238
Portishead, 235
possession, 200–201, 241, 248
"Post-Nationalist Geographies" (essay), 221, 250
Pottinger, Sonia, 164
Presley, Elvis, 28, 186
Pressure Sounds (record label), 25
Price, Billy, 164
Prince Alla, 126
Prince Buster, 75, 94, 142, 190, 212, 230, 240
Prince Far I, 16, 225, 228
Prince Jammy. *See* King Jammy
Prince Jazzbo, 55, 152, 158
Prince Patrick (sound system), 127
Professionals, the, 169, 171
Professor, 41
Prophet, Michael, 134, 230
Prophets, the, 121, 122
Protestant hymns, 27, 156
Prysock, Arthur, 28
psychedelia, 8, 18, 34, 80, 82–85, 128, 157, 200, 202, 209, 224, 235, 242
Public Enemy, 194, 248
Public Image, Ltd., 226
punk music, 3, 222, 225–26, 228, 233, 258

quadrille, 27
Queens, 9

Radio Jamaica Rediffusion (RJR), 49, 50
Radio London, 226
Radiodiffusion Française (studio), 40
ragga, 13, 17, 29, 62, 172, 187–88, 190–91, 195, 199, 247. *See also* dancehall music
Ramsey, Guthrie P., 23
Randy's Impact (record label), 168. *See also* Randy's Studio
Randy's Studio, 47, 50, 53, 62, 125, 143; Errol "Errol T." Thompson's association with, 10, 19, 105, 112, 124, 145, 163–64, 166, 169–70; Lee "Scratch" Perry's association with, 144, 145, 147, 148, 150, 151; photo, 180
Ranglin, Ernest, 29, 41, 123, 189
Ranking, Peter, 135, 137
rap, 193, 258
rapping. *See* toasting
Rastafari, 21, 82, 110, 134; beliefs of, 14, 15–16, 198; growth of, 15–16; importance of ganja to, 17, 18, 80; in Africa, 199; in the United Kingdom, 222; influence on Bob

Marley and the Wailers, 4, 15, 144, 190, 217; influence on contemporary Jamaican music, 193; influence on other musicians, 81, 166, 217; influence on reggae, 5, 7, 11, 16, 18, 33, 80, 99, 144, 186, 187, 190, 200, 241; influence on ska, 30; music of, 27, 122, 145, 156, 159, 200; mysticism in, 241; narratives of, 187, 190, 192, 198, 202, 213, 223, 248, 250, 259; popular images of, 225; slang, 61–62; themes in song lyrics, 67, 88, 106, 122, 200, 201, 202, 217
raves, 85, 233, 243, 257, 259–60
Ray Symbolic (sound system), 53, 86
Reagan, Ronald, 186, 187
Record Plant (studio), 37
Red Hills, 109
Redding, Otis, 119, 157
Redwood, Rudolph "Ruddy," 52, 112
"Reflections on Exile" (essay), 198
reggae, 196, 201, 218, 219; as an African-derived music, 16, 70, 250; as communal art form, 215; as source material, 75, 246, 247; "country" reggae, 157; creation of, 31–34; decline of, 185–88; devotional reggae, 166; economics of, 47–49, 161; emphasis on Africa, 199; fusion with jazz, 151; history of, 2, 4–7, 13, 31–34, 44, 76, 91, 95, 99, 102–3, 119, 128, 131, 134–35, 143, 144–45, 159, 163–64, 185–88, 190–92; in the United Kingdom, 221–23, 225–27, 228, 231–32, 251; in the United States, 8, 9, 240–41, 258; influence on other musical styles, 162; innovations in, 9, 46, 57–61, 87, 93, 133; musical traits of, 105, 120, 121, 142, 145, 146, 147, 150, 166–67, 193, 213, 238; Rastafari influence on, 11, 15, 16, 17, 187, 200, 210, 217; relationship to dub, 34, 63, 140, 212, 224, 243–44; relationship to ganja, 17, 18, 80, 81; relationship to Jamaican culture, 14, 23, 35–36, 190, 214, 216, 250; relationship to neo-dub, 229, 230, 231, 234, 242; scholarship on, 23–25, 141; sound quality of, 21, 60, 71–72, 80, 81, 97, 132, 210, 258; uptown reggae, 50. *See also* dancehall music; dub; Marley, Bob; ragga
Reich, Steve, 3, 39
Reid, Arthur "Duke," 169, 223; as producer, 29, 30, 33, 34, 49, 50–51, 146; as sound system operator, 42, 109, 142; as studio owner, 46, 52, 96, 105, 112, 117. *See also* Treasure Isle; Trojan

Sinker, Mark, 243

Sir Coxsone's Downbeat (sound system), 42, 55, 98, 141, 241

Sir George (sound system), 109

Sir Jessus, 223

Sir Mike (sound system), 109

Sixteen, Earl, 125, 230

Size, Roni, 233

ska, 14, 29–31, 32, 33, 35, 95, 141, 142, 190, 221

Skatalites, the, 8, 30, 46, 190

Skin, 170

slackness songs, 5, 16, 79, 141, 163

slave orchestras, 27

slavery, 23, 26, 27, 186, 197, 204, 205, 209, 213

Slemon, Steven, 203

Sly & Robbie, 5, 58, 70, 85, 128, 131, 134, 136, 172, 227; photo, 178. *See also* Dunbar, Lowell "Sly"; Shakespeare, Robbie

Small Acts (book), 252

Small, Millicent, 221

Smart, "Prince" Philip, 132, 133; collaboration with King Tubby, 19, 60, 124–26; comments and interviews, 33, 57, 82, 108, 110, 111, 112, 113, 114, 115, 116, 123, 124–26, 127, 148, 185, 188; life abroad, 206; photo, 176; works by, 126

Smith, Byron, 50, 105, 108

Smith, Earl "Chinna," 59

Smith, Mikey, 62

Smith, Patti, 225, 227

Smith, Slim, 52, 112

Smith, Wayne, 188

Smithies, Grant, 229

Solid Foundation (book), 141

Soul Jazz (record label), 132

soul music, 5, 30, 119, 128, 145, 147, 149, 150, 156, 193, 225, 243, 246, 247; "post-soul," 243–44

Soul Syndicate, 46, 118, 131, 170, 188

Sound Dimension, the, 98

sound equipment: Alice mixing console, 150–51, 153; API mixing console, 135; Electro-Harmonix Small Stone (phase shifting device), 153; Fuzz Face distortion pedal, 98; Grantham reverberation unit, 151; Marantz amplifier, 151; MCI mixing console, 113–14, 115, 119, 121, 123; Mutron Bi-Phase (phase-shifting device), 153; MXR Phase 45 (phase-shifting device), 153; MXR Phase 90 (phase-shifting device), 153; MXR Phase 100 (phase-shifting device), 153; Neve mixing console, 210; Pultec

equalizer, 97–98; Roland Space Echo (delay device), 153, 154, 158; Scully recorder, 49; Sound City amplifier, 98; Sound Technique console, 170; Soundcraft mixing console, 153; Soundimension mixing console, 98, 100; Tannoy monitors, 112; Teac 3340 recording console, 150; Teac mixing console, 150; Telefunken speaker, 71

Sound of Africa (book), 24

"Sound of Culture, The" (essay), 250

sound processing, 2, 9, 37, 38, 51, 59, 61, 62, 63, 71–78, 83, 84, 86, 93, 126, 130, 136, 155, 158, 168, 208, 213, 235, 238, 260; accumulation, 67–70, 248; backward sound, 75; backward tape manipulation, 37, 45, 84, 144; bleed-through, 74, 118, 138; clicks and cuts, 236; delay effect, 72–73, 74, 76–77, 78, 79, 98, 100, 106, 110, 121–22, 123, 128, 129, 130, 131, 137, 138, 149, 153, 154, 171, 197, 198; disruption, 72, 73, 86–87, 129, 200, 205, 206–7; distortion, 75, 93, 158, 167, 194; double-tracking, 84, 100; dropout, 52, 88, 102, 118, 119, 120–21, 126, 129, 130, 138, 152, 156, 166, 172, 220; echo effect, 8, 72, 73, 78, 80, 83, 93, 98, 106, 110, 118, 121–22, 123, 129, 137, 138, 144, 147, 149, 151, 156, 158, 172, 192, 197, 198, 201–2, 220; equalization, 36, 51, 73–74, 77, 86, 88, 132, 133; erasure, 196; extraneous material, 74, 131, 147, 158, 168, 171, 194; feedback, 45, 127, 152; filtering, 73, 88, 118, 119, 120, 126, 130, 131, 138, 153, 232; fragmentation, 2, 56, 57, 64–66, 70, 71, 77, 79, 107, 120–21, 123, 138, 152, 158, 194, 196, 197, 199–200, 202, 203–4, 206, 216, 224, 233, 234, 235, 247, 256, 258–59; incompletion, 57, 248; overdubbing, 37, 57, 118, 133, 144, 168, 171, 172, 194, 206, 230; panning, 71, 84, 128, 130; phase shifting, 84, 101, 120, 153–54, 156, 157, 232, 241; reverberation, 7, 8, 36, 71–72, 74, 77, 80, 98, 100, 115–16, 118, 120, 121, 123, 126, 127, 128, 130, 137, 138, 144, 145, 147, 149, 153, 156, 168, 170, 171–72, 192, 197, 198, 199, 200, 201–2, 234; sampling, 3, 172, 193, 194, 228, 233, 235, 236, 245–46, 247–48, 249, 253; scratching, 235, 245–46, 248; sequencing, 3; sound effects, 37, 74, 89, 118, 132, 133, 144, 149, 168, 170, 171, 172, 190, 194–95, 230; talk-overs, 88; tape loops, 3, 72, 115, 157; tape noise, 100, 101, 156, 158; tape speed manipulation; 75, 87, 88, 149, 168, 213; tape splicing, 37, 75

We, 249
West Indies Records (WIRL), 49, 96, 143
West Kingston, 10, 13, 29, 60, 109, 110, 150, 151
Western Recorders (studio), 37
White, Timothy, 12
Whiteley, Sheila, 84
Whitfield, Norman, 149
Williams, Ranford, 145
Williams, Raymond, 17
Williams, Willie, 132
Wilson, Brian, 37
Wilson, Chris, 25
Wilson, Delroy, 116, 141, 164
Wilson-Tagoe, Nana, 212
Wonder, Stevie, 4
Woodbridge, Christine, 227
Woodstock, 84

World's Fair, 40
Wright, Winston, 143, 147

Yabby You, 9, 74, 116–17, 121, 122, 134, 165, 217, 218, 230
Yap, Justin, 30
Yellowman, 11, 134
Yinger, J. Martin, 215
Young, LaMonte, 3

Zamora, Lois, 203
Zap Pow, 153
Zappa, Frank, 75, 147
Zen Buddhism, 250
Zero, Earl, 66
Zion Initiation, 8
Zukie, Tappa, 55, 67, 125, 126, 231
Zurich, 162, 185

MUSIC / CULTURE

A series from Wesleyan University Press.

Edited by Harris M. Berger and Annie J. Randall

Originating editors: George Lipsitz, Susan McClary, and Robert Walser

Setting the Record Straight: A Material History of Classical Recording
by Colin Symes

False Prophet:
Fieldnotes from the Punk Underground
by Steven Taylor

Any Sound You Can Imagine:
Making Music/Consuming Technology
by Paul Théberge

Club Culturers:
Music, Media and Sub-cultural Capital
by Sarah Thornton

Dub:
Songscape and Shattered Songs in Jamaican Reggae
by Michael E. Veal

Running with the Devil:
Power, Gender, and Madness in Heavy Metal Music
by Robert Walser

Manufacturing the Muse:
Estey Organs and Consumer Culture in Victorian America
by Dennis Waring

The City of Musical Memory:
Salsa, Record Grooves, and Popular Culture in Cali, Colombia
by Lise A. Waxer

ABOUT THE AUTHOR

Michael Veal is an associate professor of music at Yale University. He received his M.A. and Ph.D. in ethnomusicology at Wesleyan University. He is the author of *Fela: The Life and Times of an African Musical Icon* (Temple University Press, 2000), a sociocontextual biography of the late Nigerian musician Fela Anikulapo-Kuti that uses the life of one of the most influential African musicians of the post–World War II era to explore themes of African postcoloniality, musical and cultural interchange between cultures of Africa and the African diaspora, and the political uses of music in Africa.